Older Adults' Misuse of Alcohol, Medicines, and Other Drugs

Anne M. Gurnack MSW, PhD; Editor

Dr. Gurnack is an Associate Professor of Political Science at the University of Wisconsin–Parkside. She is also a clinical social worker and the author of numerous publications in the field of social gerontology, including substance use and misuse among older adults.

Dr. Gurnack lives in Racine, Wisconsin, on Lake Michigan.

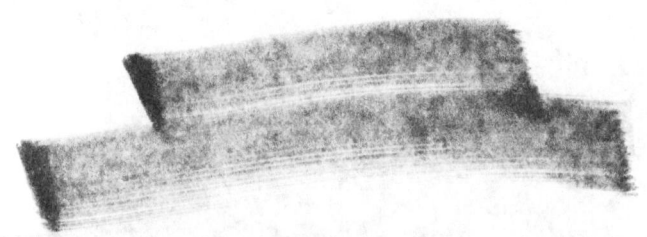

Older Adults' Misuse of Alcohol, Medicines, and Other Drugs

Research and Practice Issues

Anne M. Gurnack
Editor

 SPRINGER PUBLISHING COMPANY

Springer Publishing Company, Inc.
536 Broadway
New York, NY 10012–3955

Cover design by Margaret Dunin
Production Editor: Susan Gamer

91 92 93 94 95 / 5 4 3 2 1

Library of Congress Cataloging-in-Publication Data

Older adults' misuse of alcohol, medicines, and other drugs: research and practice /
    Anne M. Gurnack, editor.
      p.   cm.
    Includes bibliographical references and index.
    ISBN 0-8261-9500-8
    1. Aged—Alcohol use.   2. Aged—Drug use.   3. Aged—Drug abuse.
    4. Medication abuse.   I. Gurnack, Anne Marie.
    HV5138.043   1997
    362.29'2'0846 — dc20   96-35208
                                              CIP

DEDICATION

This book is dedicated to the memory of the late William J. Gurnack, my father; and the late William E. Gurnack, MD, my brother. Their lives in many ways served as an inspiration for this book.

Contents

Contributors

Wendy Adams, M.P.H., M.D.
University of Nebraska Medical Center
Section of Geriatric and Geronology

Roland Atkinson, M.D.
Psychiatry Services,
V.A. Medical Center, Portland, Oregon

Narra Smith Cox, Ph.D.
Department of Health and Human Issues
Division of Outreach
University of Wisconsin-Madison

Sara De Hart, Ph.D.
University of Minnesota
School of Nursing

Lawrence DuPree, Ph.D.
Florida Mental Health Institute
University of South Florida

Richard Finlayson, M.D.
Mayo Clinic
Rochester, Minnesota

Anne M. Gurnack, Ph.D., Editor
University of Wisconsin-Parkside

Norman G. Hoffmann, Ph.D.
Omega Institute, St. Paul, Minnesota

Carol Joseph, M.D.
Division of Geriatric Medicine,
V.A. Medical Center, Portland, Oregon

Joseph Liberto, M.D.
University of Maryland, Baltimore
V.A. Medical Center

David Oslin, M.D.
University of Pennsylvania
Department of Psychiatry

Helen Rosenberg, Ph.D.
Department of Sociology
University of Wisconsin-Parkside

Lawrence Schonfeld, Ph.D.
Florida Mental Health Institute
University of South Florida

David M. Smith, M.D.
Oregon Health Sciences University, Portland

James W. Smith, M.D.
Shick Shadle Hospital, Seattle, Washington

Foreword

Edith S. Lisansky Gomberg

The proportion of older persons in the population continues to increase in the United States and in most industrialized nations. In 1900, people 65 years and older constituted 4% of the population. The percentage of people 65 and older in the general population is now 13%, and it is anticipated that this will increase slowly and steadily until the year 2011. In that year, most baby-boomers will be turning 65, and a large spurt in the proportion of elderly in the population is anticipated. These demographics relate to the fact that life expectancy has increased, but it is of interest that life expectancy continues to vary by gender and by ethnicity. In 1992, life expectancy for white females was 79 years, for white males, 73. In the same year, life expectancy for black females was 74; for black males, 65.

Increasingly, social scientists are recognizing the necessity of studying the whole life course. Traditionally, developmental study has progressed through infancy, childhood, and adolescence; but the importance of studying adulthood, middle age, and the older years has become evident. Development and change do not cease as one leaves adolescence behind. One of the behaviors which change through the life course is the use and abuse of alcohol and drugs, but the understanding of alcohol-related and drug-related behaviors is possible only in the context of studying the whole person, including general health, family life, social networks, role behaviors, and mental health.

The percentage of men and women who drink, moderately or immoderately, drops at age 60. There are various explanations for this drop, which is observed across nations (Fillmore et al., 1991), including economics, health problems, changes in alcohol metabolism, and cohort effects. Interestingly enough, older problem drinkers who present with nonspecific signs—e.g., self-neglect, falls or injuries, depression, and the like—may often be mistaken as having diseases related to dementia (Atkinson, 1984). We have just begin the task of alerting primary care physicians to the diagnosis and treatment of elderly problem drinkers (American Medical Association, 1995).

This book deals with many aspects of older peoples' alcohol and drug misuse. Some of the issues are epidemiological; (see chapter 1). where an important research area is definition and screening: What are the criteria for defining alcohol or drug problems among older people? Chapter 3 is a medical report on "additional problems resulting from the interaction of age-related changes in physiology and heavy alcohol intake." We agree with the conclusion of DeHart and Hoffmann in chapter 2, that "in treatment, older and younger adults do not differ on the constellation of individuals' lifetime diagnostic indicators." We have found (Gomberg, 1995) that elderly women problem drinkers show remarkable similarity in histories and patterns of drinking behavior to younger women problem drinkers. We have also found that the older problem drinkers who were studied showed remarkably similar development in the time course of alcohol-related problems. The older problem drinkers interviewed reported similar phasic development whether they were in treatment or not in treatment, whether they were male or female, and whether they were African-American or white (Gomberg, 1994). Similar sequencing has been reported in other age groups (Schuckit, Anthenelli, Bucholz, Hesselbrook, & Tipp, 1995).

The problematic use of prescribed psychoactive drugs by older people is discussed in chapter 7. The widespread use of such drugs by older persons, particularly older women, is an issue that needs addressing. Recent surveys indicate that 21% of the men and 32% of the women in the age group 60 to 74 use prescribed psychoactive drugs. Is such a difference linked to observed psychiatric symptomatology or to prescribing practices? The use of psychoactive medications as a form of behavior control in nursing homes (see chapter 10) is a related phenomenon. The extent of abuse of banned substances ("street drugs") among older adults is discussed by Rosenberg in chapter 9; patterns of compliance and noncompliance with medical prescriptions are also relevant. And the unique aspects of treating alcohol or drug problems in the elderly are presented by Schonfeld and Dupree in chapter 5.

One of the most interesting research problems is the questions of early versus late onset of alcoholism (chapter 4). Although this dichotomy relates to problem drinkers in all age groups, it seems of particular interest with the elderly. We prefer the phrase "early versus *recent* onset" and we have found, as have others, that recent onset is more frequently reported by elderly *female* than by elderly male problem drinkers (Gomberg, 1995; Osterling & Berglund, 1994). This finding raises some interesting questions about widowhood, the finances of older men and women, the likelihood of remarriage, depression, the proportion of older men and older women who live alone, and the transmission of problem drinking from male to female. At age 65, 41% of women are living alone, compared with 15% of men in the same age group. Poverty is much more likely to be an issue with elderly women than with elderly men.

There are many challenging questions about the elderly population. We are just beginning to explore differences in attitudes and social status of older people in the different subcultures of America: the Caucasians, the African-Americans, the Hispanic-Americans, the Asian-Americans, and the Amerindians. Does the status of the elderly, for example, among Asian immigrants, change with assimilation or do permissible drinking patterns remain as they were in the old country? It is of great interest that while older white men show an increased tendency to suicide with aging, this phenomenon does not appear among African-American elderly men.

There is much that needs to be learned both in the field of gerontology and in alcohol and drug studies; this book is a good beginning.

REFERENCES

American Medical Association. (1995). *Alcoholism in the elderly: Diagnosis, treatment, prevention.* Chicago, IL: American Medical Association, Department of Geriatric Health.

Atkinson, R. A.(ed.) (1984), *Alcohol and drug abuse in old age.* Washington, DC: American Psychiatric Press.

Fillmore, K. M., Hartka, E., Johnstone, B. M., Leino, E. V., Motoyoshi, M. E., & Temple, M. T. (1991). A meta-analysis of life course variation in drinking. *British Journal of Addictions, 86,* 1221–1268.

Gomberg, E. S. L. (1994). The phasic development of alcohol dependence among older persons [abstract]. *Alcoholism: Clinical and Experimental Research, 19,* 473.

Gomberg, E. S. L. (1995). Older women and alcohol: Use and abuse. In M. Galanter (Ed.), *Recent developments in alcoholism: Volume 12. Alcoholism and women.* p. 61–79. New York: Plenum.

Osterling, A., & Berglund, M. (1994), Elderly first time admitted alcoholics: A descriptive study on gender differences in a clinical population. *Alcoholism: Clinical and Experimental Research, 18,* 1317–1321.

Schuckit, M. A., Anthenelli, R. M., Bucholz, K. S., Hesselbrock, V., & Tipp, J. (1995). The time course of development of alcohol-related problems in men and women. *Journal of Studies on Alcohol, 56,* 218–225.

Introduction

Anne M. Gurnack, MSW, PhD; Editor

I am delighted to introduce and highlight the contents of this very important book, which represents 4 long years of hard work. Drug abuse among the elderly has received little empirical attention. However, scholars and practitioners are recognizing the need for models of drug misuse that pertain specifically to later life. Since the number of older Americans is increasing at a rapid pace, the problems and human service needs of the elderly must be better understood if we are to adequately meet these needs in the future.

Five major reasons for heightened concern about drug misuse in later life have been identified:

1. Census figures document that there will be well over 32 million older Americans by the year 2000 (Gurnack & Thomas, 1989). The sheer number of elders and expectations that their number will increase justify concern about substance misuse in later life.
2. Gerontologists have noted that characteristics of older cohorts, including their likelihood of using a wide range of health services, are changing (Gurnack & Hoffmann, 1992). Researchers expect future cohorts to make greater use of available services than do contemporary elders, as the average educational level of the elderly increases and attitudes toward the need for health and human services become more positive.
3. Scholars have noted that successively younger cohorts include fewer abstainers and more heavier consumers of alcohol and drugs. These experts thus predict increased rates of problems resulting from alcohol and drug misuse in later life.
4. Several authorities have noted that physicians and other health providers are likely to mistake the effects of alcohol misuse in older patients for other conditions, such as irreversible dementia or senility. The impact of such mislabeling can be devastating since inappropriate care may be provided.

5. The high costs of health care associated with alcohol and drug misuse continue to be a serious concern. Recent researchers have drawn attention to the Medicare dollars being spent on health services related to this problem (Adams, Yuan, Barboriak, & Rimm, 1993). Therefore, mechanisms for early identification of alcohol and drug misuse in this population, and options and models for effective intervention, must be devised to curtail later expensive institutionalization.

The chapters in this volume offer the latest thinking and research findings related to the area of alcohol and drug misuse in later life. The authors of these contributions are nationally and internationally known scholars in this field. However, the study of alcohol and drug problems for older adults still remains a young area of inquiry. Additional knowledge is required to more fully comprehend the complexity of the problems associated with these individual cohorts of older adults. Issues related to the life course of alcohol and drug misuse must be addressed on a regular basis as the special needs of this population are identified now and in the future.

The chapters fall into two sections. Chapters 1 through 6 deal primarily with aspects of alcohol abuse. The first contribution, by Adams and Cox (chapter 1), describes the prevalence of alcohol misuse and a range of characteristics of elderly users diagnosed with these problems. Next (chapter 2), DeHart and Hoffmann examine the state of the art of screening and diagnosis of "alcohol abuse" and "dependence" in great depth. They see a need to evaluate the sensitivity and specificity of newer screening instruments for "alcohol abuse" in the elderly. This analysis is followed by Smith's comprehensive discussion of the physical and mental problems associated with alcoholism in older adults (chapter 3). Liberto and Oslin then proceed to delineate issues related to the age of onset of alcohol-related problems (chapter 4). They point to findings from epidemiological studies which suggest that there are a significant number of older alcoholics ("late onset") who first began to drink alcohol "abusively" in their later years. This discussion is followed by an article (chapter 5) by Schonfeld and Dupree, who summarize the alternative treatment approaches available to elderly persons who misuse alcohol. They suggest that there is evidence for better outcomes for age-specific treatment. Then, Smith and Atkinson (chapter 6) devote their attention to aspects of alcoholism and dementia. They provide an informative classification and differentiation of persons within various types of dementia.

Chapters 7 through 10—the next section of the book—address a number of issues related to drug misuse among the elderly. Finlayson's contribution (chapter 7) addresses drug misuse as it pertains to inappropriate diagnoses and prescription of medicines by physicians, as well as the problems of older adults who find themselves misusing these substances. The case studies presented in this article illustrate these situations well.

Adams, in the next contribution (chapter 8), discusses the major interactions between alcohol and other drugs. She reports that the major adverse clinical outcomes of drug-alcohol interactions are altered blood levels of the medication or of alcohol, lower toxicity, gastrointestinal inflammation and bleeding, sedation and delirium disulfiram-like reactions, and interference with the desired effect of medication.

In the next article (chapter 9), Rosenberg provides a description of the characteristics of older adults who misuse illicit drugs. She reviews past trends in drug misuse among the elderly, the lifestyle of those addicted to drugs, and the problems the elderly face with traditional treatment programs. She suggests an agenda for future research.

The concluding chapter, by Joseph (chapter 10), points to the fact that problems associated with use of alcohol and drugs by nursing home residents are frequently overlooked, with potentially devastating consequences. She finds that effective intervention requires that substance misuse problems be actively sought out, carefully delineated, and appropriately treated.

We hope that this volume will stimulate an interest in this subject and be a catalyst for continued development and refinement of research issues.

REFERENCES

Adams, W. L., Yuan, Z. & Barboriak, J. J., & Rimm, A. A. (1993). Alcohol-related hospitalizations in elderly people:Prevalence and geographic variation in the United States. *Journal of the American Medical Association, 270*,1222–1225.

Gurnack, A. M., & Hoffmann, N. G., (1992). Elderly alcohol abuse. *International Journal of the Addictions, 27*, 869–878.

Gurnack, A. M., & Thomas, J. L. (1989). Behavioral factors related to elderly alcohol abuse:Research and policy issues. *The International Journal of the Addictions, 24*, 641–654.

Acknowledgments

This book is a revised and expanded version of a special issue of the *International Journal of the Addictions* (Gurnack, 1995). I am very grateful to Stanley Einstein, editor-in-chief of that journal, for his tenacious and thorough review of the manuscripts of all the contributors. I also feel very indebted to Nancy Osgood from the Medical College of Virginia for her very fine review of the book manuscript. These individuals were of great help in producing this very high-quality and much-needed volume. And I must make a special note of thanks to the contributors of this book. They were always patient and understanding when I asked them to revise their chapters just one more time. They were always willing to do their very best.

Finally, I am grateful to Bill Tucker and his staff at Springer Publishing Company for their assistance with and enthusiastic support of this project. It was a genuine pleasure to work with them.

Anne M. Gurnack
Kenosha, Wisconsin
February 8, 1996

REFERENCE

Gurnack, A. M. (Ed.) (1996). Special issue on drugs and the elderly: Use and misuse of drugs, medicines, alcohol, and tobacco. *International Journal of the Addictions, 30* (13,14).

1

Epidemiology of Problem Drinking among Elderly People

Wendy L. Adams, MD, MPH
Narra Smith Cox, PhD

INTRODUCTION

The significance of alcohol-related problems in elderly people is becoming increasingly evident as the population continues to age. Recent epidemiologic studies have greatly improved our understanding of how alcohol use affects this segment of our population. *Epidemiology* may be defined as the study of the distribution and determinants of diseases and injuries in human populations (Mausner, 1985). Epidemiologic studies of problem drinking among elderly people give us an understanding of the scope of problem drinking in this population. They report on the prevalence of problem drinking, describe increases in morbidity related to alcohol use, and identify societal and medical costs associated with problem drinking among elderly people. They also identify variations in problem drinking according to such characteristics as age, gender, and geographic location, and identify variations over time. By recognizing and understanding the broad patterns of problem drinking in the elderly population, clinicians may better understand the individual cases they see. In addition, epidemiologic studies of problem drinking among the elderly can help administrators better plan for the future health care needs of our population. Readers can enhance their understanding of these studies by appreciating some of the challenges involved in designing and conducting the research. In this chapter we will discuss some of the relevant epidemiological issues, review research findings regarding alcohol problems among elderly people in the community and in health care settings, and discuss the implications of these studies for the health care system in the coming decades.

ISSUES IN EPIDEMIOLOGICAL RESEARCH

The Problem of Definitions

Problems of measurement and definition are prominent among the challenges facing researchers who conduct studies of alcohol use and misuse. Variable definitions of "alcoholism," "alcohol abuse," "heavy drinking," and "drinking problems" have plagued researchers in the field for many years. The lack of consensus regarding a definition of "problem drinking" is problematic for both those who conduct and those who read and interpret research studies. The criteria used may include high levels of alcohol consumption, symptoms of alcohol dependence or withdrawal, and adverse consequences of alcohol use. Since different studies employ different definitions, it is very difficult to compare the results of various studies. For instance, in the 1960s, one study evaluated structured interview results on a case-by-case basis to decide whether or not the responses or the respondent's behavior during the interview justified a diagnosis of "probable alcoholism" (Bailey, Haberman, & Alksne, 1965). Another, somewhat later study used very different criteria. Smart and Liban identified seven symptoms of "problem drinking," including automobile accidents, fights and job problems related to drinking, and 7 symptoms of "dependency," including feeling a need to cut down or quit drinking, blackouts, shakes, and morning drinking. Yet another study described those with self-reported "drinking problems" and those whose lives had "been made worse" in health, finances, or relationships by drinking practices (Meyers, Hingson, Mucatel, & Godlman, 1982). Since people who meet criteria for problem drinking in one study might not in another, comparing the prevalence of alcoholism or problem drinking from one study to another when there is no standardized definition is not really possible. In the 1980s the *Diagnostic and Statistical Manual of Mental Disorders (3rd ed.) (DSM–III)* (see below) helped to standardize the definitions of alcohol abuse and alcoholism. Since not all researchers agree that these are the most appropriate definitions for the elderly population, however, variability continues.

   Studies of "heavy drinking" also use inconsistent definitions. In the 1960s, Cahalan and Cisin (1968, pp. 131–151) defined "heavy drinkers" as those who drank "typically, nearly every day with five or more drinks at a sitting at least once in a while; or at least weekly with usually five or more drinks on most occasions." Barnes (1979, pp. 244–250) classified "heavy drinking" as a range of alcohol use, including "a pattern of drinking one or two drinks three or more times a day or a pattern of drinking only a couple of times a month but usually consuming at least five or six drinks at a time." Molgaard, on the other hand, defined "severe drinking" as weekly consumption of 2 or more six-packs of beer or more than 8 glasses of wine or liquor (Molgaard, Nakamura, Stanford, Peddecord, & Morton, 1990). Since people may fall into the "heavy" or "severe" category in one of these studies but not others, conclusions about heavy drinkers in one study may differ greatly from those in another. When attempting to discern at what level alcohol use becomes a risk factor for adverse health or social consequences, consistency from study to study is essential.

In 1980, the third edition of the *Diagnostic and Statistical Manual of Mental Disorders* (DSM–III) (American Psychiatric Association, 1980) was published. That manual, its subsequent revised edition *(DSM–III–R),* and the present edition *(DSM IV)* have helped to standardize diagnostic criteria for psychiatric illnesses, including alcohol dependence and alcohol abuse. The authors developed criteria for alcohol abuse and dependence based on problems that can result from drinking behavior. Keystones of a *DSM* diagnosis of "alcohol dependence" are: Loss of control over drinking, withdrawal symptoms, tolerance to alcohol, and social decline resulting from drinking. "Alcohol abuse" is characterized by either continued use of alcohol despite problems it has caused, or recurrent use of the substance in hazardous situations. After 1980, several studies used the *DSM* criteria to define alcohol abuse and dependence. These studies can be compared with one another more easily than could previous studies.

Some researchers believe that although the *DSM* criteria have been helpful in standardizing the definitions of alcohol abuse and dependence, these criteria exclude a substantial number of elderly problem drinkers. Because of physical and psychosocial age-related changes, older people may have problems caused by their drinking practices even though they do not appear to meet the *DSM* criteria. Elderly people may differ in their presentation of the key symptoms of alcoholism and alcohol abuse (Atkinson, 1984; Graham, 1986). For instance, "tolerance" is characterized by requiring increasing amounts of alcohol to achieve the same effect. Because of changes in the absorption (Pozzato et al., 1995; Seitz, 1993) and distribution of alcohol in the body with increasing age, older people obtain higher blood alcohol levels per amount consumed (Vestal, McGuire, & Tobin 1976). Thus elderly alcoholics may quite honestly report consuming a smaller amount of alcohol to achieve the same effect as previously, although they have the same liver enzyme induction that causes tolerance in younger people. Another alcohol-related problem likely to present differently in older people is "social decline." Those who are not employed will not have problems at work; those who are widowed will not have marital problems; those who have stopped driving will not be cited for driving while intoxicated. Subtle presentations such as a gradual decline in self-care may be the rule and may be attributed to other age-related illness or impairment.

Because of these differences in the clinical presentation of alcohol misuse in older people, researchers sometimes choose to use a broader definition of alcohol problems or criteria of quantity and frequency of alcohol consumption as a surrogate for alcohol abuse or dependence in order to detect these elderly problem drinkers. In this chapter, we will use the term "problem drinking" to include alcohol abuse, alcohol dependence, and drinking which causes social or medical problems whether or not *DSM* criteria are met.

Identifying Cases

In addition to the way in which a case of problem drinking is defined, the way in which the cases are identified may also affect the accuracy of a study. Information about drinking behavior may be elicited in various ways, including mailed surveys, personal interviews, telephone interviews, diet records, and medical record review. These approaches vary in their ability to detect problem drinkers. For example, Werch (1989) found that elderly respondents gave higher estimates of their alcohol consumption when they kept a drinking diary than when they filled out 7- or 28-day recall instruments. This effect has also been seen in studies of younger people (Lemmens, Knibbe, & Tan, 1988; Redman, Sanson-Fisher, Wilkinson, Fahey, & Gibberd, 1987), but has not been consistent in all studies, (Giovannucci et al., 1991; Goodwin et al., 1987). Medical record review shows lower rates of alcohol abuse or dependence than interviews (Curtis et al., 1989; Kirkpatrick, Johnson, Earp, & Fletcher, 1988). To complicate matters further, even if we are able to assume reliable reporting and accurate diagnosis, people seem to move in and out of problem drinking status over time (Moos, Brennan, & Moos, 1991; Vaillant, 1983), so a person who meets diagnostic criteria for alcoholism at a given time may not meet the same criteria several months later.

Diagnosing problem drinking depends heavily on self-reported drinking practices, which presupposes honest reporting on the part of subjects. Many alcoholics deny their heavy drinking, so this is somewhat problematic. The reliability of self-reported drinking practices may be further compromised by cognitive impairment. Up to 10% of those 65 and older and up to 33% of those 85 and older suffer from dementia (Katzman, 1986; Skoog, Nillson,

Palmertz, Andreasson, & Svanborg, 1993). The most common causes are Alzheimer's disease and multiple cerebral infarcts. Heavy alcohol use also causes cognitive impairment, so the prevalence of dementia is especially high among elderly people who misuse alcohol (Finlayson, Hurt, Davis, & Morse, 1988). The lack of standardized instruments for detecting alcohol misuse is also problematic in this population. Although several questionnaire and interview instruments have been developed for detecting problem drinking, none has been extensively tested among elderly people. Researchers at the University of Michigan have developed a geriatric version of the Michigan Alcohol Screening Test, which may be useful in future studies of alcohol problems in elderly people, but tests of its sensitivity and specificity have not yet been reported. The reader is referred to chapter 2, on diagnosis of alcoholism, for further details on diagnostic instruments.

Other Methodologic Challenges

Another challenge facing researchers is how to select a sample of the population to study. Since the 1960s, researchers have conducted a few nationwide general population surveys to study drinking practices. However, much of the population-based research examining drinking practices among elderly people has not been based on national samples. Important factors that may influence the findings of smaller studies are the size, age range, gender ratio, and geographic location of the population sample studied. A small sample may not be large enough to include many problem drinkers. One sample might comprise predominantly "young-old" people, who tend to be in better health and are often still working, and another "old-old" people, who are more likely to be frail or ill. Samples may also vary in the ethnic, religious, educational, and economic backgrounds of their participants. Thus, various samples of "elderly" people may differ substantially from one another in ways that systematically affect the alcohol consumption of the participants. Since at all ages and in many locations women drink less than men (Barnes, 1979; Bristow, & Clare, 1992; Cornoni-Huntley, 1986; Helzer, Burnham, & McEvoy, 1991), the gender ratio of the sample must be considered. There is variation in per capita consumption of alcohol from one geographic region to another, which is also important to appreciate when reading studies of problem drinking.

Research in various settings has contributed to our understanding of problem drinking among elderly people. Surveys of the general population as well as epidemiological research based in clinical settings are important when considering this problem. Alcohol problems among people in hospitals, nursing homes, and other health care settings may have characteristics and implications different from those associated with alcohol problems in the community. Some studies have examined problem drinkers in treatment programs. Since relatively few problem drinkers are in treatment (Shapiro et al., 1984), this represents a highly select population that probably differs from the general population in many ways. Studies of alcohol problems in older people have also been done in health care settings. While important to consider in their context, findings based on clinical studies cannot be generalized to a broader population.

When reading and comparing studies of problem drinking in elderly people, we must appreciate the various methods of defining problem drinking and identifying the cases. Was a DSM-III definition of alcoholism used, or were there other criteria? Did the researchers send out a mailed survey, or do personal interviews? We must also consider the characteristics of the sample population. What was the age of the participants? Were both men and women included? Were the subjects healthy people living at home, or were they hospitalized? All these things must be taken into account in order to understand how the study under consideration applies to the reader's own situation.

EPIDEMIOLOGICAL FINDINGS

Alcohol Problems in the Community

Several population-based studies have examined alcohol use and misuse among elderly people. There has been a wide range of prevalence in these studies, partly due to the variability in case definition and method of detecting alcohol problems, as well as other factors discussed above. Table 1.1 gives a summary of several prominent epidemiologic studies arranged in chronological order.

One of the first population-based studies of alcoholism was reported in 1965 by Bailey et al. Using a structured interview designed for the study, these researchers surveyed residents of the Washington Heights section of New York City. Among those aged 65–74, the population prevalence of "probable alcoholism" was estimated at 22 per 1000, and among those aged 75 and older 12.5 per 1000. "Probable alcoholism" was defined as positive reponses to interview questions on health, job, social, legal, or financial problems resulting from drinking or abnormal drinking behavior observed during the interview. Respondents were asked about themselves and family members. The investigators determined on a case-by-case basis whether the responses and observed behavior constituted probable alcoholism, which renders the definition virtually impossible to reproduce.

TABLE 1.1   Population-based Studies of Alcohol Problems among Elderly People

Study	Population	Type of problem drinking	Prevalence	Comments
Bailey et al. (1965)	3959 households in Washington Heights District of New York City. 17.8% respondents were ≥65 years old	Probable alcoholism (See text for definition)	22 per 1000 age 65–74 12 per 1000 age 74 and older	Geographically limited urban population. Definition of alcoholism somewhat subjective, based on investigators' interpretations of respondents' answers to questions and behavior during interview.
Cahalan & Cisin (1968)	National sample. 257 men and 367 women age 60 and older͏	Heavy or binge drinking (See text for definition)	20% of men 2% of women	Definition of "heavy drinking" complex and hard to compare with other studies.
Barnes (1979)	100 men and 137 women age 60 and older in two Western New York State Counties	Heavy or binge drinking (3 or more drinks per day or 5 or more per occasion)	16% 1%	Geographically limited rural population. Household survey, n-home interviews.
Smart & Liban (1981)	142 noninstitutionalized residents of Toronto (probability sample) age 60 and older	Dependency symptoms (See text for definition) "Problem symptoms" (See text for definition)	10.6% 3.5%	Urban population 68% response rate.
Meyers et al. (1982)	928 noninstitutionalized residents of Boston age 60 or	Heavy drinking (2 or more drinks per day) older drinking	6% Self-reported problem	Urban population (Boston). In-home interviews. 60% 1% response rate.

continued

TABLE 1.1 *continued*

Epidemiologic Catchment Area Study Blazer et al. (1987) Eaton et al. (1984) Meyers et al. (1989)	805 men and 1305 women age 65 and older in four separate geographic locations	DSM–III Alcohol Abuse or Dependence	1.4% North Carolina 3.0% New Haven 3.7% Baltimore 3.0% St. Louis	Methodologically rigorous study, strict diagnostic criteria.
Paganini-Hill et al. (1986)	11,888 California retirement community residents age 60–89	Heavy drinking (3 or more drinks per day)	31% of men 22% of women	Special population: retirement community residents with high socioeconomic status.
Alexander and Duff (1988)	260 retirement community residents, median age 76	Heavy drinking (2 or more drinks per day)	20%	Special population: retirement community residents with high socioeconomic status.
Molgaard (1990)	955 randomly sampled residents of San Diego County, California age 65 and older	Heavy drinking (12 or more cans of beer or 8 or more glasses of wine or liquor)	8.2% age 65–74 6.4% age 75 and older	Lower limits on "heavy drinking" than most studies. Included more African-American and Mexican-American people than most studies.

Cahalan and Cisin (1968), reported on a national survey of the quantity and frequency of drinking. They classified 20% of men and 2% of women aged 60 and older as heavy drinkers, using an index of drinking behavior developed for the study. The definition of heavy drinking included but was not completely limited to either drinking nearly every day as well as five or more drinks per occasion at times or binge drinking. Again, the definition of heavy drinking as reported in this study is very difficult to reproduce.

In 1979, Barnes surveyed a random sample of Western New York State residents and found that 7% of those age 60 and older (16% of men and 1% of women) were heavy drinkers. This study used a more standardized definition of heavy drinking: either 3 or more drinks per day regularly or 5 or more per occasion at times.

A study from Canada found that 3.5% of elderly residents of Ontario reported at least one "drinking problem symptom" in the year prior to the study and 10.6% reported at least one symptom of alcohol "dependency" (Smart & Liban, 1981). The seven problem symptoms included "feeling the effects of alcohol on the job," "being told to leave a place because of drinking," and other behavioral consequences of drinking. The seven dependency symptoms included "feeling the need to cut down or stop drinking altogether," blackouts, and morning tremors. Since many nonalcoholic people have felt "the need to cut down," the inclusion of this symptom may account for the higher prevalence of "dependency" than "problem" symptoms in that study. In 1982, Meyers et al. reported on a sample of 928 elderly (65 and older) residents of Boston. They found that 6% consumed more than 2 drinks per day, only 1% were self-reported "problem drinkers," and 3% reported that drinking had "made their lives worse in at least one of six life areas."

The most methodologically rigorous population-based study of alcohol problems in elderly people is part of the Epidemiologic Catchment Area (ECA) Study. Researchers in that project interviewed people in five separate geographic locations (New Haven, Baltimore, St. Louis, Los Angeles, and Durham, NC). There were 805 male and 1305 female respondents age 65 and older. They used the Diagnostic Interview Schedule (DIS) (Robins, Helzer, Cronghan, & Ratcliffe, 1981), a structured psychiatric interview developed for that study, to make *DSM–III* diagnoses of psychiatric problems, including alcohol abuse and alcoholism. Using the *DSM–III* criteria, researchers in the ECA study found considerable geographic variation in the prevalence of alcohol abuse and dependence. The prevalence ranged from 1.5% among elderly adults in the Piedmont area of North Carolina to 3.7% in Baltimore. In addition, a much higher percentage of people had less severe alcohol problems or were heavy drinkers (Helzer, Burnham, & McEvoy, 1991). Men consistently had higher rates than women, and the prevalence declined with increasing age (Blazer, Crowell, & George, 1987; Myers et al., 1984). Over a one-year period, the ECA study was also able to calculate incidence rates, i.e., rates of newly developed cases of alcohol abuse and alcoholism. Though these rates also declined with age up to age 60, they began to increase again for both men and women over age 60 (Eaton et al., 1989), and were particularly notable for men age 75 and older. This increasing incidence in older people is based on a very small number of cases, however, and must be interpreted with caution.

A study of the alcohol consumption of 2105 randomly sampled residents of San Diego County, California, found that 8.2% of respondents aged 65–74 and 6.4% of those aged 75 or older were heavy drinkers (12 or more cans of beer or 8 or more glasses of wine or liquor per week) (Molgaard et al., 1990). This definition of heavy drinking is based on a substantially lower quantity than in previous studies. They did not report on drinking-related problems. Whites were more likely to use alcohol than African-American or Mexican-American people in that study. As in other studies, men used considerably more alcohol than women.

As they age, many people move to communities designed specifically for older people. Whether and how this phenomenon affects the drinking practices of these people is of some interest. Three studies have reported on drinking practices in such retirement communities. Alexander and Duff surveyed 260 people aged 57–97 years (median age 76), who lived in California and Oregon retirement communities. They found a 20% prevalence of heavy drinking (2 or more drinks per day) (Alexander & Duff, 1988). Another study also found a surprisingly high prevalence of heavy drinking among retirement community residents. In a study of 11,888 California retirement community residents, Paganini-Hill, Ross, and Henderson (1986) reported that 31% of men and 22% of women age 60 and older consumed more than 3 drinks per day. However, in a survey of 317 older (mean age 83) Wisconsin retirement community residents, Adams (1995) found that only 8% were daily drinkers, and less than 1% scored positive on the CAGE questionnaire. The difference may have been due to the older age and larger proportion of women in the Wisconsin sample or to a combination of these and other factors.

In summary, the literature indicates considerable variation in estimates of the frequency with which older adults drink heavily or experience problems associated with alcohol use. Although the studies show consistently lower rates among elderly than among young and middle-aged people, the prevalence remains high enough to warrant serious attention from those who plan, study, and provide health care to this population. In some settings, as noted above, as many as 20% of older people are heavy drinkers (Alexander & Duff 1988; Paganini-Hill, 1986). Up to 4% of elderly people in some locations meet criteria for alcohol abuse or dependence (Blazer, Crowell, & George, 1987; Eaton et al., 1989; Molgaard et al., 1990; Myers et al., 1984). Women at all ages, including older women, are substantially less likely than men to be heavy or problem drinkers. In addition to gender differences, there is considerable geographic variation in the prevalence of alcohol problems. The influence of age is also important and is discussed below.

Changes in Alcohol Use and Abuse with Increasing Age

Several cross-sectional studies have shown a decline in alcohol use and misuse in old age (Barnes, 1979; Cahalan & Cisin, 1968; McKim & Quinlan, 1991; Meyers, Goldman, Hingson, & Scotch, 1981–82; Smart & Liban, 1981). Among those 75 years of age and older, cross-sectional studies have shown a particularly low rate of heavy alcohol use and a high proportion of abstainers (Adams, Garry, Rhyne, Hunt, & Goodwin, 1990; Barnes, 1979; Douglass Schuster, & McClelland, 1988). A decline seen in cross-sectional studies, however, could represent a decline in alcohol use over time or a cohort effect; that is, people born at one time may have had different lifelong drinking practices from those born at other times. For example, today's elderly population lived through Prohibition and the Great Depression, which may well have contributed to lighter drinking habits throughout their lives. In order to distinguish between these effects, longitudinal studies, which follow the same people over a period of time, are needed. Several have been done, and they generally confirm that heavy alcohol use does decline with increasing age after age 65 (Adams et al., 1990; Fillmore, 1987; Glynn, 1985; Stall, 1986; Temple & Leino, 1989). Longitudinal studies also have limitations, however. Studies of drinking behavior are subject to secular trends, i.e., changes in the environment or in societal attitudes that affect the phenomenon under investigation during the time period of the study. This may be the effect seen in the Framingham Study, which, in contrast to other longitudinal studies, showed an increase over time in the mean alcohol intake of those who drank in all age groups (Gordon & Kannel, 1983). The rate of increase was most impressive among women. In the group over age 60, however, it was substantially lower . During the same time period, per capita consumption of alcohol in the United States increased considerably (U.S. Bureau of the Census, 1975). So those 60 and older did follow the trend of the population in general as it increased its alcohol consumption, but at a rate lower than that of younger people. Another longitudinal study is the Normative Aging Study, which followed men in Boston during a period when per capita consumption rose only slightly (1973–1982). In that study, men aged 65 and older at the onset of the study decreased their alcohol intake over time. Those who moved from the middle-aged into the elderly group during the study, however, increased their alcohol consumption over time (Glynn et al., 1985).

There are other plausible contributors to the decline in alcohol use and misuse seen in these studies. These include changes in the gender ratio of the populations and the health status of the individuals. Men have higher mortality rates at all ages, so the female-to-male ratio of the population increases with age. In cross-sectional studies, women of all ages are less likely to use or misuse alcohol. Because of the increase in the female to male ratio as a population ages, we see a decline in alcohol use in the older population. However, this phenomenon by no means accounts for all of the decline in alcohol use with age. Separate longitudinal studies of alcohol use in men (Glynn et al., 1985; Stall, 1986; Temple, 1989) and in women (Fillmore, 1987) both show a decrease in alcohol consumption with increasing age.

Health problems contribute to the decrease in the proportion of alcoholics seen with increasing age in two ways. Misuse of alcohol causes considerable illness and injury. As alcoholics age, therefore, many of them die or are institutionalized because of alcohol-related illness or injury (Barnes, 1987). Unless these people are replaced by new-onset alcoholics, this will cause a decline in the prevalence of problem drinking in the population. People also develop chronic illnesses that are not related to alcohol as they age. They may then decrease their alcohol intake to avoid aggravating their illnesses. Those taking medications may stop drinking to avoid potential drug-alcohol interactions. Some studies have asked respondents who had decreased or stopped drinking why they did so. In those studies, health problems were indeed commonly cited as a reason for a decrease in alcohol consumption (Barnes, 1979; Bristow & Clare, 1992; Meyers, 1981).

In general, it appears that people become less likely to use and especially to misuse alcohol as they age. Several studies, however, describe a phenomenon known as "late onset alcoholism" (Atkinson, Tolson & Turner, 1990; Finlayson, 1988). As noted above, the ECA study confirms an increase in the incidence of alcohol abuse and alcoholism after age 60. Approximately one-third of elderly alcoholics in treatment have had relatively recent onset of their problem drinking. Those who begin to drink abusively in old age probably have social and medical characteristics somewhat different from long-term alcoholics who survive into old age (Atkinson et al., 1990; Buchsbaum, Buchanan, Lawton, & Schnoll, 1991; Finlayson et al., 1988; Hurt, Finlayson, Morse, & Davis, 1988; Schonfeld, 1991). This phenomenon has not yet been well-studied, however, and preliminary results are not consistent. Long-term alcoholics often have alienated family members and friends, whereas late-onset problem drinkers may be more likely to have intact social resources. For example, in one study of elderly alcoholics in a treatment program, late-onset alcoholics were more likely to be widowed but less likely to be divorced or separated than early-onset alcoholics (Hurt et al., 1988). This finding has not been corroborated in other studies, and may vary depending on the group studied. In some cases, late-onset alcohol problems may start as a reaction to losses and stresses related to aging, but this has also not been consistently shown in all studies.

It is important to bear in mind that elderly alcoholics, like their younger counterparts, are a heterogeneous group who cannot be expected to have homogeneous social characteristics. Some alcoholics die in middle age of alcohol-related illness or injury. Of those who survive, some cease their harmful drinking behavior as they age and others do not. Still others seem to develop problematic drinking in their older years. Further studies will be valuable in identifying the social characteristics salient to treating the alcohol problems of these people as well as in clarifying the medical complications of alcoholism most important in this age group.

Alcohol Problems in Health Care Settings

Since heavy drinking is known to cause increased morbidity and mortality from medical illness, it is not surprising to find that the prevalence of alcohol problems is considerably higher in health care settings than in the community (see Table 1.2). Primary care settings, which are quite similar to general population settings, show only slightly increased prevalence. Using the Diagnostic Interview Schedule, Buchsbaum, Buchanan, Welsh, Centor, and Schnoll (1992) interviewed 323 outpatients age 60 and older in a medical school clinic. Thirty-three percent had a lifetime history of alcohol problems, and 6% had current problems. Jones, Lindsey, Yount, Soltys, and Farani-Enayat (1993) interviewed 154 elderly primary care patients (59% female) in another teaching hospital clinic. Sixteen percent met DSM–III–R criteria for lifetime alcohol abuse or dependence and 3.8% for current abuse or dependence. The female predominance of these samples may have contributed to the relatively low prevalence. Magruder-Habib, Saltz, and Barron (1986) found that 10% of elderly veterans in a primary care clinic screened positive on the Veterans Alcohol Screening Test (VAST). The only study of primary care patients outside the academic or Veterans Affairs settings comes from England. In a sample of 241 older old (75 and older) general practice patients in London, Iliffe and colleagues (1991) found that 3.6% of men and 3.2% of women reported drinking more than the safety limits of the Royal College of Psychiatrists.

The prevalence is considerably higher in the emergency room setting. Adams, Magruder-Habib, Trued, and Broome (1992) found that 14% of

Table 1.2 Alcohol Problems in Medical Settings

Study	Population and setting	Definition of problem drinking	Prevalence	Comments
McCusker et al. (1971)	54 inpatients age 50 and older at Harlem Hospital, New York City	Alcohol abuse (frequent intoxication and/or impairment in social, family, occupational or physical functioning)	63% of men aged 50–69 56% of men aged 70 and older 35% of women aged 50–69 0% of women aged 70 and older	Small urban inner-city population; only 18 patients age 70 and older.
Magruder-Habib et al. (1986)	178 male outpatients age 55 and older at an urban Veterans Administration clinic	Current alcoholism (Veterans Alcoholism Screen Test)	10% of patients aged 65 and older	Veterans Administration Cli Clinic patients may differ from general population.
Curtis et al. (1989)	171 inpatients age 60 and older at inner city teaching hospital. 50% women,	Lifetime alcoholism (Short Michigan Alcohol Screening Test of CAGE)	26% of patients aged 60–69 15% of patients aged 70 and older	Urban population measured lifetime alcoholism. 11% of elderly patients for alcoholism reported consuming 35 oz. or more of alcohol per week.
Iliffe et al. (1991)	239 general practice outpatients age 75 and older (65% women) in London	Current heavy drinking (168g ethanol/wk for men 112 g ethanol/wk for women)	4% of men 3% of women	Older population: "heavy drinking" limit set lower than some other studies.

continued

Table 1.2 *continued*

Buchsbaum et al. (1991)	323 outpatients age 60 and older in a university clinic	Active DSM–III Alcohol abuse or dependence	6% for women.	Lifetime prevalence of alcohol abuse, dependence, or problem drinking was much higher: 63% for men and 22% for women.
Tabisz et al. (1991)	493 Emergency Department patients age 65 and older in Winnipeg	Alcoholism (Brief Michigan Alcohol Screening Test of CAGE)	14%	
Bristow & (1992)	327 men and women inpatients over age 65 at two London hospitals	Current heavy drinking (168 g ethanol/wk for men 112g ethanol/wk for women)	9% of men 0% of women	Older population (mean 76 for women, 74 for men). Clare
Adams et al. (1992)	205 Emergency Department patients age 65 and older in North Carolina; 66% women	Current alcoholism (CAGE positive or self-reported "drinking problem" and current use)	14%	
Mangion et al. (1993)	543 medical inpatients age 65 and older (mean 77) at two British hospitals	Alcohol abuse (168 g ethanol/wk for men 112 g ethanol/wk for women of CAGE positive)	13% of men 2% of women	24% of alcoholics' admissions were clearly alcohol-related
Jones et al. (1993)	154 outpatients age 65 and older at university outpatients clinic. 59% women	DSM–III Alcohol abuse or dependence	16% lifetime 4% current	

elderly emergency room patients in North Carolina had positive scores on the CAGE questionnaire and acknowledged current alcohol use. Interestingly, few of these patients presented with trauma, in contrast to the presentation of younger problem drinkers to emergency departments. Medical illness, particularly gastrointestinal complaints, was the rule. Using the Brief Michigan Alcohol Screening Test and CAGE, Tabisz and colleagues (1991) also found a 14% prevalence of alcohol problems among elderly people who came to an emergency department in Winnipeg. Another study examined blood alcohol levels of elderly trauma patients in the emergency department. Of 128 people 65 and older who presented to the ED with trauma, 12.6% had blood alcohol concentrations over 100 mg/dl (Rivara et al., 1993).

The prevalence of alcohol problems among hospital inpatients is even higher. Curtis et al. (1989) found that 21% of elderly medical inpatients at Johns Hopkins Hospital screened positive for alcoholism on either the CAGE or Short Michigan Alcohol Screening Test (Curtis, Geller, Stoker, Levine, & Moore, 1989). Patients age 70 and older had a lower prevalence than those age 60–69: 15% vs. 26%. Ninety-one percent of patients who screened positive for alcoholism were men, though the sample overall was predominantly female. In London, Bristow and Clare (1992) found that 9% of men but less than 1% of women admitted to medical and geriatric services met Royal College of Psychiatrists' criteria for unsafe quantities of alcohol consumption. Another British study reported an 8% prevalence of alcohol abuse among patients 65 and older admitted to 2 hospitals; in 24% of those cases (2% of all geriatric admissions) the admissions were clearly the result of alcohol misuse (Mangion, Platt, & Syam, 1992). Several years ago, a study of medical inpatients at Harlem Hospital in New York found that 60% of men and 34% of women over age 50 were alcohol abusers based on a scale of alcohol abuse designed for the study (McCusker, Cherubin, & Zimberg, 1971). The prevalence declined with increasing age.

Psychiatric settings also show a high frequency of alcohol problems among older adults. In a study of 2309 elderly people referred to a geriatric psychiatry outreach program, Reifler et al. reported that 10% were referred for alcohol abuse. Simon, Epstein, and Reynolds found that 23% of elderly psychiatric inpatients were alcoholic, by psychiatric interview.

Alcohol problems in long-term care settings have been studied very little. The reader is referred to chapter 10, on alcoholism in the nursing home, for further information on this subject.

Another approach to studying the epidemiology of alcohol problems among elderly inpatients has been to examine hospital discharge diagnoses. This allows the researcher access to a larger number of patients than is feasible in an interview study. The information acquired in this type of study is necessarily limited, however, to problems that required hospitalization, were identified by the physicians caring for the patients, noted in the medical record, and transcribed to a list of discharge diagnoses. This method almost certainly results in a marked underestimate of the frequency of alcohol abuse and alcoholism. The National Hospital Discharge Survey collects data from a national sample of hospitals to determine the frequency of various illnesses. Using data from that survey, researchers have reported that, while the highest rate of alcohol-related diagnoses among inpatients occurred in the 45–64 year old age group, alcohol-related hospitalizations were slightly more common among elderly people than among those aged 25–44 (Stinson, Dufour, & Bertolucci, 1989). That is particularly interesting in contrast to the population-based ECA study, which shows a clear decline in the prevalence of alcohol abuse and dependence with age from the 25–44 year age group to the group age 65 and older (Molgaard et al., 1990). One possible interpretation of this finding is that, although there are fewer elderly problem drinkers, they suffer more alcohol-related medical problems than their younger counterparts. In an analysis of Medicare billing records for the entire United States, Adams et al. (1993) have confirmed a high frequency of alcohol-related hospitalizations among people aged 65 and older. There was considerable geographic variation; the prevalence of alcohol-related hospitalizations ranged from 19/10,000 population in Arkansas to 77/10,000 in Alaska. Rates were higher for men than for women in every state. To put the rates in perspective, the authors compared their findings to the rates of myocardial infarction as studied by the same method in the same population. The frequency of alcohol-related hospitalizations was slightly higher than the frequency of hospitalizations for myocardial infarction.

In general, it appears that the prevalence of alcohol problems among elderly people is higher in health care settings than in the general population. Medical settings that provide relatively intense levels of medical care, such as hospitals and emergency departments, have the highest prevalence of alcohol-related problems. Though the prevalence of problem drinking in the general population declines with increasing age, the prevalence of alcohol-related hospitalizations does not. This very likely reflects the high level of morbidity and mortality known to be associated with alcoholism (Barnes, 1987).

CLINICAL IMPLICATIONS AND EXPECTATIONS FOR THE FUTURE

There are several clinical implications of these epidemiologic findings. Although problem drinking does decline with increasing age, it remains a very substantial problem among elderly people, especially in health care settings. The prevalence clearly warrants routine screening by health care providers in many settings. Alcohol misuse clearly increases the risk of health problems such as liver disease, dementia, gastrointestinal problems, trauma, and drug-alcohol interactions. Emerging epidemiologic data suggest that elderly people may be more susceptible to some alcohol-related health problems than younger people. Hospitalization for alcohol-related problems is very common among older adults. For older people, the threat of cognitive impairment is a particularly frightening complication of alcoholism which often leads to loss of independence and nursing home placement (Willenbring, 1988). Because of the morbidity and mortality associated with alcoholism, clinicians need to be able to identify and intervene with older persons at risk for problem drinking. Brief intervention strategies currently being tested may offer primary care physicians a feasible way to address problem drinking effectively in the office. In addition, the time has come for development of more treatment programs specific to the needs of older adults. Further research is needed to clarify risk factors related to population subgroups of older adults, including people 75 and older, socioeconomic groups, minority groups, and groups by gender. More research is also needed to focus on risks associated with patterns of drinking, including late-onset drinking.

Currently 11% of the U.S. population is age 60 or older; the percent is increasing, and it has been estimated that by the year 2030, 25% of the U.S. population will be age 60 or older (U.S. Department of Health and Human Services, 1990). Similar changes are occurring in the age distributions of other industrialized countries. Since the elderly population is expanding, we will see an increase in the absolute number of older problem drinkers over the next few decades, even if the prevalence of problem drinking remains constant. If, as the above studies suggest, approximately 10% of older people are heavy drinkers and 2–4% are alcoholic, the impact on the health care system will be substantial in the coming decades. Some studies suggest that the cohort currently middle-aged will increase its alcohol consumption as it ages. Changing social mores have also made drinking among women more acceptable, so in future years we may see an increase in the number of older women who use and abuse alcohol. The female predominance of the elderly population may no longer help to limit the extent of the problem as much as it appears to currently. Since heavy drinkers appear to have a higher frequency of alcohol-related medical problems as they age, we can expect a seriously increased demand on the health care system for treatment of these problems. Perhaps the most important implication of problem drinking among elderly people is the need for a proactive approach to the problem. It is incumbent on health care providers and administrators to plan for the expected increase in the number of older people with alcohol-related medical and social problems. The personal, family, and societal costs associated with problem drinking also demand that health care providers, researchers, and planners look to effective prevention as a way to reduce the morbidity and mortality associated with problem drinking in this population.

REFERENCES

Adams, W. L., Garry P. J., Rhyne, R., Hunt, W. C., & Goodwin, J. S. (1990). Alcohol intake in the healthy elderly. *Journal of the American Geriatrics Society, 38,* 211–216.

Adams, W. L., Magruder-Habib, K., Trued, S., & Broome, H. L. (1992). Alcohol abuse in elderly emergency department patients. *Journal of the American Geriatrics Society, 40,* 1236–1240.

Adams, W. L. (1995). Potential for adverse drug-alcohol interactions in elderly retirement community residents. *Journal of the American Geriatrics Society, 43,* 1021–1025.

Adams, W. L., Yuan, Z., Barboriak, J. J., & Rimm, A. A. (1993). Alcohol-related hospitalizations in elderly people: Prevalence and geographic variation in the United States. *Journal of the American Medical Association, 270,* 1222–1225.

Alexander, F., & Duff, R. W. (1988). Social interaction and alcohol use in retirement communities. *The Gerontologist, 28,* 632–636.

American Psychiatric Association. (1980). Diagnostic and statistical manual of mental disorders (3rd ed.). Washington, DC: Author.

Atkinson, R. M. (1984). Substance use and abuse in late life. In R. M. Atkinson (Ed.). *Alcohol and drug abuse in old age* (pp. 1–21). Washington, DC: American Psychiatric Press.

Atkinson, R. M., Tolson, R. L., & Turner, J. A. (1990). Late versus early onset problem drinking in older men. *Alcoholism: Clinical and Experimental Research, 14,* 574–579.

Bailey, M. B., Haberman, P. W., & Alksne, H. (1965). The epidemiology of alcoholism in an urban residential area. *Quarterly Journal of Studies on Alcohol, 26,* 9–40.

Barnes, G. M. (1979). Alcohol use among older persons: Findings from a western New York State general population survey. *Journal of the American Geriatrics Society, 27,* 244–250.

Barnes, H. N. (1987). The etiology and natural history of alcoholism. In H. N. Barnes, M. D. Aronson, & T. L. Delbanco (Eds.), *Alcoholism: A guide for primary care physicians* (pp. 21–23). New York. Springer-Verlag.

Blazer, D., Crowell, B. A., & George, L. K. (1987). Alcohol abuse and dependence in the rural South. *Archives of General Psychiatry, 44,* 736–740.

Bristow, M. F., & Clare, A. W. (1992). Prevalence and characteristics of at-risk drinkers among elderly acute medical inpatients. *British Journal of Addictions, 87,* 291–294.

Buchsbaum, D. G., Buchanan, R. G., Lawton, M. J., & Schnoll, S. H. (1991). Alcohol consumption patterns in a primary care population. *Alcohol and Alcoholism, 26,*215–220.

Buchsbaum, D. G., Buchanan, R. G., Welsh, J., Centor, R. M., & Schnoll, S. H. (1992). Screening for drinking disorders in the elderly using the CAGE questionnaire. *Journal of the American Geriatrics Society, 40,* 662–665.

Cahalan, D., & Cisin, A. (1968). American drinking practices: Summary of findings from a national probability sample. *Quarterly Journal of Studies on Alcohol, 29,* 29:139–151.

Cornoni-Huntley, J., Brock, D. B., Ostfeld, A. M., Taylor, J. O., & Wallace, R. B. (1986). *Established populations for epidemiologic studies of the elderly.* Washington, DC: U.S. Dept of Health and Human Services (NIH Publication No. 86–2443,) pp. 196–199.

Curtis, J. R., Geller, G., Stokes, E. J., Levine, D. M. & Moore, R. D. (1989). Characteristics, diagnosis, and treatment of alcoholism in elderly patients. *Journal of the American Geriatrics Society, 37,* 310–316.

Douglass, R. L., Schuster, E. O., & McClelland, S. C. (1988). Drinking patterns and abstinence among the elderly. *International Journal of Addictions, 23,* 399–415.

Dunham, R. E. (1981). Aging and changing patterns of alcohol use. *Journal of Psychoactive Drugs, 13,* 143–152.

Eaton, W. W., Kramer, M., Anthony, J. C., Dryman, A., Shapiro, S., Locke, B. Z. (1989). The incidence of specific DIS/DSM–III mental disorders: Data from the NIMH Epidemiologic Catchment Area program. *Acta Psychiatrica Scandinavica, 79,* 163–178.

Fillmore, K. M. (1989). Prevalence, incidence, and chronicity of drinking patterns and problems among men as a function of age: A longitudinal and cohort analysis. *British Journal of the Addictions, 82,* 77–83.

Fillmore, K. M. (1987). Women's drinking across the adult life course as compared to men's. *British Journal of Addictions, 82,* 801–811.

Finlayson, R. E., Hurt, R. D., Davis, L. J., Morse, R. M. (1988). Alcoholism in elderly persons: A study of the psychiatric and psychosocial features of 216 inpatients. *Mayo Clinic Proceedings, 63,* 761–768.

Giovannucci, E., Colditz, G., Stampfer, M. J., Rimm, E. B., Litin, L., Sampson, L., Willett, W. C. (1991). The assessment of alcohol consumption by a simple self-administered questionnaire. *American Journal of Epidemiology, 133,* 810–17.

Glynn, R. L., Bouchard, G. R., Lo Castro, J. S., Laird, N. M. (1985). Aging and generational effects on drinking behaviors in men: Results from the Normative Aging Study. *American Journal of Public Health, 75,* 1413–1419.

Goodwin, J. S., Sanchez, C. J., Thomas, P., Hunt, C., Garry, P. J., Goodwin, J. M. (1987). Alcohol intake in a healthy elderly population. *American Journal of Public Health, 77,* 173–177.

Gordon, T., Kannel, W. B. (1983). Drinking and its relation to smoking, BP, blood lipids, and uric acid. *Archives of Internal Medicine, 143,* 1366–1374.

Graham, K. (1986). Identifying and measuring alcohol abuse among the elderly: Serious problems with existing instrumentation. *Journal of Studies on Alcohol, 47,* 322–326.

Helzer, J. E., Burnham, A., McEvoy, L. T. (1991). Alcohol abuse and dependence. In Robins, L. N. & Regier, D. A., (Eds.). *Psychiatric disorders in America: The Epidemiologic Catchment Area Study* (pp. 81–115). New York: Macmillan.

Hurt, R. D., Finlayson, R. E., Morse, R. M., & Davis, L. J. (1988). Alcoholism in elderly persons: Medical aspects and prognosis of 216 inpatients. *Mayo Clinic Proceedings, 63,* 753–760.

Iliffe, S., Haines, A., Booroff, A., Goldenberg, E., Morgan, P., Gallivan, S. (1991). Alcohol consumption by elderly people: A general practice survey. *Age and Ageing, 20,* 120–123.

Jones, T. V., Lindsey, B. A., Yount, P., Soltys, R., & Farani-Enayat, B. (1993). Alcoholism screening questionnaires: Are they valid in elderly medical outpatients? *Journal of General Internal Medicine, 8,* 674–678.

Katzman, R. (1986). Alzheimer's disease. *New England Journal of Medicine, 314,* 964–973.

Kirkpatrick, B., Johnson, M. S., Earp, J. A., & Fletcher, R. H. (1988). Accuracy of chart diagnosis of alcoholism in patients with a history of psychosis. *Psychiatric Medicine, 6,* 65–71.

Lemmens, P., Knibbe, R. A., & Tan, F. (1988). Weekly recall and diary estimates of alcohol consumption in a general population survey. *Journal of Studies on Alcohol, 49,* 131–135.

Magruder-Habib, K., Saltz, C. C., & Barron, P. M. (1986). Age-related patterns of alcoholism among veterans in ambulatory care. *Hospital and Community Psychiatry, 37,* 1251–1255.

Mangion, D. M., Platt, J. S., & Syam, V. (1992). Alcohol and acute medical admission of elderly people. *Age and Ageing, 21,* 362–367.

Mausner, J. S., & Kramer, S. (1985). *Epidemiology: An introductory text.* Philadelphia, PA: Saunders.

McCusker, J., Cherubin, C. E., & Zimberg, S. (1971). Prevalence of alcoholism in a general municipal hospital population. *New York State Journal of Medicine,* 751–754.

McKim, W. A., & Quinlan, L. T. (1991). Changes in alcohol consumption with age. *Canadian Journal of Public Health, 82,* 231–234.

Meyers, A. R., Goldman, E., Hingson, R., & Scotch, N. (1981–82). Evidence for cohort or generational differences in the drinking behavior of older adults. *International Journal of Aging and Human Development, 14,* 31–43.

Meyers, A. R., Hingson, R., Mucatel, M., & Goldman, E. (1982). Social and psychological correlates of problem drinking in old age.*Journal of the American Geriatrics Society, 30,* 452–456.

Molgaard, C. A., Nakamura, C. M., Stanford, E. P., Peddecord, K. M., & Morton, D. J. (1990). Prevalence of alcohol consumption among older persons.*Journal of Community Health, 15,* 239–251.

Moos, R. H., Brennan, P. L., & Moos, B. S. D. (1991). Short-term processes of remission and nonremission among late-life problem drinkers. *Alcoholism: Clinical and Experimental Research, 15,* 948–955.

Myers, J. K., Weissman, M. M., Tischler, G. L., Holzer, C. E., Leaf, P. J., Orvaschel, H., Anthony, J. C., et al. (1984). Six month prevalence of psychiatric disorders in three communities. *Archives of General Psychiatry, 41,* 959–967.

Paganini-Hill, A., Ross, R. K., & Henderson, B. E. (1986). Prevalence of chronic disease and health practices in a retirement community. *Journal of Chronic Disease, 39,* 699–707.

Pozzato, G., Moretti, M., Franzin, F., Croce, L. S., Lacchin, T., Benedetti, G., Sablich, R., Stebel, M., & Campanacci, L. (1995). Ethanol metabolism and aging: The role of "first pass metabolism" and gastric alcohol dehydrogenase activity. *Journal of Gerontology, 50,* B135–41.

Redman, S., Sanson-Fisher, R. W., Wilkinson, C., Fahey, P. P., & Gibberd, R. W. (1987). Agreement between two measures of alcohol consumption. *Journal of Studies on Alcohol, 48,* 104–108.

Reifler, B. V., Kethley, A., O'Neill, P., Hanley, R., Lewis, S., & Stenchever, D. (1982). Five-year experience of a community outreach program for the elderly. *American Journal of Psychiatry, 139,* 220–223.

Rivara, F. P., Jurkovich, G. J., Gurney, J. G., Seguin, D., Fligner, C. L., Ries, R., Raisys, V. A., & Copass, M. (1993). The magnitude of acute and chronic alcohol abuse in trauma patients. *Archives of Surgery, 128,* 907–913.

Robins, L. N., Helzer, J. E., Croughan, J., & Ratcliffe, K. (1981). National Institute of Mental Health Diagnostic Interview Schedule: Its history, characteristics, and validity. *Archives of General Psychiatry, 38,* 381–389.

Schonfeld, L., & Dupree, L. W. (1991). Antecedents of drinking for early and late-onset elderly alcohol abusers. *Journal of Studies on Alcohol, 52,* 587–592.

Seitz, H. K., Simanowski, U. A., Waldherr, R., Eckey, R., Agarwal, D. P., Goedde, H. W., & von Wartburg, J. P. (1993) Human gastric alcohol dehydrogenase activity: Effect of age, sex, and alcoholism. *Gut, 34,* 1433–37.

Shapiro, S., Skinner, E. A., Kessler, L. G., VonKorff, M. V., German, P. S., Tischler, G. L., Leaf, P. J., Benham, L., Cottler, L., & Regier, D. A. (1984). Utilization of health and mental health services. *Archives of General Psychiatry, 41,* 971–978.

Simon, A., Epstein, L. J., & Reynolds, L. (1968). Alcoholism in the geriatric mentally ill. *Geriatrics, 23,* 125–131.

Skoog, I., Nillson, L., Palmertz, B., Andreasson, L., & Svanborg, A. (1993). A population-based study of dementia in 85-year-olds. *New England Journal of Medicine, 328,* 153–158.

Smart, R. G., & Liban, C. B. (1981). Predictors of problem drinking among elderly, middle-aged, and youthful drinkers. *Journal of Psychoactive Drugs, 13,* 153–163.

Stall, R. (1986). Change and stability in quantity and frequency of alcohol use among aging males: A 19 year follow-up study.*British Journal of Addiction, 84,* 537–544.

Stinson, F. S., Dufour, M. C., & Bertolucci, D. (1989). Alcohol-related morbidity in the aging population. *Alcohol Health and Research World, 13,* 80–87.

Tabisz, E., Badger, M., Meatherall, R., Jacyk, W. R., Fuchs, D., & Grymonpre, R. (1991). Identification of chemical abuse in the elderly admitted to emergency. *Clinical Gerontologist, 11,* 27–39.

Temple, M. T., & Leino, E. V. (1989). Long-term outcomes of drinking: A 20-year longitudinal study of men. *British Journal of Addiction, 84,* 889–899.

U.S. Department of Health and Human Services (1990, January). *Seventh Special Report to the U.S. Congress on Alcohol and Health.* Public Health Service, Alcohol, Drug, and Mental Health Administration (ADAMHA), National Institute of Alcohol Abuse and Alcoholism, Rockville, MD.

Vaillant, G. E. (1983). *The natural history of alcoholism: Causes, patterns, and paths to recovery.* Cambridge, MA: Harvard University Press.

Vestal, R. E., McGuire, E. A., Tobin, J. D., Andres, R., Norris, A. H., & Mezey, E. (1976). Aging and ethanol metabolism. *Clinical Pharmacology and Therapeutics, 21,* 343–354.

Werch, C. E. (1989). Quantity-frequency and diary measures of alcohol consumption for elderly drinkers. *International Journal of the Addictions, 24,* 859–865.

Willenbring, M. L. (1988). Organic mental disorders associated with heavy drinking and alcohol dependence. *Clinics in Geriatric Medicine, 4,* 869–887.

2

Screening and Diagnosis: Alcohol Use Disorders in Older Adults

Sara S. DeHart, MSN, PhD, RN
Norman G. Hoffmann, PhD

INTRODUCTION

The extent of alcohol use disorders (abuse, dependence and at-risk drinking) by older people in the United States is not known with any degree of certainty. What is known is that alcohol use disorders in older adults have had an impact on societal resources, particularly health care resources (Adams, Zhong, Barboriak, & Rimm, 1993). These data bring into question the accuracy of the assumption that alcohol abuse is primarily a problem for members of younger age groups who "recover" or die prior to entering old age.

In 1982, Brody expressed concerns about the accuracy of published data for alcoholism rates for older adults. More than a decade later, these concerns are still valid. Estimates of the prevalence of alcohol abuse or dependence are often based on surveys, which tend to underrepresent older adults in general and older drinkers in particular (Clark & Midanik, 1982). In addition, researchers have documented that elderly drinkers frequently underreport their alcohol consumption and problems (Atkinson & Kofoed, 1982; Graham, 1986). Even the Epidemiologic Catchment Area (ECA) study (Robins, Helzer, Pryzbeck, & Reigier, 1988) may have underestimated the prevalence of alcohol abuse for this segment of the population because the criteria used in that survey have not been validated for older adults (Atkinson, 1990).

Owing to the limitations of current screening instruments and under-reporting of alcohol consumption by elderly drinkers, many researchers believe that substance use disorders, including alcohol abuse and dependence, are not identified in older adults in the early, most easily treatable stages of the disease (Atkinson, 1990; Beresford, Blow, Brower, Adams, & Hall, 1988; Gomberg, 1987; Graham, 1986). One troublesome issue is that clinical guidelines for "at-risk drinking" have not been established, so there is wide variance among health care providers in their assessment of this category. Part of the problem in identifying alcohol use disorders stems from the reluctance of some health care professionals to consistently address this issue in the older adult population (Studies of alcohol abuse and alcoholism among the aged, 1988).

CONCEPTUAL AND OPERATIONAL DEFINITIONS

Older Adults

Use of such terms as "the elderly" and "elderly alcoholics" implies that chronological age confers homogeneity. This view frequently clouds important issues as researchers try to sort out the effects of alcohol abuse on aging. One recent report describes aging as a complex process that entails important cellular-genetic, organismic, psychosocial, and cultural dimensions. The interaction of these factors produces great diversity and heterogeneity among older adults. "In affected individuals, substance abuse interacts with, and complicates, all features of aging, illness, and dysfunction" (Atkinson, Ganzini, & Bernstein, 1992, p. 516).

Researchers define elderly alcoholics in a variety of ways. In 1978, Schuckit and Paster defined elderly alcoholics as persons of ages 55 and older. More recently, some researchers in the field of alcohol abuse have used Neugarten and Neugarten's (1986) terminology to categorize older adults as "young-old" and "old-old," but have used differing age breaks to categorize these groups (Atkinson, 1990; Counte, Salloway, & Christman, 1982; Moos & Finney, 1988). Geriatric demographers currently use a "middle-old" category for ages 75–84, and reserve the term "old-old" for persons of ages 85 and older (Atchley, 1991). Although care must be taken to determine how such terms are defined, chronological age categories are useful to examine large data bases for potential differences among older adults. By contrast, most researchers report broad age categories in alcohol abuse studies (e.g., > 55, > 60, or >65).

Diagnostic Criteria

In the United States current diagnostic criteria used to ascertain alcoholism are set forth in the *Diagnostic and Statistical Manual of Mental Disorders* (4th edition), which differentiates between alcohol *abuse* and alcohol *dependence* (American Psychiatric Association [APA], 1994) (See Table 2.1 for a comparison of DSM and ICD–10 classification systems). The *DSM–IV* defines alcohol *abuse* as a maladaptive pattern of alcohol use leading to clinically significant impairment or distress, as manifested by:

(a) one (or more) of the following symptoms within a 12-month period: recurrent substance use resulting in a failure to fulfill major role obligations at work, school, or home; recurrent substance use in situations in which it is physically hazardous; recurrent substance-related legal problems; continued substance use despite persistent or recurrent social or interpersonal problems, and

(b) the substances have never met the criteria for Substance Dependence for this class of substances (APA, 1994, p. 112). By contrast, alcohol *dependence* is characterized by seven symptom categories: tolerance; withdrawal; increased amounts or over a longer period than was intended; persistent desire or unsuccessful efforts to cut down or control use; a great deal of time spent in activities necessary to obtain the substance; important social, occupational, or recreational activities are given up or reduced; the substance use is continued despite knowledge of having a persistent or recurrent physical or psychological problem that is exacerbated by the substance. According to the DSM–IV guidelines three (or more) of these indicators must be present for a diagnosis of alcohol dependence to be established.

The World Health Organization's (WHO's) nosology presented in the proposed International Classification of Diseases-10 (ICD–10) and the DSM–IV use somewhat different terminology to designate alcohol abuse and dependence (APA, 1994; WHO, 1990). The ICD classification of "harmful use of alcohol" is similar to the DSM classification of "alcohol abuse," while the ICD alcohol dependence syndrome (ADS) is similar to the DSM term "alcohol dependence." Later in this chapter, we will discuss some reasons why older adults provide unique challenges to alcohol abuse and dependence classification systems, as does psychiatric comorbidity (Atkinson, 1990; Naitonal institute of Alcohol Abuse and Alcoholism, (NIAAA), October 1991).

The diagnostic formulations of DSM–III (APA, 1980) which grouped symptoms into three categories (pathological use, social impairments and physiological symptoms); DSM–III–R (APA, 1987) with nine categories;

TABLE 2.1 Comparisons of *DSM–III–R*, *DSM–IV*, and ICD–10 Criteria for Alcohol Dependence[1]

DSM–III–R	DSM–IV	ICD–10
Marked tolerance (7)	Tolerance (1)	Tolerance (d)
Characteristic withdrawal (8)	Withdrawal (2a)	Physiological withdrawal (c)
Use in larger amounts or over longer period than intended (1)	Use in larger amounts or over longer period than intended (3)	Control of use in terms of onset, level, termination (b)
Desire or efforts to cut down (2)	Desire or efforts to control use (4)	Difficulties in controlling substance-taking behavior (b)
A great deal of time is spent to obtain, use, or recover from use (3)	A great deal of time is spent to obtain, use, or recover from (3)	Time necessary to obtain, take, or recover from use effects (e)
Giving up or reducing social, occupational, or recreational activities (5)	Giving up or reducing social, occupational, recreational activities (6)	Progressive neglect of alternative recreational interests (e)
Continued use despite persistent or recurrent social, psychological, or physical problems (6)	Continued use despite persistent or recurrent physical or psychological problems (7)	Persistent use despite harmful consequences (f)
Impaired when expected to fulfill obligations (4)	[Substance abuse criterion]	[Harmful substance use criterion]
Use to relieve or avoid withdrawal (9)	Use to relieve or avoid withdrawal (2b)	Use for relieving or avoiding withdrawal (c) Strong desire or compulsion to use (a)

[1] Parentheses identify number/letter of each system criterion. Each system requires three or more of the above symptoms for a dependence diagnosis (APA, 1987, 1994; WHO, 1990).
Source: Adapted from DeHart, S. S., & Hoffmann, N. G. (1995). Screening and diagnosis of alcohol abuse and dependence in older adults. *International Journal of the Addictions, 30,* 1720, table 1.

DSM–IV (APA, 1994) with seven categories; or the proposed ICD–10 (WHO, 1990) with eight categories of dependence symptoms are predominantly based on consensus formulations by expert panels on how the behavioral indicators should be structured to define an addiction syndrome. All these diagnostic criteria tend to encompass a domain of signs and symptoms that are assumed to indicate an addiction problem. The predominant differences among the criteria appear to involve how those signs and symptoms should be divided into symptom categories, and how these respective categories are assigned importance or diagnostic significance. It is important to understand that classification systems are dynamic rather than static and that over time, changes will be made.

Examination of a large database (> 26,000 adult alcoholics) monitored by CATOR (Comprehensive Assessment and Treatment Outcome Research) suggests yet another structuring of indicators. Subjects whose data were analyzed for this study include individuals meeting DSM–III–R criteria for alcohol abuse or dependence at one of 89 treatment programs monitored by CATOR (New Standards, Inc., 1993). The treatment programs represented in this sample are largely private, nonprofit facilities providing residential or intensive outpatient services.

Factor analysis of 23 addiction symptom variables yields a four-factor solution: pathological use, behavioral consequences, physiological symptoms, and loss of control. The *first* factor includes scheduling one's day to accommodate use, use to alleviate emotional and physical discomfort, and persistent preoccupation with use. The *second* involves such indicators as becoming violent when using, missing work or school, blackouts, neglect of duties, and injury during use. The *third* factor, physiological symptoms, includes experiencing delirium tremens and other withdrawal symptoms, use to relieve withdrawal, and the need for consistent use. Factor *four* includes an inability to stop drinking following initiation of alcohol use and drinking more alcohol than intended (Doyle, Hoffmann, & Smith, 1994).

One important finding in this study is the fact that tolerance did not emerge as a strong symptom on any of the factors and did not load on the physiological factor. Its strongest correlation was with items on the pathologic use factor (e.g., scheduling to accommodate use and preoccupation). It correlated only minimally with withdrawal or other variables loading on the physiological factor.

An interpretation of these findings and other evidence suggests that tolerance should not necessarily be considered a cardinal indicator of alcohol addiction for two reasons. The first is that in the factor analysis, tolerance appears to be more a product of use; therefore, it can be acquired through moderately heavy use in the absence of any addiction. Secondly, tolerance is a multifactorial phenomenon with pharmacodynamic, pharmacokinetic, psychological, and genetic factors contributing to its presence (Beresford, 1991; Schuckit, 1989). This may account for tolerance not emerging as a factor on the data used to develop the Michigan Alcohol Screening Test—Geriatric Version (F. C. Blow, personal communication, 1993) or on the CATOR data (Doyle, Hoffmann, & Smith, 1994).

One can also make the argument that current diagnostic criteria may not be as appropriate for seniors as for younger individuals. Older persons may not be as likely to manifest apparent tolerance or other symptoms, such as work performance problems and other impairment indicators, because they no longer have such responsibilities. To ensure that criteria categories are appropriate for older persons, Atkinson has suggested that the minimum number required for a diagnosis for dependence be reduced for older adults or that criteria be studied by age group (Atkinson, 1990).

In any case, the terms "alcohol dependence" and "alcohol abuse," as defined by the DSM criteria (APA, 1980, 1987, 1994) are gradually replacing "alcoholism" and other terms in the scientific literature. Various researchers have employed a wide array of terms (e.g., heavy drinking, alcoholism, alcohol dependence, alcohol abuse, substance use disorders, and chemical dependence) to refer to one or more types and/or levels of severity of alcohol and other chemical abuse problems (Donovan, 1988). The lack of clear, operationally defined terms continues to cause confusion in some reports.

Even with clear definitions, however, the distinctions made for one age group may be less relevant for others. For older people, alcohol abuse is not necessarily less harmful than alcohol dependence. Both can cause loss of independence and functional ability through illness or injury (e.g., fractures, confusion, or dementia); therefore, in the discussion that follows, we will make no differentiation between terms intended to signal alcohol abuse or dependence. Instead, we will use "alcohol abuse" to designate both alcohol abuse and alcohol dependence, *except* where a differentiation is needed to discriminate between them in the context of special issues applicable to screening and diagnosis.

Screening and Assessment

Screening is the exercise of making a probability estimate that a given individual has a specific condition with incomplete diagnostic evidence. By contrast, making a determination with complete criteria allows for full *diagnostic assessment*.

Sensitivity and Specificity

Sensitivity refers to the accuracy of a test in identifying persons with a particular problem. In the case of alcohol detection, it is the proportion of individuals who both abuse alcohol and have an abnormal test result (also termed "true positives"). *Specificity* refers to a test's accuracy in identifying persons who do not have a particular problem. In the case of alcohol abuse detection, it is the proportion of persons who do not abuse alcohol and have normal test results. Any alcohol screen should capture *true positives*, the highest number of persons with the condition, while minimizing the risk of capturing *false positives*, persons without the condition.

ALCOHOL USE DISORDERS IN LATER LIFE

Epidemiology: Incidence and Prevalence

The true incidence of alcohol abuse cases among older adults is not accurately known, and to some extent it is a hidden problem (Osgood, Wood, & Parham, 1995). Estimates of the prevalence (existing cases) of alcohol abuse among older adults, based on epidemiologic studies, range from as low as 2% to 10% in community living groups to as high as 26% in hospitalized older adults (Beresford, Blow, & Brower, 1990). The discrepancy between rates in community versus clinical samples is not surprising, given that alcohol abusers use a disproportionate amount of medical care and constitute a significant proportion of medical patients (Hoffmann et al., 1989; Hoffmann, Harrison, & Ninonuevo, 1988; Zook, & Moore, 1980). A recent study, based on the Medicare Provider Analysis and Review Record (MEDPAR) database, provides further evidence that medical costs are substantial for older adults who abuse alcohol. Adams et al. (1993) report that for patients age 65 and older, the prevalence of hospitalizations for alcohol-related medical conditions and for myocardial infarctions are similar. These researchers conclude that as the population ages, "a potentially preventable problem of this magnitude among the elderly should be addressed by clinicians and researchers alike" (p. 1225).

While some health care providers dismiss the problem of alcohol abuse as inconsequential in old age, use of alcohol remains fairly high among people in their sixties and early seventies (Atkinson & Kofoed, 1982). On the basis of prevalence data from a number of published reports, Atkinson (1990) challenges assertions that abstainers outnumber drinkers after age 65. Thus it would appear that consumption of alcohol remains high during the later years in the "young-old" (people age 60 to age 75), especially in men (Atkinson, 1990).

The biases of some health and social service providers often preclude them from considering the possibility of alcohol abuse in geriatric patients (Atkinson, 1990; Osgood et al., 1995; Studies of alcohol abuse and alcoholism in the aged, 1988). Several hospital studies have found substantial incidence of underrecognition, underreporting, and underreferral (Beresford et al., 1988; Curtis, Geller, Stokes, Levine, & Moore, 1989; Moore et al., 1989; Stinson, Dufour, & Bertolucci, 1989). One reason for this is that many older persons who abuse alcohol are middle-class and do not conform to societal stereotypes of the down-and-out or antisocial alcoholic. Also, many health and social service providers have accepted the findings of early studies, which asserted that the risk of new alcoholism cases ends in the forties and that drug abuse "matures out" after age 45 (Drew, 1968; Winick, 1962). These studies perpetuated the myth that, due to high early mortality and spontaneous recovery in survivors, these disorders are uncommon after middle age (Atkinson, 1990).

While some individuals, families, and health care providers are pessimistic about treatment prospects for older adults, there is growing evidence that recovery (measured by long-term abstinence) for this group is matched or superior to that for younger adults (Atkinson, 1990). Nor is this pessimistic view supported by studies that demonstrate a 2-year post-treatment recovery (i.e., abstinence) rate of 65% for older adults and a significant decrease in hospital days used at 1 and 2 years after alcoholism treatment for persons who remain abstinent (Hoffmann, DeHart, & Fulkerson, 1993; Rode, Hoffmann, & Fulkerson, 1991;).

Clinicians and researchers often argue that abuse of alcohol in older adults is overlooked, in part, because of the difficulties of eliciting adequate clinical information about problem drinking in this population (Atkinson, 1990; Beresford et al., 1988; Graham, 1986). However, other researchers have documented that screening questions about alcohol use and potential abuse often are not asked by health care providers unless an obvious problem is evident (Atkinson & Kofoed, 1982; Cohen, Kern, & Hassett, 1986; Coulehan, Zettler-Segal, Block, McClelland, & Schulberg, 1987; Searight, 1992; Graham, Parran, & Jaen, 1992). An active commitment to detecting cases of alcohol abuse is typically not part of the services provided by community outreach agencies (Raschko, 1990). Therefore, many older persons who abuse alcohol will continue to be overlooked simply because too few health and social care providers consistently inquire about the problem.

Signs and Symptoms

Signs and symptoms of substance use disorders in older adults can be subtle or atypical or can mimic symptoms of other geriatric illnesses, thereby making diagnosis difficult (Atkinson, 1990; Atkinson & Kofoed, 1982). Substance abuse can produce delirium or dementia, which the clinician may falsely attribute to other causes (Freund, 1984). Nonspecific presenting signs and symptoms (e.g., poor grooming; malnutrition; bladder and bowel incontinence; gastrointestinal symptoms and/or worsening of ongoing medical problems; muscle weakness; gait disorders; recurring falls; burns; head traumas; or accidental hypothermia) may in fact be caused by unsuspected alcohol or drug abuse (Schuckit, 1990; Searight, 1992).

Gender

There is evidence that regardless of age, women are less likely than men to have their alcoholism diagnosed. Blume (1990) reports that Moore and his colleagues performed alcoholism screening on more than 2,000 patients admitted to Johns Hopkins Hospital. In this study, the highest proportion of missed alcohol abuse diagnoses by the medical staff were among women and persons of higher income and education levels (Moore et al., 1989).

Although older men are at least two times more likely than older women to have alcohol-related problems or alcoholism, late-life onset alcoholism is more commonly found in women than in men (Atkinson, 1990; Holzer et al., 1984). A sharp increase in the lifetime prevalence of alcoholism among female probands in recent birth cohorts and in female first-degree relatives of more recently born alcoholic probands of both sexes indicates that alcohol abuse rates will rise for elderly women (Cloninger, Reich, Sigvardsson, von Knoring, & Bohman, 1987; Reich, Cloninger, Van Eerdewegh, Roce, & Mullancy, 1988). However, in general medical populations that represent a broad age distribution, the prevalence of alcohol abuse is twice as high for males as it is for females (Hoffmann et al., 1989).

From the perspective of screening older women's alcohol abuse, many screening instruments (e.g. CAGE, MAST) have been normed on men. The question that must be raised is whether or not instruments are equally valid for women and men. Later in this chapter we will discuss screening items which have some potential for discerning alcohol consumption patterns for both older women and men.

INFLUENCE OF MODELS ON SCREENING PRACTICES

Chronic versus Acute Models

An important issue, whether or not the disease model of alcoholism is valid, is beyond the scope of this chapter and reviewed elsewhere (Babor, Kranzler, & Kadden, 1986; Vaillant, 1983). The Harm Reduction Model, for example, rejects the disease model (Marlatt & Tapert, 1993). What is important across models is whether alcoholism is viewed as an acute or chronic condition. A model that conceptualizes alcohol dependence as acute and episodic promotes discrete interventions with little or no long-term followup. This is often translated into policy decisions whereby health care is provided for a limited number of lifetime episodes. However, when alcohol dependence is viewed as a condition with the potential for remission and exacerbation, assessment and followup of persons in both active and remission phases then become important components of health care management. What is different about alcohol dependence recovery compared with some other chronic health problems, is that individuals can be taught about the potential of lifelong vulnerability to relapse and the positive effects of maintaining recovery.

While all persons with either active or inactive alcohol dependence problems need to be identified, recognizing these phases in older adults is especially important. Older people with an active alcohol consumption problem need appropriate intervention and treatment. For those who are in remission, identification of their recovery status has important implications for medical management of some illnesses, particularly with regard to prescribing analgesic, tranquilizer, or antihypertensive medications (Erfurt, & Foote, 1992; Graham et al., 1992; Hoffmann et al., 1988).

Multidimensionality

Many researchers now believe that rather than being a single, unitary condition, alcohol dependence is more accurately conceptualized as a group of disorders with common symptoms but differing etiologies (Babor et al., 1986; Counte et al., 1982; Schuckit, 1989). This multidimensional perspective identifies more than one type of alcoholism (e.g., Type I and Type II), makes a distinction for older adults between early and late onset alcoholism, and reflects a constellation of behaviors, events, and physical manifestations (Atkinson, Tolson, & Turner 1990; Cloninger, Bohman, & Sigvardsson, 1981; Graham et al., 1995; Graham, Ziedman, Flower, Saunders, & White-Campbell, 1989;).

Atkinson et al. (1990) delineate three alcohol abuse subgroups. The early-life onset subgroup consists of people who manifest their first alcohol problems at or before age 40; the midlife onset group ranges from 41 to 59 years; and the late-life onset group exhibits signs of alcohol abuse at or after age 60. Although the incidence of late-life alcohol abuse is not reliably known, data from both community and clinical samples suggest that late-life onset alcohol problems are not uncommon and may comprise approximately one-third of older alcohol abusers (Atkinson, 1990). See Chapter Four in this volume for a review of early versus late onset of alcoholism in older adults.

The issue of differing etiologies and various subtypes of alcohol dependence is confounded by the variety of dimensions that may be considered and the lack of consistency or overall vision of how to conceptualize the condition. Thus, some researchers have focused on genetic and symptom differentials, while others have looked toward age of onset as a distinguishing feature. Further research is needed to adequately conceptualize subtypes of alcohol problems that include the empirical and theoretical demands of these classifications, their advantages and limitations, as well as unresolved critical issues. While provisional models have been suggested (Atkinson et al., 1990; Graham et al., 1995; Graham et al., 1989), a comprehensive research-based model that identifies definitive subtypes for either alcohol dependence or abuse in older adults is not yet available.

Psychiatric Comorbidity

Assessment of psychiatric and alcohol abuse comorbidity provides a unique challenge to clinicians. A comprehensive review of pertinent issues that need to be considered with alcohol abuse and co-occurring psychiatric disorders may be found elsewhere (United States Department of Health and Human Services [USDHHS], 1994; National Institute of Alcohol Abuse and Alcoholism [NIAAA], 1991a). An understanding of these issues is important for assessment, treatment and prevention efforts. Assessment of alcoholism and co-occurring psychiatric disorders is complex and determination of whether alcohol abuse is primary or secondary may not be possible with certainty. Some clinicians suggest that if an alcohol abuse disorder begins after the age of 45, an associated mental disorder should be sought (APA, 1987). This view is refuted by Atkinson (1994) who presents substantial data documenting that primary alcohol abuse can and does occur after midlife. With respect to treatment issues, persons exhibiting comorbid alcohol-related and medical or psychiatric disorders often do not fit into the health care system because of administrative distinctions among addiction, medical, and mental health-related services. This may lead to assessment and treatment for one disorder without consideration for the other (NIAAA, 1991a). A continuing unresolved issue in the broad area of available services for the persons with dual diagnoses is that once they are so labeled, there may be barriers to getting needed care because of time lapses between linking research and policy making, and ongoing gaps between science and service.

Accurate data on the prevalence and incidence of alcoholism and psychiatric co-occurring disorders for older adults are not available. For example, Helzer and Pryzbeck's (1988) report on the ECA study is based on lifetime symptoms of comorbidity. This document reports an increase in depressive disorder among alcoholics as compared to the general population (odds ratio 1.7) and essentially no increase in anxiety disorder. While Petty (1992) reports that alcoholism is a consequence of depression in 5% or less of the cases, and that the prevalence of alcoholism in patients who have primary depression is probably no higher than that of the general population, these data may not accurately reflect co-occurring depression, anxiety, and late-life onset alcoholism. Although few geriatric studies have focused specifically on these phenomena, secondary depression and anxiety disorders may complicate alcohol abuse in elderly persons (Atkinson, 1990). On the other hand, it should not be assumed that late-life alcoholism is secondary to a co-occurring disorder. Atkinson (1994) reports several recent studies of male veterans which show that primary alcohol use disorders can and do begin in late middle age and later.

It is important to diagnose dementias and other organic mental syndromes which may co-occur with, or mask, alcoholism. For example, Raskind and Peskind (1992) report that Wernicke's encephalopathy, a thiamine-deficiency disorder, may be underrecognized prior to the onset of dementia. The importance of recognizing Wernicke's encephalopathy and chronic alcoholic dementia (Korsakoff's syndrome) are evident. Wernicke's encephalopathy is effectively treated with thiamine, and cessation of alcohol ingestion is associated with improved cognitive function in the majority of patients with alcoholic dementia (Raskind & Peskind, 1992). Alcoholism and dementia are reviewed by Smith and Atkinson in Chapter Six of this volume.

BIOLOGICAL MARKERS

Biological markers for alcohol consumption are generally categorized into three types: trait markers, state markers, and markers of organ damage. Trait markers are designed to determine which individuals are at risk for alcohol dependence. State markers reflect either chronic or acute consumption of alcohol. Markers of organ damage reflect the effect of alcohol consumption over time on specific organs such as the liver. See Rosman (1992) for an in-depth review of the utility and evaluation of various types of biological markers of alcohol consumption.

The search for a biological state marker as a "gold standard" for alcohol consumption remains elusive. Biological markers have proven to have relatively poor sensitivity and specificity. Many early-stage alcoholics have not yet developed biological indicators. Conversely, a host of nonalcohol-related conditions can produce abnormal biological findings which are similar to medical consequences of alcoholism.

The sensitivity of most biological markers ranges between 30% to 50%, which is considerably below that of most self-report scales and clinician screens. Rosman's (1992) comparative analysis has established a 50% sensitivity for gamma-glutamyl transpeptidase (GTT), 35% for mean corpuscular volume (MCV), 35% for aspartate aminotransferase (AST), 30% for alanine aminotransferase (ALT), and 30% for high density lipoprotein-cholesterol (HDL–C). While these markers lack sufficient sensitivity and specificity to be used for screens of alcoholic abuse in ambulatory patient care settings, they can be helpful to corroborate clinical suspicion of alcohol abuse.

Rosman (1992) also includes a detailed review of newly developed laboratory markers of alcohol abuse that have increased diagnostic accuracy. One potentially promising marker is serum carbohydrate-deficient transferrin (CDT) which is reported to have a sensitivity rate of approximately 80% for recent heavy drinking. CDT is not elevated by moderate alcohol consumption (approximately 40 grams per day) or by various medications that can elevate other markers of excessive alcohol consumption (e.g., anticonvulsant, antipsychotic, and anticoagulant medications). A false-positive CDT may be caused by primary biliary cirrhosis (Stibler, Borg, & Joustra, 1986).

While laboratory tests, as measures of the biological consequences of alcohol consumption, are helpful adjuncts when confirming a diagnosis of alcohol abuse, biological markers that can be used as screens for alcohol abuse remain inconclusive. Biological tests are used to garner evidence to help health care providers overcome an individual's denial of a problem, although the efficacy of this clinical practice has not been validated. Atkinson (1990) and Beresford, Blow, and Brower, (1990) recommend using self-report scales or clinician screens combined with profiles of specific laboratory tests which are known to be elevated with alcohol abuse. However, the fact that few of the commonly used screens or the DSM criteria (APA, 1994) have been validated for older persons with diagnoses of alcohol abuse or dependence remains a problem. Until research on the criteria is conducted and replicated, current measurement techniques may not be sufficiently sensitive to screen for alcohol abuse in older adults.

Until the biological sciences are able to devise more reliable indicators of alcohol abuse, behavioral indicators remain the best screens for alcohol abuse and dependence. Given the complexity of the human body, biological markers may never prove to be generally useful for screening purposes.

SCREENING INSTRUMENTS

A major resource for alcohol assessment instruments is the NIAAA Treatment Handbook Series 2, *Alcoholism Treatment Assessment Research Instruments* which is currently under revision (Lettieri, Nelson, & Sayers, 1987). The revised edition will provide age and gender sensitivity and specificity data for alcohol screening and diagnostic instruments in current use. The following selected instruments are listed either in the Treatment Handbook Series 2 or appear in current research and clinical literature.

Michigan Alcohol Screening Test (MAST)

The MAST is a 25-item instrument that provides a quantifiable screen for alcohol abuse. It is widely used to screen for alcoholism and has published reliability (alpha = .95) and validity (r = .90) data (Selzer, 1971). The MAST incorporates indicators of early-life alcohol abuse that include psychosocial phenomena such as family disorder, arrest, and morning drinking. Some clinicians have expressed concern that these indicators may not be sensitive screening items for older adults in early stages of alcohol abuse. Because of the MAST's widespread use to screen for alcoholism in younger populations, an assumption is sometimes made that it is a valid screen for older populations as well. This assumption is not necessarily accurate, and it is unwise to define alcoholism in older persons according to criteria established for younger age groups.

In one validation study of the MAST on elderly alcoholics, Willenbring and his colleagues demonstrated high sensitivity and specificity for two versions of the MAST (Willenbring, Christensen, Spring, & Rasmussen, 1987). Although this study is limited by its small sample (52 alcoholic, 33 nonalcoholic controls) and narrow focus (hospitalized men in one V. A. hospital), they found that a cutting score of 3 on the MAST yielded a sensitivity of .96 and a specificity of .86. However, a much larger hospital study conducted by researchers from the University of Michigan Alcohol Research Center has demonstrated that many items on the MAST correlate poorly with alcohol abuse in older patients (Beresford et al., 1990).

Michigan Alcohol Screening Test—Geriatric Version (MAST-G)

The Michigan Center researchers developed a new instrument for use with geriatric patients (MAST-G). This tool was developed because many of the screens currently in use have been shown to poorly identify alcoholism among older adults. The MAST-G was validated, using *DSM-III-R* criteria for alcohol dependence as the standard, on 305 older adults that included: (1) persons currently meeting criteria for alcohol dependence, but not in treatment; (2) those currently in treatment for alcoholism; (3) those with a previous history of alcoholism and currently in recovery; (4) social drinkers; and (5) abstainers (Blow et al., 1992).

The MAST-G is a 24-item elderly-specific alcoholism screening measure with a reported sensitivity of 93.9% and specificity of 78.1%. On this scale, a score of 5 or more "yes" responses indicates an alcohol problem. Although some items on the MAST-G address current and past alcohol abuse, scores do not discriminate between active (current) and inactive (lifetime) alcohol abuse histories. A factor analysis identified five underlying symptom domains: Loss and Loneliness, Relaxation, Dependence, Loss of Control with Drinking, and Rule Making (Blow et al., 1992). Tolerance did not emerge as a factor in this analysis and does not appear to be a reliable indicator of alcohol abuse for older adults (F. C. Blow, personal communication, December 20, 1993).

CAGE Questionnaire Screen

The CAGE asks four questions: (1) Have you ever felt you should *cut down* on your drinking? (2) Have people *annoyed* you by criticizing your drinking? (3) Have you ever felt bad or *guilty* about your drinking? and (4) Have you ever had a drink first thing in the morning (*eye-opener*) to steady your nerves or to get rid of a hangover? (Ewing, 1984; Mayfield, McLeod, & Hall, 1974). Buchsbaum and his colleagues examined the sensitivity and specificity for the CAGE questionnaire on 323 patients ages 60 and older and reported a sensitivity of .86 and specificity of .78 for a CAGE score of 1 for general medicine outpatients (Buchsbaum, Buchanan, Welsh, Centor, & Schnoll, 1992). Their data are particularly interesting because they report sensitivity, specificity, and positive predictive values by gender. They also demonstrate that the CAGE effectively discriminates elderly patients with a history of drinking problems from those without a history.

In an attempt to improve screening techniques for pregnant women, two modifications of the CAGE, the T-ACE and TWEAK, were developed and tested in a Michigan prenatal clinic. The T-ACE (Sokol, Martier, & Ager,

1989) substitutes a tolerance item for guilt. The TWEAK modification assesses tolerance and worry about drinking (Russell et al., 1991). These tests are reported to increase the sensitivity and specificity over the CAGE for women of childbearing age (15–44 years). Since tolerance did not emerge as an indicator for alcohol abuse in older adults (F. C. Blow, personal communication, December 20, 1993), it is unlikely that these modifications will improve screening sensitivity and specificity for older women.

Since the CAGE questionnaire captures an alcohol abuse history but does not distinguish between active (current) or inactive (lifetime) alcohol abuse histories, the status of current drinking patterns also needs to be assessed. Recent drinking (e.g., within the past week) is one indicator of an active problem, even when current problems are denied (Kristenson, Ohlin, Hulten-Nosslin, Trell, & Hood, 1983).

Drinking Problem Index (DPI)

The Drinking Problem Index (Finney, Moos, & Brennan, 1991) is purported to assess alcohol-related problems among older adults. This 17-item measure is designed to overcome concerns that screens designed for general populations are insensitive measures of alcohol abuse for older adults. The DPI taps adverse consequences from drinking, excessive consumption, dependence symptoms, and escapist drinking. The DPI is one of the few alcohol screens that included women as well as men in the norming sample. The authors report that the cross-temporal correlation between drinking problems assessed initially and at the 1-year follow-up is .66, indicting a reasonable stability of scores across the two administrations. Further research using the DPI, particularly in conjunction with a criterion standard (DSM–IV) may provide further data about use of age-normed alcohol screens.

Self-Administered Alcoholism Screening Test

The 35-item Self-Administered Alcoholism Screening Test (SAAST) and a nine-item version of the SAAST have been used to screen medical patients for alcoholism (Davis & Morse, 1987). These investigators report that 80% of patients in their sample (520 alcoholics and 636 nonalcoholics) were classified accurately as "alcoholic" if they responded affirmatively to two items: "Do close relatives ever worry or complain about your drinking?" and "Have you ever felt the need to cut down on your drinking?"

Davis and Morse (1987) also used the 35-item SAAST to evaluate age and gender differences in the responses for patients admitted for evaluation and treatment at an alcoholism and drug dependence unit. In this study, "older adults" referred to persons over the age of 45 (mean age for men was 45, standard deviation 13.7 years and for women 47, standard deviation 14.1 years) so the data are less helpful in evaluating use of the SAAST for the young-old (ages 60–75) or middle-old (ages 76–84). An important finding is, relative to men, women are less often identified by questions about "objections by others about their drinking." According to these researchers, reasons for this phenomenon may include the fact that women attract less attention when drinking because they are less likely to engage in occupationally and socially disruptive behavior; are more likely to consume alcohol in the privacy of their own homes and other less public places; and because their alcoholism is often cloaked by other problems such as emotional consequences (Davis & Morse, 1987). It would be interesting to evaluate the SAAST with a sample that includes the young-old and middle-old adults to determine whether or not gender differences emerge for these age groups.

Alcohol Use Disorders Identification Test

The 10-item Alcohol Use Disorders Identification Test (AUDIT) (Buchsbaum, Buchanan, Welsh, Centor & Schnoll, 1992; Saunders, Aasland, Babor, T. F., de la Fluente, J. R., & Grant, 1993), based on the World Health Organization's screening instrument for harmful and hazardous alcohol consumption, needs to be carefully evaluated before it is widely accepted as a measure of alcohol abuse or dependence in older adults. One of the AUDIT's major strengths is that it is the first instrument of its kind that was developed on the basis of a cross-national study. This strength is mitigated by the fact that sensitivity and specificity data for older adults are not available; therefore, the recommendation for moderation of alcohol consumption for "harmful" use and abstinence for "hazardous" use is of particular concern. Given older adults' increased biological sensitivity to alcohol, and the prevalence of serious alcohol-related diagnoses for this age group (Adams et al., 1993), moderation of use needs to be carefully evaluated before health care providers sanction drinking by vulnerable persons as safe use of alcohol.

BONS Screen

In a randomly selected sample of 310 medical and surgical inpatients from two hospitals, research using the Substance Use Disorders Diagnostic

Schedule (SUDDS) found that an item subset identified by the acronym BONS had high sensitivity and specificity for detecting alcohol abuse in this population (Hoffmann et al., 1989). This acronym refers to the items for blackouts, objections, neglect of responsibilities, and shakes. Of the general medical and surgical patients with a current alcoholism diagnosis, 99% endorsed at least one of these four items, compared to 7% of the patients without a history of alcohol dependence. The BONS screen was cross-validated using other hospitalized medical and surgical patients in a different setting with comparable results (Hoffmann et al., 1989).

In order to determine how well the BONS items would discriminate older adults, data for 672 men and 330 women over the age of 60 in the CATOR database were examined (New Standards, 1993). These data are presented in Table 2.2 (page 44). In general, the relative prevalence or rank order of the items appears similar for both men and women. With very large samples, comparative statistical tests of significance have so much power that even small differences are significant at traditional probability values (e.g., $p \leq .05, .01, .001$). On the basis of the margin of error for the two samples, we considered absolute endorsement differences of 10% or more to compare gender differences. The only item for which women have a 10% higher level of endorsement is the item regarding use of alcohol to alleviate emotional distress. By contrast, the men have substantively higher endorsement rates on four items: blackouts, binges, missing work, and becoming violent when drinking. These items are in conformity with the stereotype of the traditional male alcoholic.

U-OPEN Screen

Another subset of five items emerged from the CATOR data that has some promise for screening older individuals. U-OPEN, the acronym by which the set is identified, denotes the items dealing with unplanned use, objections, preoccupation with use, use in response to emotional distress, and neglect of responsibilities. With older adult alcoholics, this set of screening items appears to be more sensitive than BONS.

Virtually all of the older alcoholics endorsed at least one of the U-OPEN items, and at least 95% of both men and women endorsed at least two of the five items, suggesting that these items have adequate potential sensitivity for detecting the older alcohol abuser. Particularly noteworthy is the fact that, with the U-OPEN screen, older women and men have comparable detection thresholds. Specificity data, that is how well the U-OPEN items discriminate older adults who are non-alcohol abusers, is not yet known.

General Screening Issues

Three issues need to be addressed with regard to the use of screening tests. First, it cannot be assumed that a screen validated for one group is a sensitive and specific screen for other groups. Second, screens are not meant to be used for diagnostic purposes. Rather, their usefulness resides in their ability to help select patients for in-depth interviewing and further diagnostic testing. A second level of questions needs to be directed toward characterizing the intensity and frequency of drinking and the psychological, social, and/or physical effects of drinking on a given person's current functioning (Buchsbaum et al., 1992).

There continues to be a need to evaluate the effectiveness of several different screens to determine the optimum sensitivity and specificity to identify alcohol abuse in older adults. A few well-constructed studies are now appearing in the literature that address this issue. Buchsbaum et al. (1992) provide an appropriate model to use in such validation research.

Other rarely addressed issues with use of alcohol screens are health care providers' comfort level with asking questions about alcohol use, and the training that is needed to conduct a valid and reliable interview in the face of denial or misinformation. Health care providers must consistently use and record screen results for all patients on a regular basis if the procedure is to be useful. This, unfortunately, does not happen frequently enough, as evidenced by the dearth of alcohol screening data documented in charts of patients prescribed benzodiazepines, referred for cognitive impairment evaluation, or whose alcohol abuse diagnoses were missed (Graham et al., 1992; Moore et al., 1989; Rains & Ditzler, 1993). Thus, some proportion of missed alcohol abuse diagnoses appears to be accounted for by the lack of consistent screening of medical patients.

DIAGNOSTIC ASSESSMENT

At least two structured interviews have been developed to assess alcohol abuse and dependence according to DSM diagnostic criteria. The Structured Clinical Interview for DSM–III–R (SCID) (Spitzer, Williams, Gibbon, & First, 1990) and the Substance Use Disorders Diagnostic Schedule-IV (SUDDS–IV) (Hoffmann & Harrison, 1995) are reviewed. The Composite International Diagnostic Interview (CIDI) and Schedules for Clinical Assessment in Neuropsychiatry (SCAN) that were developed for ICD criteria are reviewed elsewhere (USDHHS, 1990).

TABLE 2.2 Indicators of Lifetime Alcohol Abuse/Dependence Reported by Alcoholics ≥ Age 60

Rank		Men N=672	Women 330	Total 1002
			Percentage	
01	Objections from family/friend *,**	92	87	91
02	Unplanned use **	82	80	82
03	Emotional distress use +,**	72	86	76
04	Wanted to stop, but could not	75	74	75
05	Consistent Preoccupation with use **	68	63	67
06	Blackouts/amnesia while using +,*	66	55	62
07	Had Shakes *	61	55	59
08	Needed alcohol to keep going	56	59	57
09	Neglected responsibilities *, **	58	55	57
10	Unusual behavior while drinking	58	49	55
11	Developed tolerance	52	50	52
12	Use to relieve withdrawal symptoms	54	45	51
13	Use with medical contraindications	48	47	48
14	Scheduling day to accommodate drinking	45	48	46
15	Use to relieve physical pain	41	49	44
16	Injury while using	34	36	35
17	Experienced binges +	38	25	34
18	Missed work or school +	28	13	24
19	Became violent while drinking +	21	11	18
20	Neglect of children	13	7	11

Key: + = 10% difference between men's and women's endorsements of item is > the combined margin of error between the two samples
* = BONS Screen items
** = U-OPEN Screen items
Source: Adapted from DeHart, S. S., & Hoffmann, N. G. (1995). Screening and diagnosis of "alcohol abuse and dependence" in older adults. *International Journal of the Addictions, 30,* 1734, table 3.

While the use of formal assessment instruments can not replace experienced clinical judgment, use of a standardized instrument provides a method for quantitative comparison across patients and groups (NIAAA, 1991). Specifically, as reliability and validity data for older adults becomes available through research based on structured clinical interviews, it is hoped that the alcohol abuse and dependence diagnosis will be made earlier in its course, and prior to the development of medical complications or comorbid conditions.

The validity of a diagnostic assessment instrument refers to the agreement between the diagnoses made by the assessment technique and some "gold standard." It is important to recognize that a gold standard for alcohol abuse does not exist and to designate a validating instrument as a "gold" standard is misleading. For research purposes, the NIMH Diagnostic Interview Schedule (NIMH–DIS) is one standard that is frequently used to validate newly developed instruments (Robins, Helzer, Croughan, & Ratcliff, 1981).

Structured Clinical Interview for *DSM–III–R*

The Structured clinical interview for *DSM–III–R* (SCID) (Spitzer et al., 1990) is a semistructured interview for making *DSM–III–R* Axis I and Axis II diagnoses (APA, 1987). A 6-hour videotape is available as a supplement to the manual to train clinicians to reliably administer the SCID. Clinicians can use specific modules of the SCID to confirm a suspected diagnosis, e.g., psychoactive substance use disorder, and researchers may use part or all of the interview to include or exclude specific study subjects. The diagnoses covered in the SCID modules include psychotic disorders, mood disorders, substance use disorders, snxiety disorders, somatoform disorders, eating disorders, adjustment disorder, and personality disorders.

The SCID has undergone extensive reliability testing. Agreement, measured by the kappa statistic, between trained interviewers is comparable to those reported for the NIMH Diagnostic Interview Schedule (Robins et al., 1981). According to the manual, SCID interview questions are appropriate for adults, although with modification of wording they can be used with adolescents. There are no data reported in the manual about use of the instrument with young-old and middle-old adults.

Section E.1 of the SCID includes 35 questions directed to discerning alcohol dependence or abuse. If there is no suggestion of excessive alcohol use or alcohol-related problems after 6 probes, the interviewer can exit and skip to Nonalcohol Psychoactive Substance Use Disorders (section E.6). The interviewer scores each *DSM–III–R* criterion according to four levels of data: ? = inadequate information; 1= absent or false; 2 = subthreshold; and 3 = threshold or true. Three of the nine criteria must be present in order to diagnose alcohol dependence. Separate questions are directed toward discerning the chronology and severity of alcohol dependence, and partial or full remission (Spitzer et al., 1990). The alcohol module can be administered by a skilled clinician in 20 to 30 minutes.

Substance Use Disorders Diagnostic Schedule

The Substance Use Disorders Diagnostic Schedule–IV (SUDDS–IV) is a structured series of 64 questions designed to elicit information essential to the diagnosis of substance use disorders using DSM–IV criteria (Hoffmann & Harrison, 1995). Fifty-three questions discern alcohol and other drug and tobacco use; additional questions (with subcategories) screen for current and past stress, anxiety, and depression symptoms. The questions are objective and generally require a "yes" or "no" response rather than a clinical interpretation. The average length of the full interview is 45 to 60 minutes; the alcohol section takes about 20 minutes to administer.

Unlike the SCID, the SUDDS specializes in the diagnosis of alcohol and drug dependence rather than covering a range of psychiatric diagnoses. Also, since it is a structured rather than a semistructured interview, administration and scoring are relatively routine. A manual and 35-minute video of a mock interview provide sufficient training for most routine clinical applications. Results, like those of the SCID, should be interpreted by a qualified professional.

The SUDDS reliably differentiates current from prior alcohol abuse (Hoffmann et al., 1989). This version of the SUDDS is available in clinician-interview and computer-interview formats. Davis and his colleagues report reliability data on the SUDDS demonstrating that the two formats are equivalent. Overall agreement between the two forms of administration and clinician's diagnosis (validity) was 100% for the computer-generated diagnosis of current alcohol dependence (Davis, Hoffmann, Morse, & Luehr, 1992).

The SUDDS has been used successfully in research studies and clinical trials to document the diagnosis of alcohol and other substance use disorders. Research has established that the SUDDS provides excellent documentation of alcohol or other drug abuse and/or dependence when used either as a structured interview or as a computer-administered interview (Davis et al., 1992). DeHart and Hoffmann (1991) reported on use of the computerized and in-person versions of SUDDS for alcohol assessment with older adults.

CONCLUSIONS AND DIRECTIONS FOR RESEARCH

The CATOR data indicate that, once in treatment, older and younger adults do not differ on the constellation of individual, lifetime diagnostic indicators. This implies that older persons are quite similar to younger persons in the later phases of an addiction syndrome. It also implies that diagnostic strategies that focus on specific events and behaviors may be effective in identifying a lifetime history of alcohol dependence in older as well as younger adults.

However, screening for current alcohol abuse in older adults raises the concern that the criteria used to define an active diagnosis need to be revised. For example, typical indicators of a current addiction in younger individuals center on vocational and interpersonal problems. By contrast, older alcoholics may have neither vocational demands nor frequent family contacts; therefore, they may have fewer responsibilities where lack of performance might indicate a problem. Social isolation and a reduced sphere of responsibilities may also increase the difficulty of detecting and diagnosing the older adult who has a current alcohol abuse problem.

Researchers need to reassess the reliability and validity of screening instruments that are frequently recommended for detecting alcohol abuse and dependence. Many screens emphasize late-stage symptoms, thereby making early detection unlikely. Others that do tap earlier-stage symptoms may not be as sensitive for older individuals, especially older women. Because many geriatric cases of alcohol abuse are not properly identified, evaluation and validation of new instruments used to screen for alcohol abuse in older adults, such as the DPI, MAST–G or U–OPEN items, should be a research priority.

Age-stratified response analysis of proposed national and international diagnosis criteria and specific geriatric patterns of alcohol abuse should be part of field-tested research trials. Further, researchers and clinicians need to identify older adults' alcohol abuse in the early, most easily treatable stages and prior to the development of comorbid conditions. There is an ongoing need to train health care providers to conduct alcohol abuse interviews accurately, particularly under typical clinical and field conditions rather than artificial experimental environments.

Further research on the typology of alcohol problems in older people is also warranted (Yates & Meller, 1993). Graham et al. (1989) developed a provisional model with three types of cases: (1) primary, lifelong alcohol problems; (2) reactive alcohol problems following major loss; and (3) alcohol problems coexisting with dementia or other major psychiatric problems. This model needs additional refinement and clarification, since it does not differentiate some cases of late-life onset alcohol abuse that are precipitated by older persons' increased physiological sensitivity to alcohol and living in environments conducive to drinking (e.g., retirement centers or high-rise settings, where the milieu for social drinking is present and socially sanctioned).

In summation, research and clinical practice that seeks to address alcohol abuse and dependence in older populations should receive greater emphasis than is currently the case (Gurnack & Hoffmann, 1992). The myth that alcoholism afflicts only younger segments of the population must be carefully examined. As the population of the United States ages, the effects of alcohol abuse and at-risk drinking in older individuals will have an increasing impact on family, friends, communities, health care, nursing home admissions, and public welfare. Society must pursue solutions or find itself pursued by even more pervasive problems.

REFERENCES

Adams, W. L., Zhong, Y., Barboriak, J. J., & Rimm, A. A. (1993). Alcohol related hospitalizations of elderly people. *JAMA, 270,* 1222–1225.

American Psychiatric Association. (1980). *Diagnostic and statistical manual* (2nd ed.) Washington, DC: Author.

American Psychiatric Association. (1987). *Diagnostic and statistical manual* (3rd ed., revised). Washington, DC: Author.

American Psychiatric Association. (1994). *Diagnostic and statistical manual* (4th ed.) Washington, DC: Author.

Atchley, R. C. (1991). *Social forces and aging.* Belmont, CA: Wadsworth.

Atkinson, R. M. (1990). Aging and alcohol use disorders: Diagnostic issues in the elderly. *International Psychogeriatrics, 2,* 55–72.

Atkinson, R. M. (1994). Late onset problem drinking in older adults. *International Journal of Geriatric Psychiatry, 9,* 321–326.

Atkinson, R. M., Ganzini, L., & Bernstein, M. J. (1992). Alcohol and substance use in the elderly. In J. E. Birrin, R. B. Sloane, & G. D. Cohen (Eds.), *Handbook of mental health and aging* (pp. 515–555). New York: Academic.

Atkinson, R. M., & Kofoed, L. L. (1982). Alcohol and drug abuse in old age: A clinical perspective. *Substance and Alcohol Actions/Misuse, 3,* 353–368.

Atkinson, R. M., Tolson, R. L., & Turner, J. A. (1990). Late versus early onset problem drinking in older men. *Alcoholism: Clinical and Experimental Research, 14,* 574–579.

Babor, T. F., Kranzler, H. R., & Kadden, R. M. (1986). Issues in the definition and diagnosis of alcoholism: Implications for a reformulation. *Progress in Neuropsychopharmacology and Biological Psychiatry, 10,* 113–128.

Beresford, T. P. (1991). The nosology of alcohol research. *Alcohol Health and Research World, 15,* 260–265.

Beresford, T. P., Blow, F. C., & Brower, K. J. (1990). Alcoholism in the elderly. *Geriatrics, 16,* 38–43.

Beresford, T. P, Blow, F. C., Brower, K. J., Adams, K. M., & Hall, R. C. W. (1988). Alcoholism and aging in the general hospital. *Psychosomatics, 29,* 61–72.

Blow, F. C., Brower, K. J., Schulenberg, J. E., Demo-Dananberg, L. M., Young, K. J., & Beresford, T. P. (1992). The Michigan Alcoholism Screening Test: Geriatric version (MAST–G): A new elderly-specific screening instrument. (Abstract). *Alcoholism: Clinical and Experimental Research, 16,* 172.

Blume, S. B. (1990). Chemical dependency in women: Important issues. *American Journal of Drug Alcohol Abuse, 16,* 297–303.

Brody, J. A. (1982). Aging and alcohol abuse. *Journal of the American Geriatrics Society, 30,* 123–126.

Buchsbaum, D. G., Buchanan, R. G., Welsh, J., Centor, J. R. M., & Schnoll, S. H. (1992). Screening for drinking disorders in the elderly using the CAGE questionnaire. *Journal of the American Geriatrics Society, 40,* 662–665.

Clark, W. B., & Midanik, L. (1982). Alcohol use and alcohol problems among U. S. adults. *NIAAA: Alcohol consumption and related problems* (Alcohol and Health Monograph No. 1, DHHS Publication No. ADM 82–1190 (pp. 3–52). Washington, DC: U.S. Government Printing Office.

Cloninger, C. R., Bohman, M., & Sigvardsson, S. (1981). Inheritance of alcohol abuse. *Archives of General Psychiatry, 38,* 861–868.

Cloninger, C. R., Reich, T., Sigvardsson, S. von Knoring, A. L., & Bohman, M. (1987). The effects of changes in alcohol use between generations on the inheritance of alcohol abuse. In R. M. Rose & J. E. Barrett (Eds.), *Alcoholism: Origins and outcomes* (pp. 49–74). New York: Raven.

Cohen, M., Kern, J. C., & Hassett, C. (1986). Identifying alcoholism in medical patients. *Hosp. Community Psychiatry, 37,* 398–400.

Coulehan, J. L., Zettler-Segal, M., Block, M., McClelland, M., & Schulberg, H. C. (1987). Recognition of alcoholism and substance abuse in primary care patients. *Archives of Internal Medicine, 147,* 349–352.

Counte, M. A., Salloway, J. C., & Christman, L. (1982). Age and sex related drinking patterns in alcoholics. In W. G. Wood & M. F. Elias (Eds.), *Alcoholism and aging* (pp. 17–27). Boca Raton, FL: CRC.

Curtis, J. R., Geller, G., Stokes, E. J., Levine, D. M., & Moore, R. D. (1989). Characteristics, diagnosis and treatment of alcoholism in elderly patients. *Journal of the American Geriatrics Society, 37,* 310–316.

Davis, L. J., Hoffmann, N. G., Morse, R. M., & Luehr, J. G. (1992). Substance Use Disorder Diagnostic Schedule (SUDDS): The equivalence and validity of a computer-administered and interviewer-administered format. *Alcoholism: Clinical and Experimental Research, 16,* 250–254.

Davis, L. J., Jr., & Morse, R. M. (1987). Age and sex differences in the responses of alcoholics to the self-administered alcoholism screening test. *Journal of Clinical Psychology, 43,* 423–430.

DeHart, S. S., & Hoffmann, N. G. (1991). Using microcomputers to identify substance use disorders in the elderly [Abstract]. *The Gerontologist, 31,* 158.

Donovan, D. M. (1988). Assessment of addictive behaviors: Implications of an emerging biopsychosocial model. In D. M. Donovan & G. A. Marlatt (Eds.), *Assessment of addictive behaviors* (pp. 3–48). New York: Guilford.

Doyle, S. S., Hoffmann, N. G., & Smith, M. B. (1994). *Factor structure of alcohol dependency symptoms.* Unpublished manuscript. (Available from New Standards, Inc. 1080 Montreal Ave., St. Paul, MN 55116.)

Drew, L. R. H. (1968). Alcoholism as a self limiting disease. *Quarterly Journal of Studies on Alcohol, 29,* 956–967.

Erfurt, J. C., & Foote, A. (1992). Who is following the recovering alcoholic? *Alcohol Health and Research World, 16,* 154–159.

Ewing, J. A. (1984). Detecting alcoholism: The CAGE questionnaire. *Journal of the American Medical Association, 252,* 1905–1907.

Finney, J. W., Moos, R. H., & Brennan, P. L. (1991). The drinking problem index: A measure to assess alcohol-related problems among older adults. *Journal of Substance Abuse, 3,* 395–404.

Freund, G. (1984). Aging and alcoholism: Neurobiological relationships between aging and alcohol abuse. In M. Galanter (Ed.), *Recent developments in alcoholism,* Vol. 2 (pp. 203–221). New York: Plenum.

Gomberg, E. S. L. (1987). Drug and alcohol problems of elderly persons In T. D. Nirenberg & S. A. Maisto (Eds.), *Developments in the assessment and treatment of addictive behaviors* (pp. 319–37). Norwood, NJ: Ablex.

Graham, A. V., Parran, T. V., Jr., & Jaen, C. R. (1992). Physician failure to record alcohol use history when prescribing benzodiazepines. *Journal of Substance Abuse, 4,* 179–185.

Graham, K. (1986). Identifying and measuring alcohol abuse among the elderly: Serious problems with existing instrumentation. *Journal of Studies on Alcohol, 47,* 322–326.

Graham, K., Ziedman, A., Flower, M. C., Saunders, S. J., & White-Campbell, M. (1989). *Case study analysis of elderly persons.* Toronto: Final report to the Canadian National Health Research and Development Program. Project No. 66066-3414-43 DA (1987–1989).

Graham, K., Saunders, S. J., Flower, M. C., Timney, C. B., White-Campbell, M., & Pietropaolo, A. Z. (1995). *Addictions treatment for older adults.* Binghamton, NY: Haworth.

Gurnack, A. M., & Hoffmann, N.G. (1992). Elderly alcohol misuse. *International Journal of Addictions, 27,* 869–878.

Helzer, J. E., & Pryzbeck, T. R. (1988). The co-occurrence of alcoholism with other psychiatric disorders in the general population and its impact on treatment. *Journal of Studies on Alcohol, 49,* 219–224.

Hoffmann, N. G., DeHart, S. S., & Fulkerson, J. A. (1993). Medical care utilization as a function of recovery status following chemical addictions treatment. *Journal of Addictive Diseases, 12,* 97–108.

Hoffmann, N. G., & Harrison, P. A. (1995). SUDDS–IV manual. (To obtain, contact: New Standards Publisher, St. Paul, MN 55103.)

Hoffmann, N. G., Harrison, P. A., Hall, S. W., Gust, S. W., Mable, R. R. J., & Cable, E. P. (1989). Pragmatic procedures for detecting and documenting alcoholism in medical patients. *Advances in Alcohol & Substance Abuse, 8,* 119–131.

Hoffmann, N. G., Harrison, P. A., & Ninonuevo, F. (1988). Screening for alcoholism in general medical patients. *Alcohol and Alcoholism, 23,* 541–543.

Holzer, C. E., III, Robins, L. N., Myers, J. K., Weissman, M. M., Tischler, G. L., Leaf, P. J., Anthony, J., & Bednarski, P. B. (1984). Antecedents and correlates of alcohol abuse and dependence in the elderly. In G. Maddox, L. N. Robins, & N. Rosenberg (Eds.), *Nature and extent of alcohol problems among the elderly* (National Institute of Drug Abuse Research Monograph No. 14) (pp. 217–244). U. S. Government Printing Office.

Kristenson, H., Ohlin, H., Hulten-Nosslin, M., Trell, E., & Hood, P. (1983). Identification and intervention of heavy drinking in middle aged men: Results and follow up of 24–60 months of long term study with randomized controls. *Alcohol Clinical and Experimental Research, 7,* 203–209.

Lettieri, D. J., Nelson, J. E., & Sayers, M. A. (1987). *NIAAA Treatment Handbook Series 2: Alcoholism treatment assessment research instruments.* Rockville, MD: NIAAA. DHHS Publication No. (ADM) 87–1380.

Marlatt, G. A., & Tapert, S. F. (1993). Harm reduction: Reducing the risks of addictive behaviors. In J. S. Baer, G. A. Marlatt, & R. J. McMahon (Eds.), *Addictive behaviors across the life span: Prevention, treatment and policy issues* (pp. 243–273). Newbury Park, CA: Sage.

Mayfield, D. G., McLeod, G., & Hall, P. (1974). The CAGE questionnaire: Validation of a new alcoholism screening instrument. *American Journal of Psychiatry, 131,* 1121–1123.

Moore, R. D. Bone, L. R., Geller, G., Manon, J. A., Stokes, E. J., & Levine, D. M. (1989). Prevalence, detection and treatment of alcoholism in hospitalized patients. *Journal of American Medical Association, 261,* 403–408.

Moos, R. H., & Finney, J. W. (1988). A systems perspective on problem drinking among older adults. In G. Maddox, L. N. Robins, & N. Rosenberg, (Eds.), *Nature and extent of alcohol problems among the elderly* (pp. 151–173). DHHS Research Monograph No. 14: Proceedings of workshop Nov 3–4, 1988 sponsored by NIAAA, NIMH and NIA.

National Institute of Alcohol Abuse and Alcoholism (1991b). Assessing alcoholism. *Alcohol Alert, 12.*

National Institute of Alcohol Abuse and Alcoholism. (1991a). Alcoholism and co-occuring disorders. *Alcohol Alert, 14.*

Neugarten, B. L., & Neugarten, D. A. (1986). Changing meanings of age in the aging society. In A. Fifer & L. Bronte, (Eds.), *Our aging society: Paradox and promise* (pp. 33–51). New York: Nortor.

New Standards, Inc. (1993). *Comprehensive Assessment and Treatment Outcomes Research (CATOR).* St. Paul, MN: Author.

Osgood, N. J., Wood, H. E., & Parham, I. A. (1995). *Alcoholism and aging.* Westport, CT: Greenwood.

Petty, F. (1992). The depressed alcoholic: Clinical features and medical management. *General Hospital Psychiatry, 14,* 258–264.

Rains, V. S., & Ditzler, T. F. (1993). Alcohol use disorders in cognitively impaired patients referred for geriatric assessment. *Journal of Addictive Diseases, 12,* 55–64.

Raschko, R. (1990). Gatekeepers do the casefinding in Spokane. *Aging, 361,* 38–40.

Raskind, M. A., & Peskind, E. R. (1992). Alzheimer's disease and other dementing disorders. In J. E. Birren, R. B. Sloane, & G. D. Cohen (Eds.), *Handbook of mental health and aging* (pp. 477–513). New York: Academic.

Reich, T., Cloninger, C. R., Van Eerdewegh, P., Roce, J. P., & Mullancy, J. (1988). Secular trends in the familial transmission of alcoholism. *Alcoholism (New York), 12,* 458–464.

Robins, L. N., Helzer, J. E., Croughan, J., & Ratcliff, K. S. (1981). National Institutes of Mental Health diagnostic interview schedule: Its history, characteristics, and validity. *Archives of General Psychiatry, 38,* 381–389.

Robins, L. N., Helzer, J. E., Pryzbeck, T. R., & Reigier, D. A. (1988). Alcohol disorders in the community: A report from the epidemiologic catchment area. *Alcoholism: Origins and outcomes* (pp. 15–30). New York: Raven.

Rode, S. S., Hoffmann, N. G., & Fulkerson, J. A. (1991). Medical care utilization before and after alcoholism treatment for the elderly. *The Southwestern: Journal of Aging for the Southwest, 6,* 140–148.

Rosman, A. S. (1992). Utility and evaluation of biochemical markers of alcohol consumption. *Journal of Substance Abuse, 4,* 277–297.

Russel, M., Martier, S. S., Sokol, R. J., Jacobson, S., Jacobson, J., & Bottoms, S. (1991). Screening for pregnancy risk-drinking: TWEAKING the tests [abstract]. *Alcoholism-Clinical and Experimental Research, 15,* 368.

Saunders, J. B., Aasland, O. G., Babor, T. F., de la Fluente, J. R., & Grant, M. (1993). Development of the Alcohol Use Disorders Identification Test (AUDIT): WHO collaborative project on early detection of persons with harmful alcohol consumption II. *Addiction, 88,* 791–804.

Schuckit, M. A. (1989). *Drug and alcohol abuse: A clinical guide to diagnosis and treatment* (3rd ed.) New York: Plenum.

Schuckit, M. A. (1990). Introduction: Assessment and treatment strategies with the late life alcoholic. *Journal of Geriatric Psychiatry, 23,* 83–89.

Schuckit, M. A., & Pastor, P. A. (1978). The elderly as a unique population. *Alcoholism: Clinical and Experimental Research, 2,* 31–38.

Searight, H. R. (1992). Screening for alcohol abuse in primary care: Current status and research needs. *Family Practice Research Journal, 12,* 193–204.

Selzer, M. L. (1971). The Michigan Alcoholism Screening Test (MAST): The quest for a new diagnostic instrument. *American Journal of Psychiatry, 127,* 1653–1658.

Sokol, R. J., Martier, S. S., & Ager, J. W. (1989). The T–ACE questions: Practical prenatal detection of risk drinking. *American Journal of Obstetrics and Gynecology, 160,* 463–470.

Spitzer, R. L., Williams, J. B., Gibbon, M., & First, M. B. (1990). Structured Clinical Interview for DSM–III–R (SCID). Washington, DC: American Psychiatric Press.

Stibler, H., Borg, S., & Joustra, M. (1986). Micro anion exchange: Chromatography of carbohydrate-deficient transferrin in serum in relation to alcohol consumption. *Alcoholism: Clinical and Experimental Research, 10,* 535–544.

Stinson, F. S., Dufour, M. C., & Bertolucci, D. (1989). Alcohol-related morbidity in the aging population. *Alcohol Health and Research World, 13,* 80–87.

Studies of alcohol abuse and alcoholism among the aged. (1988, December 13). *Federal Register, 53,* 50168.

U.S. Department of Health and Human Services. (1990). *Seventh special report to the U. S. Congress on alcohol and health* [DHHS Publication No. (Adm) 90–1656]. Rockville, MD: National Institute on Alcohol Abuse and Alcoholism.

U.S. Department of Health and Human Services. (1994). *Eighth special report to the U.S. Congress on alcohol and health* [NIH Publication No. 94–3699]. Rockville, MD: National Institute on Alcohol Abuse and Alcoholism.

Vaillant, G. E. (1983). *The natural history of alcoholism.* Cambridge: Harvard University Press.

Willenbring, M. L., Christensen, K. J., Spring, W. D., Jr., & Rasmussen, R. (1987). Alcoholism screening in the elderly, *Journal of the American Geriatrics Society, 35,* 864–869.

Winick, C. (1962). Maturing out of narcotic addiction. *United Nations Bulletin on Narcotics, 14,* 1–7.

World Health Organization (1990). *Proposed 10th revision of the international classification of diseases (1CD–10): Diagnostic criteria for research.* Geneva: the Organization.

Yates, W. R., & Meller, W. H. (1993). Comparative validity of five alcoholism typologies. *American Journal of Addictions, 2,* 99–108.

Zook, J., & Moore, F. D. (1980). High cost users of medical care, *New England Journal of Medicine, 302,* 996–1002.

3

Medical Manifestations of Alcoholism in the Elderly

James W. Smith, MD

INTRODUCTION

The effects of alcohol are, in general, very similar at any age. However, the physiologic concomitants of aging, together with the physiologic concomitants of heavy alcohol intake, lead to a number of age-related differences. These differences generally are in *degree* of organ injury or other adverse consequences rather than in *type* of injury, although there does appear to be more trauma in younger people and more medical illness in older people. In studying these differences, it is perhaps wise to start at the beginning, that is, with alcohol consumption itself.

Age-Related Statistical Differences in Alcohol Consumption

A good deal of research has consistently found that alcohol consumption levels are lower and alcohol abuse is less prevalent in persons in their sixties and older (Dufour & Fuller, 1995). There are, however, newer studies that cast doubt on these conclusions and point out that those early studies were cross-sectional in nature and compared different age groups at one point in time. When longitudinal studies are done that follow individuals over a number of years, consumption patterns do not change much at all. They tend to remain remarkably stable as the person ages (Stall, 1968). These latter findings suggest that the cross-sectional differences in consumption in older persons may represent a cohort effect influenced by different cultural and historical experiences of each generation (National Institute on Alcohol Abuse and Alcoholism [NIAAA], 1988; Stinson, Dufour, & Bertolucci, 1987). Nevertheless, despite the relative stability of alcohol consumption over the years, whenever changes in consumption occurred, the direction was toward a decreased intake much more often than toward an increase (Glynn, Bouchard LoCastro, & Hermos, 1984). Stall (1968, 1986) reported that approximately two-thirds of older male drinkers remained stable in quantity and frequency of alcohol intake over a period of 19 years. The one-third who changed consumption levels were more than twice as likely to decrease their consumption.

There may be socioeconomic explanations, such as decreased income, for these decreases or unrelated chronic health problems may preclude alcohol use. Nevertheless, age-related changes in physiology may also play a significant role in decreasing alcohol intake. One well-known factor is the decrease in lean body mass with aging. Between age 20 and age 70, lean body mass decreases about 10% (Bienefeld, 1987). Because of this, the total body water content accounts for a smaller percentage of body weight (DuFour, Archer, & Gordis, 1992). Since alcohol is distributed only in the body water and not the fat this means that each drink of alcohol results in a higher blood alcohol level in the same person when he or she is elderly than during a young adulthood. Therefore, without any other age-related effect accounted for, the elderly individual gets more intoxication per drink consumed.

Age-Related Biological Factors in Alcohol Metabolism

Another factor is an age-related decrease in the gastric alcohol dehydrogenase enzyme (ADH). This enzyme is responsible for the first step in the metabolism of alcohol. The majority of alcohol metabolism takes place in the liver. However, a significant amount of alcohol metabolism is also known to take place in the gastric mucosa with gastric ADH. With aging, gastric ADH levels decrease. They are also noted to be lower in females of all ages. In addition, certain medications such as H2 blockers (e.g., Tagamet, Zantac, Axid and others) further decrease gastric ADH levels, these are frequently taken by elderly patients. As a consequence, less alcohol is metabolized in the stomach, which contributes further to an increased blood alcohol level per unit of alcohol consumed (Lieber, 1988; Moreno, Pares, Ortiz, Enriqvez & Pares, 1994; Schuckit, Oct. 1982). This also increases the alcohol burden on the liver. The metabolism of alcohol in the liver is not significantly altered with aging (Schuckit & Miller, 1976; Scott, 1989). The liver enzymes responsible for this metabolism seem to be as efficient in the aged as in the young person (Scott, 1989). Despite this, as noted above, a given dose of alcohol imposes a greater metabolic burden on the liver of an older person than on that same person when young.

Once the alcohol is in the bloodstream, it affects all tissues in the body. It has been shown that measurable physical damage is detectable in *every* system of the body. Fortunately, in most systems the damage is not fatal or even permanently disabling. In others, however, the damage is life-threatening. Some reports indicate that over 90% of actively drinking older alcoholics have presented with a major health problem (Schuckit & Miller, 1976).

ALCOHOL-RELATED PHYSICAL DAMAGE

Skeletal System

Aging tends to be associated with a decrease in bone density (osteopenia) in both males and females. When extreme, it leads to an abnormal degree of rarefaction of bone (osteoporosis). Alcoholic drinking[1] accelerates this bone loss and may lead to compression fractures of vertebrae (Moniz, 1994). Drinking also leads to poor mobility and a marked increase in falls (Ziring & Adler, 1991). The result is an increase in fractures. In an elderly person fractures tend to heal more slowly than in a younger individual and tend to be associated with more complications, e.g., thromboembolism.

The head of the femur also has a rather tenuous blood supply, and even without injury heavy alcohol intake can cause an interruption of circulation to the bone, resulting in aseptic necrosis of the head of the femur. This leads to deformity of the bone, fragmentation, and osteoarthritis of the joint and usually requires hip replacement surgery (Rosenkranz, 1983). Alcohol-induced endocrine changes may also lead to osteopenia and aseptic necrosis (Rico, 1990).

Bone Marrow and Blood

Red Blood Cells

Virtually no aspect of blood cell development, survival or function escapes the toxicity of alcohol (Hillman, 1982). Interference with cell development may occur at the point of stem cell proliferation or during cell maturation. Cell survival in the circulation may be shortened because of intracellular abnormality or a change in the vascular environment.

In cases where inflammation of the liver (alcoholic hepatitis) or inflam-

FIGURE 3.1 Some Consequences of Alcoholism

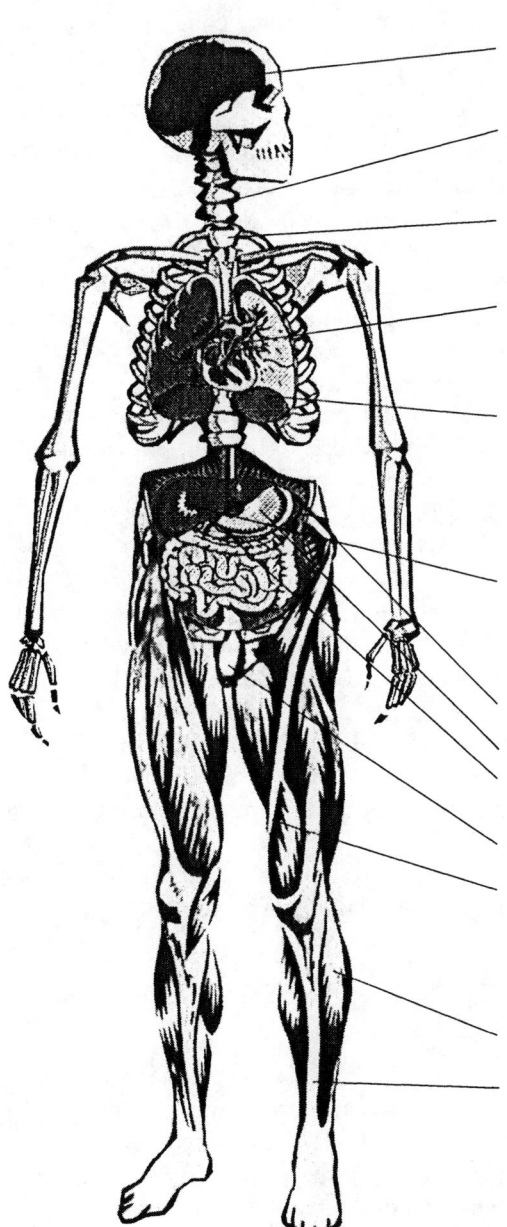

The Brain. Brain atrophy and dementia.

Pharynx. Cancer of the pharynx is increased tenfold for drinkers who smoke.

Esophagus. Esophagitis and esophageal varices.

Heart. Alcoholic cardiomyopathy, a heart condition which is reversible only in its early stages.

Lungs. The lower resistance of the problem drinker is thought to lead to greater incidences of tuberculosis, pneumonia and emphysema.

Liver. An acute enlargement of the liver, which is reversible, as well as the irreversible alcoholic's liver (cirrhosis).

Spleen. Hypersplenism.

Stomach. Gastritis and ulcers.

Pancreas. Acute and chronic pancreatitis.

Testes. Atrophy of the testes.

Long Nerves. Peripheral neuropathy, a generally reversible condition, which is characterized by loss of sensation, weakness and pain.

Muscles. Alcoholic myopathy.

Blood and Bone Marrow. Coagulation defects and anemia.

mation of the pancreas (pancreatitis) occurs, the production of an essential hormone, erythropoietin, may be suppressed. This inflammatory suppression of erythropoietin leads to a lower than normal production of red blood cells, leading to anemia ("hypoproliferative anemia"). A more common abnormality is a defect in red cell maturation. This leads to a progressive anemia with red blood cells that are larger than normal ("macrocytic anemia") (Eichner & Hillman, 1970). The vitamin folic acid appears to be a critical factor in the development of this macrocytic anemia. Folic acid is an essential vitamin for humans and is required whenever cells are actively dividing (as in the bone marrow). If the diet is severely restricted, deficiencies may occur. Elderly persons are often subject to poor nutrition. When alcoholism is added, food intake may be further reduced. Even when the diet is adequate, large amounts of alcohol interfere with absorption of the vitamin from the small intestine (Halsted, Griggs, & Harris, 1967). An even more important toxic effect of alcohol involves disruption of the internal pathways of folic acid supply to marrow precursor cells and causes a dramatic drop in serum folic acid levels, despite adequate supplies in the liver or diet (Hillman, McGuffin, & Campbell, 1977). There also appears to be a direct toxic effect on the developing red cell (Seppa & Sillanavkee, 1994).

Even in the absence of bleeding, red cell survival is commonly reduced by alcohol ingestion. One factor is that abnormal red cells (e.g., macrocytes) have a shortened survival time in the circulation. Cell survival may also be influenced by changes in the vascular environment. Three hemolytic syndromes have been identified in alcoholics: acanthocytosis and acquired stomatocytosis, both characterized by distorted red cells, and Zieve's Syndrome, a complication of alcoholic fatty liver (Hillman, 1973). Still another hazard to red cells is hypersplenism. With severe alcoholic cirrhosis, one concomitant may be an enlarged spleen which then traps and destroys more than the normal amount of red cells.

All of these factors lead to anemia. When these are added to other factors that lead to anemia in the aging person, it is not surprising that significant anemia is a common finding in the elderly alcoholic (An'ia, Suman, Fairbanks, & Melton, 1994).

White Blood Cells

Decreased levels of white blood cells, or leukopenia, are frequently found in alcoholics (Eichner & Hillman, 1970). It has also been demonstrated that the granulocyte reserve available in the marrow to respond to infections is reduced in alcoholics. Not only are there fewer white cells to respond to infection, but those that are present are not as effective. Alcohol reduces the ability of a granulocyte to move toward invading bacteria and engulf them (chemotoxis) (Brayton, Stokes, Schwartz, & Louria, 1970; Crowley & Abramson, 1971).

It is well known that pneumonia and other infectious diseases are increasing mortality risks for elderly persons. The alcohol-induced decrease in leukocyte numbers and effectiveness further increases this mortality risk.

Platelets

Decreased level of blood platelets, or thrombocytopenia, is a common laboratory finding in alcoholics (Cowan, 1969; 1971). Older persons often take medications to inhibit the agglutination of platelets in order to prevent stroke, myocardial infarction, or other complications of inappropriate thrombus formation. It is unusual for the alcohol-induced thrombocytopenia to be severe enough (by itself) to induce bleeding. However, when these "antiplatelet" medications are added, bleeding complications become a much more real concern. Fortunately, the platelet count usually rapidly returns to normal after 4-10 days once alcohol intake has stopped (Cowan, 1969; Eichner & Hillman, 1970).

Immune System

The direct effect of alcohol on the immune system is difficult to determine with precision in alcoholics because of the presence of concurrent disorders in so many cases (e.g., liver disease, malnutrition). Nevertheless, numerous clinical studies have reported that alcoholics have an increased susceptibility to infection (Adams & Jordan, 1984; Andersen, 1975). Animal studies show an alcohol-related decrease in the response to infection (Bluckman, Dvorak, & MacGregor, 1975; Colle, Forestier, Quero, Bourrinet, & German, 1982). Likely factors involved in this deficient response to infection include:

- Decreased production of certain white blood cells (polymorphonuclear leukocytes [PMN]) in the bone marrow (fewer cells to fight invading organisms) (National Institute on Alcohol Abuse and Alcohilism, 1990).
- Defects in the movement toward infection (chemotoxis) (Rajkovic, Yousif-Kadaru, Wyke, & Williams, 1984).
- Impaired ability of PMNs to adhere to cell (Brayton, Stokes, Schwartz, & Louria, 1970) (an essential step in migration to the site of infection and ingestion of invading organisms).
- Lowered production of other white blood cells (lymphocytes) leading to deficiencies of "cell-mediated immunity" (believed to be responsible for the increased incidence of tuberculosis in alcoholics, as well as an increase in virus-associated head and neck cancers) (Martinez, 1970; Mutchnick & Lee, 1988).

- Impairment of the response of lymphocytes to infection or other activating substances. Certain lymphocytes (T-lymphocytes), which are important in fighting infection, are reduced in number in alcoholics with liver disease. The cells are also deficient in their ability to undergo transformation into an activated form leading to a poor response to test antigens and failure to develop immune response to new antigens (Cook et al., 1995; Lundy, et al., 1975). This appears to be a direct effect of alcohol, since incubating lymphocytes from nonalcoholics in an alcohol solution leads to the same failure of transformation (Roselle & Mendenhall, 1982). Alcohol by itself is shown to inhibit the function of B-lymphocytes (which produce antibodies) in humans as well as animals (Aldo-Benson, 1988; Gilhus & Matre, 1982). This inhibition may contribute to the increased incidence of pneumonia and peritonitis in alcoholics. Alcohol also has an adverse effect on still another type of lymphocyte, the "natural killer cell." This cell is an important part of the body's defense against spontaneously arising tumors and metastases. One study showed a reduction of over 50% of the cells in mice who were fed alcohol chronically (Abdallah, Starkey, & Meadows, 1988). Even a modest amount of alcohol decreases this "killer" activity (Bounds, Betzing, Stwart, & Holcombe, 1994).

Elderly persons show a decline in immunologic competence. The additional impairment of their immune system caused by heavy alcohol consumption dramatically increases their risk of succumbing to pneumonia or other infections and enhances their vulnerability to cancer.

Cancer

Cancer is a worry for individuals of any age, but as one ages, both the risk and the worry tend to increase. Alcohol abuse adds considerably to that risk. There is substantial epidemiologic evidence linking heavy alcohol intake with an increased incidence of certain cancers, notably those of the liver, esophagus, larynx, nasopharynx, colon, and prostate (Decker & Goldstein, 1982; Driver & Swann, 1987). Alcoholics with a variety of cancers have poorer chances of survival and greater chances of developing another primary tumor than do nonalcoholics with the same cancer (Driver & Swann, 1987).

The effect of alcohol on the immune system appears to play a significant role, as noted above. In addition, alcohol may affect enzymes controlling carcinogens, as demonstrated by the synergistic effect of alcohol consumption plus smoking in the development of cancer of the head, neck, and esophagus (Driver & Swann, 1987). Animal studies show an alcohol-related deficient ability to repair DNA damage produced by carcinogens leading to the development of precancerous lesions (Garr, Espina, & Lieber, 1986).

Muscles

With advancing age, the muscle mass of the body decreases (Bienefeld, 1987). Alcohol can add to that effect. Approximately 50% of alcoholics have alcoholic muscle disease (Preedy, Salisbury, & Peturs, 1994). Chronic alcoholic myopathy may cause muscle wasting and weakness, most commonly involving the proximal muscles of the extremities, the pelvic and shoulder girdle and the muscles of the thoracic cage (Smith, 1982b). Even without evidence of muscle wasting, muscle strength is diminished. One study concluded that skeletal muscle strength declined as the estimated lifetime dose of alcohol increased (Urbano-Marquez, et al., 1989). Women appear to be more sensitive to this type of damage than men (Urbano-Marquez, Esturch, Fernandez-Solas, Pare, & Rubin, 1995).

Acute alcoholic myopathy is a syndrome of muscle pain, tenderness, and edema occurring after an excess of alcohol ingestion (Smith, 1982b). Again, the proximal muscles of the extremities and the pelvic and shoulder girdles are the most common sites of involvement. Laboratory findings include elevated levels of the enzymes CPK, LDH, aldolase, and AST. In some cases, muscle necrosis may occur and be severe enough to produce myoglobinemia which in turn may produce acute renal tubular necrosis. This is a serious complication and may lead to death unless renal dialysis is carried out (Smith, 1982b). Treatment for any type of myopathy is abstinence and nutritional repair.

Increased weakness from myopathy or any other cause can increase the possibility of falling, which is a danger even in healthy elderly people.

Cardiovascular System

The cardiovascular system is one of the systems of the body in which heavy alcohol intake may result in death or permanent disability. Cardiovascular disease is the leading cause of death in the United States (Levy, 1985). Alcoholics have a marked increase in mortality from these complications. On average, alcoholic men have a death rate from atherosclerotic and degenerative heart disease 1.74 times that of nonalcoholic men. In alcoholic women, the death rate is 4.1 times that of nonalcoholic women (Schmidt & DeLint, 1972). A 15-year prospective study showed a similar increased mortality with "problem drinking" (Dyer et at. 1977). These adverse effects occur as a result of both direct and indirect injury to the system.

Direct Effects on the Heart

In normal test animals, alcohol produces a decrease in contractile velocity and a decrease in peak tension of heart muscle (Mitchell & Cohen, 1970).

That is, both the speed of contraction and the maximum tension produced by that contraction is reduced in the presence of alcohol. As a result the heart becomes a less efficient pump.

Individuals who are alcoholic have been reported to show a similar decrease in heart function (Zakhari, 1991). Not only alcoholics are affected. In individuals who are not alcoholic but have cardiac disease, as little as 2 ounces of whisky caused a decrease in cardiac output and a decrease in coronary artery circulation (Gould, Azhir, DeMartino, & Comprecht, 1971). Exercise testing of nonalcoholics with known angina pectoris and proven coronary artery disease revealed that a decreased duration of exercise was required to produce angina and abnormal electrocardiographic changes (increased ischemic ST segment depression) after 2 to 5 ounces of alcohol (Orlando et al., 1976).

These findings are of grave concern for the elderly population because coronary artery disease is so prevalent in that population and because alcohol has often been prescribed to treat the symptoms. Heberden, in 1786 (Heberden, 1929), first suggested the use of alcohol for the treatment of angina pectoris. As physiologists learned of the ability of alcohol to cause the blood vessels of the skin to dilate, this effect seemed to confirm the validity of alcohol as a legitimate cardiac drug, since arterosclerotic vascular disease produces its deleterious effect on the heart by narrowing the coronary arteries, thus depriving the heart muscle of adequate blood flow. Alcohol, therefore, should dilate these vessels and improve blood flow. Unfortunately, alcohol does *not* dilate coronary arteries as it does the vessels of the skin and, as noted above, it often causes further deterioration in cardiac function. The practice of prescribing alcohol to treat angina pectoris can no longer be supported on the basis of scientific evidence, despite the fact that alcohol frequently relieves the chest pain (probably because it is a rather effective analgesic).

Alcohol, at least in larger amounts, has a direct toxic effect on the heart. Injury to the walls of myocardial cells allows the leakage of intracellular contents into the bloodstream, including potassium, phosphate, and cardiac enzymes. In individuals who are alcoholic, this leakage does not occur at blood alcohol levels of 0.10% (the blood level many states use as legal proof of intoxication), but leakage occurs readily at 0.20%, a level often obtained by alcoholic individuals (Mitchell & Cohen, 1970).

The heart directly metabolizes alcohol to form a class of compounds called fatty acid ethyl esters. These compounds may cause damage to the mitochondria of the cardiac muscle, and thus they may be a direct link to alcohol-induced cardiomyopathy (Lang & Kinnanen, 1987). Alcoholic cardiomyopathy is defined as a syndrome of cardiac dysfunction in which the heart muscle is the site of the disease and in which the remainder of the cardiovascular system is relatively unaffected (Smith, 1982b). In the United

States, up to half of all people with idiopathic cardiomyopathy are alcohol-dependent (Wang, Mallon, Alterman, & McLellan, 1987). It is further estimated that 20 to 30% of all cardiomyopathy cases can be attributed to alcohol abuse (Regan, 1990). Regular consumption of large amounts of alcohol for 10 or more years appears to be required to produce the condition (Urbano-Marquez et al., 1989). One estimate was "at least 80 grams of ethanol daily for at least a decade" (Cohen, 1985). Electron microscopy of the heart muscle reveals swollen, fragmented mitochondria and various degrees of disruption of the contractile proteins (myofibrils). The clinical findings in alcoholic cardiomyopathy are those of congestive failure, arrhythmia, or both. They include decreased tolerance of exercise, tachycardia, dyspnea, othopnea, edema, palpitations, and nonproductive cough. The clinical manifestations of idiopathic and alcoholic cardiomyopathy are the same; however, the prognosis is quite different. The prognosis for idiopathic cardiomyopathy is poor, regardless of treatment, but alcoholic cardiomyopathy is reversible in about 30% of patients if they become abstinent (Lang & Kinnanen, 1987; Wang et al., 1987). Even in young (age 20–24) healthy men, a single intoxicating dose of alcohol (mean blood alcohol concentration 0.123%) has impeded recovery from exercise by decreased myocardial performance (Markiewicz & Cholewa, 1982); this might be viewed as the first small step toward cardiomyopathy. As with alcoholic myopathy, women are more sensitive than men to the toxic effects of alcohol on the heart (Urbano-Marquez et al., 1995).

Blood Pressure

Alcohol also has an adverse effect on blood pressure, even in relatively modest amounts (Marmot et al., 1994). A significant elevation in blood pressure (with its well-known increased risk of myocardial infarction and stroke) is caused by three or more drinks a day. This effect is seen most strongly in men, Caucasians, and people over age 55. Blood pressure readings in the range of definitive hypertension were more prevalent in persons over age 50 who consumed six or more drinks daily (Criqui, Wallace, Mishkel, Barrett-Connor, & Hess, 1981). Some individuals showed substantial or complete regression of their hypertension when they become abstinent.

Coronary Artery Disease

"Heart attacks" and other complications of coronary artery disease are the leading cause of death in the United States; the risk increases with age (Levy, 1985). Numerous studies show that the risk of coronary artery disease and related mortality in both men and women is increased by heavy drinking (Crombie, Smith, Tavendale, & Tunstall-Pedoe, 1990; Schmidt & deLint,

1972). The issue relates to total alcohol intake, rather than type of beverage, and is incrementally increased with each average daily drinking level (Bianchi, Negri, LaVecchia, & Franceschi, 1993; Urbano-Marquez et al., 1989).[2] Since there is no longer any question that heavy alcohol use causes an increase in cardiac mortality, the only remaining question is whether or not small amounts may actually be beneficial.

Elderly persons are generally well aware that coronary heart disease is a leading cause of death. Many take pains to do those things that are generally believed to reduce this risk, including taking regular exercise, maintaining a low cholesterol diet and the like. Over a number of years, several epidemiologic studies have reported that up to one or two drinks a day may *reduce* the risk of coronary heart disease. In fact, some report that moderate drinkers have a lower mortality rate than total abstainers (Boffetta & Garfinkel, 1991; Coate, 1993; deLabry et al., 1992; Jackson, Scragg, & Beaglehole, 1992; Lang & Kinnanen, 1987; Suh, Shaten, Culler, & Kuller, 1992). An argument to support the beneficial effect of moderate alcohol intake is that it leads to an increase in high-density lipoprotein (HDL) which is known to be associated with a decreased risk of coronary artery disease (Linn et al., 1993; Razay, Heaton, Bolton, & Hughes, 1992; Smith, 1982b). This argument does not appear to be valid, since the subfraction of HDL that is protective (HDL2) is not appreciably affected. HDL3, a nonprotective subfraction, is the one that is responsive to alcohol intake (Lang & Kinnanen, 1987), and some fail to find any change in the HDL-cholesterol ratio (Seppa, Sillanoukee, Pitkajorri, Nikkcla, & Kowula, 1992). Other concepts suggest that moderate alcohol use increases fibrinolytic factors (Hendriks, Veenstra, Velthuis-te-Wierik, Schaafsma, & Klufr, 1994) and decreases platelet aggregation (Renaud & deLorgerilt, 1992), all of which decrease clot formation, which in turn decreases risk of myocardial infarction.

Other studies question the validity of the concept of a "U-shaped curve" where moderate drinkers have a lower *total* and *cardiovascular* mortality than either total abstainers or heavy drinkers. On the basis of a large prospective study of British men, the light-drinking group, who had the lowest cardiovascular mortality rate, also had the lowest proportion of smokers, the lowest mean blood pressure, and the lowest proportion of manual workers (Schaper, 1991). On the other hand, a high proportion of the abstainers had previously been heavy drinkers (Wannamethee & Schaper, 1988). The ex-drinkers were also older, a high proportion were cigarette smokers, and their incidence of hypertension and obesity was similar to that in the heavier drinkers (and higher than in the lifelong teetotalers, who were similar to the light drinkers). The former heavy drinkers also had the highest rates of history of angina, myocardial infarction, diabetes, and other significant illnesses assessed. The lifelong teetotalers were similar to the light drinkers in prevalence of hypertension and evidence of ischemic heart disease.

In a very large (11,000 subjects) prospective study comparing vegetarians with meat eaters, the issue of the "U-shaped curve" was also assessed. There was no U-shaped curve found at all. Instead, significant differences in risk were related to dietary practices, particularly in the women (Gavaler, et al., 1991)

The official position of the surgeon general of the United States has not changed since the 1988 report. That position is: "The use of alcohol, even in moderate quantities, for its possible effects on [coronary heart disease] is not recommended" (National Institute on Alcohol Abuse and Alcoholism, 1988). A similar conclusion was reached as a result of a large British study (Schaper, 1991; Schaper, Wannamethee, & Walker, 1994;).

Alcohol and Cardiac Arrhythmia

Cardiac rhythm disturbances associated with alcohol intake have been well-known for years. The "holiday heart syndrome" is perhaps the best-known example; it consists of episodes of abnormal cardiac rhythms following a heavy bout of drinking. The dysrhythmia may be either atrial or ventricular (Ettinger et al., 1978; Zakhari, 1991). In one study, 35% of all new-onset atrial fibrillation was attributed to alcohol intoxication. In those under age 65, alcohol accounted for 63% of cases (Lowenstein, Gabow, Cramer et al., 1983). Another study reported 62 percent of cases of atrial fibrillation were heavy users of alcohol (Rich, Siebold, & Campian, 1985). Ventricular arrhythmias may also be involved, with ventricular premature beats or sustained ventricular tachycardia (Ettinger et al., 1978). Because these symptoms tend to occur after a binge rather than during a period of intoxication, it has been suggested that a mild degree of alcohol withdrawal syndrome may be the cause (Lang & Kinnanen, 1987).

In older age groups, coronary heart disease and pulmonary disease are prominent causes of atrial fibrillation. Lowenstein et al. (1983) reported that in those over age 65 with new-onset atrial fibrillation, coronary artery disease was the causative agent in 29% and pulmonary disease was the cause in 33% while alcohol accounted for only 10%. Persons with established ischemic heart disease, a condition frequently encountered in the elderly, are especially susceptible to arrhythmias precipitated by a heavy bout of drinking (Kentala, Luurila, & Salospuro, 1976; Rich et al., 1985). These may result in sudden death from ventricular fibrillation (Ashley & Rankin, 1980; Deutscher, Rackette, & Krishnaswami, 1984; Zakhari, 1991).

Cerebrovascular System

Death or disability from stroke is an increasing risk as one ages. Alcohol increases the risk. Hemorrhagic strokes as well as cerebral infarctions are markedly increased in heavy drinkers. After adjustment for hypertension, cigarette smoking, and medication, the relative risk for stroke in the heavy drinkers has been found to be four times that of nondrinkers (Gill, Zezulka, Shipley, Gill, & Beevers, 1986). This is true even in younger age groups (age 16 to 40) (Hillbom et al., 1995). Heavy alcohol intake is associated with a significant increased incidence of intracranial bleeding, including subarachnoid hemorrhage as well as intracerebral hemorrhage (Monforte, Estruch, Graus, Nicolas, & Urbano-Marquez, 1990). Both hypertension and heavy alcohol use are risk factors for intracerebral hemorrhage, but the lesions are in different areas. The alcohol-related lesions tend to be located in the cerebral lobes, in contrast to the typical location of hypertensive hemorrhages in the basal ganglia (Monforte et al., 1990). When compared with nondrinkers, even light drinkers (1–14 ounces of alcohol per month) more than doubled their risk for hemorrhagic stroke (Donahue, Abbott, Reed, & Yano, 1986). This increased risk for hemorrhagic stroke, even in moderate drinkers, has been confirmed by other studies (Shinton, Sagar, & Beevers, 1993; Stampfer, Colditz, Willett, Speizer, & Hennekens, 1988).

Conclusions

All things considered, there seems to be nothing to recommend even moderate amounts of alcohol, and much in the cardiovascular system to recommend against the use of large amounts of alcohol for older people.

Effects of Alcohol on Reproductive and Endocrine System

Men

It is well known that alcoholic men frequently have disorders of the reproductive system, including impotence, low sperm counts, low testosterone levels, and testicular atrophy (North & Walter, 1984; Smith, 1982a; Van Thiel, 1983). They may also show gynecomastia, which may be associated with elevated estrogen levels. Alcohol appears capable of directly suppressing testosterone production in the testes (Ellingboe & Varanelli, 1979). It has not yet been clearly determined what role alcohol effects in the hypothalamus and pituitary may play in this process.

The precise role played by alcohol in alcohol-induced sexual dysfunction has not been defined, but it is probably a combination of primary and secondary hypogonodism and neurotoxicity interrupting the neurogenic arc that controls sexual function (Heinz et al., 1995; Hugues et al., 1980).

Women

Studies involving alcoholic women suggest that they have a higher prevalence of anovulation, amenorrhea, pathologic ovarian changes, and accelerated onset of menopause (Gavaler, 1985; Moskovic, 1975). Repeated or sustained episodes of alcohol intoxication may also suppress hormonal activity in women (Mendelson et al., 1987). However, recent studies show that moderate amounts of alcohol (e.g., comparable to two drinks a day) are associated with an increase in estrogen levels and might account for the 40% to 100% greater risk of breast cancer in these women compared with women who abstain from alcohol. (Reichman et al., 1993; Van den Brandt, Goldblom, & Van't Veer, 1995).

Other Endocrine Effects

Alcohol also affects most other endocrine organs. The findings vary depending on the dose, duration, and timing of the measurement with respect to alcohol intake. Alcoholics may have elevated plasma cortisol levels and even show pseudo—Cushing's syndrome (elevated corticosteroids with normal ACTH levels), a condition that resolves after a few weeks of abstinence (Heinz et al., 1995; Reese, Besse, Jeffcoate, Goldie, & Marks, 1977). In addition to adrenocortical effects, alcohol causes an increased output of adrenal catacholamines (epinephrine and norepinephrine) (Koob, 1983). Elevated serum catecholamines have an obvious implication in the alcohol-induced elevation of blood pressure.

Other endocrine effects include decreased thyroid hormone levels, decreased growth hormone levels, and decreased vasopressin (Hegedus, 1984). Liver disease appears to be a factor in this process, but alcohol may also have a direct toxic effect on the thyroid since a decreased thyroid size has been observed in patients with alcoholic cirrhosis but not in those with non-alcoholic cirrhosis (Hegedus et al., 1988).

Conclusions

Again, alcohol, particularly in large amounts, is found to have deleterious effects on an important system: reproductive and endocrine. These effects may be most distressing to older males who may be having concerns about sexual functioning, even without the added functional impairment produced by the alcohol.

Nervous System

Central Nervous System

Brain dysfunction. Hippocrates was one of the first to associate excessive alcohol use with serious, even fatal brain dysfunction. Later Greek and Roman physicians made similar observations (Hankoff, 1972). Subsequent observations through the present time have consistently confirmed these

findings. Both the physical findings and the behavioral findings of this alcoholic brain syndrome resemble closely the changes induced by aging. The
behavioral changes include impaired learning, difficulty concentrating,
impaired abstract thinking, impaired judgment, impaired short-term memory,
impaired problem solving, and impaired perception. On tests of adaptive
ability, alcoholics scored closer to brain-damaged subjects that to non-brain-
damaged controls (Fitzhugh, Fitzhugh, & Reitan, 1965; Smith, Burt, &
Chapman, 1973). Mental aging index scores show a significant acceleration
of mental aging in alcoholics. They showed more test-measured signs of
mental aging at every chronological age, a finding that was more prominent
in the older cohorts (Williams, Ray, & Overall, 1973). This same study suggested that the alcoholics showed two distinct patterns of deterioration, of
which one is consistent with general organic brain syndrome and one is more
closely associated with aging (Williams et al., 1973).

   Alcoholic dementia. Alcohol-induced dysfunction is rather common.
Alcoholic dementia accounts for 10 to 20% of all admissions to state mental
hospitals in the United States (Emmerson, Dustman, & Shearer, 1988; Still,
Jackson, Brandes, Abramson, & Macera, 1990). This condition is also
found in about the same frequency in other countries and cultures where
alcohol is used (Ikeda, 1991; Ishii, 1983; Park, Ko, Park, & Jung, 1994).
Neuropsychological testing reveals some degree of dysfunction in 45 to 70%
of detoxified alcoholics without clinical evidence of organic brain syndrome
(Eckhardt & Martin, 1986; Smith, Burt, & Chapman, 1982). Some studies
even suggest measurable alcohol-related cognitive impairment in nonalcoholic social drinkers, in which a dose-response relationship between alcohol
consumption and lower scores on certain neuropsychological tests is seen
(Parker, Parker, Brody, & Schoenberg, 1983). Other studies, however, throw
doubt on these conclusions and the issue is still unresolved (Emmerson et al.,
1988; Parsons, 1986). Studies of alcohol-induced dementia identify age as
the most important risk factor in the severity of the dementia. This clinical
finding is supported by CT scans showing significant cerebral atrophy, particularly in older alcoholics (Miller, Belkin, & Gold, 1991).

   Autopsy findings include brain atrophy, with histologic loss of the dendritic tree of neurons in various brain regions (including the hypocampus and
cerebellum), and a variety of chemical changes in brain synaptic functions
(Freund, 1984). Numerous other studies have reported cortical atrophy or
cerebellar (or both) atrophy at autopsy in deteriorated alcoholics (Butters &
Cermak, 1983). Similar antemortem findings have been demonstrated with
computerized tomography (CT) scans and other imaging techniques (Harper
& Kril, 1985; Lee, Maller, Hardt, Havbek, & Jensen, 1979). Widening of the
lateral ventricles and the third ventricle is also noted (Bergman, 1987;
Pfefferbaum, Rosenbloom, Jernigan, & Brain, Crusan, 1988). Enlargement

of the third ventricle is associated with impairment of paired-associate tasks (Gebhardt, Naeser, & Butters, 1984). Those with widened lateral ventricles show a consistent trend toward more neuropsychological deficits in general intelligence, verbal learning and retention, and short-term memory (Bergman, 1987). This trend is more pronounced in middle-aged or older alcoholics and becomes exaggerated with age (Bergman, 1987; Pfefferbaum et al., 1988). Studies in women show changes similar to those in men, but an important finding is that the evidence of brain atrophy in women occurs after significantly shorter and less intense periods of drinking (Jacobsen, 1986).

Structural damage. The issue of whether or not moderate amounts of alcohol intake are associated with structural damage is still not clear. Some CT scans show evidence of atrophy (Cala, 1985). So, as with the issue of cognitive deficits associated with moderate alcohol use, the findings are inconsistent, and a final judgment has not been made.

Alcohol and Alzheimer's Disease

In Alzheimer's Disease (AD), a special case of what has been called "pathological aging" (Freund, 1982), cognitive performance declines severely. Postmortem examination of the brain of alcoholic and nonalcoholic AD patients showed that alcohol and AD had different effects on different regions of the brain and suggests that the effects of alcohol may have contributed further to the dementia of the AD patients (Freund & Ballinger, 1992).

Recovery of Function with Abstinence

A number of studies show that abstinence for months to years may lead to recovery of some or all cognitive function and even reversal of at least some brain atrophy (Carlen, Wortzman, Holgate, Wilkinson, & Ranking, 1978; Goldman, 1982; Shear, Jernigan, & Buttirs, 1994; Smith, Johnson & Burdick, 1971). Abstinent alcoholics under age 40 have been found to recover visiospatial capacity more frequently than older abstinent alcoholics (Goldman, Williams, & Klisz, 1983). On the other hand, even after 5 years of abstinence, young alcoholics did not reverse memory and learning deficits (Brandt, Butters, Ryan, & Bayog, 1983). Other studies do confirm some long-term cognitive deficits in abstinent alcoholics, despite various functional improvements (Fabian & Parsons, 1983; Yohman, Parsons, & Leber, 1985).

Peripheral Neuropathy

Peripheral neuropathy is frequently seen in clinical practice. Statistics from large municipal hospitals show that alcoholic peripheral neuropathy is more common than all other forms combined (Merritt, 1979). The condition is generally believed to result from nutritional deficiency, principally of the B vitamins. The nerve lesions begin in the longest peripheral nerves (those leading to the feet and hands). Initially, demyelination of the nerves takes place, resulting in decreased conduction velocities in the affected nerves. As the process becomes more severe, degeneration of the axon, occurs with a process of "dying back" from the distal end proximally.

The onset of symptoms is usually slow, extending over weeks or months, but occasionally may present rapidly over the course of only a few days (Merritt, 1979). Involvement is usually bilateral and symmetrical. The first symptoms may be pain in the calf muscles or feet. At other times, the first symptoms are a burning, tingling, or prickling sensation of the lower extremities, often progressing to numbness of the feet and legs. Later, similar symptoms may occur in the hands and arms.

The sensory symptoms start peripherally and progress centrally, so that the discomfort and numbness usually begins in the feet and works its way up the leg. As the process continues, muscle weakness and wasting may occur. The first noticeable effect may be a "foot-drop gait." Later, the legs may become completely paralyzed. Proprioception is often impaired and this, in concert with weakened muscles, leads to an ataxic wide-based gait.

Treatment for alcoholic peripheral neuropathy is simple and straightforward. Abstinence from alcohol, a nutritious diet and supplementary vitamins are the main factors. Thiamine has been the vitamin most heavily emphasized, but it may not be the only vitamin of importance in the pathogenesis of the condition (D'Amour, Bruneau, & Butterworth, 1991). In clinical practice large doses of B vitamins (in addition to thiamine) are administered in amounts much larger than the minimum daily requirements. Recovery occurs rapidly in early cases in which only demyelinization has occurred. When degeneration of the axon fiber has occurred, recovery is much slower, in some cases requiring months to a year or more (Merritt, 1979).

Age-Specific Considerations

In older patients, diabetic peripheral neuropathy is often the first diagnosis considered. When this diagnosis proves false, too often a great deal of time and expense is wasted on searching for uncommon causes of neuropathy (for example, pharmacologic agents, toxic agents, or other metabolic diseases) while the most common cause, alcoholism is not considered at all. This generally occurs because the patient does not fit the physician's mental image of an alcoholic.

Conclusions

Once more, it appears that alcohol, particularly in large quantities, is a further substantial burden to deficits inherent in both normal aging and "pathological aging."

Gastrointestinal System

Esophagus

Frequent use of alcohol may cause esophagitis and gastritis and exacerbate existing peptic ulcers (Kurata & Halle, 1984). The relative risk of carcinoma of the esophagus is high in alcoholics (Driver & Swann, 1987). Most studies do not calculate the increased risks. One study from China (Gao et al., 1994) reported the odds ratio to be 1.4 for men who drank alcohol ("primarily heavy drinkers"). When heavy smoking and heavy drinking were combined, the effect was dramatically increased (odds ratio 12.0). In a South American study (De Stefani, Munoz, Esteve, Vasallo, & Victor, 1990) the relative risk was 12.2 for those drinking over 2.5 liters of a local alcoholic beverage (called *mate*). Smoking in addition to this heavy alcohol intake increased the relative risk to 22.6.

Esophagitis is more prevalent in alcoholics than in others because of the increased acid production in the stomach and frequent vomiting. In addition, intoxication predisposes to reflux of stomach contents into the esophagus (Fenster, 1982). Vomiting, with severe retching, may tear the mucosa at or just below the gastroesophageal junction, leading to profuse bleeding and hematemesis (the Mallory-Weiss Syndrome) (Fenster, 1982).

One of the most common consequences of heavy alcohol intake is erosive gastritis. Alcohol increases gastric acid secretion, but of even more importance, it also reduces the mucosal cell barrier, allowing back-diffusion of the acid into the mucosa (Fenster, 1982). The mucosal damage caused in this process leads to swelling, inflammation, and a friable surface which is prone to bleeding. If aspirin (as is commonly prescribed for older people), is added to this combination, the process is accelerated (Overholt, 1969). The symptoms may include epigastric distress, nausea, and vomiting. A major complication is gastric bleeding, which may be life-threatening (Fenster, 1982). Alcohol may also exacerbate existing peptic ulcer disease. If bleeding occurs, it may be more difficult to control in an older person with more rigid vessels. Even in nonpredisposed individuals, alcohol consumption increases the risk of major gastric and duodenal bleeding (Kaufman, Koff, Laszlo, Wiholm, & Shapiro, 1995).

Small Intestine

Chronic alcoholism leads to malabsorption of a variety of nutrients, including fat, xylose, folic acid, and vitamin B12 (Mezey, 1975). The malabsorption syndrome thus induced may further impair the nutritional status of the individual. Alcohol also impairs normal peristalsis (Mayer, Grabowski, & Fisher, 1978) and may cause a variety of structural changes, including flattening of the villi, loss of certain enzymes, and inhibition of amino acid and glucose transport mechanisms (Dinda & Beck, 1977).

Pancreas

Heavy alcohol consumption and gallstones are the two leading causes of pancreatitis. Acute pancreatitis, or inflammation of the pancreas, is manifested by severe upper abdominal pain, nausea, vomiting, ileus, fever, and sometimes hypovolemia with hypotension and electrolyte disturbances (Fenster, 1982), none of which are well tolerated by elderly people. About 20% of these patients have a much more severe form which may even lead to death (in under 5% of cases) or severe complications, such as pancreatic abscess, pseudocyst, or peripheral fat necrosis involving pleura, pericardium, bones, and joints (Fenster, 1982).

Chronic pancreatitis may occur insidiously, and many such patients have no previous history of acute attacks (Fenster, 1982). Over 75% of patients with chronic pancreatitis have a history of heavy alcohol consumption (Van Thiel et al., 1981). It may be associated with chronic pain which may in turn lead to narcotic dependence (Fenster, 1982). Within 3 or 4 years of the initial attack, many of these patients develop insulin-dependent diabetes mellitus. This occurs as a result of progressive destruction of the insulin-producing cells of the pancreas. In addition, the reduced production of pancreatic digestive enzymes may lead to malabsorption, particularly of fat, leading to weight loss, malnutrition and foul-smelling bulky stools, often with diarrhea (Fenster, 1982). Both the acute effects (pain, nausea, vomiting, etc.), the associated stress, and the chronic effects such as malabsorption and diabetes are poorly tolerated by elderly patients.

Alcohol and the Liver

The liver is the principal site of alcohol metabolism. Liver damage from excessive use of alcohol has been recognized since ancient times; descriptions of cirrhosis of the liver were given by Hippocrates (Leibowitz, 1967). There are three types of alcohol-induced liver disease. In order of increasing severity they are:

- Fatty liver
- Alcoholic hepatitis
- Cirrhosis

Among heavy drinkers, 90 to 100% show some evidence of fatty liver; 10 to 35% show alcoholic hepatitis; and 10 to 20% develop cirrhosis (Grant,

Dufour, & Hartford, 1988). Other studies suggest that cirrhosis may be underdiagnosed, since autopsy findings reveal that 40% of cirrhosis was not detected before death (Lieber, 1982).

It was assumed for many years that the principal cause of liver damage in alcoholics was their tendency to drink and neglect to eat a nutritionally adequate diet (Hartroft & Porta, 1966). This nutritional insult to the liver certainly can, and undoubtedly does, produce damage in many cases. In more recent years, however, it has been found that alcohol by itself has the capacity to damage liver cells in spite of a nutritionally adequate diet (Lieber, 1995). This has been demonstrated in animal studies (Rubin & Lieber, 1974) and human studies, both in alcoholics (Lieber, 1966) and in nonalcoholics.

Fatty liver. The precise amount of alcohol that is required to induce liver damage is still rather uncertain. One study showed that in young, nonalcoholic research volunteers, the substitution of alcohol for carbohydrates in the diet for 1 week caused fat accumulation and ultrastructure change in liver cells (Rubin & Lieber, 1968). The alcohol intake was well below intoxication levels. The primary cause of fat accumulation in the liver appears to be simply the manner in which alcohol is metabolized in liver cells. The major route of metabolism involves the action of the enzyme alcohol dehydrogenase (ADH), which removes a hydrogen atom from the alcohol and transfers it to the coenzyme nicotinamide adenine-dinucleotide (NAD), which then converts NAD into its reduced form NADH. The NAD– NADH system is required in a multitude of metabolic processes in the liver. Metabolism of relatively large amounts of alcohol results in an excess of NADH, which in turn leads to a variety of metabolic effects, including reduced glycogen formation and both *increased* production and *decreased* oxidation of lipid (Lieber, 1976). The net effect is an accumulation of lipids within liver cells. Virtually all actively drinking chronic alcoholics show increased fat accumulation in liver cells on a liver biopsy (Fenster, 1982). This "alcoholic fatty liver" is generally not associated with distressing clinical symptoms. The liver may be enlarged and biochemical tests of liver function may be mildly deranged. Occasionally, in a binge-drinking alcoholic, "acute fatty liver" may develop and be associated with abdominal pain, anorexia and jaundice (Fenster, 1982). This may pose a diagnostic challenge, since it might be confused with alcoholic or viral hepatitis or cholecystitis. The course of fatty liver of any variety is generally benign. Abstinence from alcohol and normal nutrition results in a rapid return to normal structure and function (including normal liver function tests) in a few weeks to 2 months or so (Fenster, 1982).

Alcoholic hepatitis. In some alcoholics, for reasons not yet completely understood, continued heavy drinking leads to alcoholic hepatitis. Microscopic examination of liver tissue shows an active inflammatory process, areas of necrosis, fibrosis, and Mallory bodies (glassy-appearing membrane structures). The process may develop insidiously and progress gradually over a period of months or years. In other cases, it may present in a fulminant form, advancing to death over a course of only a few weeks (Fenster, 1982; Moddrey, 1988). Clinically, the alcoholic will generally show evidence of significant liver disease with hepatomegaly, jaundice, hepatic pain, fever, and leukocytosis. These acute symptoms may lead to the erroneous diagnosis of cholecystitis, a condition not uncommon in older persons. This can be a deadly miscalculation, since these patients have a high death rate following surgery; for this reason, alcoholic hepatitis has been called a "surgical trap" (Fenster, 1982; Mikkelsen, Turill, & Kern, 1968).

Alcoholic hepatitis is a serious condition and may progress to death. Its reversibility is variable and depends on its severity and chronicity. Abstinence from alcohol is a prerequisite for healing. However, even with permanent abstinence, some degree of scarring may remain (Fenster, 1982; Moddrey, 1988).

Cirrhosis. The most advanced form of alcoholic liver disease is alcoholic cirrhosis, also known as Laennec's cirrhosis. It is characterized by fibrosis (scarring) leading to disruption of the normal liver lobular architecture in which nodules of liver parenchyma are surrounded by fibrous tissue (Lieber, 1995). As cirrhosis progresses, the patient is likely to develop portal vein hypertension, leading to esophageal varices which may rupture and bleed massively (a complication poorly tolerated by older people). In addition, edema and ascites may develop. In older persons with emphysema, the increased intra-abdominal pressure from ascites may seriously compromise the movement of the diaphragm and further impair respiration.

The symptoms may present insidiously, with anorexia, fatigue, and weakness, and a gradual onset of jaundice. The condition may progress to liver failure, in which products of manufacture by the liver are no longer produced in adequate quantities (e.g., decreased serum protein levels and decreased prothrombin levels, which may lead to bleeding). Equally dangerous is the accumulation of excessive levels of certain chemicals normally removed by the liver, (e.g., bilirubin, leading to progressive jaundice; or ammonia, leading to hepatic encephalopathy and coma). Mortality from cirrhosis is ranked as the ninth leading cause of death in the United States (NIAA, 1988).

Individual differences. As noted earlier, the amount or duration of excessive alcohol use leading to liver injury has not been definitely established. It is well established, however, that there are marked individual differences in susceptibility to the alcohol damage (Moddrey, 1988). An increased risk of developing fatty liver is found with alcohol consumption of 80 grams a day for men and 20 grams a day for women (Grant et al., 1988). The severity of liver damage tends to increase with increasing daily intake to over 180 grams per day, or about 14 standard bar drinks (Grant et al., 1988). When daily alcohol consumption increases to 210 grams for 22 years, the probability of developing cirrhosis is 50%, and after 33 years it is 80% (Lelbach, 1974).

Genetic factors also play a role. Identical twins show an increased concordance for cirrhosis (Hrubec & Omenn, 1981). A specific gene, coding for type I collagen (the type most prominent in dense fibrosis), was found more frequently in alcoholics with cirrhosis than in those without cirrhosis or than in controls (Weiner, Eskreis, Compton, Orrego, & Zern, 1988). Women are found to be more likely to develop alcohol-induced liver damage, and they do this with less alcohol and for a shorter duration of use than is the case with men (Lieber, 1995).

It should be emphasized that not all cases of cirrhosis are caused by alcohol. Viral hepatitis also makes a significant contribution, particularly hepatitis B and hepatitis C. Chronic hepatitis C is also significantly correlated with the severity of alcoholic cirrhosis (Mendenhall et al., 1991) and may influence the progression of alcoholic liver disease (Schiff, 1992). Markers for hepatitis B have been found in some patients with alcoholic liver disease, especially those with portal hypertension, and may be a risk factor for the development or progression of alcohol-induced liver disease (Lieber, 1984). Evidence also suggests that the reverse is true, and that alcohol consumption intensifies hepatitis B-induced liver disease (Nomura et al., 1988).

Age-specific considerations. About 25% of alcoholic liver disease is seen in persons older than 60 years (Potter & James, 1987). Of the younger persons with alcoholic liver disease, only a minority have cirrhosis. In contrast, the majority of the elderly with alcoholic liver disease have cirrhosis (Scott, 1989). Whereas the clinical findings of cirrhosis in an older alcoholic are no different from those in a younger one, the prognosis is quite different. In the first year after diagnosis of cirrhosis, 50% of those over the age of 60 die, in contrast to 7% of those under age 60 (Potter & James, 1987; Scott , 1989).

Treatment of cirrhosis in the elderly is similar to that for younger people; however, again there are special considerations. Diuretics are frequently required to treat edema or ascites. Great care must be used when giving diuretics to elderly cirrhosis patients, since their total body water may already be decreased, making them more susceptible to fluid and electrolyte depletion (Scott, 1989). If potassium-sparing diuretics are not used, hypokalemia may occur, which may in turn lead to cardiac arrhythmia, particularly those patients who may also be taking digitalis preparations.

If bleeding esophageal varices become one of the complications, vasopressin is sometimes used in the treatment. However, vasopressin may also compromise the blood flow in coronary arteries, a situation that is especially dangerous in the elderly (Scott, 1989). In any event, bleeding is less well tolerated by the elderly. It may be necessary to treat the varices by reducing the pressure in the portal vein system by a major surgical procedure in which the portal vein is connected to the inferior vena cava (portacaval shunt). This, too, is a procedure poorly tolerated by the elderly.

If hepatic encephalopathy becomes a complication, it may pose a diagnostic dilemma. Hepatic encephalopathy progresses through four recognized stages (Scharschmidt, 1985, pp. 852–859):

- Stage 1 is associated with a variety of symptoms including apathy, lack of awareness, euphoria, anxiety, restlessness or shortened attention span.
- Stage 2 is associated with lethargy, drowsiness and/or disorientation.
- Stage 3 is associated with deep somnolence (but at least transient arousal is possible).
- In stage 4, coma (absent verbal response) is present.

In stages 1 and 2 it may be difficult to distinguish effects of liver disease from organic brain syndrome, in which case appropriate treatment for the liver disease may be delayed, with unfortunate results.

The issue of cancer is prominent in the older population. Primary liver cancer is relatively rare in North America and Europe; however, the disease is associated with cirrhosis. A series of studies showed that 64% to 90% of persons with *either* condition had *both* conditions. The reported population of alcoholics with cirrhosis who develop cancer ranges from 5 to 30% (Driver & Swann, 1987).

Skin

Rosacea

When the average person thinks about dermatologic manifestations of alcoholism, rosacea (also known as acne rosacea) generally is the first to come to mind. The condition is more common in the later decades of life (fourth, fifth and sixth). The central region of the face (central forehead, nose, cheeks and chin) develops erythema and telangiectasias and occasionally acne-like papules. A more extreme form of rosacea, rhinophyma, involves a lobulated thickening of the lower portion of the nose and is recognized by many as the stereotypic red, bulbous nose of alcoholics. Rosacea and rhinophyma are stimulated by alcohol, but the condition is not caused by alcoholism and may occur in people who never were alcoholic (Pochi, 1988). Even without rosacea, persistent redness of the face is a common finding in alcoholics ("plethoric facies") and is believed to result from chronic vasodilitation and loss of vasoregulatory control. Fine telangiectasia are also characteristic (Higgins & duVivier, 1992).

Skin changes

Skin changes associated with alcoholic liver disease include jaundice, palmar erythema ("liver palms"), spider nevi, Dupuytren's Contracture, white nails, and "paper money skin" (fine threadlike capillaries scattered in a random manner, like the fine silk threads in paper money) (Higgins & duVivier, 1992).

Psoriasis

Psoriasis, while not caused by alcohol ingestion, is often made worse by heavy alcohol intake (Higgins, du Vivier, & Peters, 1992). Abstinence from alcohol is often associated with clinical remission of the dermatosis (Vincenti & Blunden, 1987).

Eczema

Discoid eczema, characterized by well-circumscribed, nummular plaques of dermatitis, is generally found on the lower legs. The condition tends to be particularly recalcitrant to treatment and has a strong association with heavy alcohol intake (Higgins & du Vivier, 1992).

Skin infections

Skin infections such as cellulitis are also more frequent in alcoholics. Fungal infections are also more frequent, including tinea pedis, onychomycosis and chronic tinea vesicolor (Higgins et al., 1992).

Age-Specific Considerations

Rosacea has a definite age relationship, and psoriasis was found much more frequently in alcoholics age 65 and older than in the general population of the same age (Hurt, Finlayson, Morse & Davis, 1988). All of the inflammatory skin conditions (psoriasis, discoid eczema, and superficial infections) may interfere with sleep, may promote agitation and, in general, tend to be less well tolerated by older persons.

ALCOHOL AND NUTRITION

Factors Leading to Decreased Intake and Absorption

There are many ways in which excessive alcohol consumption can interfere with adequate nutrition. The first way, obviously, is for the alcohol budget to compete with the food budget. In low-income alcoholics, the alcohol budget may win to the point where food stamps are sold to purchase alcohol, with the result that less food is purchased. If alcoholic gastritis is present, appetite may be diminished and ingested food may be vomited. Alcohol damage to the intestine or pancreas may impair absorption of vitamins, amino acids, and fats (Israel, Valenzuela, Salazar, & Ugarte, 1969; Lieber, 1995). For example, after alcohol ingestion, thiamine (Vitamin B1) absorption is reduced 40–60% (Israel, 1969), and chronic alcohol intake significantly reduces protein synthesis (Sinclair, 1972). Prolonged intake of alcohol injures the mucosa of the small intestine—this, among other things, intensifies folate deficiency, which separately impairs active absorption of trace nutrients (Schuckit, 1982).

Nutritional Consequences of Alcohol Metabolism

The metabolism of alcohol also places an increased demand on the utilization of thiamine (Dreyfus, 1974) as well as other water-soluble vitamins, which are lost through the kidneys at an accelerated rate with heavy drinking. All of these factors promote malnutrition in alcoholics of all ages. Nutrient intakes decline with age (Klein & Iber, 1991). Many body functions and metabolic pathways decline throughout the life cycle; all of them measurably decrease after age 65, and many before that age (Munro, Suter, & Russell, 1987). Chronic disease is also common in the elderly and may further contribute to nutritional impairment. Social factors such as decreased income, decreased mobility, or living alone may also contribute to failure to purchase and prepare an adequate diet. The additional burden of alcoholism is cause for further concern for the nutritional status of elderly alcoholics.

Alcohol metabolism provides energy intermediate to that of fats and carbohydrates at 7 kcal per gram. However, it contains virtually no nutrients. The energy requirement for an average retired elderly person living in an apartment with no organized outings is about 1,600 to 1,800 kcal per day (Klein & Iber, 1991) The usual serving of beer or wine contains about 100 kcal, so that four or five portions (less than a six-pack of beer) may provide over 20% of the daily energy requirement in a form almost devoid of nutrients (Klein & Iber, 1991). Severe malnutrition may be expected in persons with disease or physical incapacity and in those consuming a high percentage of their daily caloric intake as alcohol (e.g., 25% or more) (Iber, 1990). Deficiencies in some nutrients (e.g., folic acid, pyridoxine, potassium, phosphorus, magnesium) occur after only a rather brief time (less than 21 days) of heavy alcohol use. Others require an intermediate (1–4 months) duration of use (for example, thiamine, nicotinamide, ascorbic acid, zinc, and selenium). Still others require a rather long period, 4 months to several years, of excessive intake (for example, protein, essential fatty acids, iron, vitamins B12, A, D, and E) (Iber, 1990).

Conclusions on Alcohol and Nutrition

All alcoholics are at risk for malnutrition. Elderly alcoholics are at considerably increased risk and require even greater attention to nutritional repair in the course of treatment.

PSYCHIATRIC MANIFESTATIONS

Acute Withdrawal

Psychiatric complications of dependence on alcohol (or other drugs) are similar in all age groups with some shift in emphasis in the older population. Anxiety and depression are well known to be associated with alcoholism. The direct effect of alcohol or any other depressant drug is mood sedation. After physical dependence is established, withdrawal of alcohol leads to increased catecholamine blood levels with tremor, agitation, and sleeplessness. With more severe withdrawal symptoms, frank psychotic symptoms may develop, with delusions and hallucinations. It is not possible to accurately predict what percentage of those showing symptoms of alcohol withdrawal will progress to hallucinosis, since much depends on what, if any, treatment has been received for the mitigation of those symptoms. One recent study of 532 male patients in a Veterans Administration Hospital inpatient treatment program found that 10% exhibited alcoholic hallucinosis (Tsuang, Irwin, Smith, & Schuckit, 1994) Those who developed hallucinosis tended to be younger at the onset of their alcohol problems, consumed more alcohol per drinking occasion, developed more alcohol-related life problems, and had higher rates of other drug experimentation than those who did not hallucinate (Tsuang et al., 1994). It is generally agreed that alcoholic hallucinosis and delirium tremens are the result of long-term heavy alcohol intake (Hemmingsen, & Kamp, 1988; Tsuang, Irwin, Smith et al., 1994).

When hallucinations or delusions occur, they are particularly troublesome in the elderly, who may already have diminished vision and hearing and are thus predisposed to misperception. Alcoholic hallucinosis generally follows a relatively benign course in which the individual remains oriented and communicative, and it is not generally associated with panic or paranoia (Butz, 1982). Delirium tremens is the most severe form of alcohol withdrawal and is characterized by marked tremor, anxiety, insomnia, anorexia, paranoia, disorientation, and hallucination. It may also be associated with fever, vomiting and diarrhea. Tachycardia and tremor are the rule (Butz, 1982). In about one-third to as many as 97% of cases, delirium tremens is preceded by an alcohol withdrawal seizure (Sellers & Kalant, 1982). All of these severe withdrawal reactions are physically, as well as emotionally, stressful and pose an increased mortality risk for older persons who may already have marginal cardiovascular function.

Depression

Depressed mood is present in most alcoholics, particularly in the immediate postintoxication period. Part of this is undoubtedly the result of some of the life consequences of alcoholic drinking, including isolation from family and friends who will no longer put up with the drinking behavior. This leads to a spiral of loneliness and dysphoria (Bienefeld, 1987). In addition, the neuro-chemical disturbances induced by a heavy bout of drinking lead to a depressed mood ("alcoholic sadness") which is temporary and will clear after 2 or 3 weeks of abstinence (Schuckit, 1982). However, some alcoholics have primary depression which is present even in periods of prolonged abstinence. These individuals require treatment for their depression in *addition* to treatment for their alcoholism (Schuckit, 1982).

Suicide is a particularly common problem associated with alcohol dependence and has been estimated to be as high as 32 times the risk for the general population (Sexias, 1982). Next to advancing age, dependence on alcohol and other drugs is among the greatest risk factors for suicide. Men are more likely to commit suicide than women. In 57 countries studied, the ratio of men to women varied, but suicide among women was always "considerably lower" (La Vecchia, Lucchini, & Levi, 1994). Suicide rates for the elderly rose from 1955 to 1989, particularly in Canada and the United States, Australia, and New Zealand (La Vecchia et al., 1994). The elderly are clearly weighted toward suicide as a complication of alcoholism (Atkinson & Schuckit, 1983).

GENERAL HEALTH STATUS

General health is an area of substantial concern in actively drinking elderly persons. One study showed that over 90% of the actively drinking older alcoholics presented with a major health problem (Schuckit & Miller, 1976). In surveys of self-perceived health status of a large stratified sample of men and women over age 60, those who were classified as heavy drinkers were most likely to see themselves as in poor health (Monk, Cryns, & Cabral, 1977). The major health problems tend to be a consequence of chronic heavy drinking and its associated lifestyle, rather than alcohol withdrawal symptoms (Schuckit, Anthenelli, Bucholz, Hessbrock, & Tipp, 1995; Schuckit, Morrissey, & O'Leary, 1978). All-cause mortality has a significant linear relationship to quantity of alcohol consumption (Rehm & Sempos, 1995).

CONCLUSIONS

Alcoholism may lead to a great many physical and mental problems in individuals of any age. Elderly alcoholics often have additional problems resulting from the interaction of heavy alcohol intake with age-related changes in physiology. There seems to be no area in which even moderate alcohol intake is of positive benefit, and there are some areas in which even small amounts are detrimental.

NOTES

1. "Characterized by impaired control over drinking, preoccupation with the drug alcohol, use of alcohol despite adverse consequences" (Morse & Flavin, 1992, pp. 1012–1014).
2. Relative risk increases from 1.2 for more than one to two drinks per day, to 1.4 for more than two to three drinks per day, to 2.6 for more than three drinks per day (Bianchi et al., 1993).

REFERENCES

Abdallah, R. M., Starkey, J. R., & Meadows, G. G. (1988). Toxicity of chronic high alcohol intake on mouse natural killer cell activity. *Research Communications in Chemistry, Pathology, and Pharmacology, 59,* 245–258.

Adams, H. G., & Jordan, C. (1984). Infections in the alcoholic. *Medical Clinics of North America, 68,* 179–199.

Aldo-Benson, M. A. (1988). Alcohol directly suppresses B cell response to antigen. *Federation Proceedings, 2,* 6.

An'ia, B. J., Suman, V. J., Fairbanks, V. F., & Melton, L. J., III. (1994). Prevalence of anemia in medical practice: Community versus referral patients. *Mayo Clinic Proceedings, 69,* 808–809.

Andersen, B. R. (1975). Host factors causing increased susceptibility to infection in patients with Laennec's cirrhosis. *Annuals of the New York Academy of Science, 252,* 348–352.

Ashley, M. J., & Rankin, J. G. (1980). Hazardous alcohol consumption and diseases of the circulatory system. *Journal of Studies on Alcoholism, 41,* 1040–1070.

Atkinson, J. H., & Schuckit, M. A. (1983). Geriatric alcohol and drug misuse and abuse. *Advances in Substance Abuse, 3,* 195–237.

Benzer, D. G. (1994). Management of alcohol intoxication and withdrawal. In N. S. Miller (Ed.), *Principles of Addiction Medicine.* (pp. 1–7). Chevy Chase, MD: American Society of Addiction Medicine.

Bergman, H. (1987). Brain dysfunction related to alcoholism: Some results from the KARTAD project. In O. A. Parsons, N. Butters, and P. E. Nathan (Eds.), *Neuropsychology of alcoholism: Implications for diagnosis and treatment* (pp. 21–24). New York: Guilford

Bergman, H., Arelson, G., Idestrom, C. M., Borg, S., Hindmarsh, T., Makower, J., & Mutzell, S. (1983). Alcohol consumption and computer-tomographic findings in a random sample of men and women from the general population. *Pharmacology, Biochemistry and Behavior, 18,* 501–505.

Bianchi, C., Negri, E., Lavecchia, C., & Franceschi, S. (1993, August). Alcohol consumption and the risk of acute myocardial infarction in women. *Journal of Epidemiology and Community Health, 47,* 308–311.

Bienefeld, D. (1987). Alcoholism in the elderly. *American Family Physician, 36(2),* 163–169.

Bluckman, S. J., Dvorak, V. C., & Macgregor, R. R. (1975). Host defences during prolonged alcohol consumption in a controlled environment. *Archives of Internal Medicine, 137,* 1539–1543.

Boffetta, P., & Garfinkel, L. (1991). Alcohol drinking and mortality among men enrolled in an American Cancer Society prospective study. *Epidemiology, 1,* 342–348.

Bounds, W., Betzing, K. W., Stewart, R. M., & Holcombe, R. F. (1994). Social drinking and the immune response: Impairment of lymphokine activated killer activity. *Americal Journal of Medical Sciences, 307,* 391–395.

Brandt, J., Butters, N., Ryan, C., & Bayog, R. (1983). Cognitive loss and recovery in long-term alcohol abusers, *Archives of Gerneral Psychiatry, 40,* 435–442.

Brayton, R. G., Stokes, P. E., Schwartz, M. S., & Louria, D. B. (1970). Effect of alcohol and various diseases on leukocyte mobilization, phagocytosis and intracellular bacterial killing. *New England Journal of Medicine, 282,* 123–128.

Butters, N., & Cermak, L. S. (1983). Acute loss of autobiographical memories in an amnesic patient with Korsokoff's Syndrome. *Society of Neurosciences Abstracts, 9*(Part 1), 29.

Butz, R. H. (1982). Intoxication and withdrawal. In N. J. Estes & M. E. Heinemann (Eds.), *Alcoholism: Development, consequences and interventions* (pp. 102–108). St. Louis: Mosby.

Cala, L. A. (1985). CT demonstration of the early effects of alcohol on the brain. In M. Galanter (Ed.), *Recent developments in alcoholism: Vol. 3* (pp. 253–264). New York: Plenum.

Callen, K. J., Knuiman, M. W., & Ward, N. J. (1993). Alcohol and mortality in Brusselton, Western Australia. *American Journal of Epidemiology, 137,* 242–248.

Carlen, P. L., Wortzman, G., Holgate, R. C., Wildinson, D. A., & Rankin, J. C. (1978). Reversible cerebral atrophy in recently abstinent chronic alcoholics measured by computed tomography scans. *Science, 200,* 1076–1078.

Coate, D. (1993). Moderate drinking and coronary heart disease mortality: Evidence from HNANES I and HNANES I follow-up. *American Journal of Public Health, 83,* 799–801.

Cohen, S. (1985, November). Alcoholism: Cardiovascular consequences. *Drug and Alcoholism Newsletter, 14,*

Colle, J., Forestier, F., Quero, A. M., Bourrinet, P., & German, A. (1982). The effect of alcohol ingestion on the susceptibility of mice to viral infections. *Alcoholism New York, 6,* 239–246.

Cook, R. T., Ballas, Z. K., Waldschmidt, T. J., Vandeuteen, D., Labrecque, D. R., & Cook, B. L., (1995). Modulation of T-cell adhesion markers, and the CD45R and CD57 antigens in human alcoholics. *Alcoholism: Clinical and Experimental Research, 19,* 555–563.

Cowan, D. H. (1969a). Effect of alcohol on circulating platelets. *Blood, 34,* 850–854.

Cowan, D. H. (1969b). Thrombokinetics in alcoholism. *Journal of Laboratory Clinical Medicine, 74,* 865–870.

Cowan, D. H. (1971). Thrombocytopenia of severe alcoholism. *Annals of Internal Medicine, 74,* 37–43

Criqui, M. N., Wallace, R. B., Mishkel, M., Barrett-Connor, E., & Hess, G. (1981). Alcohol consumption and blood pressure: The Lipid Research Clinics prevalence study. *Hypertension, 3,* 552–565.

Crombie, I. K., Smith, W. C., Tavendale, R., & Tunstall-Pedoe, H. (1990). Geographical clustering of risk factors and lifestyle for coronary heart disease in the Scottish Heart Health Study. *British Heart Journal, 64,* 199–203.

Crowley, J. P., & Abramson, P. M. (1971). Effect of ethanol on complement mediated chemotoxis. *Clinical Research, 19,* 415.

D'Amour, M. L., Bruneau, J., & Butterworth, R. F. (1991). Abnormalities of peripheral nerve conduction in relation to thiamine status in alcoholic patients. *Canadian Journal of Neurological Sciences, 182,* 126–128.

De Stefani, E., Munoz, N., Esteve, J., Vasallo, A., & Victor, A. C. (1990). Mate drinking, alcohol, tobacco, diet and esophageal cancer in Uruguay. *Cancer Research, 50,* 426–431.

Decker, J., & Goldstein, J. (1982). Risk factors in head and neck cancer. *New England Journal of Medicine, 306,* 1151–115.

deLabry, L. O., Blynn, R. J., Levenson, M. R., Hermos, J. A., Locastro, J. S., & Vokonas, P. S. (1992). Alcohol consumption and mortality in an American male population: Recovering the U-shaped curve: Findings from the mormative aging study. *Journal of Studies on Alcohol, 53,* 25–32.

Deutscher, S., Rackette, H. E., & Krishnaswami, V. (1984). Evolution of excessive alcohol consumption on myocardial infarction risk in coronary disease patients. *American Heart Journal, 108,* 988–995.

Dinda, P. K., & Beck, I. T. (1977), On the mechanism of the inhibitory effect of ethanol on intestinal glucose and water absorption. *American Journal of Digestive Diseases,* *22,* 529–533.

Donahue, R. P., Abbott, R. C., Reed, D. M., & Yano, K. (1986). Alcohol and hemorrhagic stroke. *JAMA, 255,* 2311–2314.

Dreyfus, P. M. (1974). Diseases of the nervous system in chronic alcoholics. In B. Kissin & H. Begleiter (Eds.), *The biology of alcoholism, Vol. 3, Clinical Pathology,* (chap. 7, pp. 265–290). New York: Plenum.

Driver, H. E., & Swann, P. F. (1987). Alcohol and human cancer. *Anticancer Research, 7,* 309–320.

Dufour, M. C., Archer, L., & Gordis, E. (1992). Alcohol and the elderly. *Clinics in Geriatric Medicine, 8,* 127–141.

Dufour, M., & Fuller, R. K. (1995). Alcohol in the elderly. *Annual Review of Medicine, 46,* 123–132.

Dyer, A. R., et al. (1977). Alcohol consumption, cardiovascular risk factors, and mortality in two Chicago epidemiologic studies. *Circulation, 56,* 1067–1074.

Eckardt, M. J., & Martin, P. R. (1986). Clinical assessment of cognition in alcoholism. *Alcoholism New York,* 123–127.

Eichner, E. R., & Hillman, R. S. (1970). The evaluation of anemia in alcoholic patients. *American Journal of Medicine, 50,* 218–232.

Ellingboe, J., & Varanelli, C. E. (1979). Ethanol inhibits testosterone biosynthesis by direct action on Leydig cells. *Research Communications in Chemistry, Pathology and Pharmacology, 24,* 84–102.

Emmerson, R. Y., Dustman, D. A., & Shearer, D. E. (1988). Neuropsychological performance of young nondrinkers, social drinkers, and long-and-short-term sober alcoholics. *Alcoholism: Clinical and Experimental Research, 12,* 625–629.

Ettinger, P. O., W, C. F., De La Cruz, C., Weisse, A. B., Ahmed, S. S., & Regan, T. J. (1978). Arrhythmias and the holiday heart: Alcohol associated cardiac rhythm disorders. *American Heart Journal, 95,* 555–561.

Fabian, M. S., & Parsons, O. A. (1983). Differential improvement of functions in recovering alcoholic women. *Journal of Abnormal Psychology, 921,* 87–95.

Fenster, L. F. (1982). Alcohol and disorders of the gastrointestinal system. In N. J. Estes & M. E. Heinemann (Eds.), *Alcoholism Development, consequences, and interventions,* (pp. 136–143). St. Louis: Mosby.

Fitzhugh, L. C., Fitzhugh, K. B., & Reitan, R. M. (1965). Adaptive abilities and intellectual functioning of hospitalized alcoholics: Further considerations. *Quarterly Journal of Studies in Alcohol, 26,* 402–411.

Freund, G. (1982). The interaction of chronic alcohol consumption and aging on brain structure and function. *Alcoholism: Clinical and Experimental Research, 6,* 13–21.

Freund, G. (1984). Neurotransmitter function in relation to aging and alcoholism. In J. T. Hartford and T. Samorojski (Eds.), *Alcoholism in the elderly.* New York: Raven.

Freund, G., & Ballinger, W. E. (1992). Alzheimer's Disease and alcoholism: Possible interactions. *Alcohol, 9,* 223–240.

Gao, Y. T., Mclaughlin, J. K., Blot, W. J., Ji, B. T., Benichou, J., Dai, Q., & Fraumeni, J. F., Jr. (1994). Risk factors for esophageal cancer in Shanghai, China: I. Role of cigarette smoking and alcohol drinking. *International Journal of Cancer, 58,* 192–196.

Garr, A., Espina, N., & Lieber, C. (1986). Ethanol and the repair of DNA. *Alcohol Health and Research World, 10,* 26–27.

Gavaler, J. S. (1985). Effect of alcohol on endocrine function in post-menopausal women: A review. *Journal of Studies on Alcohol, 46,* 495–516.

Gavaler, J. S., Love, K., Van Thiel, D., Farbolt, S., Gluud, C., Montiero, E., Galvao-Teles, A., Ortega, T. C., & Cuervas-Mons, V. (1991). An international study of the relationship between alcohol consumption and postmenopausal estrodial levels. *Alcohol,* (Suppl. 1), 327–330.

Gaziano, J. M., Burning, J. E., Breslow, J. L., Goldhaber, S. Z., Rosner, B., Van Denburgh, M., Willett, W., & Hennekens, C. H. (1993). Moderate alcohol intake, incrased levels of high-density lipoprotein and its subfractions and decreased risk of myocardial infarction. *New England Journal of Medicine, 329,* 1829–1934.

Gebhardt, C. A., Naeser, M. A., & Butters, N. (1984). Computerized measures of CT scans of alcoholics: Thalamic region related to memory. *Alcohol, 1,* 133–140.

Gilhus, N. D., & Matre, R. (1982). In vitro effect of ethanol on subpopulations of human blood mononuclear cells. *International Archives of Allergy and Applied Immunology, 68,* 382–386.

Gill, J. S., Zezulka, A. V., Shipley, M. J., Gill, S. K., & Beevers, D. G. (1986). Stroke and alcohol consumption. *New England Journal of Medicine, 315(17),* 1042–1046.

Glynn, R. M., Bouchard, G. R., Locastro, J. S., & Hermos, J. A. (1984). Changes in alcohol consumption behaviors among men in the normative aging study. In G. Maddox, L. N. Robins, & N. Roseberg, (Eds.) *Nature and extent of alcohol problems among the elderly (Research Monograph No. 14).* (DHHS Pub. No. (ADM) 84–1321) (pp. 101–116). Washington, DC: U.S. Government Printing Office.

Goldman, M. S. (1982). Reversibility of psychological deficits in alcoholics: The interaction of aging with alcohol. In D. A. Wilkinson (Ed.), *Cerebral deficits in alcoholism* (pp. 79–105). Toronto: Addiction Research Foundation.

Goldman, M., Williams, D., & Klisz, D. (1983). Recoverability of psychological functioning following alcohol abuse: Prolonged visual-spatial dysfunction in older alcoholics. *Journal of Consulting and Clinical Psychology, 51,* 370–378.

Gould, L., Azhir, M., Demartino, A., & Comprecht, R. F. (1971). Cardiac effects of a cocktail. *JAMA., 218,* 1799–1802.

Grant, B. F., & Zobeck, T. C. (1989). *Liver cirrhosis: Mortality in the United States, 1972–1986.* (Surveillance Report No. 11) Rockville, MD: National Institute on Alcohol Abuse and Alcoholism.

Grant, B. F., Dufour, M. C., & Hartford, T. C. (1988). Epidemiology of alcoholic liver disease. *Seminars in Liver Disease, 8,* 12–25.

Halsted, C. H., Griggs, R. C., & Harris, J. W. (1967). The effect of alcoholism on the absorption of folic acid (H3 PGA) evaluated by plasma levels and urine excretion. *Journal of Laboratory Clinical Medicine, 69,* 116–131.

Hankoff, L. P. (1972). Ancient descriptions of organic brain syndrome: The "Kordiakos" of the Talmud. *American Journal of Psychiatry, 129,* 233–236.

Harper, C., & Kril, J. (1985). Brain atrophy in chronic alcoholic patients: A quantitative pathological study. *Journal of Neurology Neurosurgery and Psychiatry, 48,* 211–217.

Hartroft, W. S., & Porta, S. A. (1966). Experimental alcoholic hepatic injury. *Nutr. (Rev.),* 97–101.

Heberden, W. (1929). *Heberden, William 1710–1801: An Introduction to the Study of Physic.* New York: P. B. Hoeber.

Hegedus, L. (1984). Decreased thyroid gland volume in alcoholic cirrhosis of the liver. *Journal of Clinical Endocrinology and Metabolism, 58,* 930–933.

Hegedus, L., Rasmussen, N., Ravn, V., Kastrup, J., Krogesgaard, K., & Aldershvile, J. (1988). Independent effects of liver disease and chronic alcoholism on thyroid function and size: The possibility of a toxic effect of alcohol on the thyroid gland. *Clinical and Experimental Metabolim, 37,* 229–233.

Heinz, A., Pommelspocher, H., Graf, K. J., Kurten, I., Otto, M., & Baumgartener, A. (1995). Hypothalamic-pituitary-gonadal axis, prolactin, and cortisol in alcoholics during withdrawal and other three weeks of abstinence: Comparison with healthy control subjects. *Psychiatry Research, 56,* 81–95.

Hemmingsen, R., & Kramp, P. (1988). Delirium tremens and related clinical states: Psychopathology, cerebral pathophysiology and psychochemistry: A two-component hypothesis concerning etiology and pathogenesis. *Acta Psychiatrica Scandinavica Supplementum, 345,* 94–107.

Hendriks, H. F., Veenstra, J., Velthuis-Te-Wierik, E. J., Schaafsma, G., & Kluft, C. (1994). Effect of moderate dose of alcohol with evening meal on fibrinolytic factors. *British Medical Journal, 308,* 1003–1006.

Higgins, E. M., & Duvivier, A. W. P. (1992). Alcohol and the skin. *Alcohol and Alcoholism, 27,* 595–602.

Higgins, E. M., Duvivier, A. W. P., & Peters, J.J. (1992). Skin disease and alcohol abuse. *Alcohol and Alcoholism, 27(Suppl.),* 95.

Hillbom, M., Haapaniemi, H., Juvela, S., Palomaki, H., Numminen, H., & Kaste, M. (1995). Recent alcohol consumption, cigarette smoking and cerebral infarction in young adults. *Stroke, 26,* 40–45.

Hillman, R. S. (1973). Hematologic disorders in alcoholism. *Journal of Clinical Investigation, 52,* 584–588.

Hillman, R. S. (1982). Hematological disorders of alcoholism. In N. J. Estes & M. B. Heinemann (Eds.), *Alcoholism development, consequences, and interventions* (pp. xxx). St. Louis: Mosby.

Hillman, R. S., Mcguffin, R., & Campbell, C. (1977). Alcohol interference with the folate enterohepatic cycle. *Transactions of Association of American Physcians, 90,* 145–149.

Hrubec, Z., & Omenn, G. S. (1981). Evidence of genetic predisposition to alcoholic cirrhosis and psychosis: Twin concordances for alcoholics and its biological end points by zygosity among male veterans. *Alcoholism (New York), 5,* 207–215.

Hugues, J. N., Cofte, T., Perret, G., Jaryle, M. S., Sebaoun, J. & Modybani, E. (1980) Hypothalamo-pituitary ovarian function in 31 women with chronic alcoholism. *Clinical Endocrinology, 12,* 543–551.

Hurt, R. D., Finlayson, R. E., Morse, R. M., & Davis, L. J., Jr. (1988). Alcoholism in elderly persons: Medical aspects and prognosis of 216 patients. *Mayo Clinic Proceedings, 63,* 753–760.

Iber, F. L. (1990). Alcoholism and associated malnutrition in the elderly. *Progress in Clinical and Biological Research, 326,* 157–173.

Ikeda, H. (1991). Clinical and epidemiological studies of alcoholic dementia. *Arukoru*

Kenkyu to Yakubutsu Ison [Japanese Journal of Alcohol Studies and Drug Dependence], 26, 341–348.

Ishii, T. (1983). a comparison of cerebral atrophy in CT scan findings among alcoholic groups. *Acta Psychiatrica Scandinavica Supplementum, 309,* 1–30.

Israel, Y., Valenzulla, J. E., Salazar, I., & Ugarte, J. (1969). Alcohol and amino acid transport in the human small intestine. *Journal of Nutrition, 98*(2), 222–224.

Jackson, R., Scragg, R., & Beaglehole, R. (1992). Does recent alcohol consumption reduce the risk of acute myocardial infarction and coronary death in regular drinkers? *American Journal of Epidemiology, 136,* 819–824.

Jacobsen, R. (1986). Female alcoholics: A controlled CT brain scan and clinical study. *British Journal of Addiction, 81,* 661–669.

Kaufman, D. W., Koff, R. S., Laszlo, A., Wiholm, B. E., & Shapiro, S. (1995). Alcohol consumption and the risk of major upper gastrointestinal bleeding. *American Journal of Gastroenterology, 90,* 1058–1064.

Kentala, E., Luurila, O., & Salospuro, M. F. (1976). Effects of alcohol ingestion on cardiac rhythm in patients with ischaemic heart disease. *American Journal of Epidemiology, 121,* 549–554.

Klatsky, A. L., Friedman, G. D., Siegelaub, A. B., & Gerard, M. J. (1977). Alcohol consumption and blood pressure. *New England Journal of Medicine, 296,* 1194–1200.

Klein, S., & Iber, F. L. (1991). Alcoholism and associated malnutrition in the elderly. *Nutrition, 7,* 75–79.

Koob, G. (1983). Interaction of vasopressin and corticotropin releasing factors with stress. In T. Cicero (Ed.), *Ethanol tolerance and dependence: Endocrinological aspects* (pp. 217–230). Washington, DC: U. S. Government Printing Office.

Kurata, J. H., & Halle, B. E. (1984). Epidemiology of peptic ulcer disease. *Clinics in Gastroenterology, 13,* 289–307.

Lang, L. G., & Kinnanen, P. M. (1987). Cardiovascular effects of alcohol. *Advances in Alcohol and Sbstance Abuse, 6,* 47–52.

Lavecchia, C., Lucchini, F. & Levi, F. (1994, July). Worldwide trends in suicide mortality, 1955–1989. *Acta Psychiatrica Scandinavica, 90,* 53–64.

Lee, K., Moller, L., Hardt, F., Haubek, A., & Jensen, E. (1979). Alcohol-induced brain damage and liver damage in young males. *Lancet, 2,* 759–761.

Leibowitz, J. O. (1967). Studies in the history of alcoholism: II. Acute alcoholism in ancient Greek and Roman medicine. *British Journal of Addiction, 62,* 83–86.

Lelbach, W. K. (1974). Organic pathology related to volume and pattern of alcohol use. In R. J. Gibbins, Y. Israel, H. Kolant, R. E. Popham, W. Schmidt, & R. G. Smart (Eds.), *Research advances in alcohol and drug problems* (pp. 93–198). New York: Wiley.

Levy, R. I. (1985). Prevalence and epidemiology of cardiovascular disease. In J. B. Symgaarden and L. H. Smith (Eds.), *Cecil textbook of medicine* (18th ed., pp. 155–158). Philadelphia: Saunders.

Lieber, C. S. (1982). *Medical disorders of alcoholism: Pathogenesis and treatment.* Philadelphia: Saunders.

Lieber, C. S. (1976). The metabolism of alcohol. *Scientific American, 234,* 25.

Lieber, C. S. (1966). Hepatic and metabolic effects of alcohol. *Gastroenterology, 50,* 119–133.

Lieber, C. S. (1984). Alcohol and the liver: 1984 update. *Hepatology, 4,* 1243–1260.

Lieber, C. S. (1988). Metabolic effects of ethanol and its interaction with other drugs, hepatotoxic agents, vitamins and carcinogens: A 1988 update. *Seminars in Liver Disease, 8,* 47–68.

Lieber, C. S. (1995). Medical disorders of alcoholism. *New England Journal of Medicine, 333,* 1058–1065.

Linn, S., Carroll, M., Johnson, C., Fulwood, R., Kalsbeek, W., & Biefel, R. (1993). High density lipoprotein, cholesterol and alcohol consumption in U.S. white and black adults: Data from HNANES II. *American Journal of Public Health, 83,* 799–801.

Lowenstein, S. R., Gabow, P. A., Cramer, J., Oliva, P. B., & Ratner, K. (1983). The role of alcohol in new-onset atrial fibrillation. *Archives of Internal Medicine, 143,* 1882–1885.

Lundy, J., Raaf, J. H., Deakins, S., Wanebo, H. J., Jacobs, D. A., Lee, T., Jacobowitz, D., Spear, C., & Oettgen, H. F. (1975). The acute and chronic effects of alcohol on the human immune system. *Surgery, Gyneocology & Obstetrics, 141,* 212–218.

Maddrey, W. C. (1988). Alcoholic hepatitis: Clinicopathologic features and therapy. *Seminars on Liver Disease, 8,* 91–102.

Markiewicz, k., & Cholewa, M. (1982). The effect of alcohol on the circulatory system adaptation to physical effort. *Journal of Studies on Alcohol, 43,* 812–822.

Marmot, M. G., Elliott, P., Shipley, M. J., Dyer, A. R., Ueshima, H., Beevers, D. G., Stamler, R., Kesteloot, H., Rose, G., Stamler, J. (1994). Alcohol and blood pressure: The INTERSALT study. *BMJ, 308,* 1263–1267.

Martinez, I. (1970). Retrospective and prospective study of carcinoma of the esophagus, mouth and pharynx in Puerto Rico. *Boletin—Asociacion Medica de Puerto Rico, 62(6),* 170–178.

Mayer, E. M., Grabowski, C. J., & Fisher, R. S. (1978). Effects of graded doses of alcohol upon esophageal motor function. *Gastroenterology, 75,* 1133–1136.

Mendelson, J. H., Mello, N., Cristofano, P., Ellingbo, J., Skupny, A., Plamieri, S. L., Benedikt, R., & Schiff, I. (1987). Alcohol effects on naloxone-stimulated luteinizing hormone protactin and estradiol in women. *Journal of Studies on Alcohol, 48,* 187–194.

Mendenhall, C. L., et al. (1991). Antibodies to hepatitis B and hepatitis C virus in alcoholic hepatitis and cirrhosis: Their prevalence and clinical relevance. *Hepatology, 14,* 581–589.

Merritt, H. H. (1979). *A textbook of neurology.* Philadelphia: Lea & Febiger.

Mezey, E. (1975). Intestinal function in chronic alcoholism. *Annals of the New York Academy of Science, 252,* 215–227.

Mikkelsen, W. P., Turill, F. L., & Kern, W. H. (1968). Acute hyaline necrosis of the liver: A surgical trap. *American Journal of Surgery, 116(2),* 266–272.

Miller, N. S., Belkin, B. M., & Gold, M. S. (1991). Alcohol and drug dependency among the elderly: Epidemiology, diagnosis and treatment. *Comprehensive Psychiatry, 32,* 153–165.

Mitchell, J. H., & Cohen, L. S. (1970). Alcohol and the heart. *Modern Concepts of Cardiovascular Disease, 39(7),* P Suppl., pp. 109–113.

Moddrey, W. C. (1988). Alcoholic hepatitis: Clinicopathologic features and therapy. *Seminars in Liver Disease. 8(1),* 91–102.

Monforte, R., Estruch, r., Graus, F., Nicolas, J. M., & Urbano-Marquez, A (1990). High ethanol consumption as risk factor for intracerebral hemorrhage in young and middle-aged people. *Stroke, 21,* 1529–1532.

Moniz, C. (1994). Alcohol and bone. *British Medical Bulletin, 50,* 67–75.

Monk, A., Cryns, A. G., & Cabral, R. (1977, November). *Alcohol consumption and alcoholism as a function of adult age.* Paper presented at 30th Annual Scientific Meeting of the Gerontological Society, San Francisco, CA.

Moreno, A., Par'es, A., Ortiz, J., Enriquez, J., Par'es, X. (1994). Alcohol dehydrogenase from human stomach: Variability in normal mucosa and effect of age, gender, ADH3 phenotype and gastric region. *Alcohol and Alcoholism, 26,* 663–671.

Morse, R. M., & Flavin, D. K. (1992). The definition of alcoholism. *JAMA, 268,* 1012–1014.

Moskovic, S. (1975). Effect of chronic alcohol intoxication on ovarian dysfunction. *Srpski Arhiv Za Celokupno Lekarstvo, 103*(9), 751–758.

Munro, H. N., Suter, P. M., & Russell, R. M. (1987). Nutritional requirements for the elderly. *Annual Review of Nutrition, 7,* 23–49.

Mutchnick, M. G., & Lee, H. H. (1988). Impaired lymphocyte proliferative response to mitogen in alcoholic patients: Absence of a relation to liver disease activity. *Alcoholism (New York), 12,* 155–158.

National Institute on Alcohol Abuse and Alcoholism. (1988). Alcohol and aging. *Alcohol Alert, 2,* 1–4.

National Institute on Alcohol Abuse and Alcoholism. (1990). *Seventh Special Report to the U.S. Congress on alcohol and health from the Secretary of Health and Human Services.* U.S. Department of Health and Human Services, Public Health Service, Alcohol, Drug Abuse and Mental Health Administration, p. 120.

Nomura, H., Kashiwagi, S., Hayashi, J., Kajuyama, W., Ikematsu, H., Noguchi, A., Tani, S., & Goto, M. (1988). An epidemiological study of effects of alcohol in the liver in heptatis B surface antigen carriers. *American Journal of Epidemiology, 128,* 277–284.

North, R. N., & Walter, R. M. (1984). The effects of alcohol on the endocrine system. *Medical Clinics of North America, 68,* 133–146.

Orlando, J., Aronow, W. S., Cassidy, J., & Prakash, P. (1976). Effect of ethanol on angina pectoris. *Annals of Internal Medicine, 84,* 652–655.

Overholt, B. F. (1969). Comment on acid, aspirin, alcohol and bleeding. *Gastroenterology, 56,* 637–638.

Park, J., Ko, H. J., Park, Y. N., & Jung, C. H. (1994). Dementia among the elderly in a rural Korean community. *British Journal of Psychiatry, 164,* 796–801.

Parker, D. A., Parker, E. S., Brody, J. A., & Schoenberg, R. (1983). Alcohol use and cognitive loss among employed men and women. *American Journal of Public Health, 73,* 521–526.

Parsons, O. A. (1986). Cognitive functioning in sober social drinkers: A review and critique. *Journal of Studies on Alcohol, 47,*101–114.

Pfefferbaum, A., Rosenbloom, M., Crusan, K., Jernigan, T. L., & Brain, C. T. (1988). Changes in alcoholics: Effects of age and alcohol consumption. *Alcoholism (New York), 12,* 81–87.

Pochi, P. E. (1988). Acne vulgaris and rosacea. In R. E. Rakel (Ed.), *Conn's current therapy* (pp. 655–659). Philadelphia: Saunders.

Potter, J. F., & James, O. F. (1987). Clinical features and prognosis of alcoholic liver disease in respect to advancing age. *Gerontology, 33,* 380–387.

Preedy, V. R., Salisbury, J. R., & Peters, R. J. (1994). Alcoholic muscle disease: Features and mechanisms. *Journal of Pathology, 173,* 309–315.

Rajkovic, I. A., Yousif-Kadaru, A. G. M., Wyke, R. J., & Williams, R. (1984). Polymophonuclear leukocyte locomotion and aggregation in patients with alcoholic liver disease. *clinical and Experimental Immunology, 58,* 654–662.

Razay, G., Heaton, K. W., Bolton, C. H., & Hughes, A. O. (1992). Alcohol consumption and its relation to cardiovascular risk factors in British women. *British Medical Journal, 304,* 80–83.

Razoni-Boroujerdi, S., Savage, S. M., & Spori, M. L. (1994). Alcohol induced changes in immune response: Immunological effects of chronic ethanol intake are genetically regulated. *Toxicology and Applied Pharmacology, 127,* 37–43.

Reese, L. H., Besse, G. M., Jeffcoate, W. J., Goldie, D. J., & Marks, V. (1977). Alcohol induced pseudo Cushing's Syndrome. *Lancet, 1,* 726–728.

Regan, T. J. (1990). Alcohol and the cardiovascular system. *JAMA, 264,* 377–381.

Rehm, J., & Sempos, C. T. (1995). Alcohol and all-cause mortality. *Addiction, 90,* 471–480.

Reichman, M. E., Jude, J. T., Schatzkin, A., Clevidence, S. A., Nair, P. O., Campbell, W. S., & Taylor, P. R. (1993). Effects of alcohol consumption on plasma urinary hormone concentrations in premenopausal women. *Journal of the National Cancer Institute, 85,* 722–727.

Renaud, S., & Delorgeril, M., (1992). Wine, alcohol, platelets and the French paradox for coronary heart disease. *Lancet, 339,* 1523–1526.

Rich, E. C., Siebold, C., & Campian, B. (1985). Alcohol-related acute atrial fibrillation. *Archives of Internal Medicine, 145,* 830–833.

Rico, H. (1990). Alcohol and bone disease. *Alcohol and Alcoholism, 25,* 345–352.

Roselle, G. A., & Mendenhall, C. L. (1982). Alternation of in vitro human lymphocyte function by ethanol, acetaldehyde and acetate. *Journal Clinical and Laboratory Immunology, 9,* 33–37.

Rosenkranz, L. (1983). Aseptic necrosis of bone and chronic alcoholism. *Journal of Family Practice, 17,* 323–326.

Rubin, E., & Lieber, C. S. (1968). Alcohol-induced hepatic injury in nonalcoholic volunteers. *New England Journal of Medicine, 278,* 869–876.

Rubin, E., & Lieber, C. S. (1974). Fatty liver alcoholic hepatitis and cirrhosis produced by alcohol in primates. *New England Journal of Medicine, 290,* 128–135.

Schaper, A. G. (1991). Alcohol and mortality: A review of prospective studies. *British Journal of Addiction. 86,* 379–382.

Schaper, A. G., Phillips, A. N., Pocock, J., & Walker, M. (1987). Alcohol and ischemic heart disease in middle aged British men. *BMJ, 294,* 733–737.

Schaper, A. G., Wannamethee, G., & Walker, M. (1994). Alcohol and coronary heart disease: A perspective from the British Regional Heart Study. *International Journal of Epidemiology, 23,* 482–494.

Scharschmidt, B. F. (1985). Acute and chronic hepatic failure with encephalopathy. In

J. B. Wyngaarden & L. H. Smith (Eds.), *Cecil textbook of Medicine* (18th ed.),. Philadelphia: Saunders.

Schiff, E. R. (1992). Non-alcoholic liver disease in the alcoholic. *Newer aspects on alcohol nutrition and hepatic encephalopathy* (pp. 349–360). Thorofare, NJ: American Association for the study of Liver Disease.

Schmidt, W., & de Lint, J. (1972). Causes of death in alcoholics. *Quarterly Journal of Studies on Alcohol, 33,* 171–185.

Schuckit, M. A., & Miller, P. (1976). Alcoholism in elderly men: Survey of a general medical ward. *Annals of the New York Academy of Science, 273,* 558–571.

Schuckit, M. A. (1982). A clinical review of alcohol, alcoholism and the elderly patient. *Journal of Clinical Psychiatry, 43,* 396–399.

Schuckit, M. A., Morrissey, E. R., & O'Leary, M. R. (1978). Alcohol problems in elderly men and women. *Addictive Diseases, 3,* 405–416.

Schuckit, M. A., Anthenelli, R. M., Bucholz, K. K., Hessbrock, V. M., & Tipp, J. (1995). The time course of development of alcohol-related problems in men and women. *Journal of Studies on Alcohol, 56,* 218–225.

Scott, R. B. (1989). Alcohol effects on the elderly. *Comprehensive Therapy, 15,* 8–12.

Sellers, E. M., & Kalant, H. (1982). Alcohol withdrawal and delirium tremens. In E. M. Pattison and E. Kaufmann (Eds.), *Encyclopedic handbook of alcoholism* (pp. 149–166). New York: Gardner.

Seppa, K., & Sillanavkee, P. (1994). Women, alcohol and red cells. *Alcoholism: Clinical and Experimental Research, 18,* 1168–1171.

Seppa, K., & Sillanoukee, P., Pitkajorvi, T., Nikkela, M., & Kowula, T. (1992). Moderate and heavy alcohol consumption have no favorable effect on lipid values. *Archives of Internal Medicine, 152,* 297–300.

Sexias, F. A. (1982). Criteria for the diagnosis of alcoholism. In N. J. Estes & M. E. Heinemann (Eds.), *Alcoholism: Development, consequences and interventions* (pp. 49–66). St. Louis: Mosby.

Shear, P. K., Jernigan, T. L., & Butters, N. (1994). Volumetric magnetic resonance imagery quantification of longitudinal brain changes in alcoholics. *Alcoholism, Clinical and Experimental Research, 18,* 172–176.

Shinton, R., Sagar, G., & Beevers, G. (1993). The relation of alcohol consumption to cardiovascular risk factors and stroke: The West Birmingham stroke project. *Journal of Neurology Neurosurgery and Psychiatry, 56,* 458–62.

Sinclair, H. M. (1972). Nutritional aspects of alcoholism. *Proceedings of the Nutrional Society, 31,* 117.

Smith, J. W. (1982a) Alcohol: Its effects on sexual performance. *Consultant, 22,* 261–264.

Smith, J. W. (1982b). Alcohol and disorders of the heart and skeletal muscles. In N. J. Estes & M. E. Heinemann (Eds.), *Alcoholism development, consequences and interventions* (pp. 76–183). St. Louis: Mosby.

Smith, J. W. (1982c). Neurological disorders in alcoholism. In N. J. Estes & M. E. Heinemann (Eds.), *Alcoholism Development, consequences, and interventions* (pp. 176–183). St. Louis: Mosby.

Smith, J. W., Burt, D. W., & Chapman, R. F. (1973). Intelligence and brain damage in alcoholics. *Quarterly Journal of Studies in Alcoholism, 34,* 414–433.

Smith, J. W., Johnson, L. D., & Burdick, J. A. (1971). Sleep, psychological and clinical changes during alcohol withdrawal in NAD-treated alcoholics. *Quarterly Journal of Studies in Alcoholism, 32,* 982–994.

Stall, R. (1968). Respondent-identified persons for change and stability in alcohol consumption as a concomitant of the aging process. In C. R. Janes, R. Stall, & S. M. Gifford, (Eds.), *Anthropology and epidemiology: Interdisciplinary approaches to the study of health and disease* (pp. 275–302). Boston: Reidel.

Stall, R. (1986). Change and stability in quantity and frequency of alcohol use among aging males: A 19-year follow-up study. *British Journal of Addiction, 81,* 537–544.

Stampfer, M. J., Colditz, G. A., Willett, W. C., Speizer, F. E., & Hennekens, C. H. (1988). A prospective study of moderate alcohol consumption and the risk of coronary disease and stroke in women. *New England Journal of Medicine, 319,* 267–273.

Still, C. N., Jackson, K. L., Brandes, D. A., Abramson, R. K., & Macera, C. A. (1990). Distribution of major dementias by race and sex in South Carolina. *Journal of the South Carolina Medical Association, 86,* 453–456.

Stinson, F. S., Dufour, M. C., & Bertolucci, D. (1987). Alcohol related morbidity in the aging population. *Alcohol Health and Research World, 13,* 80–87.

Suh, I., Shaten, B. J., Culler, J. A., & Kuller, L. H. (1992). Alcohol use and mortality from coronary heart disease: The role of high-density lipoprotein cholesterol. *Annals of Internal Medicine, 116,* 881–887.

Tsuang, J. W., Irwin, M. r., Smith, T. L., & Schuckit, M. A. (1994). Characteristics of men with alcoholic hallucinosis. *Addiction, 89,* 73–78.

United States Department of Health and Human Services. (1988). *The Surgeon General's report on nutrition and health* (DHHS Pub. No. 988–50210). Washington, DC: U. S. Government Printing Office.

Urbano-Marquez, A., Estruch, R., Fernaandez-Solas, J. M., Par'e, J. C. & Rubin, E. (1995). The greater risk of alcoholic cardiomyopathy and myopathy in women compared with men. *JAMA, 194,* 149–154.

Urbano-Marquez, A., Estruch, R., Navarro-Lopez, F., Graw, J. M., Mont, L., & Rubin, E. (1989). The effects of alcoholism on skeletal and cardiac muscle. *New England Journal of Medicine, 320,* 409–415.

Van Den Brandt, P. A., Goldblom, R. A. & Van't Veer, P. (1995). Alcohol and breast cancer from the Netherlands cohort study. *American Journal of Epidemiology, 141,* 907–915.

Van Thiel, D. H. (1983). Ethanol: Its adverse effects on the hypothalamic-pituitary gonadal axis. *Laboratory and Clinical Medicine, 101,* 21–33.

Van Thiel, D. H., Lipsitz, H. D., Porter, L. E., Schade, R. R., Gottlieb, G. P., & Graham, T. O. (1981). Gastrointestinal and hepatic manifestations of chronic alcoholism. *Gastroenterology, 81,* 594–615.

Vincenti, G. E., & Blunden, S. M. (1987). Psoriasis and alcohol abuse. *Journal of the Royal Army Medical Corps, 133,* 77–78.

Wang, R., Mallon, J., Alterman, A. I., & Mclellan, A. T. (1987). Alcohol and dilated cardiomyopathy: Incidence and correlation with clinical outcome. *Journal of Substance Abuse Treatment, 4,* 209–213.

Wannamethee, G., & Shaper, A. G. (1988). Men who do not drink: A report from the British Regional Heart Study. *International Journal of Epidemiology, 17,* 307–326.

Weiner, F. R., & Eskreis, D. S., Compton, K. V., Orrego, H., & Zern, M. A. (1988).

Haplotype analysis of a type I collagen gene and its association with alcoholic cirrhosis in man. *Molecular Aspects of Medicine,* Elmsford, NY: Pergamon, 159–168.

Williams, J. D., Ray, G. G., & Overall, J. E. (1973). Mental aging and organicity in an alcoholic population. *Journal of Consulting and Clinical Psychology, 41,* 392–396.

Yohman, J. R., Parsons, O. A., & Leber, W. R. (1985). Lack of recovery in male alcoholics' neuropsychological performance one year after treatment. *Alcoholism (New York), 9,* 114–117.

Zakhari, S. (1991). Vulnerability to cardiac disease. *Recent Developments in Alcoholism, 9,* 225–260.

Ziring, D. J., & Adler, A. G. (1991). Alcoholism: Are you missing the diagnosis? *Postgraduate Medicine, 89,* 139–144.

4

Early versus Late Onset of Alcoholism in the Elderly

Joseph G. Liberto, MD
David W. Oslin, MD

INTRODUCTION

Many researchers agree that alcoholism has multiple etiologies involving interactions among genetics, environment, and personality (Atkinson, 1984; Finney & Moos, 1984). Alcoholism typologies, based on a variety of clinical characteristics, are suggested in an effort to group alcoholics with similar etiologies. Such categorization may lead to a better understanding of the clinical course and ultimately to the most efficacious treatment approaches for individual patients. In particular, the age of onset of alcohol-related problems is one typology that is gaining prominence among clinicians.

Since the late 1950s, descriptions of elderly alcoholics have included two groups of problem drinkers: (1) early onset, those who began having alcohol-related problems early in life and continue to have problems late into life; and (2) late onset, those having alcohol-related problems late in life (Simon, Epstein, & Reynolds, 1968). Recent studies suggest that early- and late-onset elderly drinkers may differ in their etiologies, clinical characteristics, and responses to treatment. This chapter reviews the current available information on early- and late-onset alcoholism in the elderly. Following this review, clinical and treatment issues for these patients are discussed, and future research directions are considered.

DEFINITION

While most authors agree that the age of onset of alcoholism is the age when "alcohol-related problems" or a "pattern of heavy drinking" first develops, there are two major difficulties in defining the early- and late-onset populations. The first difficulty, as discussed by Liberto, Oslin, and Ruskin (1992), is that there is no standard definition of alcoholism in the elderly. The second difficulty is in defining the appropriate cutoff age for early versus late onset.

Early- and late-onset groups have been identified using a variety of criteria. The age at which a person develops "alcohol-related problems" is one criterion that has been used to determine age of onset of alcoholism. "Alcohol-related problems" have generally been defined by dysfunction in one of several areas of life, including legal problems (DWI, arrest); social problems (family, friends, or spouse); occupational problems (school, job, military); or medical problems (cirrhosis, falls, motor vehicle accidents) (Finney, Moos, & Brennan, 1991). The first treatment for an alcohol use disorder, or the first attendance at Alcoholics Anonymous, has also been used by some authors (Parrella & Filstead, 1988). There is no consensus as to what specific "alcohol-related problems" should be assessed, nor is there any definitive understanding of how "drinking pattern" is related to the diagnosis of alcohol abuse and dependence as defined in *Diagnostic and Statistical Manual of Mental Disorders* (4th ed). *(DSM–IV)* (American Psychiatric Association, 1994). This problem of definition is highlighted in data reported by Parrella and Filstead (1988) on a younger population sample. Each one of five different definitions of "alcohol problems" used to determine age of onset changed the proportions of individuals classified as late or early onset.

At least two authors have suggested that the construct of "alcoholism onset" should be viewed on the basis of personality development, which is essentially complete by age 25 (Parrella & Filstead 1988; Von-Knorring Palm, & Anderson, 1985). Most reports, however, use older cutoff ages, with the etiology of late onset being viewed as related to the physiologic and psychologic changes associated with the aging process. The cutoff ages used in the studies reviewed in this chapter ranged from 25 to 60, with the majority of studies using a cutoff age of 40, 45, or 50. The cutoff age used is important, as Atkinson (1984), in a group of 36 elderly patients followed in a VA alcoholism clinic, reported the percentage of late-onset drinkers changed from 61%, using a cutoff age of 40; to 11%, using a cutoff age of 60.

Despite these difficulties with defining the age of onset of alcohol-related problems, there appears to be enough consistency between studies to make some meaningful comparisons and to be clinically helpful. The studies that report on the most common "alcohol-related problems" and the studies that utilize a cutoff age of 40 to 60 will be the focus of this chapter.

EPIDEMIOLOGY

Most studies rely heavily on self-reports for determining the age of onset of alcohol-related problems. In support of this data collection method, while it was not specifically used for determining the age of onset in his sample, Werch (1989) found that use of retrospective self-reports of consumption is a reliable method to classify elderly subjects in drinking class categories. Graham (1986), on the other hand, has called into question the validity of self-reports in elderly alcoholics, suggesting that memory of past events may deteriorate as a consequence of the aging process and long-term alcohol use. While we feel that self-reported data provide clinically useful information, we caution that the specificity with which retrospective self-reports can be viewed remains somewhat unclear.

Prevalence

Some people argue that onset of alcoholism in older life is uncommon. In fact, the *Diagnostic and Statistical Manual* (3rd ed., revised) (DSM III–R) states that, in males, alcohol use disorders rarely occur after age 45 (American Psychiatric Association, 1987). *DSM–IV* states that the "large majority of those who develop Alcohol-Related Disorders do so by their late 30s" (American Psychiatric Association, 1994, p. 202). In addition, Meyers, Hingson, Mucatel, and Goldman (1982) concluded from a Boston community sample in 1977 that there was no support for categorizing alcoholics into late and early onset. Despite this criticism, however, there is a large body of recent evidence that supports this distinction. In his review, Atkinson (1984) noted that late-onset problem drinking occurred in 4 to 88% of elderly alcoholics.

Studies looking at clinical populations have reported significant proportions of late-onset alcoholism among elderly alcoholics (see Table 4.1). Schuckit and Miller (1976) found that 11 of 20 patients age 65 and over (55%) with a diagnosis of alcoholism on a VA medical ward had developed alcohol-related problems after the age of 40. Ten percent of the elderly alcoholics developed their first alcohol-related problems after age 60. Three studies examined patients in psychiatric clinics or wards (Gaitz & Baer, 1971; Hubbard, Santos, & Santos, 1979; Simon et al., 1968). The prevalence rate of late-onset disease among alcoholics in these studies was 11 to 30%. Studies examining patients in alcohol treatment programs showed a distribution of late-onset drinking problems between 11 and 61% (Adams & Waskel, 1991b; Atkinson, 1984; Atkinson, Turner, Kofoed, & Tolson, 1985; Atkinson, Tolson, & Turner, 1990; Bahr, 1969; Hurt, Finlayson, Morse, &

TABLE 4.1 Characteristics and Findings of Selected Studies Related to Late-Onset and Early-Onset Alcoholism in the Elderly.

Author	Year of Study[a]	Cohort description	Gender (% Males)	Race (% Caucasian)	Late-onset age cutoff	Number of early onset (%)	Number of late onset (%)	Diagnostic criteria
Simon, Epstein, & Reynolds	1959	534 patients age 60+ admitted to a psychiatry ward	NR	NR	60	86 (70)	37 (30)	"Clinical" diagnosis
Bahr	1969	94 alcoholics in a skid row community	100	NR	45	87 (93)	7 (7)	Quality/ Frequency index
Bahr	1969	104 patients in a public alcohol hospital	100	NR	45	83 (80)	21 (20)	Quality/ Frequency index
Gaitz & Baer	1971	100 consecutive admissions, age 65+, to a county psychiatric screening ward	60	76	50	39 (89)	5 (11)	DSM–III Abuse/ Dependence
Schuckit & Miller	1974	113 consecutive admissions age 65+ to a VA medical ward	100	96	40	9 (45)	11 (55)	Alcohol-related problems
Meyers, Hingson, Mucatel, et al.	1977	928 noninstitution- alized Bostonians age 60+	NR	NR	late-life	40 (100)	0 (0)	Alcohol-related problems

continued

TABLE 4.1 *continued*

		Sample						Criterion
Abrahams & Patterson	1978	445 people age 65+ in a New England community	"nearly all male"	"mostly"	65	2 (29)	5 (71)	Alcohol-related problems
Wiens et al.	1978	87 patients age 65+ admitted to a potential alcohol treatment unit	69	99	50	8 (12)	60 (88)	Drinking "out of control" by self-report
Hubbard et al.	1979	250 admissions to a mental health outreach program	NR	NR	later years	20 (40)	12 (24)[b]	"Clinical" diagnosis
Atkinson et al.	1985	36 patients aged 53+ admitted for an out-patient treatment program	92	NR	40 / 60	14 (39) / 32 (89)	22 (61) / 4 (11)	DSM–III Abuse/ Dependence
Mulford & Fitzgerald	1986	785 Iowans age 55+ who had their license revoked after an arrest for a DWI	90 overall	NR	55	187 (59)	130 (41)	Age received DWI
		243 Iowans age 65+ who had their license revoked after an arrest for a DWI	90 overall	NR	55	45 (50)	45 (50)	Age received DWI
Hurt et al.	1988	216 inpatients age 65+ admitted to an Alcohol Treatment program	70	NR	60	122 (56)	89 (41)[c]	DSM III Abuse/ Dependence

TABLE 4.1 *continued*

Atkinson et al.	1990	132 male veterans age 60+ admitted to an outpatient alcohol treatment program	97	NR	45	69 (52)	63 (48)	DSM III Abuse/ Dependence
Schonfeld & Dupree	1991	170 admissions age 60+ to alcoholism day treatment program	NR	NR	50	48 (28)	100(59)[d]	Quality/ Frequency index
Brennan & Moos	1991	1884 patients age 55–65 with recent contact with one of two medical centers	68	90	50	475 (67)	229 (33)	Drinking Problems index
Adams & Waskel	1991	60 males age 60+ admitted to an Alcohol Treatment Center	100	NR	40 / 60	33 (55) / 63 (89)	27 (45) / 7 (11)	Veterans Alcohol Screnning Test

NOTES:

[a] "Year of study" indicates when study was conducted; this may differ from date of publication.

[b] 18 patients in this study were not defined as late- or early-onset.

[c] The age on onset for 5 patients was not determined.

[d] The age on onset for 22 patients was not determined.

NR: Not Reported.

Davis, 1988; Schonfeld & Dupree, 1991; Wiens, Mensutik, & Miller, 1982).

Another large community-based study exploring early- and late-onset problem drinking in the elderly is worth noting. Brennan and Moos (1991) reported on 1,884 persons age 55 and older who had recent contact with two medical centers in Palo Alto, California. Unfortunately, this study defined late- and early-onset drinkers differently from most others. Late-onset problem drinking was defined as having developed alcohol-related problems within the past 2 years, rather than after a specified age. Because their definition of late onset is more in keeping with definitions of recent onset, it is possible that some "early-onset" individuals would be defined as "late-onset" individuals by other authors. Nevertheless, all patients in this study identified as "late-onset" had their first alcohol-related problem after the age of 53. Respondents to a phone survey were placed in one of three drinking categories on the basis of their responses to alcohol-related questions on a 17-item Drinking Problems Index. This index assessed the adverse consequences related to alcohol consumption. A person who had one or more problems on the Index was considered a problem drinker. Of those patients identified as problem drinkers (704), 33% were characterized as late-onset alcoholics and 67% as early-onset alcoholics.

Only one study has explored age of onset on the basis of the *DSM–III* diagnostic criteria of alcohol abuse and dependence. Hurt et al. (1988) reviewed the charts of 216 patients over the age of 65 who were admitted to an inpatient alcohol treatment program with a *DSM III* diagnosis of alcoholism. Patients were defined as early-onset alcoholics if they had developed alcohol abuse or dependence prior to age 60. In this group of patients, early-onset alcoholism was present in 59% of the men and 51% of the women. Late-onset alcoholism was present in 39% of the men and 46% of the women. Recently, the Epidemiologic Catchment Area (ECA) study reported on the prevalence of *DSM–III* alcohol abuse and dependence in the general population (Helzer, Burnam, & McEroy, 1989). Although there was no specific category of late- or early-onset alcoholism—making it difficult to compare the ECA results with other studies—the ECA study examined the cumulative prevalence of alcohol abuse and dependence by age. In the ECA study, many elderly individuals were first diagnosed with alcohol abuse and dependence after the age of 45.

The data from these prevalence studies suggest that there are a significant number of older alcoholics who first begin to drink abusively in their later years. However, it is also important to appreciate the incidence of late-onset alcoholism in order to better understand the impact that late-onset drinking will have on treatment and prevention planning.

Incidence

A few longitudinal studies have reported on the incidence of alcohol-related problems and heavy drinking. The earliest of these was conducted by Stall (1986), who studied a San Francisco cohort of males in 1964 and reinterviewed the population in 1983. In 1964, 85 subjects age 30 to 69 were interviewed. Of this sample, 8% of men were characterized as heavy drinkers in 1983. Fifty-seven percent of the heavy drinkers had developed their pattern of heavy drinking between 1964 and 1983. Fillmore (1987) studied two national community samples with regard to their alcohol use. In one sample he found that, of the nonproblem drinkers over 50 years old in 1969, 7% became problem drinkers by 1974. In a second sample, of those over the age of 50 in 1969, 21% became problem drinkers by 1974.

Glynn, Bouchard, LoCastro, and Laird (1985) studied the drinking behavior of 1,859 healthy male veterans as part of the Boston Normative Aging Study conducted between 1973 and 1982. There were 69 men age 64 to 72 in 1973 who were studied. Of the men reporting no problems with alcohol in 1973, 1.5% had developed problems by 1982. In this same sample, there were 310 men age 55 to 63; of these, 5.1% had new-onset alcohol problems by 1982. In a recent longitudinal study of patients with medical comorbidity, Schuckit, Atkinson, Miller, and Berman (1980) followed 280 veterans age 65 and older from 1974 until 1977. There were 113 men who did not have a diagnosis of alcoholism in 1974. Of this group 5 (6%) had a diagnosis of alcoholism in 1977.

On the basis of the longitudinal studies described above, the incidence of late-onset problem drinking, especially among males, ranges from 0.2% to 4.0% of the population per year. This represents many new cases per year and suggests a significant clinical impact. As the American population ages, there may be need for a greater emphasis on primary and secondary prevention.

Demographics

The demographic configuration of late- and early-onset problem drinkers is an important aspect of the epidemiology. Perhaps the most striking finding is that most of the studies show no significant differences between the late-onset and early-onset drinker with regard to age, marital status, employment, living status, or education (Atkinson et al., 1985; Hurt et al., 1988; Schonfeld & Dupree, 1991). One demographic factor that does stand out is gender. In the studies reviewed, women accounted for a greater proportion of late-onset alcoholics than early-onset alcoholics (Brennan & Moos, 1991; Hurt et al., 1988; Koewler, 1982; Mulford & Fitzgerald, 1992; Wiens, Mensutik, Miller,

& Schmitz, 1982). Hurt et al. (1988) and Brennan and Moos (1991) found that approximately one third of late-onset problem drinkers were women compared with one fourth of early-onset problem drinkers. This may be a result of the higher incidence of late-onset alcoholism in older women or perhaps a higher mortality rate among older male alcoholics.

CLINICAL CONSIDERATIONS

Despite the epidemiologic evidence for the distinction between late and early onset, the categorization of patients into late- and early-onset groups must have clinical relevance to be meaningful.

Biopsychosocial Factors

While few demographic differences appear between early- and late-onset alcoholics, a number of studies have reported clinical differences that may affect the natural course and treatment outcome of the illness. Early- and late-onset problem drinkers appear to differ with regard to their drinking behavior. Compared with late-onset alcoholics, early-onset alcoholics report alcohol use more frequently and in greater quantities (Brennan & Moos, 1991; Mulford & Fitzgerald, 1992; Schonfeld et al., 1987). In addition, Schonfeld and Dupree (1991) reported that early-onset alcoholics were intoxicated twice as often as late-onset subjects in the 30 days preceding their last drink before admission to treatment.

Differences between late- and early-onset alcoholics have been reported in past treatment experiences and in referrals for treatment in later life. By definition, early-onset alcoholics have had alcohol-related problems for a longer time. As expected, compared with late-onset alcoholics, early-onset alcoholics are more likely to have been in an alcohol treatment program and to have used self-help groups such as Alcoholics Anonymous (Atkinson et al., 1990; Hurt et al., 1988). Atkinson et al. (1990) found that early-onset patients were typically referred by professionals, family members, friends, or themselves for pervasive social problems related to their lifelong drinking. On the other hand, late-onset alcoholics were more likely to seek treatment as a result of receiving a driving-while-intoxicated (DWI) legal charge. This suggests that elderly late-onset drinkers may not seek treatment as readily as elderly early-onset drinkers.

Medical morbidity and mortality related to the effects of longer alcohol use also appear more severe in the early-onset population (Hurt et al., 1988;

Schonfeld, Dupree, & Merritt, 1987). Compared with late-onset alcoholics, early-onset problem drinkers have more physical symptoms and are more likely to smoke (Brennan & Moos, 1991). In addition, it has been reported that early-onset alcoholics have higher rates of falling, delirium tremens, diabetes, cirrhosis, and fatty liver disease (Brennan & Moos 1991; Hurt et al. 1988; Schonfeld & Dupree, 1991). Further, early-onset patients have been found to have a higher liver enzyme gamma-glutamyltransferase (GGT) value and a lower platelet count (Hurt et al, 1988).

Differences in psychological makeup and in reaction to late-life stress may also be different between the two groups. Rosin and Glatt (1971) reported reactive factors such as bereavement and retirement as precipitating excessive drinking in a large proportion of late-onset patients. Finlayson, Hurt, Davis, and Morse (1988) reported that late-onset alcoholics have more stressful late-life events preceding relapses than do early-onset alcoholics. However, there is little additional support to suggest that one group experiences stressful life events more than the other. For instance, no differences between early- and late-onset groups were found in the Stokes/Gordan Stress Scale or the Purpose of Life Scale (Adams & Waskel, 1991b; Rosin & Glatt, 1971). In addition, it has been reported that late-life losses (i.e. retirement, moving, or death of a spouse) are about the same for both groups (Brennan & Moos, 1991; Schonfeld et al., 1987).

Early- and late-onset groups report similar antecedents to drinking. Compared with early-onset subjects, however, late-onset alcoholics more frequently report depression, sadness, or loneliness prior to their first drink on a typical day of drinking (Schonfeld & Dupree, 1991). These mood changes may be seen either as an impetus to drink or as a consequence of drinking.

Late-onset alcoholics tend to be less self-critical of their drinking, and may suffer more denial of their alcoholism, because they do not have the life-long biopsychosocial problems associated with drinking that the early-onset alcoholic usually has experienced (Hubbard et al., 1979; Mulford & Fitzgerald, 1992). Families and friends may also collude with this denial, and thus support the drinking behavior with such statements as "Let him drink; he's had a stressful time lately," or "Drinking is one of her last enjoyments in life." Early-onset alcoholics may underestimate problems with alcohol use because memories of events, and the consequences of these events, fade as a result of memory loss related to the aging process and chronic alcohol use (Finney & Moos, 1984).

Some studies have reported more emotional problems in the early-onset alcoholic (Atkinson, 1984; Atkinson et al., 1985; Schonfeld & Dupree, 1991). Results of formal psychological testing of the two groups, however, have been mixed. Atkinson (1984) and Atkinson et al. (1985), in two studies that excluded subjects with major mental disorders, found greater psychological stability in the late-onset group, as evidenced by differences in several scales of the MMPI. Schonfeld and Dupree (1991) reported that early-onset patients exhibited greater anxiety on the State-Trait Anxiety Inventory and more depression on the Beck Depression Inventory. These findings can be contrasted with those of Finlayson et al. (1988), who reported no differences in specific MMPI scales, with the exception of the L scale. Further, there have been no reported differences in BPRS or IQ scores between early- and late-onset groups (Schonfeld & Dupree, 1991; Schonfeld et al., 1987).

Social differences between the two groups also hold promise in distinguishing late- from early-onset alcoholics. Findings by various authors have suggested that compared with the late-onset group, early-onset alcoholics tend to have more legal, employment, and financial problems and less psychosocial support in life (Atkinson et al., 1985; Atkinson et al., 1990; Brennan & Moos, 1991; Mulford & Fitzgerald, 1992; Schonfeld et al., 1987). Compared with early-onset alcoholics, late-onset alcoholics report more friends and a greater concern about their drinking from both family and friends (Brennan & Moos, 1991; Schonfeld & Dupree, 1991; Schonfeld et al., 1987). It is reasonable to suggest that this finding reflects, in part, a deterioration of the social network as a consequence of chronic alcoholism in the early-onset group. An unanswered question, though, is how much social support is available to a late-onset alcoholic compared with a nonalcoholic elderly person. It is possible that late-onset alcoholics begin problem drinking because they have fewer mature defense reactions and less social support than the nonalcoholic elderly.

Overall, these studies suggest that compared with late-onset alcoholics, early-onset alcoholics have a more debilitating life course secondary to their alcohol use. Late-onset alcoholics appear to consume less alcohol, have fewer alcohol-related problems, have less psychiatric and medical comorbidity, and have greater psychosocial supports. The greater severity of alcoholism in the early-onset group is supported by the findings among early-onset alcoholics of augmented MMPI MacAndrews scales, used to indicate the severity of alcoholism, and the scores from the Alcohol Stages Index (Atkinson et al., 1990; Mulford & Fitzgerald, 1992).

Etiologic Factors

The etiology of late- and early-onset alcoholism is largely unknown. Studies to date suggest a greater genetic etiology in early-onset patients than in late-onset patients, as evidenced by more frequent family histories of alcoholism in early-onset subjects (Atkinson et al., 1990). Several authors have postulated, on the other hand, that late-onset alcoholism is more frequently linked to subjective reactions to late-life social stressors (Atkinson et al., 1990; Brennan & Moos, 1991; Finlayson et al., 1988; Schonfeld et al., 1987). As previously discussed, late-onset alcoholics are more likely to report a relapse as a consequence of a stressful life event (Finlayson et al., 1988; Schonfeld et al., 1987). It is possible that psychosocial stressors play a larger role in initiating pathological drinking in the late-onset group. This notion is supported by findings showing that the MacAndrew MMPI scale is lower in late-onset subjects, suggesting secondary alcoholism (Atkinson, Tolson, & Turner, 1990). It is not known if the late-onset alcoholic is more reactive to stress, and thus to the initiation of alcoholism, than nonalcoholic elderly persons. Alternatively, others suggest that an increase in associated stressful life events may not be an etiologic factor, but rather represents a heightened need to rationalize alcohol abuse (Hurt et al., 1988).

Deteriorating social function may also be seen as an etiologic factor for late-life alcoholics. Alcohol misuse may begin in late life as a result of the increased sensitivity to alcohol that occurs with the physiologic changes associated with aging, increased discretionary time and money, or increased social pressures to drink in retirement settings (Atkinson et al., 1990). This biopsychosocial causation hypothesis implies that such persons may have certain physiological characteristics, personality traits, psychopathologic conditions, or social experiences that lead to the beginning of alcohol misuse (Atkinson, Tolson, & Turner, 1990; Schonfeld et al., 1987). It seems logical that all of these factors are interdependent and play significant roles in the development of alcohol abuse for both the early- and the late-onset groups.

Treatment

The ultimate goal in trying to understand the etiology and dynamics associated with late- and early-onset alcoholism is to improve our treatment strategies for elderly alcoholics. Identifying the elderly alcoholic is the first step in this treatment process. As discussed in chapter 2, several biopsychosocial issues related to the aging process often make identification of the elderly problem drinker difficult. Because red flags for alcoholism, such as severe medical problems and lack of family support systems, are less common in the late-onset group, late-onset alcoholics may be even more difficult to identify and hence less likely to be referred for treatment.

Until recently, the elderly have not been treated much differently from younger populations. Greater age-related difficulties with leisure time, medical comorbidity, and social supports, however, indicate a clear need to focus on different psychosocial issues in the older population as part of the recovery process (Adams & Waskel, 1991a). Unfortunately, there are no studies which take into account the different needs of early- and late-onset alcoholics. While some studies fail to show treatment differences in elderly patients with regard to the age of onset of alcohol-related problems (Koewler, 1982), a few studies have reported treatment differences between early- and late-onset groups,

Two studies have reported differences in treatment completion rates between late- and early-onset alcoholics treated in age-specific alcohol treatment programs (Atkinson et al., 1990; Schonfeld and Dupree, 1991). Atkinson et al. (1990) reported that in a group of 132 men, age 60 and older, the likelihood of completing a 12-month outpatient treatment program was greater with later age of onset. The frequency of attendance at weekly group meetings was also greater in the late-onset group. Similarly, Schonfeld & Dupree (1991) found that early-onset patients were less likely to expect success in treatment and less likely to complete treatment in a day alcoholism program. Relapse rates in these studies, however, did not vary with age of onset (Atkinson et al., (1990); Schonfeld & Dupree, 1991).

Moos, Brennan, & Moos (1991) reported on predictors of remission, defined as an absence of drinking problems in the last 12 months, in a group of 659 older alcoholics who utilized general medical services. Using a prospective study design, these researchers found that early-onset problem drinkers were less likely than late-onset drinkers to have remitted at 1 year follow up (23.7% vs. 40.5%). Remission and abstention in early-onset subjects was associated with less alcohol consumption on heavy drinking days, seeking support for a major life stressor, and obtaining help from a mental health professional. Early-onset subjects who reported more negative health events were more likely to remit; those who had more drinking problems and more financial stressors were more likely to abstain from alcohol.

Predictors for late-onset remission and abstention were somewhat different. Late-onset alcoholics who reported fewer drinking problems, less alcohol consumption, and friends' disapproval of drinking were more likely to remit. Abstention in the late-onset group was associated with more drinking problems, more financial problems, more health stressors, more health-related negative events, hospitalization, fewer spousal resources, and friends' disapproval of drinking.

These findings suggest a need for treatment modifications that consider the different needs of early- and late-onset alcoholics. As there are no empirical data on the efficacy of treatment models for patients with late- and early-onset alcoholism, we suggest practical considerations in treatment by two case vignettes followed by treatment approaches. The presentation and treatment approaches in these case vignettes are not intended to be guidelines, but instead suggest possible directions for future development.

Case Vignette: Early Onset

Mr. J. is a 60-year-old white male who presents to the emergency room in a general hospital with symptoms of severe abdominal pain. Medical evaluation reveals the patient to be dehydrated. Laboratory studies show elevated liver function tests consistent with alcoholic hepatitis, decreased total protein and albumin, indicating malnutrition; and an elevated amylase suggestive of pancreatitis. The patient is admitted to the medical service, hydrated, and stabilized. An addiction consultation is made.

A patient history reveals that Mr. J. first began using alcohol in his early teenage years. Alcohol use became heavy in his late teens and early twenties, with daily use beginning in his early thirties. His family history is positive for alcoholism in his father, grandfather, and two of his three siblings. With the onset of heavy drinking, several psychosocial difficulties developed. Mr. J.'s family, originally active in trying to get help for him, began to avoiding contact with him. Two marriages ended in divorce. He was arrested several times on a variety of charges, including drunk and disorderly conduct, driving while intoxicated, and disturbing the peace. He lost many jobs because of his poor work and inconsistent attendance.

His treatment history revealed numerous previous alcohol detoxifications and one admission to a 28-day inpatient rehabilitation program. In addition, he attended Alcoholics Anonymous (AA) meetings sporadically throughout the years, but he was never involved in formal outpatient treatment. He noted having experimented with illicit drugs in the past, but he denied any current use. His longest period of sobriety was the 9 months immediately following his attendance at the inpatient rehabilitation program, during which time he attended AA regularly. His pattern has been that he begins missing his AA meetings, begins associating with his drinking "friends," and then begins drinking "socially" again. His drinking quickly escalates in severity, and he again finds himself at the same level of alcohol dependence.

Mr. J. is characteristic of early-onset patients who have presented for treatment with us, often after multiple treatment attempts. He was referred by his internist because of worsening medical and psychosocial comorbidity as a consequence of his chronic alcohol use. He had estranged family and friends, resulting in a fragmented and dysfunctional social network.

For patients like Mr. J., we have found that particular emphasis must be placed on providing external psychosocial support. After detoxification and early engagement in recovery has begun, highly structured outpatient treatment programs should be considered. Outpatient rehabilitation, in addition to focusing on active addiction issues, usually needs to address issues of leisure time management. Social services, especially financial support, are also very often needed to help stabilize patients in early recovery. Supervised living arrangements, such as half-way houses, should also be considered.

Case Vignette: Late Onset

Ms. K. is a 67-year-old retired business-woman who presents to an alcoholism outpatient treatment program after being charged with driving under the influence of alcohol. Ms. K. has not had previous treatment for alcohol-related problems, nor does she admit to a family history of alcoholism. She has never attended Alcoholics Anonymous, and she is clear that the only reason that she presents for treatment is that the courts have ordered her to do so.

Ms. K. gives a history of first using alcohol in her late teenage years. She describes her drinking as mild to moderate throughout the years, but is very clear that she had no psychosocial or medical comorbidity related to her alcohol use. She retired 2 years ago, about the same time that her husband died. She notes that she felt quite depressed and alone at that time and stated that her drinking began to escalate. She is also clear that she feels her alcohol use is not a problem noting "I can stop when I want to." She characterizes her DWI arrest as an "unlucky break." She admits that her children have recently been concerned about her drinking but she does not feel that their concern is warranted.

Physical exam and laboratory studies reveal no serious pathology.

Ms. K exemplifies the difficulties we experience with denial in our late-onset patients. She is "forced" into care by the court system and doesn't see herself as an alcoholic. Despite growing concerns on the part of family and friends, she rationalizes her DWI as an "unlucky break" and supports this contention by citing no previous problems with alcohol use.

In patients like Ms. K., we feel that early treatment efforts to break down denial are paramount. It is our experience that failure to do so usually results in patients' leaving treatment when the factors that coerce them into treatment are no longer present. Since social networks are often still intact, we make every effort to engage family and significant others in participating in the patient's treatment plan. In addition, we focus on educating late-onset patients about the biopsychosocial effects of alcoholism. Further, we find that individual therapy aimed at processing the patient's late-life losses is often needed.

CONCLUSION: FUTURE RESEARCH DIRECTIONS

In this chapter, we have presented evidence to support the clinical utility of the late- and early-onset typologies. Epidemiological studies utilizing community, general medical, and alcohol-treatment population samples have demonstrated that a significant portion of elderly alcoholics develop their first alcohol-related problems later in life. Demographically, the two populations appear similar, except that the late-onset group includes a greater percentage of women.

Clinical differences emerge between late- and early-onset patients. Early-onset alcoholics appear to suffer a more chronic and debilitating natural course, as evidenced by greater biopsychosocial problems. The early-onset patients exhibit more legal, medical, and financial problems related to their alcohol use. Psychosocial support from family and friends, often intact in late-onset patients, is usually fragmented in the early-onset group. Psychologic stability may also be greater in the late-onset group.

Reaction to late-life stress and associations between psychological states and drinking episodes may also be different. Late-onset patients report a greater likelihood of experiencing a stressful late-life event preceding a drinking episode. In addition, late-onset individuals may be even more prone than early-onset individuals to experience depression, sadness, or loneliness prior to their first drink on a typical day of drinking.

These clinical differences raise questions as to possible differences in the etiology and maintenance of problem drinking in the elderly. It is fairly clear that early-onset alcoholics more frequently have family histories of alcoholism, suggesting a greater genetic etiologic component. Late-onset patients have had a greater association of late-life stress and mood states associated with their drinking behavior. It is unclear if these psychologic determinants are a causative factor for problem alcohol use in the elderly, or instead a consequence of late-onset alcoholism. Nevertheless, it appears that psychosocial stress and psychologic states play a greater role in the initiation and maintenance of drinking in the late-onset patient.

Until recently, older alcoholics were treated much the same as younger addicted populations. Treatment of older patients in age-specific alcoholism programs is a relatively new approach that has developed out of the recognition that older patients exhibit special biopsychosocial needs that may not be met in traditional treatment programs. No studies to date have examined the efficacy of different clinical approaches in the treatment outcome of early- versus late-onset alcoholics. Some studies have reported that late-onset patients complete treatment more frequently than early-onset patients and thus represent a separate typology, possibly with a better prognosis. It is our belief that treatment focus is often different in these two groups. Owing to their more dysfunctional social networks, early-onset patients need greater external psychosocial supports than do late-onset patients. On the other hand, late-onset patients tend to exhibit stronger denial that must be dealt with early in treatment if recovery is to take hold. Overall, however, if the late-onset typology is to have significant clinical meaning, several important issues need to be studied.

There remain many unanswered questions regarding early- and late-onset alcoholics that need further elaboration in order to yield relevant treatment options. As described earlier, differences in how authors define late- and early-onset alcoholism make comparison of data between studies difficult. In addition to greater consensus in the research community on diagnostic criteria for alcoholism, there needs to be more agreement on the cutoff age for the dichotomy between early- and late-onset. Further, more descriptive studies need to be performed exploring the differences between late- and early-onset groups. Particular emphasis on how these groups seek treatment differently may help to better define outreach and prevention efforts in the elderly alcoholic population. A better understanding of psychologic defensive structure and reactions to stressful life events would help highlight areas to be focused on in treatment design.

Although their efficacy has yet to be demonstrated, it seems reasonable that special older-age substance abuse treatment programs may be more beneficial to the elderly alcoholic. Prospective studies are needed to assess the efficacy of substance abuse day treatment programs, partial hospitalization, Antabuse treatment, self-help groups, individual therapy, and family intervention in the early- and late-onset alcoholic populations.

REFERENCES

Abrahams, R. B., & Patterson, R. D. (1978). Psychologic distress among the community elderly: Prevalence, characteristics and implications for service. *International Journal of Aging and Human Development, 9,* 1–18.

Adams, S. L., & Waskel, S. A. (1991b). Late onset of alcoholism among older midwestern men in treatment. Psychological Reports, 68, 432–434.

Adams, S. L., & Waskel, S. A.(1991s). Comparisons of purpose in life scores between alcoholics with early and later onset. *Psychological Reports, 69,* 837–838.

Atkinson, R. M.(1984). Substance abuse and use in late life. In R. M. Atkinson (Ed.), *Alcohol and drug abuse in old age* (pp. 1–21). Washington, DC: American Psychiatric Press.

Atkinson, R. M., Tolson, R. L., & Turner, J. A. (1990). Late versus early onset problem drinking in older men. *Alcoholism: Clinical and Experimental Research, 14,* 574–579.

Atkinson, R. M., Turner, J. A., Kofoed, L. L., & Tolson, R. L. (1985). Early versus late onset alcoholism in older persons: Preliminary findings. *Alcoholism: Clinical and Experimental Research, 9,* 513–515.

Bahr, H. M. (1969). Lifetime affiliation patterns of early and late-onset heavy drinkers on skid row. *Quarterly Journal of Studies on Alcohol, 30,* 645–656.

Brennan, P. L., & Moos, R. H. (1991). Functioning, life context, and help-seeking among late-onset problem drinkers: Comparisons with nonproblem and early-onset problem drinkers. *British Journal of Addiction, 86,* 1139–1150.

American Psychiatric Association. (1987). Diagnostic and statistical manual of mental disorders (3rd ed.), Washington, DC: Author.

American Psychiatric Association. (1994). Diagnostic and statistical manual of mental disorders, (4th ed). Washington, DC: Author.

Fillmore, K. M. (1987). Prevalence, incidence and chronicity of drinking patterns and problems among men as a function of age: A longitudinal and cohort analysis. *British Journal of Addiction, 82,* 77–83.

Finlayson, R. E., Hurt, R. D., Davis, L. J., & Morse, R. M. (1988). Alcoholism in elderly persons: A study of the psychiatric and psychosocial features of 216 inpatients. *Mayo Clinic Proceedings, 63,* 761–768.

Finney, J. W., & Moos, R. H. (1984). Life stressors and problem drinking among older adults. In M. Galanter (Ed.), *Recent developments in alcoholism* (pp. 267–288). New York: Plenum.

Finney, J. W., Moos, R. H., & Brennan, P. L. (1991). The drinking problems Index: A measure to assess alcohol-related problems among older adults. *Journal of Substance Abuse, 3,* 395–404.

Gaitz, C. M., & Baer, P. E. (1971). Characteristics of elderly patients with alcoholism. *Archives of General Psychiatry, 24,* 372–378.

Glynn, R. J., Bouchard, G. R., LoCastro, J. S., & Laird, N. M. (1985). Aging and generational effects on drinking behaviors in men: Results from the normative aging study. *American Journal of Public Health, 75,* 1413–1419.

Graham, K. (1986). Identifying and measuring alcohol abuse among the elderly: Serious problems with existing instruments. *Journal of Studies on Alcohol, 47,* 322–326.

Helzer, J. E., Burnam, A., & McEvoy, L. T. (1989). Alcohol abuse and dependence. In L. N. Robins & D. A. Regier (Eds.). *Psychiatric disorders in America: The epidemiologic Catchment Area Study* (pp. 81–115). New York: The Free Press.

Hubbard, R. W., Santos, J. F., & Santos, M. A. (1979). Alcohol and older adults: Overt and covert influences. *Social Casework,* 166–170.

Hurt, R. D., Finlayson, R. E., Morse, R. M., & Davis, L. J. (1988). Alcoholism in elderly persons: Medical aspects and prognosis of 216 inpatients. *Mayo Clinic Proceedings, 63,* 753–760.

Koewler, J. H. (1982). Differences between elderly and non-elderly alcoholics in treatments: Referral source, compliance, service provision and improvement. *Dissertation Abstracts International,* 313–B.

Liberto, J. G., Oslin, D. W., & Ruskin, P. E. (1992). Alcoholism in older persons: A review of the literature. *Hospital and Community Psychiatry, 43,* 975–984.

Meyers, A. R., Hingson, R., Mucatel, M., & Goldman, E. (1982). Social and psychologic correlates of problem drinking in old age. *Journal of the American Geriatrics Society, 30,* 452–456.

Moos, R. H., Brennan, P. L., & Moos, B. S. (1991). Short-term processes of remission and nonremission among late-life problem drinkers. *Alcoholism: Clinical and Experimental Research, 15,* 948–955.

Mulford, H. A., & Fitzgerald, J. L. (1992). Elderly versus younger problem drinker profiles: Do they indicate a need for special programs for the elderly? *Journal on Studies of Alcohol, 53,* 601–610.

Parrella, D. P., & Filstead, W. J. (1988). Definition of onset in the development of onset-based alcoholism typologies. *Journal of Studies on Alcohol, 49,* 85–92.

Rosin, A. J., & Glatt, M. M. (1971). Alcohol excess in the elderly. *Quarterly Journal of Studies on Alcohol, 32,* 53–59.

Schonfeld, L., & Dupree, L. W. (1991). Antecedents of drinking for early- and late-onset elderly alcohol abusers. *Journal of Studies on Alcohol, 52,* 587–592.

Schonfeld, L., Dupree, L. W., & Merritt, S. (1987). *Alcohol abuse and the elderly: Comparison of early and late life onset.* Paper presented at the 95th Annual Convention of the American Psychological Association, New York City.

Schuckit, M. A. (1982). A clinical review of alcohol, alcoholism, and the elderly patient. *Journal of Clinical Psychiatry, 43,* 396–399.

Schuckit, M. A., Atkinson, J. H., & Miller, P. L., & Berman, J. (1980). A three year follow-up of elderly alcoholics. *Journal of Clinical Psychiatry, 41,* 412–416.

Schuckit, M. A., & Miller, P. L. (1976). Alcoholism in elderly men: A survey of a general medical ward. *Annals of the New York Academy of Sciences, 273,* 558–571.

Simon, A., Epstein, L. J., & Reynolds, L. (1968). Alcoholism in the geriatrically mentally ill. *Geriatrics, 23,* 125–131.

Stall, R. (1986). Change and stability in quantity and frequency of alcohol use among aging males: A 19-year follow-up study. *British Journal of Addiction, 81,* 537–544.

Von-Knorring, L., Palm, U., & Anderson, H-E.(1985). Relationship between treatment outcome and subtype of alcoholism in men. *Journal of Studies on Alcohol, 46,* 388–391.

Werch, C. E. (1989). Quantity-frequency and diary measures of alcohol consumption for elderly drinkers. *International Journal of Addictions, 24,* 859–865.

Wiens, A. N., Mensutik, C. E., & Miller, S. I., & Schmits, R. E. (1982). Medical-behavioral treatment of the older alcoholic patient. *American Journal of Drug and Alcohol Abuse, 9,* 461–475.

5

Treatment Alternatives for Older Alcohol Abusers

Lawrence Schonfeld, PhD
Larry W. Dupree, PhD

Treatment of the older alcohol abuser remains a difficult problem for service providers. Older adults rarely enter addictions programs, in contrast to their relatively large proportion of the general population. As noted in a nation-wide survey of treatment programs, fewer than 6% of admissions are age 55 or older (National Institute on Drug Abuse and National Institute on Alcohol Abuse and Alcoholism [NIDA/NIAAA], 1990). On the other hand, many are found in medical hospitals being treated for secondary problems. According to a recent congressional report, 21% of hospitalized people age 60 or older had a diagnosis of alcoholism with related hospital costs as high as $60 billion (H. R. Report No. 102–852, 1992). Given these characteristics and other variables associated with later life (e.g., meager social support, reduced tolerance to alcohol, retirement, and reduced income), the older problem drinker is often viewed as a "hidden" alcohol abuser.

Inappropriate screening instruments may account for underestimation of alcohol problems among this population (Graham, 1986). For the person who does not admit to or who is unaware of the severity of his or her drinking problem, most assessment instruments are of little value. No instrument for identifying "risk" has been developed for use with older people, although there have been recent attempts to develop more age-specific alcohol assessments for older adults (e.g., Blow et al., 1992; Finney, Moos, & Brennan, 1991).

Published literature in the field of gerontological substance abuse has slowly evolved since the 1970s to the mid-1980s. During that period, the literature contained little more than reviews, incidence and prevalence estimates, and opinions about treatment based on an author's experience with younger problem drinkers. In more recent years, there has been increased focus on the nature and content of treatment to be offered to this agegroup. This chapter focuses on the recent findings concerning appropriate and effective treatment modalities for older alcohol abusers. In this discussion, we identify "traditional" approaches and more recently developed behavioral methodologies.

TRADITIONAL APPROACHES TO TREATMENT

By *traditional* approaches, we refer to a variety of psychosocial models and addictions programming, most of which have beeen used with younger substanc abusers. Unfortunately, many of these approaches have not been shown to be effective in treating younger adults, let alone older adults with alcohol problems. Nevertheless, it is necessary to discuss each approach, how it is applied to the older adult, and what outcome studies, if any, exist. These include psychodynamic, social work, counseling, 12-step, and social support approaches.

Psychodynamic Model

The modern psychodynamic model is based on classical psychoanalytic theory, which focuses on personality in the etiology of alcoholism. Pychoanalysts believe that alcoholics are fixated at the oral stage of psychosexual development, that alcohol provides oral gratification the person needs, and that alcohol serves as an indirect expression of hostile impulses. Modern psychodynamic approaches place greater emphasis on: (1) ego functioning; (2) narcissistic conflicts related to the need for noncontingent love and adoration, and expectations of noncontingent deference, control, and caregiving; and (3) forms of treatment other than classical psychoanalysis (Cox, 1987).

The model assumes that alcoholics rely on an ego defense mechanism, denial, to cope with perceived threats or anxiety (Fox, 1973). The model is very consistent with the disease concept of alcoholism advocated by Alcoholics Anonymous (AA) in that members of AA "seek to identify some basic defect in themselves (such as faulty personality structure) to which the ultimate cause of their disease can be attributed" (Cox, 1987, p. 56). In both cases, the individual must overcome the denial, recognize or accept that he or she has a problem, and implement a major change in lifestyle.

Little specific information is available concerning the model's application to the older person. Amodeo (1990) suggests that denial is a recurring theme for the older adult but offers few suggestions for dealing with denial other than to focus on the older person's physical and emotional safety—their risk for medication problems, household accidents, memory problems, etc. Solomon, Manepalli, Ireland, and Mahon (1993) suggest that late-onset male alcohol abusers experience significant conflicts regarding infantile dependency needs. Dysphoria, caused by the loss of a love object upon whom one is dependent, triggers drinking. They also suggest that older female alcohol abusers late in life are both hostile toward and dependent upon the love object with the hostile impulses coming into consciousness upon loss of the object. Subsequent "feelings" include guilt, shame, and dysphoria—all triggers for drinking. Kanas (1981) notes that "although the unconscious conflicts may be explored, only those directly related to a patient's drinking problem should be considered" (p. 1018).

Maypole (1989) states that psychoanalysis is rarely used in the treatment of alcoholism, and that because a patient may require several years of psychoanalysis, the approach "for the elderly alcoholic is limited" (p. 46). This statement may be criticized for two reasons. First, as a treatment for alcohol abuse in general, the psychoanalytic approach lacks empirical support, and its concepts are difficult to operationalize, making it difficult to test their validity (Barry, 1987; Cox, 1987; Lang, 1983). Second, Maypole's statement is ageist in its assumption that older adults cannot benefit from a treatment simply because it lasts for a number of years—although the prospect of needing treatment for years may dissuade anyone from seeking help, regardless of age.

Social Work and Counseling Approaches

Although a social work approach or mental health counseling approach is not a psychological model per se, it does provide a structure for intervention. Historically influenced by the psychodynamic model, this approach places heavy emphasis on family intervention and support groups, since it is believed that alcoholism often results from a dysfunctional family (Kelly & Remley, 1989).

However, it may be rare for older drinkers to have families with whom they interact and are in close proximity, let alone families who are willing to participate in family interventions. Older adults tend to drink in response to loneliness and have meager social support networks (Dupree, Broskowski, & Schonfeld, 1984; Schonfeld & Dupree, 1991). Schonfeld and Dupree (1991) concluded that as a result of either losses or alienation, lack of social support was a significant variable contributing to drinking problem among older adults.

The social work approach often involves recommendations for attendance at AA meetings and participation in psychosocial therapy in settings not likely to "stigmatize" older alcohol abusers. Kelly and Remley (1989) recommend the use of life-review or reminiscence therapy for older alcohol abusers only when "the client previously has demonstrated the ability to cope well with problems, has had a view of himself or herself as an individual of worth, and has possessed a positive rather than negative attitude toward life" (p. 111).

Although most of the traditional approaches stress a treatment goal of complete abstinence, Blake (1990) and Kelly & Remley (1989) suggest that expecting abstinence in all older adults may be unrealistic. In setting the treatment goal (abstinence versus limited drinking), they recommend that counselors rely on a combination of their personal convictions, their clients' wishes, and the philosophy of the agency they represent, assuming that the client and the therapist are both well informed about the nature of the specific case, the effects of alcohol, and the possible repercussions. However, they note that in group treatment, the fact that some individuals are working toward limited drinking while others are striving for abstinence may threaten group cohesiveness. The above discussion reflects recent research findings that for some people abstinence may not be a therapeutic necessity.

Blake (1990) states that the special nature of alcohol abuse in older adults provides an area in which mental health counseling may be particularly helpful. The variety of drinking behaviors in older adults suggests that a range of counseling goals may be appropriate and that "a broader range of treatment strategies is needed than has characterized traditional alcoholism treatment programs" (p. 354). To increase the number of older drinkers entering treatment, Blake recommends that mental health counselors be optimistic about the ability to help the older adult and share that optimism with others. Blake encourages diversity in approaches and settings for the older drinker, and recommends that in addition to alcohol treatment services, the treatment plan should include therapies to rebuild the social support network (e.g., family members, AA, peer groups, and self-help organizations) as well as assistance services provided by community agencies familiar with aging-related problems (e.g., aging services, case management).

Twelve-Step Approaches

The "twelve steps" of Alcoholics Anonymous or "AA" (Wilson, 1939) were developed as an alternative to the moral model of alcoholism during the

1930s. This approach requires that individuals who participate in the fellowship of AA admit that they are powerless over the "disease" and turn to a "higher power." It has its roots in the "Oxford Groups," a religious movement which stressed not only recognition of the problems one had inflicted on family, friends, etc. by his or her actions, but also a method of atoning for those actions by helping others recognize and overcome their problems. Although AA began as a fellowship for alcoholics, its philosophy soon became the central focus for many addictions programs employing a "therapeutic community" concept, in which peer groups governed the treatment interventions offered by the agency.

Much of the literature suggesting the use of the 12-step philosophy with older adults is an extension of its utility with younger alcoholics. Bienenfeld (1987) claimed that AA

> is one of the most effective elements of alcoholism treatment in general and for the elderly as well. About one-third of all AA members are over 50 years of age. AA provides nurturance, acceptance, immediate understanding, and support which is particularly meaningful to the middle-aged and older alcoholic. (p. 173)

Solomon et al. (1993) state that "although no data exist regarding this issue, clinical experience supports this modality of treatment for this population" (p. 66).

There have been several published articles citing examples of 12-step programs designed for older adults. Gordon (1988) described the Sage Crossing program in Minnesota, which offered a "less intense, slower paced program than that for younger people"; specialized services for older adults (low-cost housing, assisted living, nursing home care); and a sliding fee schedule. The program used both group and individual counseling, recreation, and other activities, and had a relatively long average length of stay (90 to 120 days).

Dunlop (1990) described a hospital-based program that offered AA meetings; life review; and group, individual, and family counseling over a 1-year period. She noted that "the participants report they enjoy the lack of profanity and opportunity to share similar life issues with others their own age" and that "specialized treatment for the older adult is resulting in successful recovery for a majority of patients at the time of this writing" (p. 32).

Between 1979 and 1981, Hinrichsen (1984) conducted a survey of 40 alcoholism programs in six states, a survey of seven programs specifically designed for older alcohol abusers, and interviews with 54 providers of services for the aging. He found that while treatment for older alcohol abusers did not differ substantially from treatment for younger individuals, staff members and experts identified age-related needs in medical services, social therapies, and assistance services (e.g., housing, transportation). He also found that "group therapy, whether based on an AA model or some other type of social support model, appears to be the single most crucial aspect of treatment for elderly people" (p. 35).

While many of these authors recommend 12-step philosophies, they note that the programs must be modified to accomodate the older person. Three basic modifications are: (1) making treatment groups age-homogeneous; (2) slowing the "pace" of the delivery of the treatment, often resulting in a longer stay; and (3) linking with services for the aging to help with special needs in housing, financial and social support, and medical intervention. However, as with any evaluation methodology, after such modifications are made, it becomes difficult to determine whether are age-specific modification or the treatment approach itself is responsible for any clinical improvement. Also, no studies are available which demonstrate, empirically, the effectiveness of the 12-step approach with older adults.

One modification incorporated by many 12-step programs is aggressive confrontation (e.g., Yablonsky, 1965). Like the psychodynamic view, the confrontational approach is based on the premise that the alcoholic must realize the seriousness of the drinking problem. When people do not admit to having a problem in the face of overwhelming evidence, they are said to be "in denial." Confrontation is used by the peer group the therapist, or both to attack the defenses of clients and accelerate recognition of the drinking problem. Hinrichsen (1984) recommended confrontation as a first step in treating older adults but warned that the "counselor should avoid the label of 'alcoholic,' as well as judgmental, blaming, or punitive statements" (p. 34). On the other hand, Schiff (1988) suggests that confrontation does not work with older adults and that they need less threatening approaches.

In one of the few outcome studies using a control group in the field of gerontological substance abuse, Kashner, Rodell, Ogden, Guggenheim, and Karson (1992) randomly assigned two groups of veterans age 45 and older (53% were 60 or older) to two treatments, each of which was 3 to 4 weeks in duration and provided individual and group therapy along with adjunct treatments. In the experimental group, 72 patients entered the Older Adult Rehabilitation (OAR) program, which emphasized peer relationships, reminiscence, self-esteem, time-limited goals, and staff members who were tolerant or understanding of patients' failures and age. In the "traditional group" 65 patients entered a program emphasizing confrontation therapy, problemsolving, vocational development, and life change. The results demonstrate that patients admitted to the supportive, "nonconfrontational"

OAR program were 2.9 times more likely than members of the traditional group at a 6-month follow-up, and 2.1 times more likely at 12 months, to report abstinence.

Miller and Rollnick (1991), in their "motivational interviewing," approach describe how, irrespective of age, individuals may fail to enter treatment or may drop out of treatment sooner when confrontation is used. As the individual who fails to recognize the seriousness of the addiction is confronted, he or she becomes more defensive about not entering treatment, as a result of cognitive dissonance. The major task of a treatment program's admissions staff should be to move the person toward the need to accept treatment, rather than to force the person to become defensive. With so few people entering addictions treatment programs, in comparison with the estimates of people needing treatment, it is imperative that we find approaches that avoid this defensiveness.

Social Support

Another treatment philosophy is to focus on improving the social support networks of older drinkers. Zimberg (1979, 1984, 1985) suggested the use of group treatment which addresses isolation and depression. In his experience with older patients, Zimberg suggests that "disulfiram, Alcoholics Anonymous, and referral to alcoholism treatment programs, frequent requirements for the treatment of younger alcoholics, were not necessary for these older patients" (p. 27).

Dupree et al. (1984) found that older alcohol abusers had meager social support networks; few friends and family were available with whom they could interact. Some of these individuals no longer had family nearby, while others had experienced the death of a spouse or adult children. Thus, while family therapy may be a possible and even desirable approach, it is unlikely to occur for many older alcohol abusers entering treatment.

In the Gerontology Alcohol Project (GAP), Dupree et al. (1984) emphasized attending to the losses experienced by the older drinker through various group treatment "modules," which taught clients to use self-management and cognitive-behavioral approaches to overcome these losses. One of these was the "social support network" module, in which clients were taught the interpersonal skills necessary to make new friends and identify and engage in new social activities. Results indicated that the GAP clients had a significant increase in the size of the social support network (the number of friends and relatives with whom the person is in contact), at discharge, and again at a 12-month follow-up.

BEHAVIORAL TREATMENT:
ALTERNATIVES TO TRADITIONAL APPROACHES

Although they are no longer "new" approaches in the field of treatment for addictions, behavioral approaches have rarely been used with older alcohol abusers. Behavioral approaches employ the principles of conditioning and learning to control or eliminate drinking. We will describe two categories of behavioral approaches: (1) those that employ basic behavioral principles focusing on easily observable behaviors, and (2) those that extend the basic techniques to covert behaviors through the use of self-management and cognitive-behavioral techniques.

Basic Behavioral Techniques

In an early review, Miller and Eisler (1976) identified several behavioral approaches used in treating alcohol abusers. These include: aversion therapy, teaching incompatible behaviors, rearranging environmental contingencies, and community reinforcers. Only one study attempted to use one of these techniques with older adults.

Wiens, Menustik, Miller, and Schmitz (1982–83) treated 78 alcoholics age 65 or older with aversion therapy, also known as counter conditioning, in a short-term (1-week) treatment program. The goal of aversion therapy is to associate consumption of alcohol with a powerful unconditioned response of illness or nausea. In this program, patients were injected with a nausea-producing drug, emetine, and were then required to drink an alcoholic beverage. Thus, consuming alcohol became associated with nausea. As sessions progressed over the 1-week treatment, nausea was prolonged more and more. Six follow-up appointments were scheduled, in which the emetine injection and alcoholic beverage were administered. Over a 1-year follow-up 51 (65.4%) of the 78 patients treated remained abstinent, with 17 of the 51 not receiving all booster sessions, demonstrating a relatively long-term effect.

Although the aversion technique may be effective in producing abstinence, the approach is not likely to be widely used, perhaps for two reasons. Aversion therapy, by itself, does not teach new, adaptive coping skills to deal with other problems besides drinking. More important, reactions to emetine may include hypotension, as well as nausea and vomiting, all of which may entail serious health risks for older people.

Somewhat similar to the use of counterconditioning, is the use of disulfiram (or Antabuse). This drug is taken orally. Should alcohol be ingested while the drug is in the system, it produces acetaldehyde toxicity, resulting in nausea, vomiting, and hypotension (Victor & Wolfe, 1973). According to Fox (1973) the drug should not be administered to any patient with a decompensated heart, overt psychosis, brain damage, or any other serious illness other than alcoholism. Therefore, like emetine, the drug is likely to be more harmful to older adults, who are more likely to have impaired health than their younger counterparts.

Self-Management and Cognitive-Behavioral Approaches

These techniques are extensions of the basic behavioral principles applied to both observable and covert behaviors. Self-management techniques require that the client or patient become an active participant or "cotherapist" in the process. With the therapist, the patient: defines tasks or homework to be conducted outside of the therapeutic environment; learns to self-monitor urges, drinking, or other target behaviors; learns to use self-reinforcement when target behaviors are accomplished; practices behaviors through behavioral rehearsal within the treatment sessions; and learns to rearrange the environment or schedules to prevent that behavior (Kanfer, 1975).

Cognitive-behavioral techniques often involve teaching the client to identify inaccurate, irrational beliefs or negative self-statements and replace them with positive and more accurate self-statements. This is intended to improve mood and reduce the probability of drinking as a method of coping (Beck, 1976; Ellis, McInerney, DiGiuseppe, & Yeager, 1988; Meichenbaum, 1977).

The model providing the best rationale for use of self-management and cognitive-behavioral approach is offered by Marlatt and Gordon (1985) in their "relapse prevention" (RP) model. Their early research (Marlatt & Gordon, 1980) indicated that after-treatment relapse was probable when the individual was faced with a "high risk situation" likely to trigger a return to drinking and lacked the skills to cope with that situation. The most common determinants of relapse were negative emotional states (such as depression, anger, frustration, etc.), peer pressure, and interpersonal conflicts (with spouse, family, a boss, etc.).

According to the RP model, in the absence of appropriate coping skills, the person experiences decreased self-efficacy as well as increased expectancy for a positive outcome from the first drink. If a "slip" or lapse does occur, it is likely to be followed by the "abstinence violation effect" (AVE), i.e., guilt and a perceived sense of loss of control following the failure to reach a goal, as exemplified by a self-statement such as: "I've really failed. I might as well continue drinking." The AVE leads to an increased probability of a full relapse.

The RP model is easily adapted to treatment programming using skills

Table 5.1. Behavioral and Self-Management Approaches in the Treatment of Alcohol Abuse

Step	Description
Behavior analysis	Counselor interviews each client to determine antecedents to his or her recent drinking and consequences which may reinforce drinking.
Functional analysis of drinking behavior	Each client is taught behavior analysis and learns to identify typical antecedents and consequences of his or her drinking identified in first step.
Self-management skills	Each person is taught the skills necessary to avoid a slip, or to prevent a slip from leading to a full relapse.
Follow-up; aftercare	Maintain contact and repeat the first three steps in the event a slip occurs.

training, self-management, and cognitive-behavioral interventions. We consider the RP model as a four-stage process of self-management and cognitive-behavioral approaches. As shown in Table 5.1, the first component is a behavior analysis or structured interview to identify the high-risk situations (both antecedents and consequences) of drinking. Second, using this information, the client is taught to recognize personal high-risk situations and to intervene earlier in the "chain" in order to prevent relapse. Next, the client is taught specific skills to cope with the identified high-risk situations. Finally, during the follow-up phase, any slips which occur are used as learning experiences from the client's perspective, to review or learn new skills to prevent the reoccurrence of the problem.

Because covert behaviors such as negative emotional states are often the determinants of relapse and continued drinking thereafter (Schonfeld, Dupree, & Rohrer, 1995; Schonfeld, Rohrer, Dupree, & Thomas, 1989), the therapist relies on self-management and cognitive-behavioral interventions to address these cognitions . Using this approach, the Gerontology Alcohol Project (GAP) was developed as an outpatient program for late onset alcohol abusers, those who began abusing alcohol after age 50 (Dupree et al., 1984). Much of the self-management and cognitive-behavioral approaches were taught in group treatment "modules" that could be taught by any staff member and easily disseminated to other treatment sites. A 1-year followup indicated a high rate of success: 75% maintained their drinking goals and there was a significant increase in the size of the social support network.

While the content of the GAP modules could be easily adapted for use with any age group, the pace and content were geared towards the older adult. Illustrative examples used in treatment modules were appropriate to older adults' lifestyles, and content of treatment often targeted depression, poor social support, and an "unstructured" life. If a client had difficulties understanding the content of a treatment module, the staff reviewed that content with him or her after the group meeting concluded. Finally, and perhaps most important, neither staff members nor clients were permitted to use confrontation.

The lack of confrontation was believed to facilitate more open discussion between staff and clients and encouraged clients to report "slips." Rather than making the client view a slip as a failure, and become reluctant to admit to such lapses in the future, the GAP staff viewed the slip as an opportunity to determine what skills the person did not use, and what the person might do the next time he or she was faced with a similar situation. The staff member reviewed the situation, in individual sessions, in group treatment, or both, using behavior analysis and diagramming the drinking "chain" on a blackboard. Such a review can benefit other clients, who might learn how to avoid or manage high-risk situations, and remain calm if a slip does occur. The technology of the GAP program was used in the Substance Abuse Program for the Elderly to treat older alcohol abusers, regardless of age of onset, and misusers of medication (Schonfeld & Dupree, 1990, 1991).

One of the earliest programs to implement behavioral interventions with alcohol abusers was developed at the VA Medical Center in Jackson, Mississippi (Miller & Mastria, 1977). This inpatient program offered individual counseling, alcohol education, self-management and problem-solving skills, vocational assistance, and marital therapy. Although it was not specifically for older patients, Carstensen, Rychtarik, and Prue (1985) conducted a follow-up study of a subgroup of 16 older veterans, ages 65–70, who had completed the program 2–4 years earlier. Results showed that eight patients abstained from alcohol for the 6 months prior to the follow-up, two had "significantly modified" their drinking behavior, and six were drinking abusively (drinking the equivalent of 8 ounces of hard liquor per day).

There are several benefits of cognitive-behavioral and self-management approaches. First, the treatment plan is individualized; each client learns specific coping skills to use in response to his or her personal antecedents to, and consequences of, drinking. Second, generalization of treatment is built in by teaching skills to be practiced within, the therapeutic environment and used outside of it. Third, the treatment plan can be modified as needed depending on the data collected by the therapist and client. Fourth, if a slip occurs, the counselor and client avoid confrontation and focus on a review of the situation and problem-solving. Fifth, success in treatment no longer is simply equated with abstinence, but rather is seen as a more complex, focusing on improvements in drinking (significantly reducing alcohol intake), emotional state, and social support; and on the acquisition and use of new skills in treatment and outside of treatment.

A final, and perhaps most important, advantage of behavioral techniques is their proven effectiveness. In the last few years there have been attempts to compare the traditional approaches with the newer behavioral interventions. Holder, Longabaugh, Miller, and Rubonis (1991) reviewed studies which had randomized clinical trials or well-matched controls, in order to compare 33 treatment modalities for effectiveness and total cost of treatment. The authors found an inverse relationship between effectiveness and cost: in the more expensive treatments were judged least effective, and the most effective treatments were the least costly. Treatments with no evidence or insufficient evidence of effectiveness—such as emetine aversion therapy, antipsychotic or psychotropic medications, acupuncture, halfway houses, various residential treatments, and insight psychotherapy—were all in the medium-high to high-cost categories. Alcoholics Anonymous, which operates on the basis of voluntary participation and donations, was in the minimal-cost category, but more important, it also fell into the "insufficient evidence of effectiveness" category. Behavioral and skills training approaches—such as brief motivational counseling, self-control training, social skills training, community reinforcement, and marital therapy—were judged the most effective treatments, but were all minimal to medium-low in cost.

AGE-SPECIFIC GROUP TREATMENT

Many of the treatment strategies we have discussed thus far can be offered as either individual or group treatment. However, with respect to group treatment, there is debate as to whether older adults benefit more from participation in "mixed-aged" groups, in which older adults are "mainstreamed" with younger adults, or from age-specific group treatment—i.e, in groups limited to older alcohol abusers. Only a few empirical studies have explored this issue.

Janik and Dunham (1983) surveyed 550 treatment programs reporting to a National Institute of Alcohol Abuse and Alcoholism database. They compared data from 3,163 older adults in treatment (age 60 or older) with data from 3,190 younger adults (ages 21–59). Results indicated that younger adults more often used other drugs in addition to alcohol and had arrest records for driving while intoxicated. Older adults more often attended AA and were more socially stable. There were no differences between adults under age 40 and those 60 or older in alcohol symptomatology, therapist's assessment of the alcohol problem, or quantity or frequency of alcohol consumed 6 months postadmission. Clients age 40–59 had the poorest treatment outcomes. The authors concluded that since younger and older adults had no differences in treatment outcomes, age-specific treatment programs were not necessary.

Kofoed, Tolson, Atkinson, Toth, and Turner (1987) argued that Janik and Dunham addressed only whether older alcohol abusers in age-mixed programs fared as well or as poorly as younger adults, and not whether age-specific treatment would lead to better outcomes. In contrast, Kofoed et al. compared two groups of outpatient veterans, ages 54 to 66, admitted to their 1-year treatment program in which participants attended weekly meetings. The first group had been admitted to a mixed-age group consisting of 6–10 members, but with only about one or two older adults per group. These groups emphasized expression of feelings and frequent peer and staff confrontations. The second group was admitted to an age-specific group treatment program, "emphasizing socialization and support, with a slower pace and less confrontation than in groups for younger patients" (p. 49). Results indicated that the "age-specific" group had better attendance and that about 68% completed 1 year of treatment. When relapses occurred they tended to take place over a longer period of time and were addressed in treatment. In contrast, the mixed-age group had worse attendance, with only 17% completing 1 year. Although the number of relapses experienced by the two groups were similar, they occurred over a shorter period of time, and they more often led to attrition for the age-mixed group.

In an attempt to identify age-related differences in treatment needs, Schonfeld et al. (1995) compared responses from behavioral interview assessments of 109 older adults (average age 65, range 55–84 years) and 47 clients in a residential program (average age 35, range 20–53). Older adults were more likely to be widowed and more likely to drink in response to depression and loneliness, as evidenced by the 74% who reported drinking at home and the 67% who drank alone. Younger adults more often drank with other people, outside of the home, and in response to a greater variety of interpersonal and intrapersonal antecedents, such as frustration, anger, and physical states such as feelings of withdrawal. These results suggest that treatment plans for older adults should more frequently focus on overcoming depression and loneliness and on rebuilding the social support network. For younger adults, other issues—such as job-hunting, dating, and relationships with family—may be more important.

Although there is evidence supporting the need for age-specific treatment, few programs provide such services. Regardless of efficacy, it is more likely that economic feasibility, profit, and availability of beds or outpatient "slots" will determine whether or not age-specific programs can be developed and implemented.

CONCLUSIONS

Much of the literature on alcohol abuse among older adults consists of reviews, incidence and prevalence studies, and a rehash of previous speculations and opinions. Little research exists regarding the assessment or effective forms of treatment for this age group, and many authors have made recommendations for the older person based on their own expertise and training, or on experiences with younger alcohol abusers.

With respect to the clinical research in this field, three questions remain to be answered: (1) Which treatment modality is most effective? (2) How do older alcohol abusers differ from older people with aging-related problems who do not abuse alcohol? (3) How do older alcohol abusers differ from younger alcohol abusers?

Effective Treatment

This is often an emotional debate, based on the personal beliefs, testimonials, and experiences of individuals who have found a particular form of treatment to be effective, or of professionals who have been trained in a particular methodology. Part of this debate concerns how we define success; the other part concerns actual outcome evaluation.

Often, success is defined as remaining abstinent after leaving treatment. Marlatt (1985) notes that "recidivism rates are notoriously high across the spectrum of addictive behaviors" (p. 34). About two-thirds of people experience relapses within the first 90 days after completing treatment. Thus, if we equate abstinence with success, there will be few successes. Miller and Rollnick (1991) suggest that the staff of many programs places clients in a "no win" situation by suggesting that if they are successful it is due to the treatment program while if they are not it is their own fault—a failure to follow tenets of the program.

Atkinson (1995) states that problem drinking in old age is unstable, particularly for late-onset older alcohol abusers, and that "neither compliance during treatment nor short term outcome after treatment may be [a] good indicator of longer term prognosis" (p. 2). He believes that outcome evaluation should take place over a substantial period of time and recommends that other nontreatment factors should be included in the outcome evaluation. These other factors are a patient's medical and psychiatric disorders, the patient's demographic characteristics and age of onset of the alcohol problem, and variables related to the program (e.g., its location, number of other participants, transportation, cost, family participation, and time of day the services are offered).

In general, outcomes of treatment programs have been poor. To explain these poor outcomes, Miller (1992) suggests that treatment programs often rely on unproven modalities rather than those with promising records, provide ineffective administration of an effective treatment, overlook short-term improvements, and provide more treatment than is necessary while failing to attend to individual differences.

On the basis of findings by Holder et al. (1991) and the few studies employing behavioral techniques with older drinkers, it would appear that behavioral techniques have the best record with respect to preventing relapse and improving quality of life (e.g., improved social support, emotional state, etc.). Although 12-step programs are easy to operate, require less staff training, and provide informal structure within sessions, there is little evidence to show that they are effective approaches for the majority of alcohol abusers. Cognitive-behavioral and self-management approaches, although effective, may be less popular since they do require significant staff training.

Why Some Older Adults Turn to Alcohol Abuse

This question may be more difficult to answer. In comparison with older people who are not problem drinkers, problem drinkers have fewer social resources, more problems in functioning, and more life stressors (Brennan & Moos, 1991). However, when comparing older mental health clients with older alcohol abusers, we have yet to identify differences between the two groups relative to demographics, frequency of recent losses and stressful events, or psychosocial assessments (Schonfeld, Garcia, & Streuber, 1985).

Differences Between Older and Younger Drinkers

This question has important implications for the design of age-specific treatment programs. Research suggests that early-onset older alcohol abusers have some similarities to younger adults who abuse alcohol with respect to personality, psychopathology, dropout rates, and quantity of alcohol con-sumed. On the other hand, late-onset and early-onset older alcohol abusers are very similar with respect to recent, pretreatment antecedents to drinking. Thus, programs which are age-specific are more likely to address issues of depression, loneliness, and poor social support.

In summary, the problems in researching alcohol abuse among older adults begin with screening and assessment and end with difficulties in evaluating outcomes of treatment. From the meager empirically based literature, we can identify six conclusions about treatment of the older alcohol abuser. These studies emphasize:

1. Age-specific, group treatment which is supportive and nonconfrontational
2. A focus on depression, loneliness, and overcoming losses (e.g., death of a spouse)
3. Rebuilding the social support network
4. Developing the pace and content of treatment appropriate for the older person
5. Employing staff members who are interested and experienced in working with older adults
6. Developing linkages with medical services, services for the aging, and institu-tional settings, for both referral into treatment and referral out, as well as "case management."

While there has been progress on treatment-related research in the past decade, additional clinical research is necessary. This research should address further the needs for appropriate assessment, design of age-specific programs, and evaluation of outcomes of treatment.

REFERENCES

Amodeo, M. (1990). Treating the late life alcoholic: Guidelines for working through denial integrating individual, family, and group approaches. *Journal of Geriatric Psychiatry, 23,* 91–105.
Atkinson, R. M. (1995). Treatment programs for aging alcoholics. In T. P. Beresford & E. S. L. Gomberg (Eds.), *Alcohol and aging,* (pp. 186–210). New York: Oxford University Press.
Barry, H. (1987). Psychoanalytic theory. In C. D. Chaudron & D. A. Wilkinson (Eds.), *Theories on alcoholism* (pp. 103–141). Toronto: Addiction Research Foundation.
Beck, A. (1976). *Cognitive therapies and the emotional disorders.* New York: International Universities Press.
Bienenfeld, D. (1987). Alcoholism in the elderly. *American Family Physician, 36,* 163–198.

Blake, R. (1990). Mental health counseling and older problem drinkers. *Journal of Mental Health Counseling, 12,* 354–367.

Blow, F. C., Brower, K. J., Schulenberg, J. E., Demo-Dananberg, L. M., Young, M. S., & Beresford, T. P. (1992). The Michigan Alcoholism Screening Test—Geriatric version (MAST–G): A new elderly-specific screening instrument. *Alcoholism: Clinical and Experimental Research, 16,* 372.

Brennan, P. L., & Moos, R. H. (1991), Functioning, life context, and help-seeking among late-onset problem drinkers: Comparisons with nonproblem and early-onset problem drinkers. *British Journal of Addiction, 86,* 1139–1150.

Carstensen, L. L., Rychtarik, R. G., & Prue, D. M. (1985). Behavioral treatment of the geriatric alcohol abuser: A long term follow-up study. *Addictive Behaviors, 10,* 307–311.

Cox, W. M. (1987). Personality theory and research. In H. T. Blane & K. T. Leonard (Eds.), *Psychological theories of drinking and alcoholism* (pp. 55–89). New York: Guilford.

Dunlop, J. (1990). Peer groups support seniors fighting alcohol and drugs. *Aging, 361,* 28–32.

Dupree, L. W., Broskowski, H., & Schonfeld, L. (1984). The Gerontology Alcohol Project: A behavioral treatment program for elderly alcohol abusers. *The Gerontologist, 24,* 510–516.

Ellis, A., McInerney, J. F., DiGiuseppe, R., & Yeager, R. J. (1988). *Rational-emotive therapy with alcoholics and substance abusers.* New York: Pergamon.

Finney, J. W., Moos, R. H., & Brennan, P. L. (1991). The Drinking Problem Index: A measure to assess alcohol-related problems among older adults. *Journal of Substance Abuse, 3,* 395–404.

Fox, R. (1973). Treatment of the problem drinker by the private practitioner. In P. G. Bourne & R. Fox (Eds.), *Alcoholism: Progress in research and treatment* (pp. 227–243). New York: Academic.

Gordon, M. (1988). Sage Crossing: A treatment program designed for elders. *Generations, 12,* 82–83.

Graham, K. (1986). Identifying and measuring alcohol abuse among the elderly: Serious problems with existing instruments. *Journal of Studies on Alcohol, 47,* 322–326.

Hinrichsen, J. (1984). Toward improving treatment services for alcoholics of advanced age. *Alcohol Health and Research World, 8,* 31–49.

Holder, H., Longabaugh, R., Miller, W. R., & Rubonis, A. V. (1991). The cost effectiveness of treatment for alcoholism: A first approximation. *Journal of Studies on Alcohol, 52,* 517–540.

H. R. Report No. 102–852 (1992). *Alcohol abuse and misuse among the elderly: A report by the Chairman of the Subcommittee on Health and Long-term Care of the Select Committee on Aging, House of Representatives* (Committee Publication No. 102–852).

Janik, S. W., & Dunham, R. G. (1983). A nationwide examination of the need for specific alcoholism treatment programs for the elderly. *Journal of Studies on Alcohol, 44,* 307–317.

Kanas, N. (1981). Alcoholism and group psychotherapy. In E. M. Pattison & E. Kaufman (Eds.), *Encyclopedic handbook of alcoholism* (pp. 1011–1021) New York: Gardner.

Kanfer, F. H. (1975). Self-management methods. In F. H. Kanfer & A. P. Goldstein (Eds.), *Helping people change: A textbook of methods* (pp. 309–355). New York: Pergamon.

Kashner, T. M., Rodell, D. E., Ogden, S. R., Guggenheim, F. G., & Karson, C. N. (1992). Outcomes and costs of two VA inpatient programs for older alcoholics. *Hospital and Community Psychiatry, 43,* 985–989.

Kelly, S., & Remley, T. P. (1989). Understanding and counseling elderly alcohol abusers. *American Mental Health Counselors Association Journal, 9,* 105–113.

Kofoed, L., Tolson, R., Atkinson, R. M., Toth, R., & Turner, J. (1987). Treatment compliance of older alcoholics: An elder-specific approach is superior to "mainstreaming." *Journal of Studies on Alcohol, 48,* 47–51.

Lang, A. R. (1983). Addictive personality: A viable construct? In P. K. Levison, D. R. Gerstein, & D. R. Maloff (Eds.), *Commonalities in substance abuse and habitual behavior* (pp. 157–235). Lexington, MA: Lexington Books.

Lyons, J. S., & McGovern, M. P. (1989). Use of mental health services by dually diagnosed patients. *Hospital and Community Psychiatry, 40,* 1067–1069.

Marlatt, G. A. (1985). Relapse prevention: Theoretical rationale and overview of the model. In G. A. Marlatt & J. R. Gordon (Eds.), *Relapse prevention: Maintenance strategies in the treatment of addictive behaviors* (pp. 3–70). New York: Guilford.

Marlatt, G. A., & Gordon, J. R. (1980). Determinants of relapse: Implications for the maintenance of behavior change. In P. O. Davidson & E. O. Davidson (Eds.), *Behavior therapy assessment: Diagnosis, design, and evaluation* (pp. 410–452.) New York: Springer Publishing.

Marlatt, G. A., & Gordon, J. R (1985). *Relapse prevention: Maintenance strategies in the treatment of addictive behaviors* New York: Guilford.

Maypole, D. E. (1989). Alcoholism and the elderly: Review of theories, treatment and prevention. *Activities, Adaptation & Aging, 13,* 43–54.

Meichenbaum, D. (1977). *Cognitive-behavior modification* New York: Plenum.

Miller, P. M., & Mastria, M. A. (1977). *Alternatives to alcohol abuse.* Champaign, IL: Research Press.

Miller, W. R., & Rollnick, S. (1991). *Motivational interviewing: Preparing people to change addictive behavior* New York: Guilford.

Miller, P. M., & Eisler, R. M. (1976). Alcohol and drug abuse. In W. E. Craighead, A. E. Kazdin, & M. J. Mahoney (Eds.) *Behavior modification: Principles, issues, and applications* (pp. 376–393). Boston: Houghton Mifflin.

Miller, W. R. (1992). The effectiveness of treatment for substance abuse: Reasons for optimism. *Journal of Substance Abuse Treatment, 9,* 93–102.

National Institute on Drug Abuse and National Institute on Alcohol Abuse and Alcoholism. (1990). *National Drug and Alcoholism Treatment Unit Survey (NDATUS): 1989 main findings report* (DHHS Publication No. (ADM) 91–1729). Rockville, MD: Author.

Schiff, S. M. (1988). Treatment approaches for older alcoholics. *Generations, 12,* 41–45.

Schonfeld, L., & Dupree, L. W. (1990). Older problem drinkers: Long-term and late-life onset abusers: What triggers their drinking? *Aging, 361,* 5–9.

Schonfeld, L., & Dupree, L. W. (1991). Antecedents of drinking for early- and late-onset elderly alcohol abusers. *Journal of Studies on Alcohol, 52,* 587–591.

Schonfeld, L., Dupree, L. W., & Rohrer, G. E. (1995). Age-related differences in antecedents to substance abuse. *Journal of Clinical Geropsychology, 1,* 219–227.

Schonfeld, L., Garcia, J., & Streuber, P. (1985). Factors contributing to mental health treatment of the elderly. *Journal of Applied Gerontology, 4,* 30–39.

Schonfeld, L., Rohrer, G. E., Dupree, L. W., & Thomas, M. (1989). Antecedents of relapse and recent substance abuse. *Community Mental Health Journal, 25,* 245–249.

Solomon, K., Manepalli, J., Ireland, G. A., & Mahon, G. M. (1993). Alcoholism and prescription drug abuse in the elderly: St. Louis University Grand Rounds. *Journal of the American Geriatrics Society, 41,* 57–69.

Victor, M., & Wolfe, S. M. (1973). Causation and treatment of the alcohol withdrawal syndrome. In P. G. Bourne & R. Fox, (Eds.), *Alcoholism: Progress in research and treatment* (137–169). New York: Academic.

Wiens, A. N., Menustik, C. E., Miller, S. I., & Schmitz, R. E. (1982–83). Medical behavioral treatment of the older alcoholic patient. *American Journal of Drug and Alcohol Abuse, 9,* 461–475.

Wilson, W. H. (1939). Sobriety: Conversion and beyond. *Maryland State Medical Journal, 26,* 85–91.

Yablonsky, L. (1965). *Synanon: The tunnel back* New York: Macmillan.

Zimberg, S. (1979). Alcohol and the elderly. In D. M. Petersen, F. J. Whittington, & B. P. Payne (Eds.), *Drugs and the elderly: Social and Pharmacological Issues* (pp.27–40). Springfield, IL: Charles C. Thomas.

Zimberg, S. (1984). Diagnosis and management of the elderly alcoholic. In R. M. Atkinson (Ed.) *Alcohol and drug abuse in old age* (pp. 24–33). Washington, DC: American Psychiatric Press.

Zimberg, S. (1985). Treating the older alcoholic. *Geriatric Medicine, 4,* 68–77.

6

Alcoholism and Dementia

David M. Smith, MD
Roland M. Atkinson, MD

Oh God, that men should put an enemy in their mouths to steal away their brains! That we should with joy, pleasance, revel, and applause, transform ourselves into beasts! (*Othello* II, iii, 279)

INTRODUCTION

Alcohol-induced dementia is a controversial disorder which entails global, persisting, and disabling cognitive impairment resulting form and temporally related to prolonged, heavy use of ethanol. The qualifiers *global, persisting,* and *disabling* bear mention. The *global* deficits of alcohol-induced dementia stand in contrast to the circumscribed memory deficits of Wernicke-Korsakoff syndrome (alcohol amnestic disorder), with which alcohol-induced dementia can be confused. Unlike the transient deficits seen during alcohol detoxification, the cognitive deficits of alcohol-induced dementia are seen as *persisting* beyond the periwithdrawal period. Finally, alcohol-induced dementia results in a disabling impairment in functioning far beyond the subtle cognitive deficits more often seen in former alcoholics.

WHY IS ALCOHOL-INDUCED DEMENTIA CONTROVERSIAL?

Recent thought on alcohol-induced dementia ranges from Lishman's contention (1981, 1986, 1990) that alcohol is just as common a cause of dementia as vascular disorders, to Victor, Adams, and Collins's (1989) that alcohol-induced dementia cannot be accepted as an independent entity until its neuropathological basis has been established. The literature on alcohol-induced dementia is limited by a number of research problems. Most studies on this disorder do not state in any rigorous way how the diagnosis of alcohol-induced dementia was established. It seems that the deficits which some authors would call alcohol-induced dementia are considered too mild or transient to be called dementia by others. Thus it is often impossible to tell if patients described in the literature actually have alcohol-induced dementia or some other diagnosis, like Alzheimer's dementia. Many studies were done in an era when comorbidity was not as popular a concept as it is today, so that some cases of mixed pathology may have gone unnoticed. It remains difficult to distinguish primary alcohol-induced pathology from brain damage due to the associated risks of the alcoholic lifestyle: vitamin deficiency, malnutrition, head trauma, liver disease, hypoglycemia, etc. The principal research problem is, then, lack of a "gold standard" for diagnosis of alcohol-induced dementia.

DIAGNOSIS: IS ALCOHOL-INDUCED DEMENTIA UNDERAPPRECIATED?

Alcohol and Cognitive Impairment

The Epidemiologic Catchment Area Study (George, Landerman, Blazer, & Anthony, 1991) reported that the incidence of *DIS/ DSM–III* alcohol use disorders is about 1.5 times greater among persons with mild or severe cognitive impairment. The Liverpool Longitudinal Community Study (Saunders, Copland, Dewey, et al., 1991) indicated that men with histories of heavy drinking were 4.6 times more likely than other men to have a subsequent diagnosis of dementia. *Heavy drinking* referred to subjects who consumed an average of 17.1 units of alcohol per week for at least a 5-year period, where 1 unit equals 8g of absolute alcohol.

Three recent studies (see Table 6.1 on the following page) report that in 21–24% of patients diagnosed with dementia, there is evidence that alcohol contributed to cognitive impairment. All three studies also showed that the association of alcohol use with the development of cognitive impairment often goes unmentioned. King (1986) used the Diagnostic Interview Schedule to elicit a history of alcohol consumption from 65 elderly patients enrolled in an Alzheimer's Disease Research Clinic in an urban area in the eastern United States. Twenty-one percent of these patients had histories of

Table 6.1 Recent Clinical Surveys of Alcohol Use and Dementia

Authors	Setting	Country	Subjects	Method: Criteria for Assessment	% of Cases Linked to Alcohol	Men	Women
Carlen, McAndrews, Weiss, et al. (1994)	Long-term Care	Canada	130	Chart review, Questionnaires	24%	37%	12%
King (1986)	Dementia registry	USA	65	DSM–III	22%	29%	17%
Smith & Atkinson (1995)	Dementia registry	USA	120	Alcohol consumption (at least 3–4 drinks/day for >1 year)	22%	22%	0%[a]

Note: All studies were noncontrolled retrospective reviews of clinical data.

[a] 5/120 were women

alcohol abuse; and of these, 64% were habitually drinking at the onset of symptoms of dementia.

Carlen, McAndrews, Weiss, et al. (1994) recently examined the prevalence of alcohol-related dementias and other dementias in residents of long-term-care facilities in northern Ontario. Using medical histories and prognosis as a basis for diagnosing alcohol-induced dementia and standard research diagnostic criteria for Alzheimer's dementia and vascular dementia, these investigators found that 24% of cognitively impaired residents suffered from alcohol-induced dementia. Alzheimer's dementia and vascular dementia accounted for 35% and 19% respectively. Patients diagnosed with alcohol-related dementia were, on average, 10 years younger than patients suffering from other dementias, yet they had been institutionalized significantly longer. However, only 25% of the residents thought to suffer from alcohol-induced dementia had any mention of this diagnosis in their medical charts.

We have recently reviewed the records of a dementia registry at a Veterans Administration Medical Center in an urban area in the Pacific Northwest and found that 21% of those listed suffered from alcohol-induced cognitive impairment (Smith & Atkinson, 1995). Ten percent of patients in this registry were diagnosed with alcohol-induced dementia. In addition, 11% of patients diagnosed with possible Alzheimer's disease had histories of heavy alcohol use temporally related to onset of cognitive impairment. *Heavy alcohol use* was here defined daily consumption of at least 5 alcoholic drinks over any 1-year period. In terms of neurological presentation and prognosis, these heavy alcohol users who had been diagnosed with possible Alzheimer's dementia differed significantly from patients diagnosed with possible Alzheimer's dementia who did not abuse alcohol. Rather, the heavy users had the same neurological, cognitive, and prognostic characteristics as patients diagnosed with alcohol-induced dementia. If, as predicted (Caracci & Miller, 1991), the number of elderly alcoholics increases, co-occurrence—and confusion—of alcohol-induced dementia with other dementias will probably also increase.

Nosology of Alcohol-Induced Dementia

Current classification systems rely on vague exclusionary criteria for the diagnosis of alcohol-induced dementia. *DSM–IIIR* (American Psychiatric Association, 1987, pp. 133–134) grouped "dementia associated with alcoholism" among the "psychoactive substance-induced organic mental disorders" and defined the diagnosis as follows:

> (A) dementia following prolonged, heavy ingestion of alcohol and persisting at least three weeks after cessation of alcohol ingestion, and

(B) exclusion by history, physical examination, and laboratory test, of all causes of dementia other than prolonged, heavy use of alcohol.

The requirement that the dementia persist at least 3 weeks excluded many patients with transitory deficits, but the main problem with *DSM–IIIR* criteria was that the disabling clinical features of alcohol-induced dementia were not specified.

DSM–IV (American Psychiatric Association, 1994, p. 154) uses the term *alcohol induced persisting dementia,* which is grouped with the other cognitive impairment disorders so as to facilitate differential diagnosis:

(A) The development of multiple cognitive deficits as manifested by both:
  (1) Memory impairment (impaired ability to learn new information or to recall previously learned information)
  (2) One or more of the following cognitive disturbances:
    (a) aphasia (language disturbance)
    (b) apraxia (impaired ability to carry out motor activities despite intact motor function)
    (c) agnosia (failure to recognize or identify objects despite intact sensory function)
    (d) disturbance in executive functioning (i.e., planning, organizing, sequencing, abstracting)
(B) The cognitive deficits in Criteria Al and A2 each cause significant impairment in social or occupational functioning and represent a significant decline from a previously higher level of functioning.
(C) The deficits do not occur exclusively during the course of a delirium and persist beyond the usual duration of Substance Intoxication or Withdrawal . . .
(D) There is evidence from the history, physical examination, or laboratory findings that the deficits are etiologically related to the persisting effects of substance use.

DSM–IV requires disabling impairment of memory and other cognitive functions so as to exclude cases with subtle cognitive deficits. The deficits must persist so as to exclude transitory cognitive impairment during recovery from intoxication or withdrawal. Still, no specific inclusionary criteria are offered to distinguish alcohol-related dementia from other dementias.

Clinical Epidemiology of Alcohol-Induced Dementia:

Nowhere is the lack of widely recognized or accepted diagnostic criteria more noticeable than in the wide range of reported incidence and prevalence of alcohol-induced dementia. Various textbooks and articles report the diagnosis as nonexistent (Palmer, 1991), rare (Kaplan & Sadock, 1990), or the most common cause of dementia after Alzheimer's disease (National Institute on Alcohol Abuse and Alcoholism, 1983). Winokur and Clayton (1986) have summarized the results of six epidemiological studies of dementia (Delaney, 1982; Freeman, 1976; Marsden & Harrison, 1972; Rabins, 1981; Smith & Kilon 1981; Victoratos, Lemmon, & Herzeberge, 1977) and reported that only 4 of 499 cases of confirmed dementia were due to alcohol. Lishman (1981, 1986, 1990) contends that alcohol is just as common a cause of dementia as vascular disorders. The APA task force report on the treatment of psychiatric disorders (American Psychiatric Association, 1989) speculates that alcohol-induced dementia could be present in as many as 10% of the patients admitted annually to psychiatric wards in the United States. Willenbring (1988), summarizing several recent epidemiological studies, reports that up to 9% of a alcoholics have cognitive deficits severe enough to impair normal functioning, and that of all dementias alcohol is believed to be the cause in about 4%. Victor et al. (1989), on the other hand, argue that most of the reported cases of alcohol-induced dementia are really a mixture of Korsakoff's psychosis, hepatic encephalopathy, Alzheimer's disease, and other dementias.

CLINICAL FEATURES OF ALCOHOL-INDUCED DEMENTIA

Gross Neuropathological and Imaging Studies

The most commonly reported findings in the brains of patients with histories of long-standing, heavy alcohol use is mild to moderate sulcal widening (especially of the frontal regions) as well as third and lateral ventricular enlargement as measured by imaging and postmortem studies (Courville, 1966; Courville & Meyers, 1954; Harper & Kril, 1990; Lynch, 1960; Mott, 1910; Ron, 1977). Victor (Victor et al., 1989) has objected to the use of the term *atrophy* to describe these changes, since he feels that the process of neuronal degeneration has not been convincingly demonstrated. Still, Lynch (1960), Harper (1982, 1987, 1990), and Kril and Harper (1989) have reported neuronal loss and shrinkage of neurons in the motor, anterior cingulate, and middle temporal gyri. Whether atrophy or not, these changes have been supported by numerous imaging studies, including pneumoencephalography, CT, and MRI (Brewer and Perrett, 1971; Harper & Blumberg, 1982; Harper & Daly, 1987; Harper & Holloway, 1985; Harper & Kril, 1985; Haug, 1968; Lishman, 1990; Ron, 1977; Ron, 1983; Ron, Acker, & Lishman, 1980; Ron,

Acker, & Shaw, 1982; Von Gall, Becker, Artmann, Lerch, & Nemeth, 1978). Although brain shrinkage is a common finding, it is not universal. Several reports indicate that sulcal widening and ventricular enlargement are commonly found in alcohol-abusing patients without obvious cognitive impairment (Brewer & Perrett, 1971; Haug, 1968; Victor et al., 1989). Furthermore, several studies report no significant association between degree of brain shrinkage and severity of cognitive impairment (Acker, Jacobson, & Lishman, 1987; Bergman, Borg, Hindmarsh, Idestrom, & Mutzell, 1980; Lee, Moller, Hardt, Haubek, & Jensen, 1979).

Microscopic Findings

Courville and Meyers (1954), Lynch (1960), Ron (1977), and more recently Akai (1991) have reviewed neuropathological studies of alcohol abuse. A major problem in interpreting this literature is the controversy over whether alcohol acts as a neurotoxin to cause neuronal death or if, instead, such damage is due to associated malnutrition or some other process in which alcohol is not directly involved. Studies on rats (Cadet-Leite, Tavares, & Paula-Barbosa, 1988; Walker, Barnes, Hornetzer, Hunter, & Kubanis, 1980) have shown that chronic alcohol consumption, even without malnutrition, leads to decreases in hippocampal pyramidal cells and dentate gyrus granule cells. Many authors (Courville, 1966; Courville & Meyers, 1954; Harper & Corbett, 1990; Harper & Kril, 1985; Lynch, 1960; Ron, 1977) have described human neuronal loss and neuroglial proliferation in the cerebral cortex; cerebella degeneration, especially in the vermis; arteriosclerotic changes; and evidence of lipid emboli. Torvik, Lindboe, and Rogde (1982) have reported lesions of the mammillary bodies in alcohol-abusing patients with global dementia, leading them to postulate a link between Wernicke-Korsakoff syndrome and alcohol-induced dementia. However, Victor et al. (1989) criticize many of the cited studies, arguing that the microscopic lesions are artifactual, nonspecific, or due to some other known disorder, like pellagra or Marchiafava-Bignami disease.

Recent pathological studies have focused on neuronal loss in subcotical brain regions in an attempt to account for global cognitive impairment. Arendt, Bigl, Arendt, & Tennstedt, (1983) reported that patients diagnosed with Korsakoff's psychosis had a significantly greater loss of large neurons in the nucleus basalis compared than nondemented alcoholics. Akai and Akai (1989) reported that postmortem studies of the brains of 9 patients diagnosed with alcohol-induced dementia also found significantly greater loss of neurons in the nucleus basalis, compared with 3 alcoholics without dementia. Akai and Akai (1989), Akai (1991), and Harper and Kril (1990) have suggested more sophisticated pathological studies to focus on both cortical and subcortical pathology.

MRI and PET Studies

Besson, Parker, Crawford, and Smith (1989) used MRI T1 (regional spin lattice relaxation times) as a rough measure of gray- and white-matter pathology in patients with Alzheimer's disease, alcohol-induced dementia, Korsakoff's psychosis, and multi-infarct dementia; and in normal controls. Patients with alcohol-induced dementia and Korsakoff's psychosis had significantly higher bilateral frontal white matter T1 than normal controls. The study also showed significant similarities in brain hypometabolism for alcohol-induced dementia and Korsakoff's psychosis. Gilman et al. (1990) used PET scans to study the brains of 14 chronic alcoholics with and without alcoholic cerebellar degeneration and 8 normal controls. As expected, patients with clinical cerebellar disease showed significant hypometabolism in the superior aspects of the cerebellar vermis, as compared with controls. The interesting finding related to alcohol-induced dementia is that all of the alcohol-abusing patients showed bilateral medial-frontal hypometabolism and a correlation between frontal hypometabolism and deficits in cognitive performance on the category test of the Halstead Impairment Index. Thus MRI and PET studies provide some support for the association of alcohol abuse, cognitive impairment, and frontal lobe pathology.

Reversible Atrophy?

A fascinating aspect of the observed sulcal widening and ventricular enlargement in patients with chronic alcohol abuse comes from several reports (Carlen & Wilkinson, 1980; Carlen, Wortzman, Holgate, Wilkinson, & Rankin, 1978; Lishman, 1990) that with abstinence, brain shrinkage is sometimes reversible. Some authors speculate that the reversibility is due to transient fluid shifts, while others (Lishman, 1990; Besson, Glen, Foreman, 1981) conjecture that alcohol may temporarily affect dendritic branching, which recovers with abstinence. MRI and pathological studies (Besson et al., 1981; McMullen, Saint-Cyr, & Carlen, 1984), however, suggest that the transient brain shrinkage is not due simply to fluid shifts.

Alcoholic Dementia and Wernicke-Korsakoff Syndrome: Part of the Same Spectrum?

Much of the controversy surrounding alcohol-induced dementia has resulted in difficulties in differentiating it from Wernicke-Korsakoff syndrome—alcohol-induced persisting amnestic disorder in *DSM–IV*. The features of Wernicke-Korsakoff syndrome are well known: acute onset of memory impairment, ataxia, ophthalmoplegia, and encephalopathy related to lesions in the mammillary bodies, certain thalamic nuclei, and surrounding basal brain regions as a result of Wernicke-Korsakoff syndrome are predominantly memory impairment, with relative sparing of other cognitive functions. The prognosis for Wernicke-Korsakoff syndrome is often considered poor, although the work of Victor et al. (1989) shows a potential for significant recovery in a sizable proportion of patients. *Alcoholic dementia,* on the other hand, usually refers to global cognitive impairment (Lishman, 1981, 1986, 1990) with significant potential for recovery with abstinence in many, if not most, cases. In spite of the appeal of a distinction between alcohol-induced dementia and Wernicke-Korsakoff syndrome, a growing body of evidence indicates considerable overlap in the described functional and pathological features of the two disorders.

Cutting (1978a, b) reviewed the records of 50 patients with Wernicke-Korsakoff Syndrome and 13 with alcohol-induced dementia. He found that patients diagnosed with Wernicke-Korsakoff syndrome were of two types. One type had the classical Wernicke-Korsakoff features—acute onset, circumscribed memory deficites, preservation of intellect, and a poor prognosis. The second type had a number of similarities to patients with alcohol-induced dementia—gradual onset, global cognitive deficits, and a better prognosis.

Autopsy studies show that despite classical Wernicke-Korsakoff brain lesions, clinical evidence of Wernicke-Korsakoff Syndrome is frequently lacking, with no history of ataxia, ophthalmoplegia, encephalopathy, or even amnesia (Lishman, 1981, 1990; McCrady & Smith, 1986; Parsons, 1977; Tarter, 1973; Torvik, Lindboe, & Rogde, 1982; Tuck & Jackson, 1991; Victor et al., 1989) report patients who at autopsy had evidence of the Wernicke-Korsakoff lesions, but who had clinical histories of global cognitive impairment rather than isolated memory impairment. Furthermore, these patients had no evidence of plaques or tangles, making it unlikely that Alzheimer's disease was the cause of the cognitive impairment. Thus, lesions of the mammillary bodies or other basal brain regions do not always lead to the dramatic, acute clinical presentation of Wernicke-Korsakoff syndrome, and may instead be associated with the global cognitive impairment commonly attributed to alcohol-induced dementia. Further evidence of a connection between alcohol-induced dementia and Wernicke-Korsakoff syndrome comes from the PET scan study by Gilman et al. (1990), which showed no difference in the brain metabolism of patients with alcohol-induced dementia and these with Wernicke-Korsakoff syndrome.

The striking similarities between alcohol-induced dementia and Wernicke-Korsakoff syndrome can be explained in either of two ways. First, because Korsakoff's syndrome is a much more heterogeneous disorder than was previously thought, alcohol-induced dementia may be subsumed under it. Second, the pathological processes of the two disorders may be interrelated in such a way as to cause significant, though by no means universal, similarities.

Neurological Findings of Alcoholic Dementia

Osuntokon et al. (1992) have recently reported the association of ataxia and peripheral neuropathy in all 13 patients with alcohol-induced dementia whom they studied. In a control group of 13 patients with probable Alzheimer's disease, only one subject had these findings. Our own data (Smith & Atkinson, 1993, 1995) indicate that patients whose cognitive impairment is associated with a history of heavy alcohol use are significantly more likely to show evidence of peripheral neuropathy and ataxia than are cognitively impaired patients with no history of heavy alcohol use. Tuck and Jackson (1991) retrospectively reviewed the charts of a large number of alcoholics and reported evidence of cerebellar damage and peripheral neuropathy in about a third of cognitively impaired alcoholics. Other neurological phenomena (seizures, amnesia, encephalopathy, dementia) affected less than 14%.

It is interesting, given the likely connection between alcohol-induced dementia and Wernicke-Korsakoff syndrome, that Victor et al. (1989) report a high degree of correlation of focal neurological findings with Wernicke-Korsakoff syndrome. In Victor's series, 87% of patients with Wernicke-Korsakoff syndrome showed some impairment of stance and gait. Polyneuropathy was also quite common, being noted in 82%. Likewise, nystagmus was reported in 85%.

Cognitive Deficits

A number of articles have reviewed the substantial literature on psychometric and neuropsychological studies of patients who abuse alcohol (Brandt, Butters, Ryan & Boyog, 1983; Cutting, 1978b; Eckardt & Martin, 1986; Fein, Bachman, Fisher, & Davenport, 1990; Harper & Kril, 1985; McCrady & Smith, 1986; Parsons, 1977; Ryan & Butters, 1986; Tarter, 1973; Tuck & Jackson, 1991). The lack of "gold standard" for diagnosing alcohol-induced dementia unfortunately makes interpreting this literature difficult, since it is not always clear if the cognitive deficits described in alcohol abusers are (a) so subtle as not to warrant the term dementia; (b) transient, so as not to persist beyond the periwithdrawal period; or (c) due to some other process, (such as hepatic encephalopathy or Alzheimer's dementia. In the majority of alcohol abusers, cognitive deficits are subtle and tend to a large extent to be reversible with abstinence. Many alcoholics will appear to perform normally on standard psychometric tests, and cognitive deficits may show up only on more specialized tests (Ryan & Butters, 1986). Although deficits in neuropsychological testing in alcohol abusers are positively correlated with age (Ryan & Butters, 1986), it is not clear if age increases a person's susceptibility to the neurotoxic effects of alcohol, or if alcohol accelerates some age-related declines in cognitive test performance.

A subgroup of alcohol-abusing patients are reported to have global, disabling cognitive deficits, and it is this subgroup that is classified as suffering from alcohol-induced dementia. Cognitively impaired alcohol abusers tend to have the most difficulty with memory, tasks requiring speed, and tests of frontal lobe function (Tarter, 1973). The deficits typically reported include difficulty with complex reasoning, planning, abstract reasoning, judgment, attention, and memory (Brandt et al., 1983; Cutting, 1978b; Fein et al., 1990; Horvath, 1975). Areas that are spared include language and verbal skills. There is ample evidence of recovery from some deficits, usually in the few weeks after cessation of drinking; but for some patients the deficits persist or improve only slowly, after years of sobriety. Saunders et al. (1991) reported that men with histories of heavy drinking, even in the remote past, had a nearly fivefold increase in risk for ultimate diagnosis of dementia.

Our data (Smith & Atkinson, 1993, 1995) show that patients with alcohol-induced dementia are significantly less likely to show evidence of an anomia than are who do not use alcohol. These patients showed an arrest of progression of dementia with abstinence, and a minority showed increases in cognitive test scores.

THEORIES OF ALCOHOL-INDUCED DEMENTIA

A number of theories have been advanced to explain the mechanism by which chronic alcohol abuse might lead to dementia (see Table 6.2).

Dual Vulnerability Hypothesis

Lishman (1990, pp. 642–643) surmises that the brain is vulnerable to both thiamine depletion and alcohol neurotoxicity. Thiamine depletion affects the basal brain regions, while alcohol acts as a neurotoxin to both basal brain

TABLE 6.2 Theories of Alcohol-Induced Dementia

Theory	Etiologic factors	Empirical findings	Unresolved issues	Author/ year
Dual vulnerability hypothesis	Genetically based susceptibility to Wernicke-Korsakoff pathology and alcohol neurotoxicity	Heterogeneous CT findings Transketolase variants Occult Wernicke-Korsakoff lesions	No accepted mechanism or neuropathology for alcohol neurotoxicity	Lishman (1990)
Cholinergic hypothesis	Wernicke-Korsakoff pathology damages Meynert nucleus	Global deficits present in cases diagnosed as Wernicke-Korsakoff disease; impaired cholinergic activity in some alcoholics	Cannot exclude coincident Alzheimer's dementia	Lishman (1986)
Coupling Hypothesis	Alcohol neurotoxicity results in dementia only when coupled with often aging, trauma, vascular damage, hepatic dysfunction	Alcohol-associated CT changes precede development of dementia by years, yet as alcohol use still a risk factor for eventual dementia	Cannot exclude other pathologies as sole cause of the dementia	Lishman (1981)
Resiliency hypothesis	Chronic withdrawal results in hyper-cortisolemia damages 5HT receptors, and cause hippocampal cell death	Long-term abstinent alcoholics show evidence of adrenocortical hypertrophy in responses to corticotropin releasing hormone challenge	No clinical tests of this hypothesis	Linnoila et al. 1991
Premature aging hypothesis	Alcohol use can accelerate age-related changes in cognitive function	Some studies show younger alcoholics have similar profiles on cognitive tests when compared with older nonalcoholics	Changes in cognitive function associated with alcohol are distinct from those seen with aging	Ryan & Butters 1980
Null hypothesis	Deficits of "Alcoholic dementia" are due to Wernicke-Korsakoff disease and a mixture of other pathologies	No neuropathological basis for alcoholic dementia has been established; autopsy studies of alcoholic dementia show diverse pathology 1989	Cannot explain alcohol-associated CT changes	Victor, Adams & Collin 1989

regions and the cerebral cortex. There is presumably considerable individual variability of response to the two insults as a result of genetic influences. Those whose brains are vulnerable to thiamine depletion are at risk of Wernicke-Korsakoff pathology. Those who are at risk for alcohol neurotoxicity are susceptible to pathology of both cortical and basal structures, and they could manifest either mild cognitive deficits, alcohol amnestic disorder, or a mixed picture. Those unlucky individuals with a susceptibility to both processes are at risk of Wernicke-Korsakoff syndrome and the global deficits of dementia. Finally, those patients who consume enormous amounts of alcohol but still remain free of cerebral impairment are presumed to be genetically resistant to both thiamine depletion and alcohol neurotoxicity. Lishman (1990) offers several therapeutic implications of his theory, including the fortification of alcoholic beverages with thiamine and the pursuit of genetic markers for persons vulnerable to alcohol neurotoxicity. Some studies (Kaczmarek & Nixon, 1983; Pratt, Jeyasingham & Shaw, 1985) have suggested that enzymes related to thiamine metabolism are genetically heterogeneous and could presumably result in the diverse vulnerabilities which Lishman supposes. Willenbring (1988) has suggested a similar combination of cortical and subcortical processes to account for both the variability and the similarities of alcohol-induced dementia and Wernicke-Korsakoff syndrome.

Cholinergic Hypothesis

In 1986, writing in *The Lancet,* Lishman hypothesized that Wernicke-Korsakoff pathological processes in the basal brain regions could damage nearby cholinergic fibers coursing to the cerebral cortex, thus accounting for distant coritcal effects. He proposed the use of cholinergic-enhancing agents as a test of this hypothesis. Akai's work (Akai, 1991; Akai & Akai, 1989) has demonstrated neuronal loss in the meynert nucleus in persons with "intellectual impairment and mental disorder in association with long periods of alcohol abuse," which gives this theory some support.

Coupling Hypothesis

Here Lishman (1981, pp. 15–16) offers yet another hypothesis. The initially benign and reversible pathology of alcohol abuse couples with other processes, including "aging, trauma, vascular changes, [and] hepatic dysfunction," leading to an irreversible cognitive decline.

Resiliency Hypothesis

This theory (Linnoila et al., 1991) is based on the idea that cognitive deficits from alcohol abuse may be related to an imbalance of various opposing serotonin receptor families. Normally, the receptor families show redilience to and are able to reverse an imbalance of receptor equilibrium. Chronic alcohol withdrawal leads to an increased adrenal response from adrenocorticotropic stimulation. The resultant hypercortisolemia disrupts the balance between the 5HT-1 and 5HT-2 receptors. The result is a decrease in 5HT-1 activity due to a loss of resilience. This somehow leads to glucocorticoid-mediated cell death in the hippocampus, thus damaging nearby cortical fiber tracts and resulting in distant cortical deficits.

Premature Aging Hypothesis

Several authors, notably Ryan and Butters (1980) and Blusewicz, Schenkenberg, Dustman, and Beck (1977a, 1977b) have suggested that, since younger alcoholics score similarly to older nonalcoholics in certain tests of learning and memory, alcohol abuse can lead to an accelerated aging process. Subsequent authors (Burger, Botwinick, & Storandt, 1987; Leber & Parsons, 1982) have disagreed with this hypothesis and have found no significant interaction between alcoholism and age. Still, there are reports (Meyer, Largen, Shaw, Mortel, & Rogers, 1984) that advanced age results in a poorer prognosis in terms of alcohol-induced cognitive deficits.

Null Hypothesis

Victor et al. (1989) make a credible case against the existence of alcohol-induced dementia. They argue that the diagnosis cannot be accepted until its pathological basis is established. They claim that the bulk of the literature supporting alcohol-induced dementia is from case studies, the majority of which are in fact cases of Wernicke-Koasakoff syndrome. Those cases where Wernicke-Korsakoff pathology is lacking are, in these authors's view, a mixture of other cerebral disorders, including Alzheimer's dementia, multi-infarct dementia, and hepatic disease. Regarding ventricular enlargement and sulcal widening, Victor et al. are at a loss for an explanation, other than to hint that reversible brain-fluid shift may be involved.

CASE EXAMPLES

The following case examples serve to illustrate the differential diagnosis of alcohol-induced dementia.

Case 1: Alcoholic Dementia

Mr. A. is 76 years old, a native of the Philippines, but a citizen of the United States for 58 years. He retired at age 65 after 37 years' employment in the same fish-processing plant. He was brought to our dementia clinic at age 70 by his wife, who complained that gradually, over several years, he had become increasingly forgetful, was no longer able to manage money or attend to hygiene, and had assaulted her several times when he could not locate objects he had misplaced. Past medical history was significant only for a slight normocytic anemia. Substance abuse history revealed that the patient had consumed between a pint and fifth of whiskey daily for over 30 years. He had been arrested several times for driving an automobile while intoxicated, and his driver's license had been revoked.

Physical exam was significant for a striking wide-based gait with marked staggering on tandem walking. Romberg test was positive. Fine hand movements were clumsy. There was a loss of vibration and position sense in feet and hands. No ocular abnormalities were noted. The rest of the physical exam was unremarkable. Except for a slightly elevated alkaline phosphatase, laboratory testing—including TSH, B12, folate, and VDRL—was unremarkable. Chest X-ray and EKG were normal. Head CT without contrast showed mild, diffuse cerebral atrophy and enlarged ventricles.

The patient's Folstein Mini-Mental Status Exam score was 23. Neurocognitive status exam was significant for a marked deficiency in recent memory and below-average performance in language repetition, judgment, and reasoning. Fund of information, naming, and arithmetic were in the low-average range.

Initial diagnosis was progressive dementia. Patient spontaneously stopped drinking, mostly because of increased supervision by his family. He has been followed now for 5 years. He continues to live at home with his wife. He has shown virtually no progression of his dementia. His latest cognitive testing shows stable deficits in short-term memory, language repetition, and judgment. His naming abilities, orientation, attention, and abstract reasoning have remained stable. His latest Mini-Mental Status score was 24. His behavioral problems—occasional aggression toward his wife—have persisted.

In this patient, years of alcohol abuse preceded the development of cognitive deficits which remained stable for 5 years. His naming abilities remained intact in the face of deficits in memory, language repetition, and judgment. His peripheral nerve abnormalities and ataxia are not commonly associated with Alzheimer's dementia.

Case 2: Probable Alzheimer's Dementia

Mr. B. is a 74-year-old Caucasian who was brought to the dementia clinic at age 68 by his wife. He was described as gradually becoming more forgetful and repeating himself. He became lost while driving the car and had begun wandering around the neighborhood at night. Past medical history was unremarkable except for tobacco dependence and emphysema. There was no history of stroke or transient ischemic attacks. His wife reported that he had been a drinker about 20 years previously but in recent years had cut down to 1–2 beers daily. Medications included only inhalant bronchodilators and aspirin. Physical exam was significant for mild hypertension. There was no evidence of gait disturbance or any other neurological abnormality. Laboratory values, EKG, and CXR were unremarkable. CT was normal for age. Mini-Mental Status Exam score was 19. Cognitive testing showed impairment of orientation, short-term memory, long-term memory, naming ability, visuoconstructional skills, abstract reasoning, and judgment. Language repetition was normal.

On the advice of his doctor, the patient stopped drinking but still showed a rapid decline in cognitive functioning. Within 1 year he was placed in a nursing home. Three years later, his impairment is so server that he cannot be assessed by routine cognitive tests. Cognitive deficits were progressive, even though he was abstinent. Rapid decline, language impairment, and lack of evidence of vascular disorder suggest Alzheimer's dementia.

Case 3: Alcohol Amnestic Disorder

Mr. C. is a 67-year-old Caucasian first evaluated on the medical service. He had a long history of alcohol abuse with many unsuccessful attempts to achieve sobriety. On the day of admission, he had been found in his apartment by his sister in an acute and unprecedented state of confusion, wearing urine-soaked clothes. The sister brought Mr. C. to the emergency room, where he was noted to have nystagmus, which resolved after thiamine and nutritional replacement. His liver function tests were slightly elevated. Blood ammonia was normal. He showed evidence of delirium with nocturnal agitation, which resolved in about 6 days. Cognitive testing at that time showed severe impairment in recent and remote memory. He was oriented to person and city, but not to date or hospital. His naming, repetition, and arithmetic skills were normal. He had a marked lack of insight into his memory impairment.

After 2 months, Mr. C. surprised his family and doctors by showing a substantial recovery from his amnestic symptoms. He challenged and successfully reversed a court-ordered guardianship. The abrupt onset, delirium, relatively circumscribed cognitive deficits, and transient nystagmus all support a diagnosis of alcohol amnestic disorder.

DIFFERENTIAL DIAGNOSIS

The possibility of improvement of alcohol-related dementia with abstinence makes consideration of this diagnosis critical in the differential diagnosis of dementia (see Table 6.3). Bearing in mind the possibility of a dementia with multiple etiologies, the principal diagnoses to consider along with alcohol-induced dementia include Alzheimer's dementia, vascular dementia, and alcohol amnestic disorder, as well as a number of other cognitive disorders including subcortical dementias, dementia syndrome of depression, and dementia associated with trauma.

Patients with *alcohol-induced dementia* should have evidence of heavy, prolonged use of alcohol, which may or may not be temporally related to onset of the dementia. (In other words, they may have stopped drinking years earlier.) Unfortunately, an accurate history of substance abuse is often difficult to obtain. A thorough neurological examination is likely to show evidence of peripheral polyneuropathy and cerebellar ataxia that cannot be explained by another disorder, such as diabetes mellitus or stroke. Patients with alcohol-induced dementia are also less likely to show evidence of anomia. Most important, their cognitive deficits should be more likely to improve, or at least not progress, with sustained abstinence from alcohol. This makes follow-up of suspected cases especially important.

Patients with *Alzheimer's dementia,* on the other hand, will be more likely to show language deficits and a progression of symptoms. Furthermore, patients with Alzheimer's dementia will be less likely to show evidence of ataxia or peripheral neuropathy not accounted for by some other disorder (e. g., diabetes or CVA).

Patients with *vascular dementias* are more likely to have evidence of acute cerebrovascular events such as CVA, TIA, motor weakness, sensory impairment, and speech deficits which occur in temporal association with onset of a dementia whose progression tends to occur in stepwise or intermittent fashion.

TABLE 6.3 Differential Diagnosis of Alcohol-Induced Dementia

	Alcohol-induced dementia	Alzheimer's dementia	Vascular dementia	Alcohol amnestic disorder
Onset of cognitive deficits	Gradual	Gradual	Acute	Acute
Progression of deficits	Improvement or arrest with abstinence	Gradual deterioration	Stepwise deterioration	Improvement or arrest with abstinence
Ataxia	Present	Absent	+/-	Present
Peripheral neuropathy	Present	Absent	+/-	Present
Anomia	Absent	Present	+/-	Absent
Cognitive deficits	Global	Global	Patchy to global	Memory deficits predominate
Prognosis	May improve or remain stable with abstinence	Poor	Variable	Substantial minority improve with abstinence and nutrition

Alcohol amnestic disorder classically involves the acute development of circumscribed, long-term memory deficits with relative preservation of other cognitive abilities which often, but not always, follows a global confusional state. The prognosis as reported by Victor et al. (1989) is variable, with a substantial minority showing some recovery.

TREATMENT OF ALCOHOL-INDUCED DEMENTIA

The first step in the treatment of alcohol-induced dementia is to consider it as a diagnosis. All dementia workups should include a thorough evaluation of past and present alcohol use, preferably confirmed with a collateral history. The possibility of Wernicke-Korsakoff pathology in cognitively impaired alcohol abusers demands immediate and aggressive vitamin and nutritional repletion. The mainstay of long-term treatment of alcohol-induced dementia is abstinence. Education of the patient and family about the role of alcohol in development of the dementia is critical, and may need to be frequently repeated.

Pilot data suggest that alcohol-induced cognitive impairment may be treatable with drugs that increase central neurotransmitters (Martin et al., 1989; McEntee & Mair, 1980; McEntee, Mair, & Langlais, 1984; Stapleton et al., 1988), but currently no medication is approved as a treatment for alcohol-related mood, anxiety, and sleep disorders. For some patients, time and abstinence will lead to a resolution of psychiatric symptoms without the risks of side effects from medication. Patients with more persistent psychiatric symptoms, including depression, anxiety, and sleep disorders, may required pharmacologic treatment.

Activity restructuring, reorientation, day treatment programs, and other nonspecific interventions for dementia may be useful. For some patients, coercive measures—including revocation of driver's license, use of locked facilities, regulation of money, and involuntary guardianship—are needed at least temporarily.

Specific treatment for alcoholism in older persons is generally built around the following principles and methods (Atkinson, 1995, pp. 186–210):

1. Participation in a supportive social peer group to replace drinking partners and fill voids in the social network and time schedule. This may vary in degree of involvement from a weekly 2-hour group to day treatment of 10 to 20 hours per week.
2. Use of cognitive behavioral methods to teach recognition of factors that predispose to relapse and alternative coping strategies.

3. Engagement of family or other caregivers in collaborative counseling and educational activities to support sobriety, settle old grievances, and make adjustments in family life to accommodate the changing clinical status of the patient.

If cognitive impairment is not severe initially, or shows improvement after months of sobriety, it may be possible to engage the demented alcoholic person successfully in alcoholism treatment. Lifelong shyness or introversion does not by itself predict inability to participate in a social alcohol treatment program, but inability to maintain attention, retain information, or control disruptive behaviors may make participation unproductive for the patient and unacceptable for others in the group. Cognitive behavioral methods—strategies that break down complex information into simple modules and stress repetition and individual pacing—may actually be an excellent approach for a mildly demented elderly person, though not for someone with marked problems of attention and memory. In the more severe cases of dementia, work with family members may be the most applicable and useful element of alcoholism treatment.

SUMMARY

1. Alcohol abuse appears to be a contributing factor in a significant percentage of patients with cognitive impairment, although this often goes unreported in the medical record.
2. Preliminary evidence suggests that dementia associated with alcohol may have distinct clinical features, imaging abnormalities, and prognosis.
3. Alcoholic dementia appears to be associated with peripheral neuropathy and ataxia.
4. The cognitive deficits of alcohol-induced dementia appear to be marked by an absence of anomia.
5. Anatomical and functional imaging data suggest that alcohol-induced dementia is associated with shrinkage of brain tissue and decreased brain metabolism, especially in frontal regions, which may be reversible with abstinence.
6. Cognitive deficits in patients with alcohol-induced dementia may improve or remain stable with abstinence; this is unlike the downhill course commonly seen in dementias of other etiologies.
7. In patients who suspected of suffering from alcohol-induced dementia, every effort should be made to ensure abstinence from alcohol. The family may be offered the hope that the condition may stabilize and perhaps improve with abstinence.
8. Prospective validation of the aforementioned clinical and prognostic features is needed, as is postmortem brain examination of patients with alcohol-induced dementia.

This review raises several issues related to professional training and clinical policy. Trainees need to be competent in the simultaneous assessment of alcohol use disorders, cognitive impairment, and the neurological exam. A systematic review of alcohol use should be part of every dementia workup, and patients referred for treatment of alcohol use disorders should undergo cognitive screening and neurological examination. Periodic reassessment of alcohol consumption, cognitive status, and neurological examination should be routine policy in dementia clinics. The documentation of a history of alcohol use should be coupled with neuroimaging, neurological examination, and postmortem data to attempt to elucidate the diagnostic features of alcohol-induced dementia. Until a criterion for alcohol-induced dementia can be established through careful epidemiologic, neuropathological, and neuroimaging research, the effectiveness of treatment interventions for, and even the existence of, this reportedly common disorder will remain in doubt.

REFERENCES

Acker, C., Jacobson, R. R., & Lishman, W. A. (1987). Memory and ventricular size in alcoholics. *Psychological Medicine, 17,* 343–348.

Akai, J. (1991). [Anatomo-pathological studies on alcoholic dementia: A review and up to date research.] *Arukoru Kenkyuto Yakubutsu Ison, 26,* 134–41.

Akai, J., & Akai, K. (1989). [Neuropathological study of the nucleus basalis of meynert in alcoholic dementia]. *Aruloru Kenkyuto Yakubutsu Ison, 24,* 80–88.

American Psychiatric Association. (1987). *Diagnostic and statistical manual of mental disorders* (3rd ed., rev., pp. 133–134). Washington, DC: Author.

American Psychiatric Association. (1989). *A Task Force Report of the American Psychiatric Association: Treatments of Psychiatric Disorder.* Washington, DC: Author.

American Psychiatric Association. (1994). *Diagnostic and statistical manual of mental disorders* (4th ed., rev., pp. 133–134). Washington, DC: Author.

Arendt, T., Bigl, V., Arendt, A., & Tennstedt, A. (1983). Loss of neurons in the nucleus basalis of Meynert in Alzheimer's disease, paralysis agitans, and Korsakoff's disease. *Acta Neuropathologica, 61,* 101–108.

Atkinson, R. M. (1995). Treatment programs for aging alcoholics. In T. P. Beresford & E. S. L. Gomberg (Eds.), *Alcohol and aging.* New York: Oxford University Press.

Bergman, H., Borg, S., Hindmarsh, T. Idestrom, C. M., & Mutzell, S. (1980). Computed topography of the brain and neuropsychological assessment of alcoholic patients. *Acta Psychiatrica Scandinavica Supplementum, 286,* 47–56.

Besson, J. A. O., Crawford, J. R., Parker, D. M., & Smith, F. W. (1989). Magnetic resonance imaging in Alzheimer's disease, multi-infarct dementia and Korsakoff's psychosis. *Acta Psychiatrica Scandinavica, 80,* 451–458.

Besson, J. A. O., Glen, A. I. M., Foreman, E. I., MacDonald, A., Smith, F. W., Hutchison,

J. H. S., Mallard, J. R., & Ashcroff, G. W. (1981). Nuclear magnetic resonance observations in alcoholic cerebral disorder and the role of vasopressin. *Lancet, 2,* 923–924.

Blusewicz, M. J., Schenkenberg, T., Dustman, R. E., & Beck, E. C. (1977a). Neuropsychological correlates of chronic alcoholism and aging. *Journal of Nervous and Mental Diseases, 165,* 348–355.

Blusewicz, M. J., Schenkenberg, T., Dustman, R. E. & Bech, E. C., (1977b). WAIS performance in young normal, young alcoholic, and elderly normal groups: An evaluation of organicity and mental aging indices. *Journal of Clinical Psychology, 33,* 1149–1153.

Brandt, J., Butters, N., Ryan, C., & Bayog, R. (1983). Cognitive loss and recovery in long term alcohol abusers. *Archives of General Psychiatry, 40,* 435–442.

Brewer, C., & Perrett, L. (1971). Brain damage due to alcohol consumption: An air encephalographic, psychometric and electroencephalographic study. *British Journal of Addiction, 66,* 170–182.

Burger, M.C., Botwinick, J., & Storandt, M. (1987). Aging, alcoholism, and performance on the Luria-nebraska neuropsychological battery. *Journal of Gerontology, 42,* 69–72.

Cadet-Leite, A., Tavares, M. A., & Paula-Barbosa, M. M. (1988). Alcohol withdrawal does not impede hippocampal granule cell progressive loss in chronic alcohol-fed rats. *Neuroscience Letters, 86,* 45–50.

Caracci, G., & Miller, N. S. (1991). Epidemiology and diagnosis of alcoholism in the elderly (a review). *International Journal of Geriatric Psychiatry, 6,* 511–515.

Carlen, P. L., McAndrews, M. P., Weiss, R. T., Doniger, M., Hill, J. M., Menzano, B., Farchik, K., Abarbanei, J., & Eastwood, M. R. (1994). Alcohol-related dementia in the institutionalized elderly. *Alcohol Clinical Experimental Research, 18,* 1330–1334.

Carlen, P. L., Wortzman, G., Holgate, R. C., Wilkinson, D. A., & Rankin, J. G. (1978). Reversible cerebral atrophy in recently abstinent chronic alcoholics measured by computed temographic scans. *Science, 200,* 1076–1078.

Carlen, P. L., & Wilkinson, D. A. (1980). Alcoholic brain damage and reversible deficits, *Acta Psychiatrica Scandinavica, 62* (Supp. 286), 103–118.

Courville, C. B. (1966). *Effects of alcohol on the nervous system of man* (2nd ed.). Los Angeles: San Lucas.

Courville, C. B., & Meyers, R. O. (1954). Effects of extraneous poisons on the nervous system: II. The alcohols. *Bulletin of the Los Angeles Neurology Society, 19,* 66–95. (From the Coroner's Service, County of Los Angeles. Section of Nervous Diseases; College of Medical Evangelists; and the Cajal Laboratory of Neruopathology, Los Angeles County Hospital, Los Angeles, CA.)

Cravioto, H., Korein, J., & Silberman, J. (1961). Wernicke's encephalopathy: A clinical and neuropathological study of 28 autopsied cases. *Archives of Neurology, 4,* 510–519.

Cutting, J. (1978a). The relationship between Korsakov's and "alcoholic dementia." *Psychiatry, 132,* 240–251.

Cutting, J. (1978b). Specific psychological deficits in alcoholism. *British Journal of Psychology, 133,* 119–122.

Delaney, P. (1982). Dementia: The search for treatable causes. *Southern Medical Journal, 75*, 707–709.

Eckardt, M. J., & Martin, P. R. (1986). Clinical assessment of cognition in alcoholism. *Clinical Experimental Research, 10*, 123–127.

Fein, G., Bachman, L., Fisher, S., & Davenport, L. (1990). Cognitive impairments in abstinent alcoholics. *Western Journal of Medicine, 152*, 531–537.

Freeman, F. R. (1976). Evaluation of patients with progressive intellectual deterioration. *Archives of Neurology, 33*, 658–659.

George, L. K., Landerman, R., Blazer, D. G., & Anthony, J. C. (1991). Cognitive impairment, In L. N. Robins & D. A. Regier (Eds.), *Psychiatric disorders in America: The Epidemiologic Catchment Area Study* (pp. 323–325) New York: Free Press.

Gilman, S., Adams, K., Keoppe, R. Berent, S., Kluin, K. J., Modell, J. G., Koll, P., & Brunberg, J. A. (1990). Cerebellar and frontal hypometabolism in alcoholic cerebellar degeneration studied with positron emission tomography. *Annals of Neurology, 28*, 775–785.

Grunnet, M. L. (1969). Changing incidence, distribution, and histopathology of Wernicke's polioencephalopathy. *Neurology, 19*, 1135–1139.

Harper, C., & Blumberg, P. C. (1982). Brain weights in alcoholics. *Journal of Neurology, Neurosurgery, and Psychiatry, 45*, 838–840.

Harper, C., & Corbett, D. (1990). Changes in basal dendrites of cortical pyramidal cells from alcoholic patients. *Journal of Neurology, Neurosurgery, Psychiatry, 53*, 856–861.

Harper, C. G., & Kril, J. J. (1990). Neuropathology of alcoholism. *Alcohol and Alcoholism, 25*, 207–216.

Harper, C., & Daly, J. (1987). Are we drinking our neurones away? *British Medical Journal, 294*, 534–536.

Harper, C., & Kril, J. (1985). Brain atrophy in chronic alcoholic patients: A quantitive pathological study. *Journal of Neurology, Neurosrugery, and Psychiatry, 48*, 211–217.

Harper, C., & Holloway, R. L. (1985). Brain shrinkage in chronic alcoholics: A pathological study. *British Medical Journal, 290*, 501–504.

Harper, C. (1979). Wernicke's encephalopathy: A more common disease than realized: A Neuropathological study of 51 cases. *Journal of Neurology, Neurosurgery and Psychiatry, 42*, 226–231.

Harper, C. (1983). The incidence of Wernicke's encephalopathy in Australia: A neuropathological study of 131 cases. *Journal of Neurology, Neurosurgery and Psychiatry, 46*, 593–598.

Haug, J. O. (1968). Pneumoencephalographic evidence of brain damage in chronic alcoholics. *Acta Psychiatrica Scandinavica Supplementrim, 203*, 135–143.

Horvath, T. B. (1975). Clinical spectrum and epidemiological features of alcoholic dementia. In J. G. Rankin (Ed.), *Alcohol, drugs, and brain damage.* Toronto: Addiction Research Foundation of Ontario.

Kaczmarek, M. J., & Nixon, P. F. (1983). Variants of transketolase from human erythrocytes. *Clinica Chimica Acta, 130*, 349–356.

Kaplan, H., & Sadock, B. (Eds). (1990). *Pocket handbook of clinical psychiatry.* Baltimore: Williams and Wilkins.

King, M. B. (1986). Alcohol abuse and dementia. *International Journal of Geriatric Psychiatry, 1,* 31–36.

Kril, J. J., & Harper, C. G. (1989). Neronal counts from four cortical regions of alcoholic brains. *Acta Neuropathologica, 79,* 200–204.

Leber, W. R., & Parsons, C. A. (1982). Premature aging and alcoholism. *International Journal of the Addictions, 17,* 61–88.

Lee, K., Moller, L., Hardt, F., Haubek, A., & Jensen, E. (1979). Alcohol induced brain damage and liver damage in young males. *Lancet, 2,* 759–762.

Linnoila, M., Oxenkrug, G. F., Deaken, J. F. W., Coppen, A., Palfreyman, M. G., Insel, R. R., Cowen, P. J., & Meltzer, H. Y. (1991). Discussion: 5-HT receptor imbalance theory of affective disturbance. In 5-hydroxytryptamine in psychiatry. M. Sandler, A. Coppen, & S. Harnett (Eds.). New York: Oxford University Press.

Lishman, W. A. (1981). Cerebral disorder in alcoholism: Syndromes of impairment. *Brain, 104,* 1–20.

Lishman, W. A. (1986). Alcoholic dementia: A hypothesis. *Lancet, 1,* 1184–1186.

Lishman, W. A. (1990). Alcohol and the brain. *British Journal of Psychiatry, 156,* 635–644.

Lynch, M. J. G. (1960). Brain lesions in chronic alcoholism. *Archives of Pathology, 69,* 342–353.

Marsden, C. D., & Harrison, M. J. G. (1972). Outcome of investigations of patients with presenile dementia. *British Medical Journal, 2,* 249–252.

Martin, P. R., Adinoff, B., Eckardt, M. J., Stapleton, J. H., Bone, G. A. H., Rubinow, D. R., Lane, E. A., & Linnoila, M. (1989). Effective pharmacotherapy of alcoholic amnesic disorder with fluvoxamine. *Archives of General Psychiatry, 46,* 617–621.

McCrady, B. S., & Smith, D. E. (1986). Implications of cognitive impairment in the treatment of alcoholism. *Clinical and Experimental Research, 10,* 145–149.

McEntee, W. J., & Mair, R. G. (1980). Memory enhancement in Korsakoff's psychosis by clonidine: Further evidence for a noradrenergic deficit. *Annals of Neurology, 7,* 466–470.

McEntee, W. J., Mair, R. G., & Langlais, P. J. (1984). Neurochemical pathology in Korsakoff's psychosis: implications for other cognitive disorders. *Neurology, 34,* 648–652.

McMullen, P. A., Saint-Cyr, J. A., & Carlen, P. L. (1984). Morphological alterations in rat CAL hippocampal pyramidal cell dendrites resulting from chronic ethanol consumption and withdrawal. *Journal Comparative Neurology, 225,* 111–118.

Meyer, J. S., Largen, J. W., Jr., Shaw, T., Mortel, K. F., & Rogers, R. (1984). Interactions of normal aging, senile dementia, multi-infarct dementia, and alcoholism in the elderly. In J. T. Hartford, & T. Samorajski (Eds.), *Aging: Vol. 25. Alcoholism in the elderly.* New York: Raven.

Mott, F. W. (1910). The nervous system in chronic alcoholism. *British Medical Journal, 2,* 1403–1408.

National Institute on Alcohol Abuse and Alcoholism. Alcohol and Health (1993). *Fifth Special Report to the U.S. Congress from the Secretary of Health and Human Services.*

Osuntokon, B. O., Hendrie, H. C., Fisher, K., et al. (1992, February). The diagnosis of alcoholic dementia. Poster session presented at the Fifth Annual Meeting of the American Association for Geriatric Psychiatry.

Palmer, T. Nora, (Ed.) (1991). *Molecular pathology of alcoholism.* New York: Oxford University Press.

Parsons, O. A. (1977). Neuropsychological deficits in alcoholics: Facts and fancies. *Alcoholism: Clinical and Experimental Research, 1,* 51–56.

Pratt, O. E., Jeyasingham, M., & Shaw, G. K. (1985). Transketolase variant enzymes and brain damage. *Alcohol and Alcoholism, 20,* 223–232.

Rabins, P. V. (1981). The prevalence of reversible dementia in a psychiatric hospital, *Hospital and Community Psychiatry, 32,* 490–492.

Rankin, J. G. (1975). Toronto: Addiction Research Foundation of Ontario.

Ron, M. A. (1977). Brain damage in chronic alcoholism: a neuropathological, neuroradiological, and psychological review. *Psychological Medicine, 17,* 103–112.

Ron, M. A. (1983). The alcoholic brain: CT scan and psychological findings. *Psychological Medicine,* Monograph supp. 3.

Ron, M. A., Acker, W., & Lishman, W. A., (1980). Morphological abnormalities in the brains of chronic alcoholics: A clinical, psychological, and computerized axial tomographic study. *Acta Psychiatrica Scandinavica, 2,* (Supp. 286). 41–46.

Ron, M. A., Acker, W., & Shaw, G. K., (1982). Computerized tomography of the brain in chronic alcoholism: A survey and follow up study. *Brain, 105,* 497–514.

Ryan, C., & Butters, N. (1986). The neuropsychology of alcoholism. In D. Wedding, A. Horton, & J. Webster (Eds.), *The neuropsychology handbook.* New York: Springer Publishing.

Ryan, C., & Butters, N. (1980). Learning and memory impairments in young and old alcoholics: Evidence for the premature-aging hypothesis. *Alcoholism: Clinical and Experimental Research, 4,* 288–293.

Saunders, P. A., Copeland, J. R. M., Dewey, M. E., Davidson, I. A., McWilliam, C., Sharma, V., & Sullivan, C. (1991). Heavy drinking as a risk factor for depression and dementia in elderly men. *British Jouranl of Psychiatry, 159,* 213–216.

Smith, D. M., & Atkinson, R. M. (1993). Alcoholic dementia in an Alzheimer's registry. Paper presented at the Sixth Annual Meeting and Symposium of the American Association for Geriatric Psychiatry, New Orleans, LA.

Smith, D. M., & Atkinson, R. M. (1995, May). Diagnostic criteria for alcohol-induced dementia. Paper presented at the Annual Meeting of the American Psychiatric Association, Miami, FL.

Smith, J. S., & Kiloh, L. G. (1981). The investigation of dementia: Results in 200 consecutive admissions. *Lancet, 1,* 824–827.

Stapleton, J. M., Eckardt, M. J., Martin, P., Adinoff, B., Roehrich, L., Bone, G., Rubinow, D., & Linnoila, M. (1988). Treatment of alcoholic organic brain syndrome with the serotonin reuptake inhibitor fluvoxamine: A preliminary study. *Advances in Alcohol and Substance Abuse, 7,* 47–51.

Tarter, R. E., (1973). An analysis of cognitive deficits in alcoholics. *Journal of Nervous and Mental Disease, 157,* 138–147.

Torvik, A., Lindboe, C. F., & Rogde, S. (1982). Brain lesions in alcoholics: A neuropathological study with clinical correlations. *Journal of the Neurological Sciences, 56,* 233–248.

Tuck, R. R., & Jackson, M. (1991). Social, neurological, and cognitive disorders in alcoholics. *Medical Journal of Australia, 155,* 225–229.

Victor, M., Adams, R. C., & Collins, G. H. (1989). *The Wernicke-Korsakoff syndrome and related neurological disorders due to alcoholism and malnutrition* (2nd ed). Philadelphia: Davis.

Victoratos, G. C., Lemmon, J. A. R., & Herzeberge, L. (1977) Neurological investigation of dementia. *British Journal of Psychiatry, 130,* 131–133.

Von Gall, M., Becker, H., Artmann, H., Lerch, G., & Nemeth, N. (1978). Results of computer tomography on chronic alcoholics. *Neuroradiology, 16,* 329–331.

Walker, D. W., Barnes, D. E., Hornetzer, S. F., Hunter, B. E., & Kubanis, P. (1980). Neuronal loss in hippocampus induced by prolonged ethanol consumption in rats. *Science, 209,* 711–713.

Willenbring, M. L. (1988). Organic mental disorders associated with heavy drinking and alcohol dependence. *Clinics in Geriatric Medicine, 4,* 869–887.

Winokur, G., & Clayton, P. (Eds.) (1986). *Medical basis of psychiatry.*

7

Misuse of Prescription Drugs

Richard Finlayson, MD

INTRODUCTION

Misuse of prescription drugs may be difficult to distinguish from normal use, especially in the elderly patient. In the United States, older people usually obtain these drugs within the legitimate context of the physician-patient relationship. Additionally, the responsibility for appropriate use is shared by the patient and the physician and sometimes another caretaker—e.g., a spouse or a child. The term *misuse* in this chapter is intended to cover a broad range of behaviors and circumstances that may contribute to impairment and decreased capacity for independent living in elderly persons who use prescription drugs. This term is used advisedly, recognizing that benzodiazepine dependence, for example, may develop in persons taking therapeutic doses of these drugs (Task Force on Benzodiazepine Dependency, 1990, p. 16). The term *iatrogenic drug dependence* has been used to describe those situations in which a physician has contributed to dependence on medication by prescribing it—e.g., without proper indications, in excessive dosage, or for an excessively long time. Self-medication and so-called recreational use represent other possibilities in the spectrum of medication use by the elderly. The terms *abuse* and *dependence* are descriptors of patterns of use and consequences as classified in *DSM–IV* (American Psychiatric Association, 1994).

The focus in this chapter is on psychoactive drugs, in keeping with the general theme of the book. The elderly are described as a "population at risk" by virtue of various factors: biologic, demographic, psychosocial, comorbidity, and physician-related. Patterns of use of prescription drugs and the adverse consequences of this use, as reported in the literature, are also discussed. The section on diagnosis utilizes two case reports which emphasize different aspects of the diagnostic and therapeutic challenges. A management approach for prescription drug misuse in different settings is discussed. Last, future research directions are considered.

A POPULATION AT RISK

Biologic Factors

Biologic processes tend to slow with advancing age. Alterations in gastrointestinal functioning in normal elderly persons are not a major factor affecting the metabolism of drugs. The distribution, hepatic metabolism, renal excretion, and changes in receptor sensitivity and neurotransmitters are affected in a clinically important manner by aging (Jenike, 1989). The elderly are at risk of being exposed to excessive amounts of drugs. Greenblatt, Harmatz, and Shader (1991), in a discussion of the pharmacokinetics of sedative and hypnotic drugs, noted the evidence for decreased clearance and increased accumulation of benzodiazepines in elderly patients, as well as evidence for increased intrinsic sensitivity to these drugs. There is a reasonably well established link between the use of benzodiazepines that have a long half-life and confusion, falls, and hip fractures, but whether the link is causal is not well established. Greenblatt and Wright (1993), in a report that focused on the commonly used benzodiazepine alprazolam, noted that clearance is decreased in the elderly and pointed out that chronic disorders such as liver cirrhosis and renal disease may add to problems of decreased clearance and accumulation.

Demographics

Gender has been demonstrated to be a risk factor for exposure to prescription drugs. Elderly women are more likely than men to consult physicians and to receive a prescription for a psychoactive drug (Baum, Kennedy, Knapp, & Faich, 1985; Cafferata, Kasper, & Bernstein, 1983; Glantz & Backenheimer, 1988; Mossey and Shapiro, 1985). Female gender, according to the data from the 1985 National Household Survey (Robbins, 1989), is a predictor of substance use for treatment of intrapsychic problems. Other factors can explain this use, including the behavior of male physicians toward female patients through sex-role stereotyping and the power dynamics of the physician-patient relationship (Ogur, 1986). Men, according to the National Household Survey, were more likely to use various substances in response to problems of social functioning. Some studies (Mellinger, Balter, Parry, Manheimer, & Cisin, 1974; Robbins & Clayton, 1989) suggest that men are more frequent users of psychoactive drugs than are women after age 65. Generalization concerning the role of gender in the use of psychoactive drugs can be problematic if one is simply referring to "the elderly."

Psychosocial Factors

There has been considerable interest in the relationship between late-life coping and substance-use disorders, especially alcoholism. Late-onset cases (usually described as starting about age 60) might be attributed to that individual's difficulty in adjusting to various stressors—e.g., retirement from job, loss of spouse, loss of physical vitality, and isolation from peers. This idea is attractive and has some support. Brown and Chiang (1983) reported that isolation is a key factor in late-life substance abuse. In the study of 117 inpatients reported by Bron and Lowack (1987), drug use had started frequently in late life in response to various losses, loneliness, isolation, and illness. Evidence that this type of stress is the predominant factor contributing to late-onset cases is inconclusive, however (Meyers, Hingson, Mucatel, & Goldman, 1982; Wells-Parker, Miles, & Spencer, 1983). Finney and Moos (1984) pointed out that an individual's coping style is probably more important than the presence of the stressors themselves. Little is known about the relative validity of the stress-coping model with respect to alcohol or prescription drugs. Data derived from the Mayo Clinic's Inpatient Addiction Program (Finlayson and Davis, 1994) revealed that late-onset (age 60 or older) cases occurred in 35% of elderly prescription drug-dependent patients.

Gomberg (1990, p. 177), summarizing the literature on social networks and social supports, noted, "Among all age groups, there is evidence that more isolated people are more likely to smoke, drink heavily, engage in minimal physical activity, and be overweight." This pattern is clearer for men than for women. Gomberg adds the observation that, "what is not clear is whether people drink heavily because they are isolated or whether their social networks become eroded by their heavy drinking." Social bonds (social control) might not play as important a role in influencing deviant or risky behavior as is assumed, according to a study by Rook, Thuras, & Lewis (1990). Structured interviews of 162 elderly persons found that social control was only weakly related to the participants' health practices—e.g., use of alcohol, drugs, and tobacco. For the participants in this study, the existence of significant role obligations and direct attempts by others to influence their health practices had little effect.

There are reasons to think that the roles of social support, social control, and coping may be different for persons using alcohol and those using prescription drugs. For example, is the older person who complains of insomnia, chronic pain, or fatigue and seeks medication for these complaints more likely to be enabled to continue on a path that can lead to drug dependence than is an older person who has obvious stigmata of alcoholism? The intrapsychic factors and culture surrounding the elderly person who uses or abuses prescription drugs often involve hypochondriasis, somatization, insomnia, depression, and strong support, rather than the resistance and rejection from others which commonly occur with alcoholics.

Comorbidity

Older persons are, as a group, the largest consumers of prescription drugs in the United States. Although they account for just 12% of the general population, they consume one-fourth to one-third of the legally distributed prescription drugs (United States General Accounting Office, 1987). The bulk of these drugs, in a nonhospital setting for those age 65 and older, are not psychotherapeutic; they are prescribed for the treatment of common medical ailments, such as heart disease, diabetes mellitus, and arthritis (U. S. Department of Commerce, 1991). This pattern of drug use is a result of the increased incidence and prevalence of major chronic medical disorders that are associated with advancing age. Although the use of psychoactive prescription drugs is not necessarily a direct result of visits to the physician for the care of chronic medical disorders, these illnesses are often associated with heightened anxiety or other psychopathology, which may be treated with drugs by the physician. A relationship between physical health and an increase in specific psychiatric disorders in homebound elderly persons compared with others has been demonstrated by Bruce and McNamara (1992).

Studies (Ostrom, Hammarlund, Christensen, Plein, & Kethley, 1985; Rossiter, 1983) have demonstrated that about one fourth of community-dwelling elderly persons use psychotherapeutic drugs on a regular basis. In elderly patients, sleep disorders and chronic pain are perhaps the most common symptoms treated by physicians, but anxiety, fatigue, and labile moods are also common. These symptoms may be manifestations of a mental disorder. Prevalence data concerning mental disorders do not in themselves suggest that elderly persons are at increased risk of misuse of prescription drugs. There is substantial evidence (Bland, Newman, & Orn, 1988; Kramer, German, Anthony, Von Korff, & Skinner, 1985; Weissman et al., 1985) that all the major categories of mental illness, except cognitive impairment, occur less often with aging. On the other hand, there is also evidence (Ancill, Embury, MacEwan, & Kennedy, 1988) that depression, for example, may be

TABLE 7.1 Mental Disorder Diagnoses among 100 Elderly Inpatients with Prescription Drug Dependence

	Female (N = 70)		Male (N = 30)		Total (N = 100)	
Disorder	Number	%	Number	%	Number	P*
Mood	26	37	6	20	32	0.11
Organic mental	19	27	9	30	28	0.81
Personality	22	31	5	17	27	0.15
Somatoform	12	17	4	13	16	0.75
Anxiety	10	14	2	7	12	-
Sleep	3	4	5	17	8	-
Adjustment	2	3	-	-	2	-

Note: Diagnoses based on criteria established by the American Psychiatric Association in the revised 3rd edition of the *Diagnostic and Statistical Manual of Mental Disorders* (1987). Some patients had more than one diagnosis.

Source: From "Prescription drug dependence in the elderly population: Demographic and clinical features of 100 inpatients," by R. E. Finlayson & L. J. Davis, 1994. *Mayo Clinic Proceedings, 69,* p. 1141. Copyright 1994 by the Mayo Foundation for Medical Education and Research. Reprinted with permission of Mayo Foundation for Medical Education and Research.

* Fisher's exact test.

commonly misdiagnosed in older persons and inappropriately treated with benzodiazepines rather than antidepressants. Table 7.1 presents data from the Mayo Clinic showing that affective disorders and other mental disorders were common in elderly patients hospitalized for treatment of prescription drug dependence. Mental disorders seem to be a risk factor for drug dependence in the elderly.

Physicians' Behavior

Physicians' behavior with respect to prescribing drugs has been a topic in two national conferences sponsored by the American Medical Association and in various studies and reviews in the medical literature (Hasday & Karch, 1981; Shorr, Bauwens, & Landefeld, 1990; Wesson & Smith, 1990). It has been suggested that physicians take responsibility for how their behavior enables the lifestyles of their patients, and that the physician and patient share responsibility for the patient's proper use of prescription drugs.

PATTERNS OF USE

Use of benzodiazepine in Western nations is quite variable. In a review, Lader (1990) noted that chronic use (12 months or more) in the adult population occurred at the following rates in four countries: Sweden 0.5%; United States, 1.8%; United Kingdom, 3.1%; and Belgium, 6.8%. The use of benzodiazepines by elderly persons is probably the major area of concern with respect to the use of psychoactive prescription drugs in this age group. The Task Force on Benzodiazepine Dependency (1990, p. 11) noted with regard to benzodiazepine dependence, toxicity, and abuse that data available at that time suggested that "benzodiazepines are widely used in clinical practice and although there is not an epidemic of use or overuse, prevalence rates in the general population indicate significant use of these compounds." The task force also noted (p. 55) that survey data did not encompass the period after 1980 and that clinical perceptions indicated a change in use after the introduction of the benzodiazepines with a short half-life. The report did not emphasize benzodiazepine use by elderly persons, but some of the general information can be applied to this population.

Much of the information concerning patterns of use has been obtained through community surveys. Mishara and McKim (1993), in their review, noted that the evidence to date does not suggest that survey data from the elderly are less valid than those from other populations. Thus, memory problems in old age do not seem to increase the rate of misreporting in these surveys.

Recent studies (Bjerrum, Christensen, & Larsen, 1993; Finlayson & Davis, 1994; Lockwood & Berbatis, 1990; Nolan & O'Malley, 1988; Szwabo, 1993) confirmed that use of benzodiazepine increases with age; that women are more likely to have this group of drugs prescribed; and that elderly persons are more likely than younger persons to receive increased doses, and for longer periods. A study by Mayer-Oakes et al. (1993) in Southern California of elderly persons living in the community revealed, however, that when health status was controlled, women were not more likely than men to use benzodiazepines. The study also demonstrated a positive correlation between use of benzodiazepine by older persons and increased use of other drugs, a history of depression, race (Caucasian), and having a college education.

The link between use of benzodiazepine and depression is intriguing, especially in late life. A link between benzodiazepine and use of antidepressants in a general practice setting has been demonstrated by North, McAvoy, and Powell (1992). Anxiety and insomnia are prominent symptoms of depressive illness and are likely to "attract" symptomatic treatment with sedative-hypnotic and antianxiety drugs, especially when the underlying depressive illness is not recognized. Adams (1991) has noted evidence from the medical literature that most patients, including the elderly, receive psychotropic medications from their primary care practitioners, and that nonpsychiatric primary care practitioners are most likely to prescribe an antianxiety agent. Psychiatrists are most likely to prescribe an antidepressant and to attempt nonpharmacologic interventions as first-line treatment for all mental disorders. These findings, according to Adams, may partly explain an apparent contradiction: a low prevalence of bona fide anxiety disorders in the elderly but a high use of antianxiety medications by the same group. Misdiagnosis of depression does not fully explain these findings. These same drugs have been implicated in either producing or complicating depressive symptoms (Ancill et al., 1988). Given the reported trend for elderly patients to use benzodiazepines for long periods, the risk of unfavorable alteration of mood is readily apparent.

Barbiturates, unlike benzodiazepines, are true neuronal depressants and thus are more dangerous (Rall, 1990). According to a study from Britain by Busto and Sellers (1991), the barbiturates and the nonbarbiturate anxiolytics and sedative-hypnotics have been largely replaced in clinical practice by the benzodiazepines. In a study of suicide patterns in New Zealand, Skegg and Cox (1991) noted a recent decline in poisoning as a method in both sexes and a decline in suicide in women, attributable to changes in barbiturate prescribing.

The elderly, according to Albrecht, Hohner, and Van Ackern (1987), are the largest group of patients with pain. Much of their pain is chronic, caused by various degenerative disorders (e.g., arthritis and neuritis), and opiates are commonly used for treatment. Insomnia is a closely related symptom and may also be treated with opiates. Modern, effective substitutes for aspirin—e.g., the nonsteroidal anti-inflammatory drugs—have greatly reduced the need for opiates. For example, the eighth *Annual Review of Drug Utilization in the U.S. 1986* (U. S. Department of Commerce, 1987) ranked acetaminophen with codeine as number 18 among the top 25 drugs specified by the prescribing physician in a nonhospital setting for persons age 65 or older. The review of 1988 (U. S. Department of Commerce, 1989) listed nonsteroidal anti-inflammatory drugs but omitted opiates. Despite this trend, the use of opiates remains a significant problem in older persons, second only to the benzodiazepines in the author's experience. A study by Jinks and Raschko (1990) in Spokane, Washington, of high-risk elderly persons living in the community confirmed this impression: the most misused drugs were diazepam, codeine, meprobamate, and flurazepam.

Misuse of prescription drugs in elderly patients may occur in association with alcoholism. A study at the Mayo Clinic by Finlayson, Hurt, Davis, and Morse (1988) demonstrated that 19% of a sample of 216 elderly alcoholic inpatients also were diagnosed as abusing or dependent on prescription drugs. Mayo Clinic data show that alcoholism in the elderly is much more common in its inpatient addiction program than drug dependence with alcoholism or drug dependence alone (Finlayson & Davis, 1994).

ADVERSE CONSEQUENCES OF MISUSE OF PRESCRIPTION DRUGS

Side Effects of Drugs

One might say that side effects are unwanted effects. For example, if a benzodiazepine is strongly hypnotic, it is attractive as a sleeping medication or sedative. But if its intended purpose is to decrease anxiety or to act as tranquilizer and it also causes the person to feel sleepy during the day, we say that sleepiness is a side effect and constitutes a problem. A drug can, of course, produce side effects without having been misused or abused. This outcome may come about simply because the physician cannot reliably predict how a given patient will respond to a particular drug. To carry this point a bit further, it is possible for a physical dependence on a drug to develop without misuse of the drug. A physician may have prescribed it for a long time, and this may have led to dependence. The patient and the patient's family may rightly complain that the drug was taken "just as the doctor ordered," but such blame may be part of an addicted elderly patient's defense system. Adverse consequences may be experienced during appropriately conducted therapy or may be an outgrowth of an elderly person's using (or a physician's prescribing) a drug for the wrong purpose, excessive dosages, or taking the drug for an excessively long time.

Confusion and Falls

Confusion and falls are probably the most written-about adverse consequences of use and misuse of psychoactive prescription drugs in older people. Adverse drug reactions correlate strongly with being elderly (Ives, Bentz, & Gwyther, 1987; Rodríguez et al., 1993). Sedative drugs, especially long-acting benzodiazepines, have been reported (Larson, Kukull, Buchner, & Reifler, 1987) as the most common cause of drug-related cognitive impairment in the elderly. A recent study from the Mayo Clinic by Rummans, Davis, Morse, and Ivnik (1993) compared learning and memory in recently detoxified benzodiazepine-dependent, alcohol-dependent, and control elderly subjects. Neuropsychologic testing revealed that the benzodiazepine-dependent subjects had more difficulty in the domain tested than did the two other groups. Foy, Drinkwater, March, and Mearrick (1986) have reported that use of benzodiazepine by the elderly was associated with confusion after admission to a hospital. The literature (Classen, Pestotnik, Evans, & Burke, 1992; Muñoz, Dagninio, Rufs, & Bugedo, 1992) concerning the adverse side effects of using sedative drugs before and during medical procedures is mixed as to the rate of complications, and it tends to stress the differential liabilities of the various drugs.

Elderly persons are vulnerable to accidents, especially falling. This risk is increased by the use of sedative and opiate drugs (Ray, Thapa, & Shorr, 1993; Shorr, Griffin, Daugherty, & Ray, 1992; Sorock & Shimkin, 1988). Accidental overdosing with opiates that leads to rather sudden death of elderly patients was the subject of one report from the United Kingdom by Whittington (1984).

DIAGNOSIS

Diagnostic Criteria: DSM

The *DSM–III–R* (American Psychiatric Association, 1987, p. 168) criteria for abuse of and dependence on psychoactive drugs have limited usefulness with regard to the elderly population. There are nine criteria for dependence on psychoactive substances, three of which are needed in order to make this diagnosis; but certain of the criteria are especially ill-suited for use in the elderly.

Criterion 3 needs some modification in order to make it applicable for misuse of prescription drugs by elderly persons: "A great deal of time spent in activities necessary to get the substance (e.g., theft), taking the substance (e.g., chain smoking), or recovering from its effects." The elderly do not typically steal prescription drugs. The "great deal of time spent" usually involves trips to the physician's office, submitting to tests, calling in for refills, and making trips to the pharmacy. The elderly patient may, in fact, also spend a great deal of time recovering from the effects of misuse of prescription drugs, but to the author's knowledge this has not been specifically studied or reported.

Criterion 7 must also be adapted to the case of the elderly: "Marked tolerance: need for markedly increased amounts of the substance (i.e., at least a 50% increase) in order to achieve intoxication or desired effect, or markedly

TABLE 7.2 Misuse of Prescription Drugs
in Elderly Patients: Associated Variables

Use of multiple psychoactive drugs

Multiple physical problems

Insomnia

Chronic pain

Anxiety disorder

Depressive disorder

Alcoholism

Falls

Cognitive impairment

diminished effect with continued use of the same amount." Although tolerance to psychoactive substances may increase in some persons, others experience age-related decrease in tolerance due to slowed biotransformation and elimination of a drug or drugs.

The newly released *DSM–IV* (American Psychiatric Association, 1994, p. 181) takes some steps to make criteria for substance abuse and dependence more applicable to the elderly. For example, in criterion 5 (*DSM–III–R* criterion 3), "visiting multiple doctors or driving long distances" is given as an example of "a great deal of time is spent in activities necessary to obtain the substance." These behaviors and others are often used as examples of what is known as "drug-seeking behavior." The requirement for an increase in tolerance of at least 50% (*DSM–III–R* criterion 7) has been eliminated. Decreased tolerance to drugs may develop in those drug-dependent elderly persons who have, for example, renal and hepatic insufficiency, dementia, or depression.

Individual variability is high in elderly patients with respect to a number of factors: biologic, psychologic, social, and illness-related. The manifestations of substance-use disorders, quite naturally, are also highly variable in this population. Table 7.2 summarizes common variables associated with misuse of prescription drugs.

The following two case histories are based on patient histories known to the author and illustrate different aspects of the misuse of prescription drugs by elderly persons. Are these patients drug-dependent according to standard criteria? Judge for yourself.

Case Study 1

A 64-year-old woman presented to her family physician 10 days after the death of her husband, with the complaint of insomnia. The physician had attended her for about 20 years and knew her medical and social background well. Her only medical problems were mild hypertension and osteoarthritis of her knees and hips. She had a normal developmental history, having attained her educational, occupational, and social goals in a satisfactory manner. She rarely drank alcoholic beverages. The physician had prescribed psychoactive medications for her on just two previous occasions: at age 45, after a drug overdose by her daughter; and at age 57, when her son and daughter-in-law were divorced. Benzodiazepines were prescribed and used for several weeks on each occasion, and there was no misuse or abuse. No member of her nuclear family had ever been diagnosed as having a mental disorder.

At the time of this visit to her family physician, she was having difficulty falling asleep, but once asleep, she slept until her usual awakening time. The physician found no evidence of depression and considered her to be experiencing uncomplicated bereavement and grief. Lorazepam, 0.25 mg at bedtime, was prescribed for 30 days. At the end of this time, the patient called her physician and stated that she was still having trouble with sleep. A single refill was given. About 2 weeks later, the patient called and asked if she could increase the dose of lorazepam to 0.50 mg at bedtime. The physician agreed but requested an office visit.

At this visit the patient appeared tired, and she gave a history of repeated awakenings during the night, loss of appetite, and a lack of interest in leaving her dwelling. The story suggested mild depression. Fluoxetine, 20 mg daily, was prescribed, and the patient was advised to discontinue the lorazepam within a week or two. Ten days later, the patient called the physician; complained that she felt "jumpy," and requested that the fluoxetine be discontinued. This was done, and the lorazepam was restarted. During the next 4 months, additional dosage increases, to 1.5 mg daily, were made by the physician after the patient complained that the medication "wasn't working any more." By this time she was awakening more frequently during the night and felt "terrible" when she awakened in the morning. Appetite, energy, interest in usual activities, and mental concentration had declined, and she remarked that she would "just as soon be dead as feel like this." She denied suicidal thoughts, however. The patient's family had begun to think that the lorazepam was making her feel worse, and they persuaded her to try to stop it; but each time she tried to stop, her insomnia increased and she experienced more daytime anxiety. About this time, her brother called the physician and requested that his sister be seen by the physician and "checked for Alzheimer's disease."

Comments on Case Study 1

Bereavement and grieving are risk factors for major depression in the elderly. Zisook and Shuchter (1991) reported that widows and widowers were more likely than a control group (whose spouses were living) to experience depressive disorders during the 12 months after the death of spouse. The patient in case study 1 experienced initial symptoms that were not consistent with major depression, and the physician's management of the case would be considered by many observers to be appropriate. The appearance of a more severe mood disturbance with neurovegetative symptoms led to treatment with fluoxetine, again a reasonable approach by the physician. At this point, the patient's situation starts on a downhill course.

This history is given as an example of misuse of prescription drugs by a physician, which in many instances is the result of a failure to diagnose depression or to treat it correctly (or both). There was no indication that the physician or another professional selected by the physician provided psychotherapy or counseling for the patient. When akathisia-like symptoms developed while the patient was taking fluoxetine, the drug was stopped, but another antidepressant trial was not started. The lorazepam was used from that point on to manage the patient; and a complex syndrome developed: depression, increasing tolerance to a benzodiazepine, behavioral deterioration, and cognitive impairment. The drug dependence in this case lacks some of the features of addiction, in that the patient did not have a history of substance abuse; she did not increase the dose of the lorazepam, except with the permission of the physician; and she did not engage in antisocial acts in order to obtain the drug.

Case Study 2

A 73-year-old retired physician, accompanied by his wife, registered at a large medical center with the chief complaint of back pain. He appeared very ill, weak, and unable to walk without his wife at his side, and his speech and mental processes were moderately slowed. The examining physician noted a history of chronic pain from an injury at age 28. The patient had subsequently had two back operations, neither of which produced lasting relief from pain. Since the injury he had used various opiates and opioids and, for the past 15 years, multiple benzodiazepines and other sedative-hypnotics. His current medications included propoxyphene, 500 to 700 mg daily; alprazolam, 3.0 mg daily; and flurazepam, 30 mg daily. It was evident from the history that he had used drugs in excess of the amount prescribed and that increased tolerance had developed to both classes of drugs. He denied having a syndrome of abstinence, but he admitted that his drug use had been uninterrupted for at least 4 years. He did, however, describe episodic increases in generalized anxiety.

The examining physician obtained this additional history. As a medical student, the patient had used amphetamines (obtained as samples of diet pills) to stay awake for examinations. Later, as a practicing physician, he obtained more drugs from drug samples kept in his office. On some occasions, he wrote prescriptions for opiates or benzodiazepines in his wife's name, but he used the drugs himself. He was once warned by the pharmacist that writing prescriptions for his wife was not a good idea; thereafter, he filled the prescriptions by mail order. In recent years, a colleague wrote prescriptions for his chronic back pain.

After the patient had been in practice for about 10 years, his wife separated from him, on the grounds that he was a workaholic and an alcoholic. He abstained from alcohol for about 6 months, and his wife returned. He describes his present drinking as social only—specifically, two to three drinks after dinner twice a week and on special occasions. His tolerance to alcohol had been decreasing. His use of alcohol had begun in young adulthood and increased at key points—e.g., when he entered practice and after a partner in the two-person practice left him. He had one charge against him of driving while intoxicated.

The family history was positive for alcoholism in his father and in a brother who committed suicide at age 49. One of his sons was a recovering alcoholic.

The examining physician in this case completed the general medical evaluation and requested a consultation with a psychiatrist.

Comments on Case Study 2

The patient had multiple, long-standing risk factors for prescription drug misuse, abuse, and dependence. In contrast to case study 1, this case is an example of an early-onset substance-use disorder—i.e., before late life. Multiple risk factors for a substance-use disorder are identified. The diagnosis of abuse of alcohol and multiple prescription drugs is readily made, and a diagnosis of dependence is tenable on the basis of the brief history provided.

MANAGEMENT STRATEGIES

Introductory Remarks

Misuse of prescription drugs, as discussed in this chapter, covers a wide spectrum of behaviors. These range from misuse, based on a lack of understanding of the nature and purpose of drugs, to behaviors in which older persons incorporate psychoactive drugs into a lifestyle characterized by the psychologic and social or behavioral features of addiction. Various points on this spectrum of drug misuse are not necessarily points on a continuum.

There is evidence from a survey by the American Association of Retired Persons (1984) of consumer use, attitudes, and behavior, that older consumers are often passive in the matter of asking questions of physicians and pharmacists. Failure to ask questions or to ask enough questions to meet the patient's needs may lead to misuse. A written prescription and a few words of instruction may not be adequate for an elderly person who is impaired. Specific, written instructions—e.g., on note cards—are an excellent way to extend supervision by the physician. In addition to communicating basic information about drugs, there is sometimes a need for counseling for elderly patients, who trade medications with their peers, fail to take the prescribed amounts and save the surplus for a rainy day, or are too embarrassed to tell the physician that they did not fill a prescription because it cost too much. The restoration of supervision by the physician is often adequate for management of this type of misuse.

There are virtually no reported studies concerning the effectiveness of formal treatment for abuse and dependence in elderly persons. The discussion that follows is, therefore, based largely on the author's clinical experience. The focus is on psychoactive substance abuse and dependence, as defined in *DSM–IV.*

Intervention

The management of substance-use disorders commonly begins with an intervention—an event in which interested persons express their concern to the person who is abusing drugs by making observations about how the abuse of drugs (or alcohol) has adversely affected that person's life, including his or her relationships with others. A recommendation that the person seek professional help is an essential part of the intervention. An intervention of this type is often necessary because denial is a feature of substance-use disorders, and denial is usually the first major obstacle to treatment.

Family members may have considerable difficulty in confronting elderly people, especially their parents, with drug or alcohol abuse and its consequences. Respect for a parent and difficulty in conceptualizing an elderly person as an "addict" or "drug abuser" often stand in the way of organizing and conducting an intervention. Nagging doubts about the cause of an older person's impairment may persist. "Is it really the drugs that are doing it to her?" "Mother is, after all, almost 70, and we can't expect her to remember everything." Even when drug-induced impairment is recognized, a family member may persist in blaming a physician, who was "the one who started her on the drugs in the first place" and may question why the elderly person should be subjected to the pressure of an intervention. At this point, education and support are important in dealing with family members. It is useful to point out, for example, that placing blame is not helpful to the recovery process. When families assume that the person's age explains the impairment, it is important to point out that age per se should not be used as an explanation of an older person's symptoms until existing illnesses are considered. The role of prescription drugs in altering sleep, memory, and mood should be discussed.

In cases of chronic pain and substance abuse, education of the family is critical in preparing for an intervention. The intervention may take place in various ways. The physician might, in less complicated cases, approach the patient on a one-to-one basis in the office and work out a plan for reversing the drug abuse and supporting the patient. If given permission, the physician could involve family members in the intervention session, as insurance against misrepresentation of what is said by the physician and to make the family aware of and involved in the treatment plan.

Intervention in case study 1 above would probably differ from intervention for case study 2, chiefly in the handling of denial. The elderly widow in case study 1 had developed a chronic and dependent pattern of use of benzodiazepine in the presence unresolved grief and major depression. Her difficulty in discontinuing the benzodiazepine could have represented recurrence of the anxiety, dysphoria, and insomnia associated with grief and depression as well as an abstinence syndrome. Overall, iatrogenic rather than addictive behaviors stand out and suggest a course of action. The fears of the brother concerning Alzheimer's disease should be addressed, of course. Detoxification, possibly on an inpatient basis, and pharmacologic and psychotherapeutic treatment of her depression and grief would be appropriate options to offer to the patient. The degree of psychologic dependence on the drug may not be evident initially. Persons who work in the field of addictions are well aware of the layers of psychopathology that can exist even in what seem like simple or less complicated cases of drug abuse. Longitudinal experience with the older patient and the patient's family, along with careful clinical observations, may be necessary to determine what the psychotherapeutic needs are and to what extent the disease model or the addiction model would be applicable.

An intervention in case study 2, a patient with long-standing substance-use disorders, would probably follow more classic lines. In the author's experience, the key to intervening in situations of prescription drug abuse and dependence and chronic pain in adults of any age involves creating a paradigm shift in the thinking of the patient and the family. They have reasoned that the pain, which has defied solution, is the cause of the person's suffering and loss of functional status. If the patient can accept the possibility that drug use is contributing to the varied symptoms associated with the chronic pain syndrome, a starting point has been achieved and treatment can begin.

The Outpatient Setting

The decision concerning whether treatment should be hospital-based or on an outpatient basis can be difficult. As a result of pressures from third-party payers and other economic factors, a larger proportion of persons are treated in outpatient programs. Unless an elderly person has general medical or other psychiatric problems that militate against outpatient treatment, he or she can be treated in these settings.

There is considerable interest, and there are some empirical data, concerning the question whether elderly alcoholics should be treated in peer groups or in mainline groups with other adults (Kashner, Rodell, Ogden, Guggenhem, & Karson, 1992; Kofoed, Tolson, Atkinson, Toth, & Turner, 1987). The same considerations apply to the elderly person who abuses or is dependent on prescription drugs. The author's experience suggests, however, that age per se may not be as important as the drug culture in which the patient has operated. For example, a 70-year-old woman who is opioid-dependent and experiencing chronic pain probably has more in common with a 30-year-old woman with similar problems than she would have with a 70-year-old alcoholic woman. The issues of pain, insomnia, and other somatic symptoms and the physician-patient relationship would be easier to identify with than the marital problems, antisocial behavior, legal difficulties, and associated culture common to alcoholism and abuse of illicit drugs. These observations might help design treatment for elderly persons.

The Inpatient Setting

The reasons for admitting elderly persons who are drug abusers and drug-dependent to hospital-based addiction treatment are similar to those for younger persons: high potential for an abstinence syndrome, serious risk of suicide, other major psychopathology, lack of social support, and failure to respond to outpatient treatment.

Elderly patients tend, however, to have higher levels of comorbidity than younger patients. It is common for elderly drug-abusing and drug-dependent persons to be admitted to inpatient treatment settings with major general medical problems, other psychiatric problems, and multiple drug problems. Uncontrolled diabetes mellitus, hypertension, cardiac arrhythmias, renal insufficiency, gait disorders, cognitive impairment, and reduced vision and hearing are examples of problems commonly encountered by clinicians who deal with this population.

The recent shift in emphasis from programmatic approaches to treatment —e.g., the 28-day Minnesota model—to a clinical care model is particularly appropriate in treatment of the elderly person who is dependent on prescription drugs. Chiauzzi and Liljegren (1993), in a review, identified "Taboo topics in addiction treatment," noting the lack of empirical support for the Minnesota model. The fact is, of course, that all existing treatment models lack such support. There are features of the traditional Minnesota model or other so-called programmatic models that could create difficulties in treatment of the elderly addicted person. Many of these elderly patients are not able to enter into and keep pace with a fast-moving program designed for younger patients who are more physically well. It should be pointed out that core elements of the Minnesota model are applicable to patient-centered, individualized treatment of the addicted person. Treatment centers that use formal individualized treatment plans for their elderly patients are in a favorable position to address this group's comorbidity.

It has been our experience at the Mayo Clinic that, in general, elderly persons retain information better if they have some one-to-one instruction and are given written material that repeats the information provided in the sessions. There is a risk in depending on traditional fast-paced programs that use lectures and films for the education of older persons. The shift to a clinical care model has, in part, been driven by third-party payers and certifying bodies such as the Health Care Financing Administration (HCFA) and the Joint Commission for Accreditation of Health Organizations (JCAHO). The addition of market pressure (i.e., competition) and the need for outcome data will, it is hoped, help to identify those factors that are most efficacious in the treatment of all substance-use disorders. Mammo and Weinbaum (1993), reporting data from the New Jersey State Department of Health, have indicated that dropping out of treatment for addiction is influenced by various factors such as health insurance coverage, occupational status, and living arrangements, suggesting the need for flexible, patient-centered treatment.

The detoxification of elderly persons from sedative-hypnotic and opiate-opioid drugs is based on the same principles as those used for younger persons. However, the choice and administration of drugs used for detoxification is based on knowledge of the physical condition of the elderly person. Although longer-acting drugs are typically chosen for detoxification, the delayed elimination of medications in the elderly must be kept in mind.

TABLE 7.3 Pharmacologic and Clinical Factors to Consider in the Use of Some Drugs for Detoxification of the Elderly Patient

Drug	Plasma half-life[a] (h)	Oral sedative dose[b] (mg)	Comment
Barbiturate			
Phenobarbital	80–120	15–40	Risk of accumulation and side effects is substantial; use with particular caution in the elderly; when tolerated, long-acting drugs lead to less drug-seeking behavior and a "smoother" detox
Secobarbital	15–40	30–50	If a barbiturate is used, secobarbital would be a desirable agent in a frail elderly person
Benzodiazepine			
Chlordiaze-poxide	5–15	15–100	This is a commonly used and quite safe drug; it may not be reliably absorbed when used IM, especially in patients with circulatory failure
Lorazepam	10–20	0.5–1.0	Does not require oxidation by the liver; use in patients with liver disease or renal insuffiency
Oxazepam	5–10	15–30	Has advantages similar to lorazepam, but available only in oral form
Opioids			
Methadone	15–40	5–10	When using opiates or opioids, exercise great caution when respiratory insufficiency or CNS disorders are present
Codeine	2–4	150–300	Best used for detox of less potent opioids

[a, b] These healthy adult half-life and dosing data, in part, from Rall (1990, p. 345).

Note: These half-life and dosing data may change depending on the age, acquired tolerance, and general medical condition of the patient. In general, it is advisable to reduce the initial dose in elderly persons by 1/3 to 1/2 of the usual adult dose, and adjust subsequent doses and dosing schedule based on the clinical response.

Abbreviations: CNS = central nervous system; detox = detoxification; IM = intramuscular.

According to a report by Miller, Whitcup, Sacks, and Lynch (1985), benzo-diazepine withdrawal symptoms may be difficult to recognize in a medically ill elderly patient. Schweizer, Case, and Rickels (1989) reported that elderly patients experienced fewer severe symptoms than younger patients when withdrawn from benzodiazepines. Be prepared, however, for that old neme-sis, heterogeneity. Some elderly persons experience withdrawal similar to that in younger persons.

Mixed substance dependence often prolongs the detoxification process and makes it more difficult. It is wise to stabilize patients for 24 to 48 hours on the drug or drugs that will be used for the scheduled taper. This is partic-ularly important for medically ill patients with high comorbidity—e.g., the elderly. When alcohol dependence coexists with dependence on prescription sedatives or hypnotics, an alcohol abstinence syndrome can generally be cov-ered by the scheduling of the sedative drug (e.g., chlordiazepoxide, Librium). Methadone, codeine, or propoxyphene (Darvon) will cover opiate or opioid withdrawal. Conversion tables that provide drug equivalents for suppression of an abstinence syndrome should be used with caution. Table 7.3, although not offered as a complete guide to detoxification, presents pharmacologic data and suggestions for the use of common drugs in the detoxification of elderly persons. The author suggests that readers consult standard textbooks for conversion tables. Careful titration of drug dosage on the basis of objec-tive physical signs and mental status is essential. Individual variability in elderly persons must be kept in mind.

The psychosocial treatment of drug dependence in elderly persons may be based on traditional concepts such as the Alcoholics Anonymous (AA) Twelve Steps and Narcotics Anonymous (NA). Actual participation in AA or NA may be difficult for some elderly persons. The elderly person who mis-uses prescription drugs may not be able to identify with a group of youthful offenders who use illicit drugs. A smoke-filled atmosphere may not be toler-ated by a frail, medically ill older person. There are groups specifically for the elderly and smoke-free groups in some cities. Other examples of psy-chosocial support and treatment for the elderly include support groups for chronic pain and individual counseling by a chemical dependence counselor or the primary care physician. A demonstrated willingness to participate in a particular type of psychosocial treatment is an important criterion in selec-tion. The treatment process may differ in order to compensate for reduced sight and hearing, cognitive impairment, and lack of social support. Communication with the elderly person's primary physician during treatment and at dismissal is extremely important. All the hard work and gains made can be lost after dismissal if the primary physician is not enlisted into the recovery plan.

The goal of total abstinence is probably the most thorny issue confronting the person diagnosed as dependent on prescription psychoactive drugs. What happens when the elderly person must have a surgical procedure? It is a commonsense conclusion that in such a case the necessary pain control would be provided, but under careful supervision and with the intent to discontinue the drug as soon as possible, avoiding openended prescriptions to be taken home by the patient. Relapse—recurrence of drug abuse and dependence—is most likely to occur in the management of chronic disorders (e.g. pain and insomnia). The attending physician can play a major role by providing strategies for the management of these complaints which will not put the older person at risk of relapse. Careful followup is the key.

The Nursing Home Setting

Misuse of psychoactive drugs by nursing home residents has been an ongoing concern in this country. In studies of intermediate care and skilled nursing facilities, Beers et al. (1988, 1992) have demonstrated that inappropriate use of psychoactive drugs was common, especially with respect to sedative-hypnotic and antipsychotic drugs. A study by Avorn et al. (1992) demonstrated that education of the nursing home staff significantly decreased the magnitude and probable inappropriateness of use of psychoactive drugs.

Although clinicians have a high degree of control over the use of psychoactive substances by residents of nursing homes, the problems encountered in managing behavior problems in this population create difficult decisions. One might, for example, encounter persons with known substance-use disorders who need psychoactive medication. Providing these elderly patients with alcoholic beverages in order to calm them, or modifying their behavior with alcohol as a reward, is not advisable. The phenomenon of crossaddiction is a reason for not prescribing a benzodiazepine to treat anxiety in a known alcoholic. This view has been challenged by Adinoff (1992) in a study of recovering alcoholics who did not relapse to drinking when treated with benzodiazepines for anxiety. This study did not focus on elderly patients. Data from Price et al. (1991) lend support to the traditional approaches to the substance-dependent person, with the primary principle being abstinence from all psychoactive substances of abuse, chiefly alcohol, benzodiazepines, barbiturates, other hypnotics, and opiates. The availability of other nonaddicting drugs, electroconvulsive therapy, and psychosocial therapies makes this possible. Anxiety in many elderly persons is secondary to depressive disorders which can be treated with an antidepressant (Tucker, 1994). The selective serotonin reuptake inhibitors (SSRIs) have been demonstrated to have antidepressant as well as antianxiety effects. Buspirone (BuSpar) is well tolerated in elderly persons generally and is effective for treatment of anxiety (Napoliello & Domantay, 1991). It should be noted, however, that a response may not be seen for 4 to 6 weeks after initiating treatment. Most important, one should be aware that excessive anxiety in older persons may result from a wide variety of circumstances, including organic illness, bereavement, and environment stress (e.g., crime), and that counseling and social support are often much preferred over drug therapy.

The Sharing of Responsibility

The problem of misuse of prescription drugs by the elderly population is a shared responsibility. Gomberg (1992, p. 370), in a discussion of medication problems and drug abuse by the elderly, described the physician's role as critical. She added, however, that "other health professionals, such as pharmacists, nurses, and social workers, can aid the process of maximizing the benefits of medication by having an understanding approach." Gomberg pointed to the role of government and public policy and suggested that the Food and Drug Administration should encourage the use of older populations in clinical trials of drugs. This author would add to that the study of the addictive process.

FUTURE RESEARCH

Dr. Jerome H. Jaffe, Associate Director for Science, Office of Treatment Improvement, National Institute of Drug Abuse (Jaffe, 1991), has made this observation:

> Knowledge about the multiple processes that can contribute to drug use and compulsive drug use continues to expand. It has proven easier to reach agreement on the processes that can influence drug using behavior (i.e., conceptual models) than to reach agreement on definitions of drug dependence that can be used for diagnostic and epidemiological purposes.

In the field of psychiatry, and addiction psychiatry particularly, there is intense discussion of how inclusive or restrictive the term *addiction* should be. Should we, for example, rely on restrictive criteria surrounding the concept of physical dependence, or should we open the door to a whole array of compulsive behaviors, e.g, sexual addiction? Jaffe commented further:

The debate about the primacy of physical dependence for clinical diagnosis comes at a time when available animal models suggest that primary reinforcing effects and associated learning may be the primary if not the sole determinants of drug self-administration.

In the case of the elderly, such reinforcement may result from increased attention and caring from friends and family, and from the physician, a powerful figure. "Sick role" behavior tends to be powerfully reinforced in our society.

Skinner (1990), in a monograph for the British Society for the Study of Addiction, identified three sequential stages necessary for validation of a diagnostic concept—in this case, drug dependence. Stage 1 is provisional description and development of operational measures; stage 2 is determination of prognosis and outcome of treatment; and stage 3 is a theoretical understanding of etiology and natural history. Skinner observed that the dependence syndrome is still within the first of these three stages. Empirical data are lacking, particularly for the elderly population. Basic data regarding incidence and prevalence, using available diagnostic criteria, are needed. The pheomenon of early versus late onset, already studied in alcoholics, has hardly been addressed with respect to prescription drugs. Although we live in a polydrug culture, there seems to be an opportunity to study the current generation of elderly persons without a major overlap with users of illicit drugs. There are reasons to think that of elderly alcoholics may differ considerably from elderly abuses of prescription drugs—with the latter being the more psychiatrically impaired population. The epidemiology and natural history of the two major categories of problem drugs among the elderly—i.e., benzodiazepines and opiates—should be compared as well. Last, future research should address the heterogeneity of the elderly populations. This chapter has already emphasized the individual variability found in older persons as a result of gender and health. Ethnicity, religious background, and social environment are additional variables that should be studied.

NOTE

A modified version of this article was published in *International Journal of the Addictions, 30*, 1647–1677 (1995).

REFERENCES

Adams, R. (1991). Anxiety and personality disorders. In J. Sadavoy, L. W. Lazarus, & L. F. Jarvik (Eds.), *Comprehensive review of geriatric psychiatry* (pp. 369–386). Washington, DC: American Psychiatric Press.

Adinoff, B. (1992). Long-term therapy with benzodiazepines despite alcohol dependence disorder: Seven case reports. *American Journal of Addictions, 1,* 288.

Albrecht, M., Hohner, E., & Van Ackern, K. (1987). Rationale einer Schmerztherapie im Alter [The rationale of pain therapy in the aged.] *Zeitschrift für Gerontologie, 20,* 23–30.

American Association of Retired Persons. (1984). Prescription drugs: *A survey of consumer use, attitudes and behavior.* Washington, DC: Author.

American Psychiatric Association. (1987). *Diagnostic and statistical manual of mental disorders* (3rd ed., rev.). Washington, DC: Author.

American Psychiatric Association. (1994). *Diagnostic and statistical manual of mental disorders* (4th ed.). Washington, DC: Author.

Ancill, R. J., Embury, G. D., MacEwan, G. W., and Kennedy, J. S. (1988). The use and misuse of psychotropic prescribing for elderly psychiatric patients. *Canadian Journal of Psychiatry, 33,* 585–589.

Avorn, J., Soumerai, S. B., Everitt, D. E., Ross-Degnan, D., Beers, M. H., Sherman, D., Salem-Schatz, S. R., & Fields, D. (1992). A randomized trial of a program to reduce the use of psychoactive drugs in nursing homes. *New England Journal of Medicine, 327,* 168–173.

Baum, C., Kennedy, D., Knapp, D., & Faich, G. (1985). *Drug utilization in the U.S.:1985: Seventh annual review.* Rockville, MD: Food and Drug Administration.

Beers, M., Avorn, J., Soumerai, S. B., Everitt, D. E., Sherman, D. S., & Salem, S. (1988). Psychoactive medication use in intermediate-care facility residents. *JAMA, 260,* 3016–3020.

Beers, M. H., Ouslander, J. G., Fingold, S. F., Morgenstern, H., Reuben, D. B., Rogers, W., Zeffren, M. J., & Beck, J. C. (1992). Inappropriate medication prescribing in skilled-nursing facilities. *Annals of Internal Medicine, 117,* 684–689.

Bjerrum, L., Christensen, P. B., & Larsen, P. H. (1993). Benzodiazepinordination i almen praksis. [Prescription of benzodiazepines in general practice.] *Ugeskrift for Laeger, 155,* 315–319.

Bland, R. C., Newman, S. C., & Orn, H. (1988). Prevalence of psychiatric disorders in the elderly in Edmonton. *Acta Psychiatric Scandinavica Supplementum, 338,* 57–63.

Bron, B., & Lowack, A. (1987). Missbrauch und Abhängigkeit von Alkohol und Medikamenten im höheren Lebensalter [Abuse and dependence on alcohol and drugs in advanced age.] *Zeitschrift für Gerontologie, 20,* 219–226.

Brown, B. B., & Chiang, C. P. (1983). Drug and alcohol abuse among the elderly: Is being alone the key? *International Journal of Aging and Human Development, 18,* 1–12.

Bruce, M. L., & McNamara, R. (1992). Psychiatric status among the homebound elderly: An epidemiologic perspective. *Journal of the American Geriatrics Society, 40,* 561–566.

Busto, U. E., & Sellers, E. M. (1991). Anxiolytics and sedative/hypnotics dependence. *British Journal of Addiction, 86,* 1647–1652.

Cafferata, G. L., Kasper, J., & Bernstein, A. (1983). Family roles, structure, and stressors in relation to sex differences in obtaining psychotropic drugs. *Journal of Health and Social Behavior, 24,* 132–134.

Chiauzzi, E. J., & Liljegren, S. (1993). Taboo topics in addiction treatment: An empirical review of clinical folklore. *Journal of Substance Abuse Treatment, 10,* 303–316.

Classen, D. C., Pestotnik, S. L., Evans, R. S., & Burke, J. P. (1992). Intensive surveillance of midazolam use in hospitalized patients and the occurrence of cardiorespiratory arrest. *Pharmacotherapy, 12,* 213–216.

Finlayson, R. E., & Davis, L. J. (1994). Prescription drug dependence in the elderly population: Demographic and clinical features of 100 inpatients. *Mayo Clinic Proceedings, 69,*1137–1145.

Finlayson, R. E., Hurt, R. D., Davis, L. J. Jr., & Morse, R. M. (1988). Alcoholism in elderly persons: A study of the psychiatric and psychosocial features of 216 inpatients. *Mayo Clinic Proceedings, 63,* 761–768.

Finney, J. W., & Moos, R. H. (1984). Life stressors and problem drinking among older adults. *Recent Developments in Alcoholism, 2,* 267–288.

Foy, A., Drinkwater, V., March, S., & Mearrick, P. (1986). Confusion after admission to hospital in elderly patients using benzodiazepines. *British Medical Journal, 293,* 1072.

Glantz, M. D., & Backenheimer, M. S. (1988). Substance abuse among elderly women. *Clinical Gerontologist, 8,* 3.

Gomberg, E. (1992). Medication problems and drug abuse. In F. J. Turner (Ed.), *Mental health and the elderly: A social work perspective.* New York: Free Press, p. 355–374.

Gomberg, E. S. L. (1990). Drugs, alcohol, and aging. *Research Advances in Alcohol and Drug Problems, 10,* 171–213.

Greenblatt, D. J., Harmatz, J. S., & Shader, R.I. (1991). Clinical pharmacokinetics of anxiolytics and hypnotics in the elderly: Therapeutic considerations: Part I. *Clinical Pharmacokinetics, 21,* 165–177.

Greenblatt, D. J., & Wright, C. E. (1993). Clinical pharmacokinetics of alprazolam: Therapeutic implications. *Clinical Pharmacokinetics, 24,* 453–471.

Haak, H. (1988). Pharmaceuticals in two Brazilian villages: Lay practices and perceptions. *Social Science and Medicine, 27,* 1415–1427.

Hasday, J. D., & Karch, F. E. (1981). Benzodiazepine prescribing in a family medicine center. *JAMA, 246,* 1321–1325.

Ives, T. J., Bentz, E. J., & Gwyther, R. E. (1987). Drug-related admissions to a family medicine inpatient service. *Archives of Internal Medicine, 147,* 1117–1120.

Jaffe, J. H. (1991, December). *Current concepts of addiction.* Paper presented at the second annual symposium of The American Academy of Psychiatrists in Alcoholism and Addictions, Naples, FL.

Jenike, M. A. (1989). Metabolic changes with aging. In M. A. Jenike (Ed.), *Geriatric psychiatry and psychopharmacology: A clinical approach.* Chicago: Year Book Medical Publishers.

Jinks, M. J., & Raschko, R. R. (1990). A profile of alcohol and prescription drug abuse in a high-risk community-based elderly population. *DICP, The Annals of Pharmacotherapy, 24,* 971–975.

Kashner, T. M., Rodell, D. E., Ogden, S. R., Guggenheim, F. G., & Karson, C. N. (1992). Outcomes and costs of two VA inpatient treatment programs for older alcoholic patients. *Hospital & Community Psychiatry, 43,* 985–989.

Kofoed, L. L., Tolson, R. L., Atkinson, R. M., Toth, R. L., & Turner, J. A. (1987). Treatment compliance of older alcoholics: An elder-specific approach is superior to "mainstreaming." *Journal of Studies on Alcohol, 48,* 47–51.

Kramer, M., German, P. S., Anthony, J. C., Von Korff, M., & Skinner, E. A. (1985). Patterns of mental disorders among the elderly residents of Eastern Baltimore. *Journal of Geriatrics Society, 33,* 236–245.

Lader, M. (1990). Drug development optimization: Benzodiazepines. *Agents and Actions, Supplements, 29,* 59–69.

Larson, E. B., Kukull, W. A., Buchner, D., & Reifler, B. V. (1987). Adverse drug reactions associated with global cognitive impairment in elderly persons. *Annals of Internal Medicine, 107,* 169–173.

Lockwood, A., & Berbatis, C. G. (1990). Psychotropic drugs in Australia: Consumption patterns. *Medical Journal of Australia, 153,* 604–611.

Mammo, A., & Weinbaum, D. F. (1993). Some factors that influence dropping out from outpatient alcoholism treatment facilities. *Journal of Studies on Alcohol, 54,* 92–101.

Mayer-Oakes, S. A., Kelman, G., Beers, M. H, Dejong, F., Matthias, R., Atchison, K. A., Lubben, J. E., & Schweitzer, S. O. (1993). Benzodiazepine use in older, community-dwelling southern Californians: Prevalence and clinical correlates. *Annals of Pharmacotherapy, 27,* 416–421.

Mellinger, G. D., Balter, M. B., Parry, H. R., Manheimer, D. I., & Cisin, I. H. (1974). An overview of psychotherapeutic drug use in the United States. In E. Josephson & E. E. Carrol (Eds.), *Drug use, epidemiological and sociological approaches* (pp. 340–359). New York: Hemisphere.

Meyers, A. R., Hingson, R., Mucatel, M., & Goldman, E. (1982). Social and psychologic correlates of problem drinking in old age. *Journal of the American Geriatrics Society, 30,* 452–456.

Miller, F., Whitcup, S., Sacks, M., & Lynch, P. E. (1985). Unrecognized drug dependence and withdrawal in the elderly. *Drug and Alcohol Dependence, 15,* 177–179.

Mishara, B. L., & McKim, W. (1993). Methodological issues in surveying older persons concerning drug use. *International Journal of Addictions, 28,* 305–326.

Mossey, J. M., & Shapiro, E. (1985). Physician use by the elderly over an eight-year period. *American Journal of Public Health, 75,* 1333–1334.

Muñoz, H. R., Dagnino, J. A., Rufs, J. A., & Bugedo, G. J. (1992). Benzodiazepine premedication causes hypoxemia during spinal anesthesia in geriatric patients. *Regional Anesthesia, 17,* 139–142.

Napoliello, M. J., & Domantay, A. G. (1991). Buspirone: A worldwide update. *British Journal of Psychiatry* Supplement 12, 40–44.

Nolan, L., & O'Malley, K. (1988). Patients, prescribing, and benzodiazepines. *European Journal of Clinical Pharmacology, 35,* 225–229.

North, D. A., McAvoy, B. R., & Powell, A. M. (1992). Benzodiazepine use in general practice: Is it a problem? *New Zealand Medical Journal, 105,* 287–289.

Ogur, B. (1986). Long day's journey into night: Women and prescription drug abuse. *Women and Health, 11,* 99–115.

Ostrom, J. R., Hammarlund, E. R., Christensen, D. B., Plein, J. B., & Kethley, A. J. (1985) Medication usage in an elderly population. *Medical Care, 23,* 157–164.

Price, R. H., Burke, A. C., D'Aunno, T. A., Klingel, D. M., McCaughrin, W. F., Rafferty, J. A., & Vaughn, T. E. (1991). Outpatient drug abuse treatment services: 1988: Results of a national survey. *NIDA Research Monographs, 106,* 63–92.

Rall, T. W. (1990). Hypnotics and sedatives; Ethanol. In A. G. Gilman, T. W. Rall, A. S. Nies, & P. Taylor (Eds.), *Goodman and Gilman's the pharmacological basis of therapeutics.* (8th ed.) (pp. 345–382). New York: Pergamon.

Ray, W. A., Thapa, P. B., & Shorr, R. I. (1993). Medications and the older driver. *Clinics in Geriatric Medicine, 9,* 413–438.

Robbins, C. (1989). Sex differences in psychosocial consequences of alcohol and drug abuse. *Journal of Health and Social Behavior, 30,* 117–130.

Robbins, C., & Clayton, R. R. (1989). Gender-related differences in psychoactive drug use among older adults. *Journal of Drug Issues, 19,* 207.

Rodríguez, F., Martínez, B., Saucedo, R., Cobos, F., García Morillas, M., Luna, J., & Puche, E. (1993). Aspectos diferenciales sobre la prescripción de fármacos en ancianos residentes de la zona nordeste de Granada: Estudio sobre 366 individuos. [Differential aspects of drug prescriptions in elderly people living in the northeast area of Granada: Study of 366 individuals.] *Medical Clinics: Barcelona, 100,* 24–27.

Rook, K. S., Thuras, P. D., & Lewis, M. A. (1990). Social control, health risk taking, and psychological distress among the elderly. *Psychology and Aging, 5,* 327–334.

Rossiter, L. F. (1983). Prescribed medicines: Findings from the National Medical Care Expenditure Survey. *American Journal of Public Health, 73,* 1312–1315.

Rummans, T. A., Davis, L. J., Jr., Morse, R. M., & Ivnik, R. J. (1993). Learning and memory impairment in older, detoxified, benzodiazepine-dependent patients. *Mayo Clinic Proceedings, 68,* 731–737.

Schweizer, E., Case, W. G., & Rickels, K. (1989). Benzodiazepine dependence and withdrawal in elderly patients. *American Journal of Psychiatry, 146,* 529–531.

Shorr, R. I., Bauwens, S. F., & Landefeld, C. S. (1990). Failure to limit quantities of benzodiazepine hypnotic drugs for outpatients: Placing the elderly at risk. *American Journal of Medicine, 89,* 725–732.

Shorr, R. I., Griffin, M. R., Daugherty, J. R., & Ray, W. A. (1992). Opioid analgesics and the risk of hip fracture in the elderly: Codeine and propoxyphene. *Journal of Gerontology, 47,* M111–M115.

Skegg, K., & Cox, B. (1991). Suicide in New Zealand 1957–1986: The influence of age, period and birth-cohort. *Australia & New Zealand Journal of Psychiatry, 25,* 181–190.

Skinner, H. A. (1990). Validation of the dependence syndrome: Have we crossed the half-life of this concept? In G. Edwards, & M. Lader (Eds.), *The nature of drug dependence* (pp. 41–73). New York: Oxford University Press.

Sorock, G. S., & Shimkin, E. E. (1988). Benzodiazepine sedatives and the risk of falling in a community-dwelling elderly cohort. *Archives of Internal Medicine, 148,* 2441–2444.

Szwabo, P. A. (1993). Substance abuse in older women. *Clinics in Geriatric Medicine, 9,* 197–208.

Task Force on Benzodiazepine Dependency. (1990) *Benzodiazepine dependence, toxicity and abuse.* Task Force Report of the American Psychiatric Association. Washington, DC: American Psychiatric Association.

Tucker, G. J. (1994). Introduction: Part I. Treatment approaches to anxiety, depression, and aggression in the elderly. *Journal of Clinical Psychiatry 55,* Supplement: 3–4.

U. S. Department of Commerce. (1987, December). *Drug utililization in the U.S. 1986: Eighth Annual Review.* Rockville, MD: Department of Health and Human Services.

U. S. Department of Commerce. (1989, April). *Drug utilization in the U.S. 1988: Tenth Annual Review.* Rockville, MD: Department of Health and Human Services.

U. S. Department of Commerce. (1991, April). *Drug utilization in the U. S. 1989: Eleventh Annual Review.* Rockville, MD: Department of Health and Human Services,

U. S. General Accounting Office. (1987, July). *Report to the Chairman, Special Committee on Aging, U.S. Senate, Medicare, Prescription Drug Issues.* Washington, DC: Author.

Weissman, M. M., Myers, J. K., Tischler, G. L., Holzer, C. E. III, Leaf, P. J., Orvaschel, H., & Brody, J. A. (1985). Psychiatric disorders (DSM–III) and cognitive impairment among the elderly in the U. S. urban community. *Acta Psychiatrica Scandinavica, 71,* 366–379.

Wells-Parker, E., Miles, S., & Spencer, B. (1983). Stress experiences and drinking histories of elderly drunken-driving offenders. *Journal of Studies on Alcohol, 44,* 429–437.

Wesson, D. R., & Smith, D. E. (1990). Prescription drug abuse: Patient, physician, and cultural responsibilities. *Western Journal of Medicine, 152,* 613–616.

Whittington, R. M. (1984). Dextropropoxyphene deaths: Coroner's report. *Human Toxicology, Supplement 3:* 175S–185S.

Zisook, S., & Schuchter, S. R. (1991). Depression through the first year after the death of a spouse. *American Journal of Psychiatry, 148,* 1346–1352.

8

Interactions between Alcohol and Other Drugs

Wendy L. Adams, MD, MPH

INTRODUCTION

Many medications have a potential for adverse interactions with alcohol. A number of different mechanisms can cause such interactions. Some medications alter the metabolism of alcohol, causing higher blood alcohol levels than expected. Alcohol, on the other hand, alters the metabolism of many drugs, affecting the levels of these drugs in the body. Alcohol can also interfere with the effectiveness of medications and exacerbate their side effects. Although some interactions between drugs and alcohol are caused only by regular heavy use of alcohol, some may occur even with only moderate drinking. Since elderly people use medications frequently and also commonly use alcohol, they are at particularly high risk for problems resulting from the concurrent use of these substances. In this chapter, I will review the epidemiologic data on use of alcohol and medications among elderly people and discuss the pharmacology and clinical importance of potential adverse drug-alcohol interactions in this population.

THE EPIDEMIOLOGIC DATA

Use of Alcohol among Elderly People

A majority of older people drink some alcohol, though many studies have shown a decrease in alcohol use and abuse in old age (Adams, Garry, Rhyne,

Hunt, & Goodwin, 1990; Barnes, 1979; Cahalan & Cisin, 1968; Fillmore, 1987; Glynn, Bouchard, LoCastro, & Laird, 1985; McKim & Quinlan, 1991; Meyers, Hingson, Mucatel, & Goldman, 1982; Smart & Liban, 1981). Light to moderate drinking is the rule, but the number of older people who are heavy drinkers and alcoholics is not trivial. One population-based study in western New York state found that 69% of people over 60 used some alcohol; 7% consumed 3 or more drinks per day (Barnes, 1979). A study from Boston showed that 47% of elderly people used some alcohol; 16% were daily drinkers (Meyers, Goldman, Hingson, & Scotch, 1981–82). In San Diego County, California, a study of drinking practices found that 62% of people aged 65–74 and 50% of people over age 75 used alcohol (Molgaard, Nakamura, Stanford, Peddecord, & Morton, 1990). Eight percent of respondents age 65–74 and 6% of those age 75 or over were heavy drinkers. Alcoholism is less common among older people than young or middle-aged people, but 2–4% of people over 65 are estimated to be alcoholics (Myers et al., 1984). Age, sex, and geographic location all have an effect on the prevalence of alcohol use and alcohol problems. An "old-old" population, age 80 and older, for instance, will have a lower prevalence of alcoholism than a "young-old" population. In virtually all studies, men are substantially more likely than women to use and abuse alcohol. Per capita consumption of alcohol varies greatly from place to place and heavy drinking varies with it.

Alcohol abuse among elderly people has a substantial impact on the health care system. In clinical settings, the prevalence of alcohol problems is higher than in population-based studies, with a prevalence of 5–10% in out-patient settings (Jones, Lindsey, Yount, Soltys, & Farani-Enayat, 1993; Magruder-Habib, Saltz, & Barron, 1986); 15% in emergency department settings (Adams, Magruder-Habib, Trued, & Broome, 1992; Rivara et al., 1993); and up to 21% in inpatient settings (Curtis, Goller, Stokes, Levine, & Moore, 1989). One study that examined the frequency of alcohol-related hospitalizations found that they were as common among people 65 and older as among those in the 25–44 age group (Stinson, Dufour, & Bertolucci, 1989). Another study found that alcohol -related hospitalizations are more common than hospitalizations for heart attacks among people 65 and older (Adams, Yuan, Barboriak, & Rimm, 1993).

Use of Medications among Elderly People

Use of medications is also very common among elderly people. The Established Populations for Epidemiologic Studies of the Elderly (EPESE) study surveyed a large sample of elderly people in geographically diverse communities. That study showed that 60–78% of people age 65 and older used prescription drugs, with some variability depending on age, sex, and geographic location; nonprescription drugs were also commonly used (Chrischilles et al., 1992). Sixty percent of men and 41% of women used alcohol in the EPESE survey, and concurrent drug and alcohol use was noted to be common, though specifics of potential drug and alcohol interactions have not been reported. Alcohol users were as likely as abstainers to be taking prescription medications.

Other studies have also shown a high frequency of use of medications among elderly people. In a study of elderly residents of low-income housing facilities, Ostrom, Hammarlund, Christensen, Plein, and Kethley (1985) found that 75% of those interviewed were using at least one prescription medication; 52% were taking three or more. The Cardiovascular Health Study found that 76% of a large sample of community-dwelling elderly respondents were taking at least one medication. In that study, the average number of medications taken per person was 2.3 (Psaty et al., 1992). Bernstein, Folkman, and Lazarus (1989) report on a small, well-educated sample of elderly San Francisco Bay area residents. Ninety-four percent of respondents in that study took medications, and 94% used some alcohol. The authors estimated the potential for adverse interactions between drugs or between drugs and alcohol. Of 46 potential drug interactions identified, 27 (59%) involved alcohol. Adams (1995) reported on a group of elderly (mean age 83) residents of a retirement community in Wisconsin. Seventy-seven percent used medications, 47% used alcohol, and 38% used alcohol concurrently with medications with a strong potential for adverse interactions. Another community-based study showed that 25% of elderly respondents used alcohol concurrently with one or more drugs with potential to interact adversely (Forster, Pollow, & Stoller, 1993).

Clearly, the high frequency of medication and alcohol use in the elderly population puts these people at a high risk for adverse interactions between the substances.

Adverse Drug Reactions among Elderly People

Although concurrent use of alcohol and medications is common in elderly people, data are lacking on actual adverse events resulting from such interactions. We do know that a preponderance of adverse drug reactions occur in elderly people. In one population-based study in Iowa, for instance, 10% of elderly respondents reported an adverse drug reaction in the year prior to the survey. Analgesics and central nervous system drugs, which often interact adversely with alcohol, were among the most commonly used (Chrischilles, Segar, & Wallace, 1992). In the outpatient setting, 25% of elderly patients in one study reported at least one adverse effect of a medication (Klein, German, Levine, Feroli, & Ardeny, 1984). Adverse drug reactions are also common in the hospital setting. Twelve percent of elderly people admitted on one inpatient general medical service had been admitted for adverse drug reactions (Colt & Shapiro, 1989). Nonsteroidal anti-inflammatory drugs, which have strong potential for adverse interactions with alcohol, were among the most common offending drugs. In a study of people admitted to the hospital for adverse drug reactions, Caranasos, Stewart, and Cluff found that 40% were elderly (1974). Whether the high frequency of adverse drug reactions among elderly people is due to an increased sensitivity to side effects of medication or is the result of other factors is somewhat controversial (Gurwitz & Avorn, 1991). As people age, they become more likely to take multiple medications. Use of multiple medications is itself associated with an increased risk of adverse effects of medication. Some studies have found that the number of medications taken was at least as important a risk factor for adverse drug reactions as advanced age (Chrischilles, Segar, & Wallace, 1992; Col, Fanale, & Kronholm, 1990; Colt & Shapiro, 1989; Hutchinson, Flegel, Kramer, Leduc, & Kong, 1986; Klein et al., 1984). Medical illness is also more common in elderly people and may predispose them to adverse drug reactions. Since the presence of medical illness is itself reflected by the number of medications an individual takes (Grymonpre, Mitenko, Sitar, Aoki, & Monrgomery, 1988), it is difficult to distinguish the separate effects of advanced age, multiple medications, and medical illness on the risk of adverse drug reactions. Few studies have been able to control adequately for the number of medications taken and the medical illnesses present when investigating whether age itself is a risk factor for adverse drug reactions. Bias in the selection of subjects and possible age-related differences in the accuracy of reporting are other factors that sometimes complicate the endeavor.

Alcohol, though a commonly used "drug," has been included in very few studies of adverse drug reactions or interactions. Simply by virtue of increasing the number of drugs taken, alcohol used in conjunction with other medication should increase the probability of an adverse drug reaction. The pharmacologic properties of alcohol make it more likely than many drugs to cause adverse reactions and interactions. We shall now examine the pharmacology of potential adverse interactions between alcohol and medications and the types of adverse events that may occur.

AGING, ALCOHOL, AND PHARMACOLOGY

Absorption

Several age-related changes in the gastrointestinal tract might be expected to affect the absorption of drugs. Gastric pH is increased and gastric emptying is prolonged with increasing age; intestinal blood flow and motility are decreased. Surprisingly, however, these phenomena affect the absorption of relatively few drugs (Cusack & Vestal, 1986; Greenblatt, Sellers, & Shader, 1982; Montamat, Cusack, & Vestal, 1989). A few notable exceptions may have an impact on the elderly person who drinks and uses medications concurrently. Some sedative benzodiazepines (Briggs, Castleden, & Kraft, 1980; Shader, Greenblatt, Harmatz, Franke, & Koch-Weser, 1977) appear to have an increased rate of absorption in older people. Because these drugs and alcohol both depress the central nervous system, there is a potential for serious toxicity when the two are combined.

Alcohol itself has effects on the gastrointestinal tract that may affect the absorption of some drugs. Acutely, alcohol may delay gastric emptying (Nimmo, 1976) and cause irritation of the gastric mucosa. This could have an impact on the absorption of some drugs, though the clinical importance of this effect has not been extensively studied. However, alcohol ingestion has been shown to increase the absorption of some benzodiazepines when they are taken concurrently (Hayes, Pablo, Radomski, & Palmer, 1977).

Alcohol is absorbed rapidly and efficiently from the stomach and small intestine (Auty & Branch, 1977). There is, however, gastric metabolism of alcohol that mediates the blood alcohol level acquired from a given amount consumed. This "first pass" effect is caused by the enzyme alcohol dehydrogenase (ADH) in the stomach (DiPadova et al., 1992; Julkunen, Dipadova, & Lieber, 1985) It is known that premenopausal women develop higher blood alcohol levels per amount consumed, largely because of a gender-related difference in gastric alcohol dehydrogenase activity (Frezza et al., 1990). Aging also appears to decrease the activity of this enzyme, at least in men; and this contributes to the higher blood alcohol levels elderly people develop per amount of alcohol ingested (Pozzato et al., 1995; Seitz et al., 1993). There is an important potential for interaction between alcohol and medications at this level. Gastric alcohol dehydrogenase is inhibited by the ulcer medications cimetidine, ranitidine, and nizatidine (Caballeria et al., 1991; Caballeria, Baraona, Rodamilans, & Lieber, 1989; DiPadova et al., 1992; Hernandez-Munoz et al., 1990) and also by aspirin (Roine, Gentry, Hernandez-Munoz, Baraona, & Lieber, 1990). The level of blood alcohol rises when alcohol is consumed after ingestion of these drugs, which are all commonly used by older people. Interestingly, cimetidine does not appear to inhibit ADH in the liver (Lieber, 1991).

Overall, the risk of drug-alcohol interactions at the level of absorption is due to an increase in the absorption of alcohol and of some benzodiazepines. There is some increase in absorption with aging alone, but some commonly used medications also cause greater absorption of alcohol. Higher blood alcohol levels per amount of alcohol consumed may cause somnolence and confusion and may impair the motor skills required for operating a vehicle or an appliance.

Distribution

There are clinically important changes in the distribution of drugs in the body with increasing age. Age-related decreases in lean body mass and total body water, as well as an increase in body fat, are largely responsible (Cusack & Vestal, 1986; Vestal et al., 1975). Drugs that are water-soluble, such as alcohol, generally have a smaller volume of distribution in the body because of these phenomena. The effect is higher blood levels of alcohol and other water-soluble drugs per dose in elderly people than in their younger counterparts (Vestal et al., 1976). Most fat-soluble drugs, however (such as many of the benzodiazepines), have an increased volume of distribution in older people and may consequently have prolonged half-lives (Greenblatt et al., 1982). Although the distribution of drugs in the body may not affect the mechanism by which drugs and alcohol interact, if a drug is in the body for a longer time or at a higher level, it will have greater opportunity to interact with alcohol. For example, a prolonged half-life of diazepam combined with an unexpectedly high blood alcohol level may cause far greater impairment in alertness and psychomotor function than the elderly consumer of the substances anticipated. The unwitting older person may find himself or herself sleepy, confused, off-balance, and unable to drive safely.

Metabolism

Many drugs are transformed by liver enzymes to metabolites that are less active and more readily excretable. This process depends both on blood flow to the liver and on the activity of the enzymes involved. Although there are decreases with age in hepatic blood flow and liver mass, studies of age-related changes in the hepatic metabolism of drugs have had varying results, and the clinical importance of these phenomena is uncertain (Cusack & Vestal, 1986; Greenblatt et al., 1982; Montamat et al., 1989; Scott & Mitchell, 1988).

In the only study of the effect of age on the metabolism of ethanol, Vestal et al., (1976) did not find an altered rate of metabolism with age. Much of the potential for interaction between drugs and alcohol, however, involves active and complex metabolic processes in the liver.

The liver cells are the site of most ethanol metabolism, though extrahepatic metabolism does occur. Alcohol dehydrogenase (ADH) is predominantly responsible for this process. The activity of this enzyme does not appear to decline with increasing age (Wynne et al., 1992). It can be inhibited, however, by medications. Chlorpromazine and possibly isoniazid inhibit hepatic ADH, causing decreased ethanol metabolism and higher blood alcohol levels. Other hepatic enzymes are also involved in the metabolism of alcohol and play an important role in the interactions of alcohol with other drugs. Many drugs are oxidized in the liver by a family of enzymes known as the cytochrome P450 system. Part of this enzyme system, known as the microsomal ethanol oxidizing system (MEOS), plays a role in ethanol metabolism, especially at high blood alcohol levels or during chronic use of alcohol (Lieber, 1991). Activity of cytochrome P450 enzymes is induced by chronic heavy alcohol use; this phenomenon is involved in many drug-alcohol interactions (Lieber, 1991). The increased enzyme activity causes more rapid breakdown of drugs. Because the drugs are being rapidly broken down, blood levels of the drugs are lowered. Some of the important medications affected by enzyme induction are the anticoagulant warfarin, the antiseizure drug phenytoin, the sedative diazepam and other benzodiazepines, the antihypertensive propranolol, and the antimicrobial isoniazid.

In contrast to the enzyme induction cause by chronic heavy drinking, short-term (acute) heavy drinking has an essentially opposite effect on drug metabolism. The most important effect of acute heavy drinking is inhibition of hepatic enzymes. The predominant mechanism by which this occurs appears to be direct competition for cytochrome P450 processes (Lieber, 1991). When a large amount of alcohol is ingested acutely, the enzyme system is occupied by the alcohol and is not as available for drug metabolism. Less of the drug is broken down, and higher blood levels result. Warfarin, diazepam, and isoniazid, as well as many other drugs, are affected by this phenomenon.

Since long-term heavy use of alcohol causes increased metabolism and short-term heavy use causes decreased metabolism of some of the same drugs, prescribing for heavy drinkers can be a nightmare for the clinician. Safe use of anticoagulants and antiseizure medications can be virtually impossible for patients who abuse alcohol.

Catalase is another enzyme capable of alcohol metabolism, but appears to play a less important role under ordinary circumstances (Lieber, 1991).

Metabolism of alcohol by all of these enzymes results in the production of acetaldehyde, a compound highly toxic to the liver. It, in turn, is metabolized by another enzyme in the liver, acetaldehyde dehydrogenase. When this enzyme is inhibited by a drug, elevated levels of acetaldehyde are produced, resulting in the unpleasant "disulfiram-like reaction" discussed below.

Excretion

Renal elimination of many drugs declines with age. Decreases in two processes in the kidney—glomerular filtration rate and tubular secretion—both contribute to a decline in creatinine clearance in a majority of elderly people (Greenblatt et al., 1982; Montamat et al., 1989). There are probably not many interactions between drugs and alcohol that occur at this stage of drug handling. Indirectly, however, alcohol may affect the excretion of some drugs. For instance, alcohol does inhibit antidiuretic hormone, and this increases urine production transiently. This could cause an increased rate of renal excretion of some drugs, but the clinical importance of this effect has not been studied.

Pharmacodynamics

Pharmacodynamics refers to the way drugs affect the body. Susceptibility to the effects of some drugs increases with age. Drugs that suppress central nervous system activity, such as benzodiazepines, narcotics and antihistamines, often cause increased sedation in elderly people (Greenblatt et al., 1991; Koch-Weser, 1983). There is also an increased risk of falls among elderly people using long-acting benzodiazepines, which implies an increased sensitivity to the CNS effects of these drugs (Ray, Griffin, Schaffner, Baugh, & Melton, 1987; Sorock & Shimkin, 1988). Alcohol, as a CNS depressant, has an additive sedative effect when combined with these drugs. The combination is well-known to cause serious impairment of the motor skills and judgment needed for driving, operating machinery, and many other activities.

There are few studies of the effects of increasing age on the response to alcohol. Those that have been done do show some increasing susceptibility to its psychomotor effects (Vogel-Sprott & Barrett, 1984). It seems probable, therefore, that there is an even greater risk of ill effects due to the combination of alcohol and sedating drugs in people of advanced age. Further research is needed to define the specifics of these effects. However, enough is known to recommend that physicians should advise patients taking CNS-depressant drugs to abstain from alcohol.

Other drug effects may also change with increasing age. Nonsteroidal anti-inflammatory drugs (NSAIDs) have been implicated in an increased risk of peptic ulcer disease and gastrointestinal hemorrhage in elderly people (Gabriel, Jaakkimainen, & Bobardier, 1991; Griffin, Ray, & Schaffner, 1991; Guess et al., 1988). There is evidence that several of the NSAIDs, when used concurrently with alcohol, increase bleeding times, and therefore increase the risk of hemorrhage. Since gastritis and gastrointestinal bleeding are common complications of alcoholism as well as of NSAIDs, there is a serious potential for bleeding from the gastrointestinal tract as a result of concurrent use of NSAIDs and alcohol.

Another interaction of alcohol and drugs at their site of action can occur with antihypertensives and vasodilators. A severe drop in blood pressure may occur acutely when alcohol is used concurrently with reserpine, methyldopa, hydralazine, nitroglycerine, and other antihypertensive or vasodilating drugs (Lieber, 1991).

To summarize, there are many ways in which alcohol and drugs may interact pharmacologically. Age-related changes in drug handling affect these processes and increase the risk of clinically important interactions. The absorption of alcohol is increased by aging as well as by some commonly used drugs. The age-related decrease in total body water also contributes to elevated blood alcohol in older people. Drugs and alcohol frequently interact at the level of metabolism in the liver. Pharmacodynamic interactions, or effects on the action of the drugs, can occur between alcohol and several medications. Alcohol may also exacerbate the disease for which a medication is prescribed, indirectly decreasing the effectiveness of a medication. Common examples are hypertension, diabetes, and peptic ulcer disease.

CLINICAL APPLICATION: DRUG-ALCOHOL INTERACTIONS

Now that we have reviewed the epidemiology and pharmacology of drug and alcohol use, let us turn to a discussion of the ways in which these interactions can manifest in clinical situations.

There are several ways in which the age-related changes in drug handling and the frequent concurrent use of alcohol and medications may work together to cause clinically important effects. The types of clinical events that may be caused by interactions between alcohol and medications are summarized in Table 8.1 and discussed below.

TABLE 8.1 Potential Drug-Alcohol Interactions

Clinical effect	Drugs involved	Comments
Increased blood alcohol levels	Cimetidine, ranitidine, aspirin levels even with moderate drinking.	This interaction can cause significant elevation of blood alcohol
Increased metabolism of drug (chronic heavy alcohol use)	Benzodiazepines, warfarin, tolbutamide, propranolol, isoniazid use.	Chronic heavy drinkers will require higher doses of these drugs. This effect may last for a few weeks after cessation of alcohol
Increased hepatotoxicity (chronic heavy alcohol use)	Acetaminophen, isoniazid, phenylbutazone	Heavy drinkers can experience liver necrosis even with therapeutic doses of these drugs.
Decreased metabolism of drug (acute alcohol use)	Narcotics, barbiturates, benzodiazepines, chloral hydrate, warfarin	Binge drinkers can develop toxicity from usual doses of these drugs during binges.
Increased bleeding time	Aspirin, NSAIDs	Can occur with moderate use.
Gastrointestinal inflammation and bleeding	Aspirin, NSAIDs	Can occur with moderate use. Binge drinkers are probably most at risk of hemorrhage.
Sedation, psychomotor impairment	Benzodiazepines, narcotics, tricyclic antidepressants, antihistamines, barbiturates	Degree of CNS impairment depends on doses of alcohol and drugs as well as individual tolerance.
Disulfiramlike reactions	Oral hypoglycemics (tolbutamide, chlorpropamide), antibiotics (metronidazole, sulfonamides, griseofulvin, cefoperazone), phenylbutazone, nitroglycerine	All patients who take these drugs should be warned about the interaction but heavier drinkers are at the highest risk.
Interference with effectiveness of drugs	Antihypertensives, antidiabetic drugs, drugs for CHF, gout, ulcer disease	When these drugs do not have their expected effect, be alert to possible heavy drinking.
Hypotension	Reserpine, aldomet, hydralazine, nitroglycerine	Heavy and binge drinkers are most at risk.

Increased Blood Alcohol Levels

As discussed above, recent studies have shown an important interaction between alcohol and certain histamine receptor antagonists, which are commonly used to treat peptic ulcer disease and other upper gastrointestinal problems (Caballeria et al., 1989; Caballeria et al., 1991; Hernandez-Munoz et al., 1990). Cimetidine, ranitidine, and nizatidine inhibit gastric alcohol dehydrogenase. After ingestion of these drugs, blood alcohol levels are 30–40% higher than would be seen after an equal amount of alcohol alone (DiPadova et al., 1992). Famotidine does not appear to have the same effect (DiPadova et al., 1992), nor does the newer ulcer treatment drug omeprazole (Roine, Hernandez-Munoz, Baraona, Greenstein, & Lieber, 1992). Even in the absence of these drugs, elderly people develop higher blood alcohol levels than younger people. A further increase due to interaction with one of these drugs may cause an unwitting elderly person to experience unexpectedly severe effects from a small amount of alcohol intake. Impaired balance may predispose to falls, slowed reaction time may lead to an automobile accident, and excessive sleepiness may interfere with many activities. It is important for physicians to make their patients aware of this interaction, advise abstention from alcohol while using these drugs, and especially to warn about the danger of driving an automobile if alcohol should be used while taking them. For patients unable or unwilling to abstain, such as chronic alcoholics, famotidine or omeprazole should probably be used preferentially for treatment of peptic ulcer disease or gastritis.

Aspirin has also been shown to decrease ADH activity in vitro and increase blood alcohol levels in vivo (Roine et al., 1990). Although physicians have less control over the use of this drug, it is commonly recommended for the prevention of adverse cardiovascular events and for pain. A warning about potential increases in blood alcohol levels should accompany the advice to use aspirin regularly for prevention of stroke or heart attack.

Altered Drug Levels and Hepatic Toxicity

As noted above, long-term heavy use of alcohol induces activity of several hepatic microsomal drug-metabolizing enzymes. The effect is an increase in the rate of metabolism of many drugs, including alcohol itself, benzodiazepines, warfarin, tolbutamide, propranolol, dilantin, and isoniazid (Lieber, 1991). Because of the increased metabolism, blood levels of the drug are lowered. Higher doses of alcohol or the drug are required to achieve the desired effect, and tolerance to alcohol and several other drugs results. These drugs have a much shorter half-life in alcoholics, and doses must be adjusted accordingly. The effect may persist up to weeks after cessation of alcohol use, so careful attention to changes in dose requirements is needed for a long period of time.

Since many people move into and out of problem drinking over time, physicians must be constantly alert to the changing potential for drug-alcohol interactions in these patients. For example, a heavy drinker who has an artificial heart valve requiring anticoagulation may need very high doses of warfarin. If this patient decides to abstain without informing the physician, he or she may suddenly become overly anticoagulated a few weeks later and suffer a hemorrhage. A patient with seizures treated with phenytoin, whose alcoholism has not been recognized, will require high doses of the drug to maintain therapeutic levels. If hospitalized for another problem, the patient will probably stop drinking alcohol, and liver enzyme activity will eventually decline. As a result, the patient's requirements for the drug decrease. If the dose is not decreased, he or she may develop phenytoin overdose . These problems and others related to fluctuating drug requirements by heavy drinkers can be prevented only by advising patients about the potential interactions and by vigilance on the part of the prescribing physician.

Another result of enzyme induction by long-term heavy use of alcohol is the increased production of metabolites toxic to the liver during the breakdown of certain drugs (Lieber, 1991). The most notable examples of this effect include the hepatotoxicity of isoniazid, phenylbutazone, and acetaminophen. An alcoholic who sprains an ankle, unaware of the potential liver toxicity from the combination of alcohol and acetaminophen, may take relatively large doses of this drug for pain. Severe liver necrosis can ensue. Since acetaminophen is easily available over the counter, appropriate labeling and public education should be the main routes for warning people about this potentially life-threatening combination. Alcoholics have an increased susceptibility to tuberculosis (MacGregor, 1986), and isoniazid is commonly used to treat it. This combination may also be highly toxic to the liver. Patients who may be heavy drinkers must be monitored especially carefully for elevations of liver enzymes while using these drugs.

Short-term alcohol consumption can inhibit hepatic drug metabolism, as discussed above. Because alcohol may compete for drug-metabolizing enzyme activity, many drugs, such as benzodiazepines, narcotics, and warfarin, will have slower metabolism and increased concentrations after ingestion of a large amount of alcohol. The clinical importance of this effect may be reflected by increased sedation or delirium from benzodiazepines or narcotics, increased prothrombin time and bleeding complications from warfarin, or other toxicities. It is incumbent on physicians, nurses, pharmacists, and other health care professionals to prevent these interactions, as far as possible, by consistently educating patients about the potential risks of using these drugs concurrently with alcohol every time they are prescribed. A history of alcohol use and a review of potential interactions with the patient's medications should be done frequently at office visits.

Gastrointestinal Inflammation and Bleeding

Arthritis and other musculoskeletal problems are among the most common problems for which older people consult physicians. Nonsteroidal anti-inflammatory drugs and aspirin are very commonly prescribed or recommended for these disorders. These drugs are known to cause peptic ulcer disease and gastrointestinal bleeding. The effects of NSAIDs alone on the GI tract appear to be more severe in older people (Griffin et al., 1991; Guess et al., 1988). Mortality from GI hemorrhage is also increased in elderly people (Guess et al., 1988). The gastrointestinal side effects of NSAIDs and aspirin have been exacerbated by alcohol in animal models (Davenport, 1969) and in humans (DeSchepper et al., 1978). Since the NSAIDs and aspirin are used very commonly by elderly people and at least half of elderly people use alcohol, the potential for gastrointestinal hemorrhage is very great. Another complication of aspirin, ibuprofen, and indomethacin when used concurrently with alcohol is an increase in bleeding time (Deykin, Janson, & McMahon, 1982), which further increases the potential for adversity due to this combination. Since ibuprofen and aspirin are available without prescription, a general warning to anyone likely to use them—e.g., people with musculoskeletal pain of any sort—is in order.

Sedation, Delirium, and Impaired Psychomotor Function

Another of the potentially most serious interactions of drugs with alcohol involves depression of the central nervous system (CNS). Alcohol itself is a CNS depressant. When it is combined with other CNS-depressant drugs, or drugs that combine synergistically with alcohol to impair consciousness or psychomotor function, the effect may be severe. Psychotropics are the category of drugs most likely to produce this effect. Benzodiazepines in particular are used very commonly by elderly people (Mayer-Oakes et al., 1993) and have a strong potential for this type of interaction. Both sedation and impairment of the skills needed for driving (Kuitunen, Mattial, & Seppala, 1990; Linnoila et al., 1990) have been documented and can cause serious adverse outcomes for elderly people. Some tricyclic antidepressants also interact with alcohol to impair alertness and motor functioning; amitriptyline and nortriptyline have been studied most (Dorian et al., 1983; Tiller, 1990). Studies of the CNS effects of drug-alcohol combinations have uniformly been done on healthy young subjects. Since elderly people are more susceptible to the effects of some benzodiazepines and are more likely to have illnesses that predispose them to adverse effects of drugs, it is quite possible, if not probable, that older people are even more likely than the subjects of most studies to experience adverse drug-alcohol interactions of this sort. It is imperative that health care providers advise their patients to abstain from alcohol while using other CNS-depressant drugs and particularly advise them not to drive a motor vehicle if concurrent use should occur.

In the past, barbiturates and alcohol used together were a common cause of severe CNS depression and death (Bogan & Smith, 1967). Fortunately, barbiturates are no longer in common use as sedatives, although phenobarbitol is still in common use as an antiepileptic. Physicians should still be cognizant of the potential for very serious interaction between this class of drugs and alcohol, and they should conscientiously warn their patients about the potential for severe adverse reactions from this combination.

Disulfiram-Like Reactions

Disulfiram (Antabuse) is an antioxidant drug that inhibits several enzyme systems. Because it inhibits aldehyde dehydrogenase, concurrent use of this drug and alcohol causes high systemic levels of acetaldehyde. An unpleasant reaction ensues, with symptoms including headache, flushing, nausea, and dyspnea. In severe reactions, hypotension and ECG changes may occur. When disulfiram is taken by abstaining alcoholics, the fear of this reaction may help them maintain sobriety. Because the effects may have more serious consequences in elderly people, physicians often avoid prescribing disulfiram for older abstaining alcoholics. However, other drugs may produce a similar reaction when taken concurrently with alcohol. These include oral hypoglycemic agents, including chlorpropamide and tolbutamide; antibiotics, including metronidazole, sulfonamides, quinacrine, and cefoperazone; some NSAIDs, including phenylbutazone; and nitrates, which may cause disulfiramlike reactions when used concurrently with alcohol (Lieber, 1992).

Interference with Effectiveness of Medications

Another type of interaction between alcohol and medications occurs when alcohol adversely affects the illness for which the medication was prescribed. Many of the illnesses common in old age can be exacerbated by alcohol. In middle-aged people, consumption of 2–3 drinks per day appears to be sufficient to contribute to hypertension (MacMahon, 1987). Since older people develop a higher blood alcohol level per drink, fewer drinks may cause this effect. Diabetes is also adversely affected by alcohol (Gordon & Lieber, 1992). Heart muscle functioning is impaired by heavy alcohol intake (Friedman, 1992), interfering with treatment of congestive heart failure. Upper gastrointestinal conditions, such as peptic ulcer disease, reflux esophagitis, and gastritis, are another group of disorders caused or aggravated by alcohol.

Before and during treatment for these conditions, it is incumbent on physicians to ask their patients about alcohol use, to intervene if appropriate, and to consider the effects of alcohol use on the illnesses for which they treat their patients. When a medication does not seem to be having the desired or expected effect, alcohol abuse may be the cause. Many older alcohol abusers have come to the attention of their physicians because of medical complications, such as blood pressure that was difficult to control or diabetes that was hard to manage.

CONCLUSION

Alcohol has great potential to interact with many of the medications in common use among elderly people. Some effects, such as induction of hepatic enzymes, require a quite heavy alcohol intake, and are a problem mainly for the 10% of elderly people who drink heavily. Other effects, such as the higher blood alcohol levels resulting from concurrent use of cimetidine and ranitidine, can occur with moderate use of alcohol. The potential for these interactions, therefore, could affect the 50% of elderly people who are light or moderate drinkers. There is little information on actual adverse events resulting from such interactions, and further research is needed to elucidate their importance. In the meantime, however, sufficient information exists to warrant increased efforts on the part of health care providers to educate elderly patients about the high potential for drug-alcohol interactions. Information about the risks of concurrent use of alcohol and medications should be provided by physicians when prescribing drugs, by pharmacists when dispensing them, and by nurses when educating patients about medication. Oral discussions, written instructions, and medication labeling could be used, as well as other modalities.

Too often, health care professionals assume that elderly people do not drink. At least half of elderly people do use alcohol, and a substantial number drink heavily. Failure to warn people about the risk of interactions between their medications and alcohol is a failure on the part of health care professionals to prevent serious morbidity and sometimes death.

Our population is aging: it has been estimated that by the year 2030, 25% of the population of the United States will be 60 or older (U.S. Department of Health and Human Services, 1990). As the elderly population expands, we will see an increase in the absolute number of older drinkers over the next few decades, even if the proportion of older people who use alcohol remains constant. Unless the health practices of these people change markedly, many of them will use medicines. It is imperative that we define the clinical importance of drug and alcohol interactions more clearly and work to prevent the many adverse effects that can occur.

REFERENCES

Adams, W. L., Garry P. J., Rhyne, R., Hunt, W. C., & Goodwin, J. S., (1990). Alcohol intake in the healthy elderly. *Journal of the American Geriatrics Society, 38,* 211–216.

Adams, W. L., Magruder-Habib, K., Trued, S., & Broome, H. L. (1992). Alcohol abuse in elderly emergency department patients. *Journal of Geriatrics Society, 40,* 1236–1240.

Adams, W. L., Yuan, Z., Barboriak, J. J., & Rimm, A. A. (1993). Alcohol-related hospitalizations in elderly people: Prevalence and geographic variation in the United States. *JAMA, 270,* 1222–1225.

Adams, W. L. (1995). Potential for adverse drug-alcohol interactions in elderly retirement community residents. *Journal of American Geriatrics Society, 43,* 1021–1025.

Auty, R. M., & Branch, R. A. (1977). Pharmacokinetics and pharmacodynamics of ethanol, whiskey, and ethanol with isopropyl, isobutyl, and isoamyl alcohols. *Clinical and Pharmacological Therapeutics, 22,* 242–249.

Barnes, G. M. (1979). Alcohol use among older persons: Findings from a western New York State general population survey. *Journal of the American Geriatrics Society, 27,* 244–250.

Bernstein, L. R., Folkman, S., & Lazarus, R. S. (1989). Characterization of the use and misuse of medications by an elderly ambulatory population. *Medical Care, 27,* 654–663.

Bogan, J., & Smith, H. (1967). Analytical investigation of barbiturate poisoning: Description of methods and a survey of results. *Journal of Forensic Science, 7,* 37–45 .

Briggs, R. S., Castleden, C. M., & Kraft, C. A. (1980). Improved hypnotic treatment using chlormethiazole and temazepam. *British Medical Journal, 280,* 601–604.

Caballeria, J., Baraona, E., Deulofeu, R., Hernandez-Munoz, R., Rodes, J., & Lieber, C. S. (1991). Effects of H2-receptor antagonists on gastric alcohol dehydrogenase activity. *Digestive Diseases Science, 36,* 1673–1679.

Caballeria, J., Baraona, E., Rodamilans, M., & Lieber, C. S. (1989). Effects of cimetidine on gastric alcohol dehydrogenase activity and blood ethanol levels. *Gastroenterology, 96,* 388–392.

Cahalan, D., & Cisin, A. (1968). American drinking practices: Summary of findings from a national probability sample. *Quarterly Journal of Studies on Alcohol, 29,* 139–151.

Caranasos, G. J., Stewart, R. B., & Cluff, L. E. (1974). Drug induced illness leading to hospitalization. *JAMA, 228,* 713–717.

Chrischilles, E. A., Foley, D. J., Wallace, R. B., Lemke, J. H., Semla, T. P., Hanlon, J. T., Glynn, R. J., Ostfeld, A. M., & Guralnik, J. M. (1992). Use of medications by persons 65 and over: Data from the Established Populations for Epidemiologic Studies of the Elderly. *Journal of Gerontology, 47,* M137–M144.

Chrischilles, E. A., Segar, E. T., & Wallace, R. B. (1992). Self-reported adverse drug reactions and related resource use. *Annals of Internal Medicine, 117,* 634–640.

Col, N., Fanale, J. E., & Kronholm, P. (1990). The role of medication noncompliance and adverse drug reactions in hospitalizations of the elderly. *Archives of Internal Medicine, 150,* 841–845.

Colt, H. G., & Shapiro, A. P. (1989). Drug-induced illness as a cause for admission to a community hospital. *Journal of the American Geriatrics Society, 37,* 323–326.

Criqui, M. H. (1987). Alcohol and hypertension: New insights from population studies. *European Heart Journal, 8* (Supp B), 19–26.

Curtis, J. R., Geller, G., Stokes, E. J., Levine, D. M., & Moore, R. D. (1989). Characteristics, diagnosis, and treatment of alcoholism in elderly patients. *Journal of the American Geriatric Society, 37,* 310–316.

Cusack, B. J., & Vestal, R. E. (1986). Clinical pharmacology: Special consideration in the elderly. In E. Calkins, P. J. Davis, & B. Ford (Eds): *The practice of geriatrics* (pp. 115–134). Philadelphia: Saunders.

Davenport, H. W. (1969). Gastric mucosal haemorrhage in dogs: Effects of acid, aspirin, and alcohol. *Gastroenterology, 56,* 439–49.

DeSchepper, P. J., Tjandramaga, T. B., DeRoo, M., Verhaest, L., Daurio, C., Steelman, S. L., & Tempero, K. F. (1978). Gastrointestinal blood loss after diflunisol and after aspirin: Effect of ethanol. *Clinical and Pharmacological Therapeutics, 23,* 669–676.

Deykin, D., Janson, P., & McMahon, L. (1982). Ethanol potentiation of aspirin-induced prolongation of the bleeding time. *New England Journal of Medicine, 306,* 852–854.

DiPadova, C., Roine, R., Frezza, M., Gentry, T., Baraona, E., & Lieber, C. S. (1992). Effects of ranitidine on blood alcohol levels after ethanol ingestion. *JAMA, 267,* 83–86.

Dorian, P., Sellers, E. M., Reed, K. L., Warsh, J. J., Hamilton, C., Kaplan, H. L., & Fan, T. (1983). Amitriptyline and ethanol: Pharmacokinetic and pharmacodynamic interaction. *European Journal of Clinical Pharmacology, 25,* 325–331.

Fillmore, K. M. (1987). Prevalence, incidence, and chronicity of drinking patterns and problems among men as a function of age: a longitudinal and cohort analysis. *British Journal of Addiction, 82,* 77–83.

Forster, L. E., Pollow, R., & Stoller, E. P. (1993). Alcohol use and potential risk for alcohol-related adverse drug reactions among community-based elderly. *Journal of Community Health, 18,* 225–239.

Frezza, M., DiPadova, C., Pozzato, G., Terpin, M., Baraona, E., & Lieber, C. S. (1990). High blood alcohol levels in women: The role of decreased gastric alcohol dehydrogenase activity and first-pass metabolism. *New England Journal of Medicine, 322,* 95–9.

Friedman, H. S. (1992). Cardiovascular effects of ethanol. In C. S. Lieber (Ed.), *Medical and nutritional complications of alcoholism: Mechanisms and management.* (pp. 383–387). New York: Plenum.

Gabriel, S. E., Jaakkimainen, L., & Bobardier, C. (1991). Risk for serious gastrointestinal complications related to use of nonsteroidal antiinflammatory drugs. *Annals of Internal Medicine, 115,* 787–796.

Glynn, R. L., Bouchard, G. R., LoCastro, J. S., & Laird, N. M. (1985). Aging and generational effects on drinking behaviors in men: Results from the Normative Aging Study. *American Journal of Public Health, 75,* 1413–1419.

Gordon, G. G. & Lieber, C. S. (1992). Alcohol, hormones, and metabolism. In C. S. Lieber, (Ed). *Medical and nutritional complications of alcoholism: Mechanisms and management.* New York: Plenum.

Greenblatt, D. J., Harmatz, J. S., Shapiro, L., Engelhardt, N., Gouthro, T. A., & Shader, R. I. (1991). Sensitivity to triazolam in the elderly. *New England Journal of Medicine, 324,* 1691–8.

Greenblatt, D. J., Sellers, E. M., & Shader, R. I. (1982). Drug disposition in old age. *New England Journal of Medicine, 306,* 1081–1088.

Griffin, M. R., Ray, W. A., & Schaffner, W. (1991). Nonsteroidal anti-inflammatory drug use and increased risk for peptic ulcer disease in elderly persons. *Annals of Internal Medicine, 114,* 257–263.

Grymonpre, R. E., Mitenko, P. A., Sitar, D. S., Aoki, F. Y., & Montgomery, P. R. (1988). Drug-associated hospital admissions in older medical patients. *Journal of the American Geriatrics Society, 36,* 1092–8.

Guess, H. A., West, R., Strand, L. M., Helston, D., Lydick, E. G., Bergman, U., & Wolski, K. (1988). Fatal upper gastrointestinal hemorrhage or perforation among users and nonusers of nonsteroidal anti-inflammatory drugs in Saskatchewan, Canada, 1983. *Journal of Clinical Epidemiology, 41,* 35–45.

Gurwitz, J. H., & Avorn, J. (1991). The ambiguous relation between aging and adverse drug reactions. *Annals of Internal Medicine, 114,* 956–966.

Hayes, S. L., Pablo, G., Radomski, T., & Palmer, R. F. (1977). Ethanol and oral diazepam absorption. *New England Journal of Medicine, 296,* 186–189.

Hernandez-Munoz, R., Caballeria, J., Baraona, E., Uppal, R., Greenstein, R., & Lieber, C. S. (1990). Human gastric alcohol dehydrogenase: its inhibition by H2-receptor antagonists, and its effect on the bioavailability of ethanol. *Alcoholism: Clinical and Experimental Research, 14,* 946–50.

Hutchinson, T. A., Flegel, K. M., Kramer, M. S., Leduc, D. G., & Kong, H. H. (1986). Frequency, severity, and risk factors for adverse drug reactions in adult outpatients: A prospective study. *Journal of Chronic Disease, 39,* 533–42.

Jones, T. V., Lindsey, B. A., Yount, P., Soltys, R., & Farani-Enayat, B. (1993). Alcoholism screening questionnaires: Are they valid in elderly medical outpatients? *Journal of General Internal Medicine, 8,* 674–678.

Julkunen, R. J., DiPadova, C., & Lieber, C. S. (1985). First pass metabolism of ethanol: A gastrointestinal barrier against the systemic toxicity of ethanol. *Life Sciences, 37,* 567–573.

Klein, L. E., German, P. S., Levine, D. M., Feroli, R., & Ardery, J. (1984). Medication problems among outpatients: A study with emphasis on the elderly. *Archives of Internal Medicine, 144,* 1185–8.

Koch-Weser, J. (1983). Psychotropic drug use in the elderly. *New England Journal of Medicine, 308,* 134–138.

Kuitunen, T., Mattial, M. J., & Seppala, T. (1990). Actions and interactions of hypnotics on human performance: Single doses of zopiclone, triazolam and alcohol. *International Clinics of Psychopharmacology, 5* (Supp. 2), 115–130.

Lieber, C. S. (1991). Hepatic, metabolic and toxic effects of ethanol: 1991 update. *Alcoholism: Clinical and Experimental Research, 15,* 573–592.

Lieber, C. S. (1992). Interactions of ethanol with other drugs. In C. S. Lieber, (Ed) *Medical and nutritional complications of alcoholism: Mechanisms and management.* New York: Plenum.

Linnoila, M., Stapleton, J. M., Moss, H., Lane, E., Granger, A., & Eckardt, M. J. (1990). Effects of single doses of alprazolam and diazepam, alone and in combination with ethanol, on psychomotor and cognitive performance and on autonomic nervous system reactivity in healthy volunteers. *European Journal of Clinical Pharmacology, 39,* 21–28.

MacGregor, R. R. (1986). Alcohol and immune defense. *JAMA, 256,* 1474–1479.

MacMahon, S. (1987). Alcohol consumption and hypertension. *Hypertension, 9,* 111–121.

Magruder-Habib, K., Saltz, C. C., & Barron, P. M. (1986). Age-related patterns of alcoholism among veterans in ambulatory care. *Hospital and Community Psychiatry, 37,* 1251–1255.

Mayer-Oakes, S. A., Kelman, G., Beers, M., DeJong, F., Matthias, R., Atchison, K., Lubben, J., & Schweitzer, S. (1993). Benzodiazepine use in older community dwelling southern Californians: Prevalence and clinical correlates. *Annals of Pharmacotherapy, 27,* 416–21.

McKim, W. A., & Quinlan, L. T. (1991). Changes in alcohol consumption with age. *Canadian Journal of Public Health, 82,* 231–234.

Meyers, A. R., Goldman, E., Hingson, R., & Scotch, N. (1981–82). Evidence for cohort or generational differences in the drinking behavior of older adults. *International Journal of Aging and Humman Development, 14,* 31–43.

Meyers, A. R., Hingson, R., Mucatel, M., & Goldman, E. (1982). Social and psychological correlates of problem drinking in old age. *Journal of the American Geriatrics Society, 30,* 452–456.

Molgaard, C. A., Nakamura, C. M., Stanford, E. P., Peddecord, K. M., & Morton, D. J. (1990). Prevalence of alcohol consumption among older persons. *Journal Community Health, 15,* 239–251.

Montamat, S. C., Cusack, B. J., & Vestal, R. E. (1989). Management of drug therapy in the elderly. *New England Journal of Medicine, 321,* 303–309.

Myers, J. K., Weissman, M. M., Tischler, G. L., Holzer, C. E., Leaf, P. J., Orvaschel, H., Anthony, J. C., et al. (1984). Six-month prevalence of psychiatric disorders in three communities. *Archives of General Psychiatry, 41,* 959–967.

Nimmo, W. (1976). Drugs, diseases, and delayed gastric emptying. *Clinical Pharmacokinetics, 1,* 189–203.

Ostrom, J. R., Hammarlund, E. R., Christensen, D. B., Plein, J. B., & Kethley, A. J. (1985). Medication usage in an elderly population. *Medical Care, 23,* 157–164.

Pozzato, G., Moretti, M., Franzin, F., Croce, L. S., Lacchin, T., Benedetti, G., Sablich, R., Stebel, M., & Campanacci, L. (1995). Ethanol metabolism and aging: The role of "first pass metabolism" and gastric alcohol dehydrogenase activity. *Journal of Gerontology, 50,* B135–41.

Psaty, B. M., Lee, M., Savage, P. J., Rutan, G. H., German, P. S., & Lyles, M. (1992). Assessing the use of medications in the elderly: Methods and initial experience in the Cardiovascular Health Study. *Journal of Clinical Epidemiology, 45,* 683–692.

Ray, W. A., Griffin, M. R., Schaffner, W., Baugh, D. K., & Melton, L. J. (1987). Psychotropic drug use and the risk of hip fracture. *New England Journal of Medicine, 316,* 363–9.

Rivara, F. P., Jurkovich, G. J., Gurney, J. G., Seguin, D., Fligner, C. L., Ries, R., Raisys, V. A., & Copass, M. (1993). The magnitude of acute and chronic alcohol abuse in trauma patients. *Archives of Surgery, 128,* 907–913.

Roine, R., Gentry, T., Hernandez-Munoz, R., Baraona, E., & Lieber, C. S. (1990). Aspirin increases blood alcohol concentrations in humans after ingestion of ethanol. *JAMA, 264,* 2406–2408.

Roine, R., Hernandez-Munoz, R., Baraona, E., Greenstein, R., & Lieber, C. S. (1992). Effect of omeprazole on gastric first-pass metabolism of ethanol. *Digestive Diseases Science, 37,* 891–896.

Scott, R. B., & Mitchell, M. C. (1988). Aging, alcohol, and the liver. *Journal of the American Geriatrics Society, 36,* 255–265.

Seitz, H. K., Simanowski, U. A., Waldherr, R., Eckey, R., Agarwal, D. P., Goedde, H. W., & von Wartburg, J. P. (1993). Human gastric alcohol dehydrogenase activity: Effect of age, sex, and alcoholism. *Gut, 34,* 1433–37.

Shader, R. I., Greenblatt, D. J., Harmatz, J. S., Franke, K., & Koch-Weser, J. (1977). Absorption and disposition of chlordiazepoxide in young and elderly male volunteers. *Journal of Clinical Pharmacology, 17,* 709–718.

Smart, R. G., & Liban, C. B. (1981). Predictors of problem drinking among elderly, middle-aged, and youthful drinkers. *Journal of Psychoactive Drugs, 13,* 153–163.

Sorock, G. S., & Shimkin, E. E. (1988). Benzodiazepine sedatives and the risk of falling in a community-dwelling elderly cohort. *Archives of Internal Medicine, 148,* 2441–2444.

Stinson, F. S., Dufour, M. C., & Bertolucci, D. (1989). Alcohol-related morbidity in the aging population. *Alcohol Health and Research World, 13,* 80–87.

Tiller, J. W. G. (1990). Antidepressants, alcohol and psychomotor performance. *Acta Psychiatrica Scandinavica Supplementum, 360,* 13–17.

U.S. Department of Health and Human Services (1990). *Seventh special report to the U.S. Congress on alcohol and health.* Public Health Service, ADAMHA, NIAAA, Rockville, MD.

Vestal, R. E., McGuire, E. A., Tobin, J. D., Andres, R., Norris, A. H., & Mezey, E. (1976). Aging and ethanol metabolism. *Clinical and Pharmacological Therapeutics, 21,* 343–354.

Vestal, R. E., Norris, A. H., Tobin, J. D., Cohen, B. H., Shock, N. W., & Andres, R. (1975). Antipyrine metabolism in man: Influence of age, alcohol, caffeine, and smoking. *Clinical and Pharmacological Therapeutics, 18,* 425–32.

Vogel-Sprott, M., & Barrett, P. (1984). Age, drinking habits and the effects of alcohol. *Journal of Studies on Alcohol, 45,* 517–521.

Wynne, H. A., Wood, P., Herd, B., Wright, P., Rawlins, M. D., & James, O. F. (1992). The association of age with the activity of alcohol dehydrogenase in human liver. *Age and Ageing, 21,* 417–20.

9

Use and Abuse of Illicit Drugs among Older People

Helen Rosenberg, PhD

INTRODUCTION

As of 1990, the study of abuse of and addiction to illicit drugs in the elderly is almost nonexistent.[1] Like the stereotype of the addict dropping from society, the study of street drug abuse among the elderly has virtually disappeared from the social science literature (Merton, 1957).[2] Why focus on the 2% of illicit drug abusers in the 50-years-and-older population when these same people are considered most vulnerable to abuse of alcohol and prescription, psychoactive, and over-the-counter drugs (Baum, Kennedy, & Forbes, 1985)?

Illicit drug abuse is considered the domain of the young. Some people argue that few over the age of 65 have ever used any street drugs, let alone become addicted to them (Cisin, Miller, & Harrell, 1978; DuPont, 1979; Glantz & Backenheimer, 1988; Pascarelli, 1974). According to DuPont (1979), 56% of the 18–21 year olds in the United States have tried marijuana, compared with only 2% of people over 50. This is supported by recent studies indicating that rates of drug abuse decline substantially after age 44 (Burke, Burke, Regier, & Rae, 1990; Myers et al., 1984). For example, Caracci and Miller (1991) reveal that lifetime prevalence rates for people 60 and over who are drug abusers comprise less than 1% of the population.

It is only among special populations, those who are not in the mainstream of society, that we find reported problems of drug abuse and addiction among the elderly. There is concern about the small population of elderly prisoners and elderly opiate addicts, whose numbers are expected to increase over time

(Franklin, Allison, & Sutton, 1992; Glantz, 1985; .Gottheil, Druley, Skoloda, & Waxman, 1985). Illicit drug abuse is reported to be as high as 60% among adults addicted to alcohol and as high as 50–75% in psychiatric populations (Caracci & Miller, 1991; Miller, Belkin, & Gold, 1991).

However, some social scientists, spurred by increasing numbers of people who became addicted to street drugs in the 1960s, continue to predict significant increases in the number of elderly drug addicts. For example, in 1963, 10% of 2,932 admissions to the United States Public Health Service Hospitals at Lexington, Kentucky, and Fort Worth, Texas, were people age 50 and over (Petersen, 1978). In 1976, the Community Treatment Foundation Methadone Information Center indicated that 0.7% of 35,000 patients registered in methadone maintenance programs were age 60 or older, up from 0.5% in 1974. By 1979, the figure rose to 1.1%, and in 1983 it was reported to be 2% (Gottheil et al., 1985; Pascarelli, 1974).

Recent trend analyses conducted by the United States Department of Health and Human Services on high school seniors from 1975 to 1993 indicate that lifetime prevalence of use of illicit drugs other than marijuana increased between 1976 and 1981 from 25% to 34%. By 1992, use of illicit drugs declined gradually to 15% (Johnston, O'Malley, & Bachman, 1994). Trend analyses from the National Household Survey on Drug Abuse underscore significant increases in drug use among those age 35 and older. Both studies suggest that as middle-aged users become older, drug use does not decline sharply, leaving this age group at risk for drug abuse and addiction (Glantz & Sloboda, 1995).

Rather than focusing on absolute numbers, these researchers are concerned with the increasing *rates* of drug abuse among the elderly. If trends in drug abuse continue across age cohorts, we face an aging population that will be accepting of drug use and will confront us with rates of drug abuse and addiction higher than in previous generations. Furthermore, not only will our society experience an increase in the number of aging drug addicts, but their homogeneous lifestyle, caused by polydrug abuse, will create a large subculture with considerable impact upon the criminal justice system and on social services (Pottieger & Inciardi, 1981).

In addition to these predicted increases in the population of elderly drug abusers is the warning that current statistics reflect only a fraction of the actual incidence of drug addiction among the elderly. The study of abuse of narcotics among the elderly has been obscured by lack of knowledge and by generalizations made from small samples, according to Pascarelli (1981). Surveys focus on accessible samples of elderly people who abuse illicit drugs, i.e., those in prison or participating in government-subsidized programs at HIV and methadone clinics. These researchers have failed to consider a large portion of the elderly population who do not have criminal records or do not get drugs off the street, but deploy relatives or caretakers to obtain their street drugs (Glantz, 1985; Gottheil et al., 1985). Furthermore, the illegality of narcotics forces users to resort to self-protective, camouflaging behaviors; social scientists therefore find it difficult to get information about the increasing numbers of addicted elderly people (Capel, Goldsmith, Waddell, & Stewart, 1972; Pottieger & Inciardi, 1981).

Thus, the debate over the significance of the number of elderly illicit drug addicts in the population continues.[3] When studying this population, we must consider several questions. Are the increases in the number of elderly people who are addicted to drugs important, and will these increases have an impact on social policy? Are we observing the entire population of elderly people who are illicit drug abusers, or only those easily accessible for study? Elderly people may define themselves as "non-drug users" because they are drug-free at a given time. Continuous drug addiction for periods of years is the exception, not the rule. Since few studies follow drug addicts for periods longer than 1 year, most research provides a fragmented view of the lifestyles of the addicted elderly.[4] Thus, we need to explore who is defined as "drug-addicted" at any given point in time and how our methods of gathering statistics affect the reported incidence of elderly addicts in the population.

An examination of the literature tells us much about social scientists' thinking in this area, but little about the prevalence of abuse of street drugs among the elderly. This chapter examines our understanding of how illicit drugs have affected the elderly over time, and why many people feel that the study of illicit drug abuse and addiction among the elderly is unimportant. I will examine the changing profile of the elderly person who is drug-addicted, the impact of illicit drugs on the lives of the elderly, and why elderly people have so much difficulty getting treatment for addictions. Throughout this discussion, I will include statements from three elderly street addicts whom I interviewed as part of an ongoing study of drug addiction conducted among street addicts in Chicago. Finally, I will examine the literature on drug abuse and addiction among the elderly from a methodological vantage point, considering unresolved issues and implications for future research.

TRENDS OVER TIME

Age Profile

With regard to drug addiction, different age groups have dominated our attention during different historical periods. Studies conducted during the late 19th and early 20th centuries report mean ages of opiate addiction varying from 20 to 50 years (Brown, 1915; Earle, 1880, Farr, 1915).[5] Differences in age across study samples can be attributed to the time period in which the study was conducted, the type of community studied, (e.g., urban versus agricultural); and the occupation and lifestyle of the respondents. As late as the 1940s, 39 was the average age of a person in treatment for opiate addiction at the United States Public Health Service Hospital in Lexington, Kentucky (Schuckit, 1977). In the United Kingdom, the majority of people addicted to illicit drugs were still 50 and older as of 1959 (Bean, 1974). However, the number of known addicts was believed to be so small that no detailed statistics were kept prior to that year.

Although more elderly people than young people were addicted through the 19th and early 20th centuries, trends in opiate addiction began to suggest a gradual decrease in the age of addicts (Terry & Pellens, 1928). A summation of research findings by Terry and Pellens (1928) from the 1900s becomes a precursor of what was to be. These authors concluded that drug users who became addicted through curiosity or their associations were likely to be younger than those who became addicted because they used opiates for medicinal purposes. Almost 40 years later, Schur (1962) noted that users who obtained drugs from their associations with other users tended to be young and lower-class, while users who obtained drugs through their professions as doctors or other medical practitioners were older and middle-class.[6]

Racial Profile

In the 1940s, most narcotic addicts in New York and other large cities were white; but later in that decade, black and Latino addicts came to outnumber whites (Ball & Chambers, 1970). In a study of narcotic addicts who were 55 and older, completed after World War II, Des Jarlais, Joseph, and Courtwright (1985) reported that 86% of their sample were white. However, Courtwright (1992) argues that white people's fear of blacks and drugs increased efforts at social control after World War II, resulting in significant increases in the number of blacks booked, arrested, and in federal treatment programs. Thus, apparent increases in drug abuse among blacks appear to have been a function of social control.

In later years, increasing numbers of people of color continued to be represented among elderly drug addicts. In a report on elderly addicts from nine programs and 32 clinics throughout the state of Washington, Schuckit (1977) found that the elderly who were addicts included a higher percentage of blacks (61%) than whites (42%), were more likely to receive treatment at a hospital, and were more likely to be in methadone treatment than younger addicts. Capel and Peppers (1978) studied 38 elderly drug abusers in 1976 who were not in treatment programs, comparing their profiles with those of elderly drug abusers from 6 years earlier. Comparisons across samples indicated that the population changed from predominantly white males to one including more blacks and females.[7]

Recent Trends

By the 1960s, concurrent with increases in drug trafficking and Mafia involvement in the drug trade, the distribution of addiction to illicit drugs had tipped toward the young, poor and lower classes (Bean, 1974; Capel and Peppers, 1978; Inciardi, 1990). In the United Kingdom in 1961, only 20% of addicts were under 35; but by 1969, this number increased to 84%. The number of addicts over 50 decreased slightly in absolute numbers but decreased markedly relative to the total population. In terms of national statistics, the large number of young people documented as drug-addicted deflected the impact of addicts age 50 and over. The number of addicts introduced to opiates by their peers began to overtake the number of those who became addicted to opiates from medical causes (Capel & Peppers, 1978).

During this period in the United States, heroin addiction came to be viewed as a minority problem. Blacks, migrating from the South to escape poverty and agricultural decline, fled to northern cities, where they encountered unemployment and racism. They replaced whites in neighborhoods where drugs were easily obtained, and they continued the pattern of illicit drug abuse throughout the 20th century (Courtwright, 1992). However, in the 1970s, Vietnam veterans who had become addicted overseas diversified the racial distribution of addicts in the United States. Superimposed on the population of black and Latino men who primarily used narcotics was a population of young, largely white users of nonopiate recreational drugs (Courtwright, 1992). During the 1970s and 1980s, opiates became an issue again because intravenous drug users contributed to the spread of HIV. By the 1980s, the AIDS epidemic and illicit drugs had become linked. Today, the high concentration of AIDS in black and Latino populations suggests a continuing trend of drug abuse among the poor and racial minorities. Furthermore, in two thirds of all AIDS cases among women in the United States, the women injected drugs themselves or had sexual partners who used drugs (Selwyn, 1992).

LONGITUDINAL STUDIES OF DRUG ABUSE AND ADDICTION

Longitudinal study of drug abuse and addiction is superior to cross-sectional analysis in helping to clarify the cyclical nature of drug addiction; the long-term effects of drug abuse, including transitional stages in drug use; lifespan issues related to drug abuse; and issues in treatment and recovery from addiction. However, much longitudinal research begins with the study of young addicts and stops when addicts approach middle age. The elderly addict continues to be neglected as a target for focused study.

Groundbreaking longitudinal research on duration of drug addiction was conducted by Winick in 1962. Winick found that drug use sharply declined by age 36. He based his conclusions on data of inactive opiate addicts who had not come to the attention of the criminal justice system for a period of 5 years and whose names were placed in an inactive file by the Federal Bureau of Narcotics.

For about 10 years after the publication of Winick's study, little research was conducted on the elderly and illicit drug addiction. However, during the 1970s, reports from methadone clinics to the federal government indicated that 5% of methadone maintenance patients were 45 or older and that 1% were over 60 (Capel & Peppers, 1978; Capel & Stewart, 1971; Pascarelli & Fischer, 1974). If this was a representation of the elderly who were registered at methadone clinics, then the actual cases of elderly people addicted to illicit drugs must have been much higher, since samples from methadone maintenance clinics are biased by self-selection and self-report (Gottheil et al., 1985; O'Donnel, 1969; Schuckit, 1977).

In sum, the dropoff of drug addicts after age 36, reported by Winick (1962), might be an artifact of the failure of treatment centers to attract aging addicts, the ability of the elderly to maintain their drug habits without much attention from others, and the reluctance of the criminal justice system to prosecute the elderly (Capel et al., 1972; Schuckit, 1977). These factors stimulated new research in the mid-1970s, which predicted that a significant number of addicts would remain alive and addicted well past age 40 (Vaillant, 1973).

For example, Vaillant (1973) followed a group of 100 male heroin addicts 20 years after their first admission to the United States Public Health Service Hospital in Lexington, Kentucky in 1951. He found that 72% of the men had survived 20 years later. About one third (N=25) were abstinent; i.e., they had gone at least 9 years without being reported as narcotics users, and they had regular jobs. Another third (N=25) were considered addicted except during periods of prolonged institutionalization. One fourth (N=17) of the men were classified as uncertain status.

Also during the 1970s, many men returning from Vietnam were experiencing great difficulty adjusting at home. Twenty percent reported addiction to narcotics as well as marital problems, unemployment, psychiatric problems, and frequent incarcerations. Furthermore, few sought treatment, and many continued to experience difficulties in adjustment 3 years after their return to the United States (Robins, 1973).

New research on narcotics addiction continued to suggest that addiction was a longer process than had previously been realized. In a meta-analysis of four studies which followed narcotic addicts for at least 4 years after initial cessation of drug use, Maddux and Desmond (1980) reported that while 25 to 43% of addicts age 13–46 were abstinent shortly after drug cessation, only a minority of users (19–40%) remained abstinent after 3 years. A still smaller percentage of addicts (3–11%) remained abstinent for 5–10 years after hospital treatment.

In a recently published study of 490 clients interviewed after 12 years as part of the Drug Abuse Reporting Program (DARP), Simpson and Sells (1990) concluded that chronological age and years of addiction were unrelated to addiction at follow-up. Throughout this study, the average length of addiction was 9.9 years, with 28% addicted 1–5 years, 33% addicted 6–11 years, 36% addicted 12–20 years, and 4% addicted for more than 20 years.

As follow-up studies of drug abuse continue to extend over longer time periods, our knowledge of the process of drug addiction improves. Research indicates that drug addiction has a complex, cyclical nature; that it may continue for many years throughout the life span; and that it is affected by cohort experiences sensitive to social, political, economic, and environmental events (Riley & Waring, 1978). However, current knowledge of drug addicts among people 50 and older is still based on small studies done a decade or more ago.

THE ELDERLY ADDICT

Lifestyle of Street Addicts

Trends in Drug Use and Cessation

One reason why addicts can survive as long as they do while still using street drugs is their ability to obtain good supplies of narcotics throughout their lives. Addicts who use good-quality drugs, use moderate amounts of alcohol, avoid complete withdrawal from heroin, use clean needles, and adjust their lifestyle can survive in the streets to old age.

Seasoned drug addicts can identify the quality of drugs and consequently alter their drug use when good drugs are unavailable. Richard, a 61-year-old heroin addict, comments on the overall quality of drugs he obtains in Chicago:

> You can't trust the heroin these days. When I was young, you got the stuff from New York and right on the streets. You knew it was good stuff and you wouldn't get hurt. . . . It wasn't the shit that you get today. (Richard, personal interview, July 1993)[8]

Richard has learned to adjust his habit as he has aged:

> When I was younger, I could handle it better. I started to slow down when I was about 50. (Richard, personal interview, July, 1993)

There are many reasons why drug addicts give up their habit. Like Richard, some say they are simply too old to hustle. Others give up opiates because they are convicted and imprisoned for many years, because they have a religious conversion, or because they have friends who die of overdoses (Maddux & Desmond, 1980). Bess, Janus, and Rifkin (1972) found that among their sample of addicts who lived to old age, traumatic events preceded their renunciation of heroin. These events included impending prostitution, threat of jail, disgust with their lives, a relative's death from an overdose, or loss of a child to the state. Fear of HIV infection is a more recent concern. Kool Aid, a 67-year-old heroin addict who has been drug-free for 6 months confided to me,

> When I was out in the street, I started worryin' about gettin' AIDS. With all the stuff I was usin' messin' around. There was two girls I knew that was comin' around and one of them had died and I got scared" (Kool Aid, personal interview, July, 1993)

Often, drug addicts die before reaching old age because of accidents, tainted drugs, or attacks on the street, rather than from overdoses (Atkinson & Schuckit, 1983; Bienenfeld, 1990).
Richard confides:

> R: I'm very careful about the drugs I get. If I don't know where they came from, I don't get them. You never know what's in them. You can get a hot shot.
> Interviewer [I]: What's that?
> R: It's tainted drugs, sometimes with battery acid in it. One time I was sitting there and we looked at a guy and he wasn't moving. Someone said, "What's wrong with him?" He wasn't moving, so everyone cleared out. No one wants trouble. (Richard, personal interview, July 1993)

Sometimes suicide is an answer to a never-ending battle of trying to survive on the streets. O'Donnell (1969) noted that middle-aged opiate addicts had a 6% suicide rate, in contrast with the 0.06% rate in the general population (U.S. Bureau of the Census, 1976).

Employment

Early studies depicted the elderly narcotics addict as an "unsuccessful sojourner" through life. In their study of Chinese heroin addicts, Ball and Lau (1966) described the typical addict as a man, age 53 and a manual laborer in the laundry or restaurant business, who worked erratically when heavily addicted. They described him as alienated from American culture and the main currents of American life. Another study supported this conclusion: most of the elderly Chinese addicts studied by Deely, Kaufman, Yen, Jue, and Brown (1979) lived alone in flophouses along the Bowery and were employed in illegal gambling houses. Sixty-five percent were working in laundries and were paid in heroin rather than cash.

A more recent study of 30 elderly drug addicts revealed that two thirds were steadily employed; working part-time; or on social security, pensions, or welfare. Only two were hustling (Capel et al., 1972). Elderly addicts whom I interviewed often worked at several jobs, both legitimate and illegitimate. José had a variety of legitimate jobs while he was dealing drugs.

> I: Tell me what you've done for a living.
>
> J: I've done a lot of things. I was a meat packer, a car refinisher, a tailor, a welder . . . I was all those things.
>
> I: How did you learn all those trades?
>
> J: Through the GI bill.
>
> I: Where did you start out?
>
> J: I started out in Texas.
>
> I: That's where you learned meat packing?
>
> J: Yeah, but I moved to Chicago, around 18th and Laflin. I worked at Swift, Armour. Then I moved to Detroit. I did Body by Fisher and I worked for Cadillac.
> (José, personal interview, July 1993)

Richard, although sporadically employed throughout his life, paid for his habit by being a petty thief.

> R: Right now I'm on disability. I can live on $1000 a month. But, when I was younger I was a thief. I was a smart thief.
>
> I: Did you ever work?
>
> R: I had three jobs in my life, but I paid for my drugs by stealing. People would walk down the street, on the way to work, I'd see 'em. I was good. I could support myself and my habit. (Richard, personal interview, July 1993)

Criminal Careers

People involved with drugs are often also involved with crime (Pottieger & Inciardi, 1981). Some can avoid the violence of the streets by becoming middle-level drug dealers, prostitutes, confidence men, or fences (Des Jarlais et al., 1985). Harrington and Cox (1979) followed 51 narcotics users in Tucson, Arizona 20 years after they had been charged with committing crimes. Of the total sample, 13 were dead, 16 were in prison, 8 were on methadone, 8 were leading stable lives, and the status of 6 was unknown.

Finally, disengagement from drugs may be simultaneous with disengagement from a criminal career. In a detailed study, Anglin, Brecht, Woodward, and Bonett (1986) found that a higher proportion of older addicts than would be expected by chance (75% versus 50%) became inactive with regard to drugs when they left their careers of crime and drug-dealing. The economic pressures toward crime are decreased, Pottieger and Inciardi argue (1981), because older addicts are satisfied with alternatives to heroin. Thus, as criminal activity decreases, drug abusers disappear from the police and narcotics registers, as well as from hospital and clinic rolls (Atkinson & Schuckit, 1983).

Compromises with Age: Modifying Drug Habits

Among the elderly, physical limitations of aging and reduced income force many to leave street life and keep a low profile, using less opiates and retreating from the fast-paced street life of younger days (Pascarelli & Fischer, 1974). One reason Kool Aid said he "did heroin" was to keep up with his younger friends.

> I'm just out there, you know, keepin' up with the crowd and the crowd. . . I didn't have no business with the crowd. The crowd was much younger than me anyway and I didn't know what I was doin' . . . you know not thinkin'. (Kool Aid, personal interview, July 1993)

Some addicts maintain a stable drug habit for years and then switch or reduce drug use as they become older:

> I started heroin by the doctor. You go and buy a #5 capsule for a dollar. The price went up a dollar, a dollar and a half, two dollars, three dollars and then five dollars. So, when it got too much, you go to something else. (Kool Aid, personal interview, July 1993)

Pascarelli and Fischer (1974) argue that older addicts have survived because they manage their habits relatively well and keep a low profile. In my interview with Richard, he told me, "Now I just take it slow. I have to be careful." I asked, "So it's your body that slows you down from doing heroin, or is it the money?" Richard replied, "It's both. I have to take care of my body. I'm getting old, but the drugs are expensive and you don't know what you're getting" (Richard, personal interview, July 1993). Many of the elderly use drugs sporadically to reduce boredom or for short periods of intensive pleasure-seeking (Jackson, 1969). Richard uses heroin on holidays and on his birthday.

With increasing age and gradual loss of contacts in the streets, many aging addicts lose access to their drug supplies. When this happens, they reduce their current drug supply or turn to other drugs (Capel et al., 1972; Glantz, 1981). Some substitute alcohol or prescription drugs; some use hydromorphone, a synthetic narcotic similar to morphine; and others turn to methadone, which is readily available through federal programs (Gottheil et al., 1985). Some use tainted heroin because it is easier to obtain, and others give up opiates for a time when they run out of money.

Comparative studies of older people who abuse illicit drugs indicate that heroin and marijuana are popular among the elderly (Chambers, 1971; DuPont, 1979). However, drugs of choice vary. For example, José prefers cocaine:

> J: You have a physical dependence on heroin. You see these guys on heroin. Their jaws are goin' up and down—jaw clicking. You don't get that with cocaine. I can shoot cocaine and not have the physical craving that heroin gives you. Someone who takes heroin has to have it every morning. I shoot up cocaine, but I don't need it every day. Now, they're doing crack . . . they call it rock cocaine. But you need so much with that. You got to get the pipe and all that stuff.
> I: But I hear that the high you get from cocaine isn't as good as with heroin, so why not heroin?
> J: Because it makes you sick and you need it all the time. I shoot up when I want.
> (José, personal interview, July 1993)

Despite variations among drugs of choice in the elderly, Whittington (1984) reports a consensus among researchers suggesting that older addicts do not consume as much of any drug as do younger addicts. This is attributed to diminished physiologic need, changes in pharmacokinetics, the unavailability of drugs, the inability to "hustle" for drugs as they once did, and constraints on obtaining large amounts of money (Bergman & Amir, 1973; Capel et al., 1972). Older addicts adapt by moderating the amount of drugs ingested and by switching from drugs of choice to other drugs, such as alcohol or hydromorphone, which have the advantage of being uncontaminated and reliable in their dosage (Atkinson & Schuckit, 1983; Capel & Peppers, 1978).

Pascarelli and Fischer (1974) found that elderly addicts kept a low profile in the community and switched to alternative drugs until they had enough money to buy heroin. Among the 38 heroin addicts age 48 to 73 studied by Capel et al., (1972), most avoided detection by the police through switching from heroin to hydromorphone. They decreased their daily intake and turned to alcohol and barbiturates when preferred narcotics were unavailable. Eighteen of the 38 reported using drugs at least once a day, and they relied on pushers they knew in their neighborhood to obtain these drugs (Petersen, Whittington, & Payne, 1979).

Elderly drug users tend to avoid crack cocaine (Petersen et al., 1979; Pottieger & Inciardi, 1981; Solomon & Stark, 1993). Kool Aid commented, "The kids today take crack and they don't even know why they takin' it. It makes you crazy" (Kool Aid, personal interview, July 1993). Richard stated, "These kids today just do drugs to do them. They don't know what they're doin'. You could be a smart person and then do crack and you don't know what's happening" (Richard, personal interview, July 1993). Both indicated that crack cocaine is a young person's drug.

Physical Complications of Drug Addiction in Old Age

Research on the effects of illicit drugs on the health of the elderly is difficult to interpret and evaluate. Compared with younger cohorts, fewer elderly people use one drug exclusively and more go through periods of sustained abstinence. Thus, there have been few controlled studies that isolate the effects of one drug on the health of elderly addicts. Indeed, such experimental control over drug ingestion is an artificial imposition that does not accurately reflect the lifestyles of addicts. Given this caveat, some people argue that heroin addiction causes no more problems for the elderly than it does for the young, while others hold that continued high doses of heroin among the aged are quite dangerous.

Strang and Gurling (1989) found no difference between high-dosage and average-dosage heroin addicts.

What was remarkable about these patients is that they were so unremarkable in their 5th, 6th, and 7th decade of life. . . . The very existence of this group of patients demonstrates that even the daily use of massive doses of heroin for many years does not inevitably lead to deterioration and death. (p. 1016)

This research is unique in that it followed seven long-term heroin addicts exposed to the drug in a pure form, in the absence of other drugs or alcohol.

In contrast, other research has found that the elderly are more susceptible to the toxins in drugs they take (Salzman, 1984). The elderly distribute drugs at a lower metabolic rate; this allows them to use less of a drug with the same effect as younger addicts experience with greater quantities (Solomon, Manepallim, Ireland, & Mahon, 1993). However, if drug dosage is not moderated, the elderly may experience more severe and prolonged drug dependence than younger abusers (Caracci & Miller, 1991). The result might be acute toxicity, abstinence from sex or food, and medical illnesses associated with long-term use of narcotics (Berger & Tinklinberg, 1977). Crack cocaine has the effect of bringing on acute paranoid schizophrenic symptoms which last longer in the elderly than in younger people. These conclusions are based on elderly people who abuse illicit drugs as well as prescription drugs and alcohol (Nambudiri & Young, 1991). Indeed, people who are diagnosed as drug-dependent rarely do not meet the criterion for alcohol dependence as well (Miller et al., 1991).

Mortality

Deaths related to drug overdoses are rare. Rather, deaths result from accidents, assaults in the streets, and medical complications (Bienenfeld, 1990). During his 20-year followup of drug addicts, Vaillant (1973) found that addicts who died all died of addiction-*related* causes, such as accidents, suicide, or murder.

Statistics reported by the Drug Abuse Warning Network (DAWN) in 1992 on mortality rates of drug addicts indicate that 10% (*N*=721) of the total drug-related deaths reported to this agency (*N*=7532) occurred among people 55 years and older (Substance Abuse and Mental Health Services Administration, 1993).[9] Causes of death were calculated on the basis of the total number of drugs mentioned as present in the person's system.[10] Among those 55 and older, the following percentages reflect the presence of the drug *in combination with other drugs,* at the time of death:

- 28% were reported to have alcohol in their systems.
- 23% were reported to have heroin or another opiate in their systems.
- 18% were reported to have cocaine in their systems.
- 1% were reported to have marijuana/hashish in their systems.

In comparison with other age groups, this age group was least likely to die from cocaine-related causes and had a higher proportion of opiate-related deaths than expected.

Leaving the Drug Culture

Although a variety of motives may be involved in dropping out of the drug culture, a significant factor is dissatisfaction with the lifestyle (Atkinson & Schuckit, 1983; Gottheil et al., 1985). Increasing age increases the likelihood that the addict will leave the culture. The inability to hustle for drugs results in lower income, which forces the elderly to compromise on their drugs of choice and to decrease their daily intake of drugs (Capel et al., 1972; Pascarelli & Fischer, 1974). Older addicts may switch to prescription drugs (Atkinson & Schuckit, 1983). In addition, drug addicts go through temporary periods of abstinence, which are either self-imposed or imposed on them by incarceration or hospitalization. Ray (1961) argues that drug addicts evaluate their lives in comparison with nonaddicts, and that their consequent attempts to quit drugs may have a cumulative effect of achieving abstinence for increasingly longer periods of time. In addition, fear of death caused by the unreliable content of street drugs and complications of using and sharing dirty needles may motivate abstinence and may contribute to the gradual isolation of the elderly from the drug culture (Pottieger & Inciardi, 1981).

Treatment

Reported increases in the number of elderly addicts in federally funded treatment programs during the 1970s seemed to imply an increase in the number of elderly people who would participate in organized treatment programs in the future (Capel & Peppers, 1978; Capel & Stewart, 1971; Pascarelli & Fischer, 1974). However, many elderly people are reluctant to enter treatment that, for the most part, is fashioned for the young. The lack of adequate facilities focusing on treatment for the elderly remains an obstacle to attracting them into drug treatment programs (Atkinson & Schuckit, 1983).

Methadone maintenance programs, developed during the 1970s, were designed to maintain heroin addicts without euphoria or withdrawal symptoms, and to help them give up the criminal careers often associated with heroin addiction (Gerstein & Harwood, 1990). Currently, these programs have targeted criminal drug users in prisons, adolescents, and people who have a dual diagnosis of mental illness along with alcohol abuse and other kinds of drug abuse. The programs often ignore the needs of elderly people who are susceptible to risks not experienced by other populations (De Leon, 1990). For example, Avorn (1985) cites the increased risks to the elderly of adverse drug reactions due to diminished hepatic metabolism, changes in body composition affecting the volume of distribution of drugs, and other

changes that occur as part of natural senescence. In addition, coexisting illnesses and risks from multiple drug interactions make this group a new challenge for treatment that many agencies refuse to consider. Pascarelli and
Fischer (1974) report that, often, elderly substance abusers do not enter treatment until severe medical problems appear which require immediate attention. Such problems include dental diseases, such as gingivitis, abscesses, or
root caries; bacterial infections, such as cellulitis and thrombophlebitis; diseases such as endocarditis, tetanus, malaria, tuberculosis, and hepatitis; and
sexually transmitted diseases, such as venereal disease and AIDS (Gambert,
1992). Schuckit (1977) reported that 6% of older addicts die in their first year
of treatment, suggesting that they enter therapy more seriously impaired than
younger addicts.

Elderly addicts who do enter methadone treatment are often dissatisfied
(Pascarelli, 1974). Richard stated, "Methadone is worse than heroin. With
heroin you develop a dependency, but it doesn't make you sick" (Richard,
personal interview, July 1993). In addition to being addictive itself,
methadone causes constipation, weight gain, myoclonic jerks, nausea, and
physical problems that are avoided by continued heroin use (Capel &
Stewart, 1971).

Not only are the elderly reluctant to enter methadone programs, but many
traditional treatment centers, such as nursing homes, are reluctant to take
elderly narcotics abusers because they have little or no experience with treating them (Pascarelli & Fischer, 1974). Polydrug abuse, in conjunction with
senescence and medical problems among the elderly, necessitates specialized
programming which includes more staff initiative and more attention to interpersonal needs than is needed with younger clients; intensive outpatient treatment; practical counseling; education and social services; and trials of
methadone coordinated with medical evaluations and follow-up (Atkinson &
Schuckit, 1983).

Yet few treatment regimens focus on elderly illicit drug abusers apart from
those who also abuse alcohol, or apart from treatment programs geared
toward the young. Indeed, Solomon et al. (1993) indicate that treatment
modalities for the drug-addicted should be no different from those for alco-
hol-addicted elderly people. Thus, they recommend a basic twelve-step
model as developed by Alcoholics Anonymous in the treatment of elderly
drug addicts. However, these authors caution that no research exists regarding
the success of such a program with this population. Even methadone programs
specific to heroin addiction focus on youthful addicts without consideration
of special needs of the elderly. In brief, there is little on treatment regimens
for elderly illicit drug abusers that is unique to this population.

THE LITERATURE:
SUGGESTIONS FOR FUTURE RESEARCH

As of 1990, there has been little consistent study of the elderly illicit drug user, and so this chapter asks more questions than it answers. At this time, there are no statistics, estimated or other, that indicate the population of elderly street addicts. Not only is knowledge of elderly drug abusers limited, but in our ignorance we confuse issues of policy and issues of treatment. Treatment programs and care facilities cannot adequately treat elderly addicts when research does not address the physical, medical, or social complications associated with their addictions. And yet the population is now tipped toward the aged. There is great concern with abuse of over-the-counter drugs, prescription medications, and alcohol among the elderly; but the elderly street addict is considered most resistant and most difficult to treat.

Is the elderly street drug abuser an important social problem? Without continued and improved systematic study, we cannot answer this question, nor can we recommend treatment regimens for this population to health care agencies. Young addicts are not hidden from view as many elderly addicts are and do not experience the physical and medical complications that elderly drug abusers and addicts experience. The young are a more exciting and methodologically "cleaner" study population than the elderly. Nevertheless, with the "baby boom" generation now reaching middle age, the need for systematic study of the elderly and illicit drugs seems obvious.

Current literature, although valuable, needs clarification and expansion. This field begs for information on more people who are followed throughout their lives. What is the process of drug addiction for the middle-aged and old?[11] In 1990, social scientists are confronted with a fragmented literature that neglects process and stops and starts during various historical periods. Much of what we do have is based on samples so small that their generalizability to the larger population is limited, at best. Longitudinal studies should include populations over age 40, should consider policy issues, and should make recommendations on the basis of the biological, social, and economic concerns of the elderly.

As part of their generation, patterns of drug use in the elderly are distinct from those of younger cohorts. Over time, their social networks have decreased, and many elderly people fear the younger, tougher street drug users. Yet, increasingly, elderly people who are drug abusers are relying on cocaine, traditionally a young person's drug, since it is often more readily available in the streets than heroin. Thus, the elderly have concerns with regard to social supports and safety.

In addition, the elderly have special needs for health care. Often, elderly people who receive methadone are treated no differently from younger peers or are spurned by health care providers who view them as unworthy of care. Health care concerns of the elderly need to be addressed so that they may be served in organized treatment programs under the care of professionals who understand their special needs.

In sum, research on drug addiction must be expanded to include the cohort of the elderly. Three types of research programs are called for:

1. Longitudinal research that distinguishes age cohorts beyond 40 years
2. Cross-sectional, retrospective data on the elderly that help us learn about the personal histories of drug addiction in this population
3. Policy-oriented research specific to the elderly that considers their unique patterns of drug use, their physiological adjustment to drugs, and their unique medical concerns.

NOTES

1. For the purposes of this chapter, the definitions of drug abuse and addiction are taken from a number of sources (Atkinson & Schuckit, 1983; Bean, 1974; Petersen, 1988). *Drug abuse* is defined as a persistent, nontherapeutic use of any illicit drug. *Drug addiction* refers to a consistent physical or psychological craving for drugs.
2. Although statistics on addiction continue to be collected by the National Institute on Drug Abuse (NIDA), the United States Department of Health and Human Services, and the United States Department of Health, Education and Welfare, few detailed studies of people 50 and older appear in the literature. Moreover, current statistics may be confused by the inclusion of alcohol with illicit drugs (National Institute on Drug Abuse, 1989).
3. Studies of illicit drug abuse and addiction among the elderly have differing age cutoffs for what they define as "elderly." In order to subsume the literature's definition of what it means to be elderly, I will consider the minimum age of an elderly person to be 50. Elderly addicts whom I interviewed for this project were at least 60.
4. See Anglin et al. (1986), Capel and Peppers (1978), Harrington and Cox (1979), Maddux and Desmond (1980), Robins (1973), Simpson and Sells (1990), and Winick (1962) for longitudinal research on drug abuse.
5. Literature from this period focuses on opium and, to a lesser extent, opium derivatives such as morphine, codeine, and heroin.
6. Schur based his conclusions on informants from five case studies of British addicts; government documents; personal interviews with narcotics officials; interviews with physicians and psychiatrists regarding their patients; question-

naire data from British medical specialists; descriptions of addict customers from pharmacists; and a sample of 147 randomly selected 21-year-olds, 9 of whom reported any personal contact with marijuana or heroin. He noted that drug addiction, not considered a serious problem in the United Kingdom during the period of his research, did not require reporting of detailed information or statistics.

7. For work which considers the lifestyles of addicted women, see *Women and Heroin Abuse: A Survey of Sexism in Drug Abuse Administration* by Ashbrook and Solley (1979); *Women and Substance Abuse* by Ettore (1992); *Women and Crack-Cocaine* by Inciardi, Lockwood, and Pottieger (1993); *Women on Heroin* by Rosenbaum (1981), and *Women Drug Users* by Taylor (1993).

8. The names of the elderly drug addicts whom I interviewed are pseudonymous.

9. Data from the 1992 Drug Abuse Warning Network (DAWN) comes from 137 medical examiner jurisdictions located in 38 metropolitan areas throughout the United States.

10. The base percentage on which these figures are calculated is 236.3%.

11. See *Careers in Dope* (Waldorf, 1973) and *Junky* (Burroughs, 1953) for accounts of the process of becoming drug-addicted.

REFERENCES

Abrams, R. C., & Alexopoulos, G. S. (1991). Geriatric addictions. In R. J. Frances & S. I. Miller (Eds.), *Clinical textbook of addictive disorders* (pp. 347–365). New York: Guilford.

Anglin, M. D., Brecht, M. L., Woodward, J. A., & Bonett, D. G. (1986). An empirical study of maturing out: Conditional factors. *International Journal of Addictions, 21,* 233–246.

Ashbrook, D. L., & Solley, L. C. (1979). *Women and heroin abuse: A survey of sexism in drug abuse administration.* Palo Alto, CA: R & E Research Associates.

Atkinson, J. H., & Schuckit, M. A. (1983). Geriatric alcohol and drug misuse and abuse. In N. K. Mello (Ed.), *Advances in substance abuse, behavioral and biological research* (pp. 195–237). Greenwich, CT: JAI Press.

Avorn, J. (1985). Geriatric drug epidemiology and health services research based on large-scale computerized data sets. In S. R. Moore & T. W. Teal (Eds.), *Geriatric drug use: Clinical and social perspectives* (pp. 86–94). New York: Pergamon.

Ball, J. C., & Chambers, C. D. (Eds.) (1970). *The epidemiology of opiate addiction in the United States.* Springfield, IL: Charles C. Thomas.

Ball, J. C., & Lau, M. P. (1966). The Chinese narcotic addict in the United States. *Social Forces, 45,* 68–72.

Baum, C., Kennedy, D. L., & Forbes, M. B. (1985). Drug utilization in the geriatric age group. In S. R. Moore & T. W. Teal (Eds.), *Geriatric drug use: Clinical and social perspectives* (pp. 63–69). New York: Pergamon.

Bean, P. (1974). *The social control of drugs.* New York: Wiley.

Berger, P. A., & Tinklenberg, J. R. (1977). Treatment of abusers of alcohol and other addictive drugs. In J. D. Barchas, P. A. Berger, R. D. Ciarnello, & G. R. Elliott

(Eds.), *Psychopharmacology: From theory to practice* (pp. 335–385). New York: Oxford University Press.

Bergman, S., & Amir, M. (1973). Crime and delinquency among the aged in Israel. *Geriatrics, 28,* 290–294.

Bess, B., Janus, S., & Rifkin, A. (1972). Factors in successful narcotics renunciation. *American Journal of Psychiatry, 128,* 851–865.

Bienenfeld, D. (1990). Substance abuse. In D. Bienenfeld (Ed.), *Verwoerdt's clinical geropsychiatry* (3rd ed.) (pp. 173–177). Baltimore, MD: Williams and Wilkins.

Brown, L. P. (1915). Enforcement of the Tennessee anti-narcotic law. *American Journal of Public Health, 5,* 323–333.

Burke, K. C., Burke, J. D., Regier, D., & Rae, D. S. (1990). Age at onset of selected mental disorders in five community populations. *Archives of General Psychiatry, 47,* 511–517.

Burroughs, W. S. (1953). *Junky.* New York: Penguin.

Capel, W. C., Goldsmith, B. M., Waddell, K. J., & Stewart, G. T. (1972). The aging narcotic addict: An increasing problem for the next decades. *Journal of Gerontology, 27,* 102–106.

Capel, W. C., & Peppers, L. G. (1978). The aging addict: A longitudinal study of known abusers. *Addictive Diseases: An International Journal, 3,* 389–403.

Capel, W. C., & Stewart, G. T. (1971). The management of drug abuse in aging populations: New Orleans findings. *Journal of Drug Issues, 1,* 114–121.

Caracci, G., & Miller, N. S. (1991). Alcohol and drug addiction in the elderly. In N. S. Miller (Ed.), *Comprehensive handbook of drug and alcohol addiction* (pp. 179–191) New York: Marcel Dekker.

Chambers, C. D. (1971). *An assessment of drug use in the general population.* New York: NY State Narcotic Addiction Control Commission.

Cisin, I., Miller, J., & Harrell, A. (1978). *Highlights from the National Survey on Drug Abuse: 1977.* Rockville, MD: National Institute on Drug Abuse.

Courtwright, D. T. (1992). A century of American narcotic policy. In D. R. Gerstein & H. J. Harwood (Eds.), *Treating drug problems* (pp. 1–62). Washington, DC: National Academy Press.

Deely, P. J., Kaufman, E., Yen, M. S., Jue, A., & Brown, E. (1979). The special problems and treatment of a group of elderly Chinese opiate addicts in New York City. *British Journal of Addiction, 74,* 403–409.

Des Jarlais, D. C., Joseph, H., & Courtwright, D. T. (1985). Old age and addiction: A study of elderly patients in methadone maintenance treatment. In E. Gottheil, K. A. Druley, T. E. Skoloda, & W. M. Waxman (Eds.), *The combined problems of alcoholism, drug addiction and aging* (pp. 201–214). Springfield, IL: Charles C. Thomas.

De Leon, G. (1990). Treatment strategies. In J. A. Inciardi & J. R. Biden, Jr. (Eds.) *Handbook of drug control in the United States* (pp. 115–138). New York: Greenwood.

DuPont, R. L. (1979). The future of drug abuse prevention. In R. L. DuPont, A. Goldstein, & J. O'Donnell (Eds.). *Handbook on drug abuse* (pp. 447–452). Washington, DC: Government Printing Office.

Earl, C. W. (1880). The opium habit: A statistical and clinical lecture. *Chicago Medical Review, 2,* 442–446; 493–498.

Ettore, E. (1992). *Women and substance use.* New Brunswick, NJ: Rutgers University Press.

Farr, C. B. (1915). The relative frequency of the morphine and heroin habits. *New York Medical Journal, 101,* 892–895.

Franklin, R. D., Allison, D. B., & Sutton, T. (1992). Alcohol, substance abuse, and violence among North Carolina prison admissions, 1988. *Journal of Offender Rehabilitation, 17,* 101–111.

Gambert, S. R. (1992). Substance abuse in the elderly. In J. H. Lowinson, P. Ruiz, R. B. Millman, & J. G. Langrod (Eds.), *Substance abuse: A comprehensive textbook* (pp. 843–851). Baltimore, MD: Williams & Wilkins.

Gerstein, D. R., & Harwood, H. J. (Eds.) (1990). *Treating drug problems.* Washington, DC: National Academy Press.

Glantz, M. D. (1981). Predictions of elderly drug abuse. *Journal of Psychoactive Drugs, 13,* 117–126.

Glantz, M. D. (1985). The detection, identification and differentiation of elderly drug misuse and abuse in a research survey. In E. Gottheil, K. A. Druley, T. E. Skoloda, & W. M. Waxman (Eds.), *The combined problems of alcoholism, drug addiction and aging* (pp. 113–129). Springfield, IL: Charles C. Thomas.

Glantz, M. D., & Backenheimer, M. S. (1988). Substance abuse among elderly women. *Clinical Gerontologist, 8,* 3–26.

Glantz, M. D., & Sloboda, Z. (1995). The elderly. In R. Coombs & D. Ziedonis (Eds.), *Handbook on drug abuse prevention* (pp. 429–444). Englewood Cliffs, NJ: Prentice-Hall.

Gottheil, E., Druley, K. A., Skoloda, T. E., & Waxman, W. M. (Eds.) (1985). *The combined problems of alcoholism, drug addiction and aging.* Springfield, IL: Charles C. Thomas.

Harrington, P., & Cox, T. J. (1979). A twenty-year follow-up of narcotic addicts in Tucson, Arizona. *American Journal of Drug and Alcohol Abuse, 6,* 25–37.

Inciardi, J. A. (1990). *Handbook of drug control in the United States.* New York: Greenwood.

Inciardi, J. A., Lockwood, D., & Pottieger, A. E. (1993). *Women and crack-cocaine.* New York: Macmillan.

Jackson, B. (1969). *A thief's primer.* London: Macmillan.

Johnston, L., O'Malley, P. M., & Bachman, J. G. (1994). *National Survey Results on Drug Use from The Monitoring the Future Study, 1975–1993.* Washington, DC: National Institute on Drug Abuse.

Maddux, J. R., & Desmond, D. P. (1980). New light on the maturing out hypothesis in opioid dependence. *Bulletin on Narcotics, 32,* 15–25.

Merton, R. K. (1957). *Social theory and social structure.* New York: Free Press.

Miller, N. S., Belkin, B. M., & Gold, M. S. (1991). Alcohol and drug dependence among the elderly: Epidemiology, diagnosis and treatment. *Comprehensive Psychiatry, 32,* 153–165.

Myers, J. D., Weissman, M. M., Tischler, G. L., Holzer, C. E., Leaf, P., Orvaschel, H., Anthony, J. C., Boyd, J. H., Burke, J. D., Kramer, M., & Stoltzman, R. (1984). Six-month prevalence of psychiatric disorders in three communities. *Psychiatric Disorders, 41,* 959–967.

Nambudiri, D. E., & Young, R. C. (1991). A case of late-onset crack dependence and subsequent psychosis in the elderly. *Journal of Substance Abuse Treatment, 8,* 253–255.

National Institute on Drug Abuse. (1989). *National Drug and Alcoholism Treatment Unit Survey (NDATUS)* (DHHS Publication No. (ADM) 91–1729.) Rockville, MD: U.S. Department of Health and Human Services.

O'Donnell, J. A. (1969). *Narcotic addicts in Kentucky.* Washington, DC: US Public Health Service.

Pascarelli, E. F. (1974). Drug dependence: An age-old problem compounded by old age. *Geriatrics, 12,* 109–115.

Pascarelli, E. F. (1981). Drug abuse and the elderly. In J. H. Lowinson and P. Ruiz (Eds.), *Substance abuse: Clinical problems and perspectives* (pp. 752–757). Baltimore, MD: Williams & Wilkins.

Pascarelli, E. F., & Fischer, W. (1974). Drug dependence in the elderly. *International Journal of Aging and Human Development, 5,* 347–355.

Petersen, D. M. (Ed.). (1978). Drug use among the aged [Special issue]. *Addictive Diseases, 3* (3).

Petersen, D. M. (1988). Substance abuse, criminal behavior and older people. *Generations, 12,* 63–67.

Petersen, D. M., Whittington, F. J. & Payne, B. P. (1979). *Drugs and the elderly.* Springfield, IL: Charles C. Thomas.

Pottieger, A. E., & Inciardi, J. A. (1981). Aging on the street: Drug use and crime among older men. *Journal of Psychoactive Drugs, 13,* 199–211.

Ray, M. B. (1961). The cycle of abstinence and relapse among heroin addicts. *Social Problems, 9,* 132–140.

Riley, M. W., & Waring, J. (1978). Age, cohorts and drug use. In D. B. Kandel (Ed.), *Longitudinal research on drug use* (pp. 225–233). New York: Wiley.

Robins, L. N. (1973). *The Vietnam drug user returns.* Washington, DC: Special Action Office for Drug Abuse Prevention.

Rosenbaum, M. (1981). *Women on heroin.* New Brunswick, NJ: Rutgers University Press.

Salzman, C. (1984). Neurotransmission in the aging central nervous system. In C. Salzman (Ed.), *Clinical geriatric psychopharmacology* (pp. 18–31). New York: McGraw-Hill.

Schuckit, M. A. (1977). Geriatric alcoholism and drug abuse. *The Gerontologist, 17,* 168–174.

Schur, E. M. (1962). *Narcotic addiction in Britain and America.* London: Social Science Paperbacks.

Selwyn, P. A. (1992). Medical aspects of human immunodeficiency virus infection and its treatment in injecting drug users. In J. H. Lowinson, P. Ruiz, R. B. Millman & J. G. Langrod (Eds.), *Substance abuse: A comprehensive textbook* (pp. 744–774). Baltimore, MD: Williams & Wilkins.

Simpson, D. D., & Sells, S. B. (1990). *Opioid addiction and treatment: A 12-year follow-up.* Malabar, FL: Robert E. Krieger.

Solomon, K., Manepallim, J., Ireland, G. A., & Mahon, G. M. (1993). Alcoholism and prescription drug abuse in the elderly: St. Louis University grand rounds. *American Geriatric Society, 41,* 57–69.

Solomon, K., & Stark, S. (1993). Comparison of older and younger alcoholics and prescription drug abusers: History and clinical presentation. *Clinical Gerontologist, 12,* 41–56.

Strang, J., & Gurling, H. (1989). Computerized tomography and neuropsychological assessment of long-term high-dose heroin addicts. *British Journal of Addictions, 84,* 1011–1019.

Substance Abuse and Mental Health Services Administration (1993 data file). *Annual Medical Examiner Data, 1992* (Statistical Series 1, No, 12–B). Rockville, MD: U.S. Department of Health and Human Services.

Taylor, A. (1993). *Women drug users.* New York: Oxford University Press.

Terry, C. E., & Pellens, M. (1928). *The opium problem.* Montclair, NJ: Patterson Smith.

U.S. Bureau of the Census. (1976). *Statistical Abstracts of the United States: 1976* (97th ed.). Washington, DC: Author.

Valliant, G. E. (1973). A 20-year follow-up of New York narcotic addicts. *Archives of General Psychiatry, 29,* 237–241.

Waldorf, D. (1973). *Careers in dope.* Englewood Cliffs, NJ: Prentice-Hall.

Whittington, F. J. (1984). Addicts and alcoholics. In E. B. Palmore (Ed.), *Handbook on the aged in the United States* (pp. 279–294). Westport, CT: Greenwood.

Winick, C. (1962). Maturing out of narcotic addiction. *Bulletin on Narcotics, 14,* 1–7.

10

Misuse of Alcohol and Drugs in the Nursing Home

Carol L. Joseph, MD

INTRODUCTION

Despite the importance of the nursing homes (NH) in the provision of care for the elderly, relatively little attention has been directed to the medical problems of NH residents. With the exception of prescription drugs, the problem of substance misuse in NHs has been almost entirely ignored. This review will discuss the use of alcohol, drugs, and tobacco among NH residents. The description of misuse of prescription medications will focus on psychoactive drugs. This discussion is based primarily on data derived from studies of NHs in the United States.

THE NURSING HOME ENVIRONMENT

Description of Facilities

In the United States, beds in nursing homes outnumber hospital beds by a ratio of 2 to 1 (Ouslander, Osterweil, & Morley, 1991). Not only the number of NH residents, but the expense of caring for them, is expected to increase rapidly over the next several decades. It is projected that half of those who reached age 65 in 1990 will enter an NH at least once in their lives, tripling or quadrupling the cost of NH care in the next 50 years (Kemper & Murtaugh, 1991; Schneider & Guralnik, 1990)

NHs are residential facilities for people who require nursing care and related medical or psychosocial services. In the United States, payment for NH care is determined by the level of service provided, skilled nursing facility (SNF) or intermediate-care facility (ICF). Estimates place the number of NHs in the United States at approximately 20,000 (Hing, 1989b). The majority are small homes with fewer than 100 beds, owned by individuals, partnerships, or corporations, but corporate chains operate a large proportion of NHs nationally (41% in 1985). A small percentage of NHs are operated by nonprofit groups (often with a religious affiliation) and government agencies (Hing, 1989b).

Because NH residents have complex medical, social, functional, and psychological problems and needs, the ideal model for NH care is an interdisciplinary team composed of physicians, nurses, recreational therapists, dietitians, social workers, physical and occupational therapists, pharmacists, the NH resident, and his or her family, who work together to develop and implement a plan of care. In practice, the physician's involvement, apart from mandatory visits, is usually minimal. Only a small percentage of physicians make NH visits, and even primary care physicians spend an average of less than 1½ hours per month in NHs (Aiken, Mezey, Lynaugh, & Buck, 1985) The norm in American NHs is one registered nurse to every 49 residents, with 90% of care delivered by nursing assistants (Aiken et al., 1985; Ouslander, 1989). In some facilities, turnover among nursing assistants is 100% in a 3-month period (Rango, 1982). Thus, direct patient care often falls to the least trained staff.

Characteristics of NH Residents

Ninety percent of the approximately 1.5 million NH residents in the United States are age 65 or older (Ouslander et al., 1991). The majority are single, white females with an income below the poverty level. Half are cognitively impaired, typically from Alzheimer's disease or cerebrovascular accidents (Hing, 1989b). NH residents have become more medically complicated and functionally dependent in the past decade (Hing, 1989a; Rubenstein, Ouslander, & Wieland, 1988). There are many possible explanations for this finding, including the continued aging of the population. Another important contributor is the Medicare "prospective payment system" (PPS) of hospital reimbursement, enacted in 1983. The PPS has significantly changed the ways in which hospitals are paid for providing care to their elderly patients. Under the PPS, hospitals are reimbursed a prespecified amount for the diagnostic-related group (DRG) to which a patient is assigned. If a patient's hospitalization is less costly than the designated reimbursement for his or her condition, the hospital makes a profit; if it is more costly, the hospital sustains a loss. Predictably, the PPS resulted in shortened hospital stays and encouraged the transfer of patients from acute-care hospitals to NHs much earlier in their convalescence (Fitzgerald, Moore, & Dittus, 1988).

Of all persons admitted to NHs, half will die or return home after a brief stay, and half will remain in the facility for more than 3 months (Keeler, Kane, & Solomon, 1981; Liu & Manton, 1984). For about one-third of persons admitted, the NH provides a transition from hospital to home, a fact which assumes significance from the standpoint of substance misuse (Fitzgerald et al., 1988; Liu & Manton, 1984).

USE OF ALCOHOL AND ILLICIT DRUGS BY NH RESIDENTS

In this section of the chapter, alcohol will be considered first, and then illicit drugs. Treatment of both kinds of abuse will then be discussed together.

Alcohol

Epidemiology

Problems with alcohol are encountered more frequently in studies of elderly medical populations than in community surveys, particularly in acute-care hospitals, where rates of alcohol-related admissions are similar to those for myocardial infarction (Adams, Yuan, Barboriak, & Kimm, 1993; Atkinson, 1984; Blazer & Pennybacker, 1984) The reported prevalence of alcohol problems among hospitalized elderly people ranges from 18% to as high as 60% among certain subgroups of patients (Atkinson, 1984; Curtis, Geller, Stokes, Levine, & Moore, 1989; McCusker, Cherubin, & Zimberg, 1971; Schuckit & Miller, 1976) Since the majority of NH admissions are from acute-care hospitals, the pattern of alcohol problems among people admitted to NHs might be expected to resemble hospital prevalence rates more closely than community prevalence rates (Rubenstein, Ouslander, & Wieland, 1988).

The few studies of alcohol problems in NHs have yielded prevalence rates which range from 2.8% to 49%, depending on settings and methods. (Department of Veterans Affairs, 1990; Douglass, 1980; Hing, 1989b; Joseph, Ganzini, & Atkinson, 1995; Linn, Linn, & Greenwald, 1972; Mehr, Fries, & Williams, 1993). Although prevalence is influenced by characteristics of residents and facilities—with generally higher rates in younger persons, males, and residents of Veterans Affairs (VA) NHs—the most important factors are probably case definition and time frame (i.e., lifetime history of alcohol problems or simply current diagnosis).

In the National Nursing Home Survey (NNHS) in 1985, alcoholism was determined by staff report of current alcohol abuse or dependence based on knowledge of the resident and information in the medical record (Hing, 1989b; Mehr et al., 1993). By this criterion, alcoholism was prevalent in 2.8% of community nursing home residents overall, and in 7.4% of men (Mehr et al., 1993). The prevalence rates for residents age 65 years old or older are slightly lower: 2.1% for women and 5.7% for men (Mehr et al., 1993). In contrast, studies relying on diagnoses report somewhat higher prevalence rates. By reviewing the first eight diagnoses of persons admitted to NHs under Medicare, Douglass found a 12% prevalence of alcoholism (Douglass, 1980). Similarly, Linn et al. (1972) reported that 12% of persons discharged to community NHs from a Veterans Affairs (VA) hospital between 1966 and 1971 had a diagnosis of "chronic alcoholism."

A survey of 120 VA NHs in 1990 found alcoholism in 15% of residents, making it the second most frequently reported mental health condition, after dementia (Department of Veterans Affairs, 1990). Mehr and coworkers (1993) surveyed VA NHs in 1986, but reported somewhat lower prevalence rates for alcoholism: 8.7% overall and 6.9% among residents who were 65 and older. In that study, the lower prevalence rate for alcoholism likely resulted from reliance on a more stringent case definition. Alternatively, it is possible that there was an increase in alcoholism among VA NH residents, or a change in admission criteria, between 1986 and 1990.

Alcoholism is consistently underdiagnosed and underreported by health care providers, especially in elderly female patients (Buchsbaum, Buchanan, Welsh, Centor, 1992; Curtis et al., 1989; Moore et al., 1989). Thus, studies employing diagnosis by the provider, rather than structured interviews, for case definition are likely to significantly underestimate the prevalence of alcoholism among NH residents. An interview study of persons admitted to a VA NH found that 49% of study participants met the *Diagnostic and Statistical Manual (DSM–III–R)* criteria for lifetime alcohol abuse or dependence, and 18% were active alcoholics (American Psychiatric Association, 1987; Joseph, Ganzini, & Atkinson, 1995).

Persons with alcohol problems who are admitted to NHs differ in significant ways from other residents. They are more likely to be male, younger, and without a current spouse (i.e., single, divorced, separated, or widowed); to have fewer social supports; and to have lower income than nonalcoholic NH residents (Douglass, 1980; Joseph et al., 1995; Linn et al., 1972).

Concomitant tobacco dependence and depressive symptomatology have also been found more often among alcoholic NH residents (Joseph et al., 1995). Depression, tobacco dependence, and lack of social and financial resources all suggest a poor long-term outlook for alcoholic NH residents, although there are no outcome studies specifically addressing this question.

Screening

Formal screening tests clearly increase the detection of alcoholism, although there is little information regarding their use in NHs (Buchsbaum et al., 1992; Curtis et al., 1989; Moore et al., 1989). Measures that are sensitive and specific among elderly persons in hospital and clinic settings are likely to perform similarly in the NH; screening techniques which are insensitive in the elderly, such as measuring quantity and frequency of alcohol consumption, are likely to be less useful (Curtis et al., 1989; Graham, 1986). The CAGE[1] is a brief, four-question, screening instrument which has been useful in a variety of settings, especially if the prevalence of alcohol problems is relatively high (Buchsbaum et al., 1992; Mayfield, McLeod, & Hall, 1974). A new screening questionnaire, the Michigan Alcoholism Screening Test-Geriatric Version (MAST–G), has recently been developed specifically for use with elderly persons (Blow, 1991). The MAST–G is a 24-item instrument composed of yes-or-no questions.

A recent study conducted among persons admitted to a VA NH compared both the CAGE and MAST–G with *DSM–III–R* criteria for lifetime alcohol abuse or dependence (Joseph et al., 1995). Both the CAGE and MAST–G performed well in this study. The CAGE had a sensitivity of 82% and specificity of 90%, while the MAST–G yielded a sensitivity of 93% and specificity of 65%. However, the study cited above was carried out in a population with a high prevalence of alcoholism; these sensitivities and specificities may not be equaled in NHs in which alcoholism is less common.

Clinical Considerations

Admission to an NH does not automatically end a resident's problem drinking. Drinking may continue surreptitiously, either in the facility or on outings. NH residents who continue to drink may suffer all of the problems traditionally associated with alcoholism (Hurt, Finlayson, Morse, & Davis, 1988). Ongoing alcohol use, especially if unrecognized, can result in adverse interactions with prescribed medications; can adversely affect existing health problems, such as cognitive impairment, depression, or cardiovascular or neurological disorders; and can result in behavioral outbursts (Atkinson, 1991). In our experience, NH residents who are unable to maintain a constant supply of beverage alcohol may consume more accessible substances, such as mouthwash or shaving lotion. Alternatively, they may experience withdrawal tachycardia, hypertension, tremor, or confusion, which may easily, and mistakenly, be attributed to other health problems. Residents may also discharge themselves before they are fully recovered in order to drink. The following case example illustrates some of the problems associated with alcohol misuse in the NH.

Case History

Mr. C., a 70-year-old man with a long history of alcohol dependence, was living in an adult foster care home when he experienced a series of grand mal seizures. He was admitted to a VA hospital, and a new diagnosis of hip fracture and malnutrition were added to his list of chronic medical problems: pressure ulcer, pancreatic pseudocyst, hypertension, chronic lung disease, anemia, and gastritis. After a surgical repair of his fracture, Mr. C. was transferred to a VA NH for convalescence and rehabilitation. He agreed to abstain from drinking and to participate in an alcohol treatment program in the NH as a condition of admission. After arrival in the NH, however, he refused to attend the alcohol treatment groups. He often refused other prescribed treatments, such as wound care and physical therapy, and frequently shouted at and cursed the NH staff. Mr. C.'s "significant other" was a friend who was often visibly intoxicated during visits. After one of these visits, Mr. C. was found to have a bottle of whiskey in his room. The negative health consequences of continued drinking were discussed with Mr. C. and he was informed of NH policy prohibiting alcohol. Mr. C. again contracted to abstain from alcohol as a condition of his continued residence in the NH. Mr. C. soon broke this contract and refused to cooperate in planning or transfer to another care facility, which he needed. Mr. C. chose instead to move to an apartment with his friend. He died 2 months later.

Unfortunately, some active alcoholics adapt poorly to the NH. They may leave only to return to living situations where they cannot obtain the level of care and support they require, such as single-room-occupancy hotels, apartments, or even the street.

Therapeutic Use of Alcohol in NHs

The moderate use of alcoholic beverages in NHs has long been advocated to enhance the sociability, appetite, and well-being of residents (Kastenbaum, Sarley, & Stepto, 1968; Kastenbaum & Slater, 1964). Observational studies employing alcoholic beverages as an accompaniment to NH activities have reported increased social interaction and a sense of well-being among participants, without negative outcomes (Chien, Stotsky, & Cole, 1973; Kastenbaum et al., 1968; Kastenbaum & Slater, 1964; Mishara, Kastenbaum,

Baker, & Patterson, 1975). It should be noted that these studies emphasized careful subject selection and a controlled, modest alcohol intake (less than 2 drinks a day). Each study has design flaws, such as small numbers of subjects, short study duration, and the impossibility of blinding the intervention. It should also be noted that a number of studies have shown that any change enriching the NH environment results in at least a transitory positive response from residents (Kane and Kane, 1987). And as an additional caveat, NH residents as a group have been getting progressively older and sicker, and it should not be assumed that the NH residents of the 1990s are comparable to those of the 1960s and 1970s, when most of these studies were conducted, in terms of the risks of even moderate drinking.

Before sanctioning alcohol use for any NH resident, the physician should ascertain that he or she is not overlooking an existing alcohol or drug problem; that there are no potential adverse alcohol and drug interactions; and that alcohol will not exacerbate preexisting conditions, such as cognitive impairment or cardiovascular disease. The following case history illustrates some of the potential problems of therapeutic alcohol use in an NH.

Case History

Mr. A. was a very malnourished 65-year-old who complained of a poor appetite when he was admitted to the NH. Mr. A. asked his physician to prescribe a beer with meals, in order to "stimulate his appetite." Believing that Mr. A.'s life expectancy was limited, his physician prescribed one beer three times a day with food, with the thought that Mr. A. should have "his only remaining pleasure," i.e., drinking. Unfortunately, Mr. A. did not eat better or gain weight. Within a few weeks routine laboratory testing uncovered a striking elevation in liver enzymes. A further investigation revealed that Mr. A. had a previously unsuspected history of problem drinking. The beer was discontinued; his liver enzymes returned to normal, and Mr A. eventually improved enough to return home.

Illicit Drugs

Epidemiology

The prevalence of illicit drug use among the elderly is not well documented, but it   appears to be much less frequent than problem drinking. Clinically, illicit drug use is most often reported among people with a history of lifetime alcohol dependence (Miller, Belkin, & Gold, 1991). The Epidemiologic Catchment Area Study reported lifetime prevalence rates of illicit drug dependence to be less than 1% in persons 60 years old or older (Caracci &

Miller, 1991). Older persons, generally the "young-old," account for a small percentage of enrollees in drug treatment programs. They are reported to make up 0.5% to 4% of clients enrolled in Methadone programs (Hall, 1983). Similarly, persons age 60 and older accounted for 4.7% of patients discharged from the VA medical system in fiscal year 1987 with a diagnosis of drug abuse or dependence (Dvoredsky, Suchinsky, & Speight, 1989).

The 1985 National Nursing Home Survey reported a 0.9% prevalence of drug abuse or dependence as a "current mental disorder" among all NH residents (Hing, 1989b). This prevalence was based on the staff's response to the following question: "According to (the patient's) medical record does he/she currently have drug abuse/dependence?" The type of drug is not defined, and these figures may include residents who abused or were dependent on prescription drugs. The prevalence is highest among men under 65 (2.7%). However, because the vast majority of NH residents are elderly, there are twice as many persons age 65 and older who abuse or are dependent on drugs as in younger age groups. Among those age 65 and older, the prevalences listed for men and women are very similar: 0.7% and 0.8%, respectively. In a VA study, illicit drug abuse or dependence was listed among the diagnoses of 1.2% of NH admissions over age 50 (Joseph, Atkinson, Ganzini, & Edwards, 1992).

Screening

The CAGE has been advocated to screen for drug use problems by replacing the word *drinking* with the words *drug use* or the name of the substance in question (Cyr & Sherman, 1993). This seems a reasonable approach, although there is no information about the sensitivity or specificity of this strategy in the elderly or among NH residents.

Clinical Considerations

The following case example illustrates some of the problems produced by active illicit drug use which may be encountered in the NH.

Case History

Mr. M. was 46 years old when he was admitted to the NH for stroke rehabilitation. He had a history of misusing alcohol and taking illicit drugs, including intravenous heroin. During his NH stay, Mr. M. was noted to have difficulty attending to therapy, was often lethargic, and was sometimes "inappropriately silly." This behavior suggested continued illicit drug use, and a urine drug screen confirmed the use of opiates. When confronted with the positive drug screen, Mr. M. stated that while away from the NH he had taken a friend's acetaminophen with codeine for a headache. Mr. M. contracted to take only medications prescribed for him in the NH and to have drug screens performed after returning from visits outside the facility. A subsequent urine drug screen was positive for opiates, precipitating his discharge from the NH. Mr. M. declined any referrals to a chemical dependency program for treatment.

Surreptitious use of an illicit drug may be difficult to detect, and it has the potential to cause serious problems in already frail or chronically ill NH residents. Providers should be alert to behavior problems or physical symptoms that may indicate continued substance use. Contracting with patients for randomly timed drug screens is one approach to monitoring this problem.

Treatment of Alcohol and Drug Misuse in the NH

Once a substance use problem has been detected, management embraces a spectrum of activities which may include any or all of the following: detoxification, treatment of medical complications and comorbidities, discussions with the patient and significant others, and referral for chemical dependency treatment.

Since the majority of NH residents are admitted from another health facility, alcohol withdrawal or illicit drug withdrawal is not likely to be encountered as frequently in the NH as in the acute care hospital (Rubenstein et al., 1988). Minor withdrawal symptoms may be treated symptomatically in the NH, but severe withdrawal is best managed in the acute care setting.

Role of the Primary Care Provider

It is important for primary care providers to give support and counseling to their NH patients with substance misuse problems. Providers should present concerns about alcohol or drug misuse directly to the patient. Involvement of family and significant others is also crucial. Failure to address substance misuse in NH residents impedes rehabilitation and interferes with a resident's ability to regain and maintain independence. Persons with continued alcohol dependency suffer significantly increased mortality compared with those who achieve remission (Bullock, Reed, & Grant, 1992). Admission to an NH is a time of crisis when people are more receptive to lifestyle changes, such as modifying their substance use. Studies suggest that older problem drinkers experiencing physical health problems and prolonged hospitalizations are more likely to stop drinking (Atkinson, 1985; Moos, Brennan, & Moos, 1991). In addition, a physician's recommendation can be a powerful motivation for abstinence (Walsh et al., 1992). Interviewing strategies that enhance the positive outcome of such provider-patient interactions have been reviewed by Atkinson and others (Atkinson, 1985; Miller, 1989).

Chemical Dependency Programs for NH Residents

NH residents with active chemical dependency, especially those who will return to the community and live independently, should be considered for referral to a chemical dependency treatment program. Even though studies show that elderly alcoholics do as well as younger people in treatment, or better, health care providers seldom refer elderly persons for alcohol treatment (Curtis et al., 1989).

There are many different models and techniques currently available for chemical dependency treatment. The actual model employed is less important than creating an individualized program matched to the patient. Key elements of chemical dependency treatment include a knowledgeable and experienced staff, an environment that supports change, adequate duration of treatment, involvement of the patient's family or friends, and use of both formal and informal support systems.

Even though NH residents may be unable to participate in traditional inpatient chemical dependency treatment programs because of physical or cognitive impairments, age-specific alcohol programs, or less intensive outpatient options, may be appropriate.

Another option is participation in chemical dependency programs or activities specifically modified to accommodate persons with physical or mental limitations. Schaschl and Straw (1989) report the development of an alcohol and drug intervention program to accommodate persons with physical disabilities. This model program provided alcohol and drug evaluations and consultations to physical rehabilitation units, while simultaneously developing a disability component within a standard chemical dependency treatment program. The disability component includes provision of personal care needs by certified nursing assistants, and a weekly support group for clients with concomitant chemical dependency and physical impairments.

Horton and Howe (1982) report the successful use of behavioral modification to combat alcohol dependence in an elderly, cognitively impaired NH resident. They instituted frequent breathalyzer testing for their patient and restricted privileges when breathalyzer readings indicated continued drinking.

Elderly alcoholics have been reported to do well in age-specific programs which emphasize peer group socialization (Kofoed, Tolson, Atkinson, Toth, & Turner, 1987). Socialization and peer support models can be modified for the NH setting. In the Portland VA NH, a weekly group is held for residents with substance misuse problems who are unable to participate in standard treatment programs (J. Dunlop, personal communication, 1994). This group is led by an addiction therapist and a staff nurse. The goal of the group is to provide education and a forum for discussion by participants about the impact of substance use on their medical and social problems.

Volunteers may also play a role in providing socialization and support for NH residents with substance misuse problems. Volunteer peer counseling programs have been useful in a variety of mental health settings (Bratter & Freeman, 1990; McGill & Patterson, 1990). The peer counseling model can be adapted to NHs, with older volunteers who have achieved stable sobriety supporting residents in abstinence, as in the following case history (Joseph, Barrington, Gardner, Atkinson, & Tolson, 1994).

Case History
Mr. R., a 57-year-old with chronic lung disease who required continuous home oxygen therapy, was admitted to a VA hospital with facial burns caused by a fire that occurred when he smoked a cigarette while intoxicated from alcohol. He had a history of alcohol dependence; 4 years previously he had participated in a residential alcohol treatment program, but he had relapsed. Mr. R. was referred for alcohol treatment after admission to the NH. On his first contact with the addiction therapist Mr. R. stated that he did not have a drinking problem but thought he'd "better quit for a while." He was paired with a peer volunteer to provide support and encouragement, and enrolled in the NH alcohol education group. After 1 month in the NH group, Mr. R. was transferred to an outpatient elder-specific alcohol treatment program, in which he has remained for more than 1 year.

This case history illustrates the integration of several approaches to alcohol problems during a resident's stay at an NH.

Alcohol and Drug-Free Environments
There will still be some NH residents for whom education, support, or treatment programs are not appropriate. In some cases long-term placement in an alcohol- and drug-free, NH, foster home, or other supervised living situation is the most effective management of continued substance misuse. In the demented patient who will not abstain and refuses care, placement by a guardian in a closed setting, or commitment for alcoholism, which is permitted in some states, may be tried.

The creation of an alcohol and drug-free facility is an active process. In our experience the following elements are useful in the initiation and maintenance of an alcohol and drug-free environment in the NH: (1) consultation from experts in the treatment of chemical dependency; (2) education for NH staff about alcohol and drug misuse; (3) cooperation from resident's council or other representatives of the NH residents; (4) creation of guidelines for responding to substance misuse in the facility.

Effectiveness
There are no outcome data regarding treatment for alcohol or drug problems in NH residents. The descriptions of modified chemical dependency treat-

ment programs for patients with physical and cognitive impairments are based on information from model programs, case reports, or pilot trials with small numbers of patients. Research is needed to define the role of chemical dependency treatment for NH residents.

TOBACCO (NICOTINE) DEPENDENCE

Over 30% of men and 25% of women age 65 or older smoke, making tobacco misuse the most common substance use disorder among elderly persons (U.S. Department of Health and Human Services, 1989). In a survey of persons admitted to a VA NH, 46% of respondents had lifetime tobacco dependence, and 28% were still smoking at the time of NH admission (Joseph, Ganzini, & Atkinson, 1995). Although NHs generally restrict smoking to designated areas inside or outside the facility, many NH residents continue to smoke (C. Boswell, personal communication, 1994).

Tobacco use contributes to chronic health problems encountered in NH residents, including pulmonary and cardiovascular disease, stroke, and cancer. Continued smoking exacerbates other common conditions, such as obstructive lung disease, osteoporosis, and peripheral vascular problems. Immediate and long-term benefits of quitting, including a substantial decrease in mortality, have been documented, even for elderly persons (Samet, 1992).

Advice and counseling from health care providers can be an important influence on quitting smoking (Schwartz, 1992). Although the majority of adult smokers quit without specialized treatment, programs employing strategies such as relaxation, social support, training in coping skills, and group counseling are appropriate for older persons, and may be adapted to the NH setting (Atkinson & Ganzini, 1994).

MISUSE OF PRESCRIPTION DRUGS IN NHs

Definitions

Misuse of prescribed medications is a major problem in NHs. Medication *misuse* includes inappropriate use, overuse, and underuse, and in NHs it encompasses virtually every class of agent, from prescription drugs such as histamine blockers and antibiotics to over-the-counter preparations such as laxatives, cold preparations, and analgesics (Beers et al., 1992; Gurwitz, Noonan, & Soumerai, 1992; Sherman, Avorn, & Campion, 1987). More medications are taken by the elderly than any other age group, with institutionalized elders taking the most (Beers et al., 1992). NH residents frequently have multiple chronic conditions, for each of which they may be prescribed one or more medications concurrently. Studies of NH prescribing patterns document an average of six to eight drugs per resident, with some persons receiving over 20 different medications (Beers et al., 1988; Office of Long-Term Care, 1976). Of particular concern are the psychoactive medications—anxiolytics, sedative-hypnotics, antipsychotics, and antidepressants, both because of the frequency with which they are prescribed and because of their potential to result in dependence and adverse effects (Miller, Belkin, & Gold, 1991; Ray, Griffin, Schaffner, Baugh, & Mellon, 1987).

Epidemiology

Prevalence of Psychoactive Drugs in NHs

Psychoactive drugs are reportedly prescribed for 34% to as high as 90% of NH residents (see Figure 10.1) (Beers et al., 1988; Buck, 1988; Burns & Kamerow, 1988; Cooper & Francisco, 1981; Garrard et al., 1992; Harrington, Tompkins, Curtis, & Grant, 1992; Ray, Federspicl, & Schaffner, 1980; Sternberg, Spector, Drugorich, Fretwell, & Jackson, 1990). Much of this variation reflects disparities in study methods. Studies differ in the number and type of psychoactive agents surveyed and in the methods used to determine drug use. For example, some studies accept any order for a psychoactive medication as drug use, while others report only those medications actually administered. Other significant study variations include the length of the survey, which may vary from a days to months; age of the patients; prevalence of comorbid psychiatric disorders; and type of facility surveyed (SNF, ICF, home for the mentally retarded). Not surprisingly, higher prevalence rates tend to be reported in studies using a more inclusive definition of psychoactive medications and more liberal criteria for drug use. Despite their methodological differences, a number of studies report use of psychoactive medications in over half of NH residents surveyed (Beers et al., 1988; Buck, 1988; Ray et al., 1980; Sternberg et al., 1990).

Medicare and Medicaid claims data reveal high rates of psychoactive drug use in NHs. A study of 5,902 Medicaid recipients over age 65 in Tennessee NHs conducted by Ray et al. (1980) found that 74% were prescribed psychoactive drugs. Similar studies of claims data in Rhode Island and Illinois NHs reported rates for use of psychoactive drugs of 54% and 60% respectively (Buck, 1988; Sternberg et al., 1990). Beers and coworkers (1988) examined both psychoactive drug prescriptions and medication administration records. They reported that 65% of residents in 12 intermediate care NHs in Massachusetts had orders for one or more psychoactive drugs, and 53% had used those drugs at least 5 days during the study month.

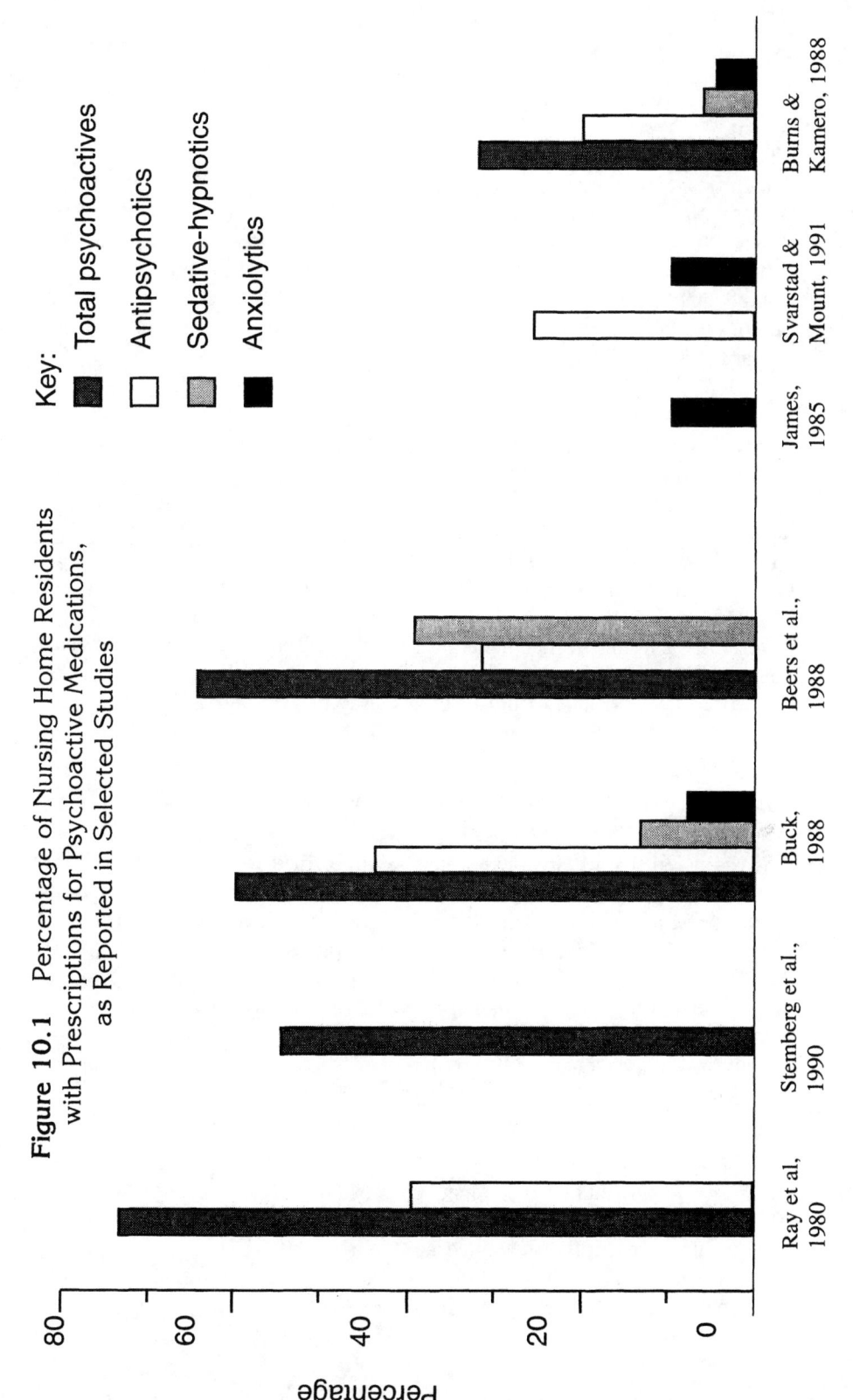

Figure 10.1 Percentage of Nursing Home Residents with Prescriptions for Psychoactive Medications, as Reported in Selected Studies

Key:
- Total psychoactives
- Antipsychotics
- Sedative-hypnotics
- Anxiolytics

Polypharmacy

A significant number of NH residents are prescribed more than one psychoactive medication. Researchers have reported that between 7% and 37% of NH residents had orders for two or more psychoactive drugs during the periods studied, although it is not always clear from the material presented whether the prescriptions were concurrent (Beardsley, Larson, Burns, Thompson, 1989; Beers et al., 1988; Buck, 1988; Burns & Kamerow, 1988; Garrard et al., 1992; Ray et al., 1980).

Antipsychotics

Antipsychotics are among the most frequently prescribed psychoactive drugs in the NH, making up as much as half to three quarters of all psychoactive agents prescribed (Beardsley et al., 1989; Buck, 1988). Large-scale studies have documented the use of antipsychotics in 21% to 44% of NH residents (Buck, 1988; Garrard et al., 1991; Harrington et al., 1992; Ray et al., 1980;) Garrard and coworkers (1991) reported a relatively low prevalence rate of 21%, but they surveyed use of only 3 antipsychotic agents. Reviews of prescriptions for Medicaid recipients in Illinois and Tennessee NHs found that 43% to 44% of residents received antipsychotic medications (Buck, 1988; Ray et al., 1980) In one of those studies (Ray et al., 1980) 9% of NH residents surveyed received at least one dose of an antipsychotic agent every day for a year.

Sedative-Hypnotics

It is estimated that sedative/hypnotics are prescribed for 7% to 40% of NH residents (Beers et al., 1988; Buck, 1988; Burns & Kamerow, 1988; Gilleard, Smits, & Morgan, 1984; James, 1985). In the past two decades, benzodiazepines and diphenhydramine have largely replaced barbiturates and chloral hydrate as the dominant sedative-hypnotic agents used in the NH. Although sedative-hypnotics are designed for short-term use only, studies show that they are frequently prescribed for months at a time, placing recipients at risk of physical dependence and chronic toxicity (Beers et al., 1988; James, 1985).

Anxiolytics

Six to twelve percent of NH residents are prescribed antianxiety agents (Buck, 1988; Svarstad & Mount, 1991; Burns & Kamerow, 1988). Benzodiazepines are the most frequently prescribed anxiolytics in the NH, with long-acting agents such as diazepam and chlordiazepoxide making up a substantial proportion of reported prescriptions (Beardsley et al., 1989; Buck, 1988).

Antidepressants

Antidepressants are prescribed for relatively few NH residents, approximately 6% to 14% (Beers et al., 1988; Buck, 1988; Burns & Kamerow, 1988; Garrard et al., 1992). Beers and colleagues found that the largest group of NH residents with an antidepressant prescription received amitriptyline, an agent with a high profile of side effects in the elderly.

Prescribing Patterns

Studies of psychoactive drugs in NHs have raised the concern that these drugs are being prescribed too often without adequate indications and administered for too long without being monitored, and that the agents and doses selected are likely to cause side effects in the frail elderly (Beers et al., 1988; Harrington et al., 1992). Several investigators have reported the prescription of psychoactive drugs without documentation of a diagnosis justifying their use (Beardsley, et al., 1989; Beers et al., 1988; Harrington et al., 1992). Thirty percent of NH residents with prescriptions for psychoactive agents studied by Burns and Kamerow (1988) lacked appropriate documentation to justify the use of these drugs, as did 21% of those examined by Beardsley et al. (1989). Beers and colleagues (1988) reported that 61% of NH residents receiving antidepresssants had no recorded diagnosis of depression.

Psychoactive drugs ordered for NH residents are often the ones likely to cause adverse drug effects in the elderly, such as amitriptyline, diphenhydramine, and long-acting benzodiazepines. (Beers et al., 1988). Beers et al. (1992) used a consensus panel to develop explicit criteria for appropriate medication use in elderly NH residents. When these criteria were then applied to prescribing practices in Los Angeles area NHs, 40.3% of residents were found to have prescriptions for at least one inappropriate drug, most often the agent in its class with the highest profile of side effects in the elderly. The dosage levels of antipsychotic agents in NHs was examined by Buck (1988), who reported that some residents received very high doses, the equivalent of 1 gram of chlorpromazine a day or more.

Garrard et al. (1992) challenged some of the negative findings and assumptions about prescribing practices in NHs in a longitudinal study of use of psychoactive drugs by NH residents. In that study, about one third of patients who were prescribed antipsychotics at NH admission were no longer taking them 3 months later. A similar number of persons without prescriptions for antipsychotics at entrance to the NH were taking them 3 months later. In addition, the majority of NH residents taking antipsychotics had dosage adjustments during their NH stay, suggesting that the medications were being monitored. In that same study population, there was a statistically significant decline in benzodiazepine use from 21% at admission to 15% 3 months later (Garrard et al., 1992).

Overuse of medications is the most common problem in NHs, but drugs may also be underused, especially in the treatment of depression and pain. Depression is estimated to affect between 9% and 38% of NH residents (Ouslander et al., 1991). Although antidepressants have proven effective in the elderly, they are not often prescribed for depressed NH residents (Heston et al., 1992; Lakshmanan, Mion, & Frengley, 1986). In a survey of 60 NHs, Heston et al., (1992) found that only 10% of residents with a diagnosis of depression were treated with an antidepressant. Pain is also a common problem of NH residents. Ferrell, Ferrell, and Osterweil (1990) reported complaints of pain in 71% of residents in one community NH. Eighty-four percent of subjects had physicians orders for analgesics, but most were to be given "as needed, " and only 15% had actually received pain medication within the previous 24 hours.

Characteristics of Residents, Facilities, and Prescribers

Particular characteristics of residents, facilities, and prescribers have been associated with drug misuse in NHs. Several studies document decreased prescribing of psychoactives for older NH residents (Buck, 1988; Garrard et al., 1992; Ray et al., 1980). Garrard et al. (1992) found that NH residents who were physically restrained were also likely to be receiving psychoactive medications, particularly antipsychotics.

Rest homes and ICFs have been reported to use more antipsychotics than SNFs (Garrard et al., 1992). Inappropriate drug use has been associated with residence in NHs that have more beds and fewer direct-care staff members per bed, suggesting that psychoactive medications are being used as chemical restraints (Beers et al., 1992; Ray et al., 1980; Svarstad & Mount, 1991).

Ray and colleagues (1980) found that physicians with larger NH practices prescribed 81% of antipsychotic medications. In contrast, Beers et al. (1993) reported that physicians who spent more time in NHs prescribed less medication overall. In that study, frequent consultation with psychiatrists was the characteristic most closely correlated with appropriate prescribing of psychoactive drugs.

Clinical Considerations

As a group, elderly NH residents have a number of characteristics that place them at high risk for adverse drug effects, including the following: (1) physiologic changes of aging which result in increased sensitivity to standard doses of many drugs; (2) multiple, coexisting, chronic diseases; (3) functional impairment; (4) need for multiple medications; and (5) deficits in cognition or speech which may delay or prevent the communication of drug-induced side effects (Beers et al., 1993; Thompson, Moran, & Nies, 1983). Medications have been implicated in numerous adverse events in the elderly, sometimes with devastating consequences. Inappropriate prescribing increases the risk of negative clinical outcomes for NH residents. Drug interactions and adverse drug effects are magnified by polypharmacy (Gurwitz, Soumerai, & Avorn, 1990).

In a study by Gerety and colleagues, (1993) central nervous system drugs were responsible for 23% of adverse drug effects among NH residents. (Gerety, Cornell, Plichta, Eimer, 1993). Common side effects of psychoactive drugs in the elderly and chronically ill include constipation, orthostasis, confusion, blurred vision, and urinary retention. (Thompson et al., 1983). The use of psychoactive agents also increases the risk of falls and hip fractures among older persons (Ray et al., 1987; Yip & Cumming, 1994). Antipsychotic drugs may have a number of unwanted effects on the central nervous system, including tardive dyskinesia, akathisia, dystonias, drug-induced Parkinsonism, seizures, and neuroleptic malignant syndrome, which is rare but potentially fatal (Keltner & Folks, 1993). Long-acting benzodiazepines have been shown to decrease psychomotor performance, worsen preexisting depression, and increase cognitive impairment in the elderly (Larson, Kukull, & Buchner, 1987; Thompson et al., 1983). Benzodiazepines used chronically may accumulate to produce daytime sedation, or induce dependence (Thompson et al., 1983).

Withdrawal

Patients who are habituated to psychoactive agents may experience withdrawal symptoms when these drugs are stopped. Gerety et al. (1993) reported that 22% of adverse drug withdrawal events in NH residents resulted from the discontinuation of central nervous system agents. Abrupt discontinuation of benzodiazepines and sedative hypnotics after many months of daily use typically results in discontinuance symptoms, such as anxiety, sleep disturbance, psychomotor agitation, difficulty concentrating, and depressed mood (Solomon, Manepalli, Ireland, & Mahon, 1993). Benzodiazepines and other psychoactive agents should be withdrawn slowly to minimize withdrawal symptoms (Schweizer, Case, & Rickels, 1989). If prescription drug dependence is detected, patients may benefit from the interventions described previously for alcohol problems, although there are no outcome data regarding treatment of prescription drug problems in NH residents.

Regulation of Psychoactive Drugs in NHs

In the United States, psychoactive medications in NHs are increasingly subject to federal regulation (Omnibus Budget Reconciliation Act, 1987; Health Care Financing Administration, 1989). Mounting evidence of poor-quality care in NHs, including an unfavorable study by the Institute of Medicine (1986), resulted in passage of the Nursing Home Reform Amendments as part of the Omnibus Budget Resolution Act of 1987 (OBRA) (Elon & Pawlson, 1992; Institute of Medicine, 1986). One goal of these regulations is to eliminate the use of unnecessary medications, especially the use of psychoactive agents for behavior control or the convenience of the NH staff.

Additional regulations and guidelines developed by the Health Care Financing Administration (HCFA) went into effect in 1990 (Health Care Financing Administration, 1989). The HCFA guidelines include specific criteria for the use of antipsychotic and other psychoactive medications (Simonson, 1991). Specific mental health diagnoses—such as schizophrenia, psychotic mood disorder, and dementia with associated psychotic or agitated features—that represent a danger to the patient or to others, or that actually interfere with the staff's ability to provide care, must be documented to justify the use of antipsychotic medications. Problem behaviors, such as wandering, anxiety, insomnia, or unspecified agitation, are not adequate indications for antipsychotic drugs, nor are antipsychotics to be used on an "as needed" basis. In addition, the regulations require drug holidays, gradual reductions of dosages, and the use of behavioral programs to replace medications. NHs that consistently fail to comply with the guidelines face stiff fines and penalties. A more detailed discussion of the OBRA regulations is available in reviews by Elon and Simonson (Elon & Pawlson, 1992; Simonson, 1991).

Impact of Regulations on Prescribing in NHs

The potential impact of the OBRA regulations was studied by Garrard and colleagues (Garrard et al., 1991). They applied the HCFA guidelines to data previously gathered about the use of antipsychotic medications in 60 Medicare and Medicaid certified NHs. In the NHs studied, half of the residents receiving antipsychotics did not have adequate documentation justifying the use of these medications. Characteristics of residents receiving unjustified antipsychotics included older age, admission from a hospital, and mental disorders not covered by the regulations.

Since implementation of the OBRA regulations, a decrease in use of psychoactive drugs has been reported by some authors (Rovner, Edelman, Cox, & Shmuely, 1992; Shorr, Fought, & Ray, 1994). A study of 17 NHs in the Baltimore area showed a 36% reduction in prescriptions for antipsychotic drugs in the 6-month period following the implementation of OBRA (Rovner et al., 1992). Shorr and colleagues (1994) reported a 26.7% decrease in the rate of use of antipsychotic drugs in Tennessee NHs after OBRA was instituted, with no change in the use of other psychoactive medications. Although the study by Shorr and colleagues demonstrated an overall reduction in use of antipsychotic drugs across all facilities, in 25% of the NHs under study the use remained the same or increased. Reduction of was greatest in NHs with older residents, a greater proportion of female residents, a higher baseline rate of use, and higher third-shift staffing (Shorr et al., 1994).

Changing Prescribing Patterns in NHs

The OBRA regulations have already had a demonstrable impact on prescribing patterns in NHs, as described above (Garrard et al., 1991; Shorr et al., 1994). However, compliance with OBRA alone does not insure improved quality of patient care. Reduction of psychoactive medication use must be accompanied by comprehensive evaluation and treatment planning, using both appropriate pharmacologic and nonpharmacologic interventions for NH residents with psychiatric disorders and behavioral problems (Board of Directors of the American Association for Geriatric Psychiatry Clinical Practice et al., 1992). Educational interventions, including specific training in nonpharmacologic approaches to behavior management, have been successful in reducing the use of psychoactive drugs without increasing the use of physical restraints or the incidence of disruptive behaviors (Avorn et al., 1992; Ray et al., 1993). Since the nursing staff is central to medication use in NHs, its members should be included in educational interventions to improve drug utilization (Avorn, et al., 1992; Gurwitz et al., 1990).

International Perspective

Although this review has concentrated on data from American NHs, similar concerns about misuse of psychoactive medication have been expressed in studies from the United Kingdom, Australia, the Netherlands, and Scandinavia (Gilbert, Owen, Innes, & Sansom, 1993; Gilleard et al., 1984; Koopmans, Van Rossum, et al., 1993; Yip & Cumming, 1994). Interventions to reduce medication for NH residents, similar to those described in the United States, have been successfully implemented in European and Australian facilities as well (Gilbert et al., 1993; Janiri et al., 1991; Koopmans, de Vaan, et al., 1993).

Unresolved Issues

Data regarding substance misuse in NHs are sketchy. The extent of alcohol and drug misuse among NH residents remains unknown. Nor has the impact of substance misuse on NHs and their residents been investigated. Research is needed to clarify the prevalence of substance misuse in NHs, and to define its effect on patient outcomes and health care costs. Perhaps most important, studies should address effective strategies for managing substance misuse in NH residents and the role of chemical dependency treatment in this population.

The prevalence of psychoactive medication in NHs is fairly well defined. However, further research is needed to establish both the frequency with which psychoactives are misused and the factors which contribute to their misuse. Clinical outcomes and strategies for decreasing inappropriate use of drugs also merit further investigation.

SUMMARY AND RECOMMENDATIONS

Alcohol and drug problems in NH residents are frequently overlooked, with potentially devastating consequences. Effective intervention requires actively looking for substance misuse, evaluating it carefully, and treating it appropriately. Additional training in the recognition and management of substance use disorders is needed for primary care providers. A simple screen for alcohol and drug abuse or dependence should be employed as part of the initial assessment for persons admitted to NHs. The Minimum Data Set (MDS) is a federally mandated assessment recorded for all NH residents in the United States. The MDS should be modified to include information about substance use disorders.

Treatment for alcoholism can be successfully initiated in the NH setting. Tobacco dependence is a preventable cause of morbidity and mortality, and quitting smoking has substantial health benefits, even among elderly persons. A range of alcohol and drug treatment programs should be available to NH residents.

Misuse of prescription medications, particularly psychoactive drugs, is a common and complex problem in NHs. Federal regulations now control the prescription of antipsychotic agents in NHs to an unprecedented degree, but education must be added to regulations if the overall quality of care in NHs is to be improved.

NOTE

1. CAGE is a mnemonic. It stands for: "Have you ever tried to *C*ut down your drinking? Has anyone ever *A*nnoyed you by criticizing your drinking? Have you ever felt *G*uilty about drinking? Do you ever have an *E*ye-opener (a drink first thing in the morning)?

REFERENCES

Adams, W. L., Yuan, Z., Barboriak, J. J., & Rimm, A. A. (1993). Alcohol-related hospital-izations of elderly people: Prevalence and geographic variation in the United States. *JAMA, 270,* 1222–25.

Aiken, L. H., Mezey, M. D., Lynaugh, J. E., & Buck C. R. Jr., (1985). Teaching nursing homes: Prospects for improving long-term care. *Journal of the American Geriatrics Society, 33,* 196–201.

American Psychiatric Association. (1987). *Diagnostic and statistical manual of mental dis-orders* (3rd ed. rev.). Washington, DC: Author.

Atkinson, R. M. (1984). Substance use and abuse in late life. In R. Atkinson (Ed.), *Alcohol and drug abuse in old age* (pp. 1–21). Washington, DC: American Psychiatric Press.

Atkinson, R. M. (1985). Persuading alcoholic patients to seek treatment. *Comprehensive Therapy, 11,* 16–24.

Atkinson, R. M. (1991). Alcohol and drug abuse in the elderly. In R. Jacoby & C. Oppenheimer (Eds.), *Psychiatry in the elderly* (pp. 819–851). Oxford and New York: Oxford University Press.

Atkinson, R. M., & Ganzini, L. (1994). Substance Abuse. In C. E. Coffey & J. Cummings (Eds.), *Textbook of geriatric neuropsychiatry* (pp. 297–321). Washington, DC: American Psychiatric Press.

Avorn, J., Soumerai, S. B., Everitt, D. E., Ross-Degnan, D., Beers, M. H., Sherman, D., Salem-Schatz, S. R., & Fields, D. (1992). A randomized trial of a program to reduce the use of psychoactive drugs in nursing homes. *New England Journal of Medicine, 327,* 168–73.

Beardsley, R. S., Larson, D. B., Burns, B. J., Thompson, J. W., & Kamerow, D. B. (1989). Prescribing of psychotropics in elderly nursing home patients. *Journal of the American Geriatrics Society, 37,* 327–330.

Beers, M., Avorn, J., Soumerai, S. B., Everitt, D. E., Sherman, D. S., & Salem, S. (1988). Psychoactive medication use in intermediate-care facility residents. *JAMA, 260,* 3016–3020.

Beers, M. H., Fingold, S. F., Ouslander, J. G., Reuben, D. B., Morgenstern, H., & Beck, J. C. (1993). Characteristics and quality of prescribing by doctors practicing in nursing homes. *Journal of the American Geriatrics Society, 41,* 802–807.

Beers, M. H., Ouslander, J. G., Fingold, S. F., Morgenstern, H., Reuben, D. B., Rogers, W., Zeffren, M. J., & Beck, J. C. (1992). Inappropriate medication prescribing in skilled-nursing facilities. *Annals of Internal Medicine, 117,* 684–89.

Blazer, D. G., & Pennybacker, M. R. (1984). Epidemiology of alcoholism in the elderly. In J. Hartford & T. Samorajski (Eds.), *Alcoholism in the elderly* (pp. 25–33). New York: Raven.

Blow, F. C. (1991). *Michigan Alcoholism Screening Test: Geriatric Version (MAST–G).* Ann Arbor: University of Michigan Alcohol Research Center.

Board of Directors of the American Association for Geriatric Psychiatry, Clinical Practice Committee of the American Geriatrics Society, and Committee on Long-Term Care and Treatment for the Elderly, American Psychiatric Association (1992). Psychotherapeutic medications in the nursing home. *Journal of the American Geriatrics Society, 40,* 946–49.

Bratter, B., & Freeman, E. (1990). The maturing peer counseling. *Generations, 24,* 49–52.

Buchsbaum, D. G., Buchanan, R. G., Welsh, J., Centor, R. M., & Schnoll, S. H. (1992). Screening for drinking disorders in the elderly using the CAGE questionnaire. *Journal of the American Geriatrics Society, 40,* 662–665.

Buck, J. A. (1988). Psychotropic drug practice in nursing homes. *Journal of the American Geriatrics Society, 36,* 409–418.

Bullock, K. D., Reed, R. J., & Grant, I. (1992). Reduced mortality risk in alcoholics who achieve long-term abstinence. *JAMA, 267,* 668–672.

Burns, B. J., & Kamerow, D. B. (1988). Psychotropic drug prescriptions for nursing home residents. *Journal of Family Practice, 26,* 155–60.

Caracci, G., & Miller, N. S. (1991). Alcohol and drug addiction in the elderly. In N. S. Miller (Ed.), *Comprehensive handbook of drug and alcohol addiction* (pp. 179–191). New York: Marcel Dekker.

Chien, C. P., Stotsky, B. A., & Cole, J. O. (1973). Psychiatric treatment for nursing home patients: Drug, alcohol, and milieu. *American Journal of Psychiatry, 130,* 543–548.

Cooper, J. W., & Francisco, G. E. (1981). Psychotropic usage in long-term care facility geriatric patients. *Hospital Formulary, 16,* 407–419.

Curtis, J. R., Geller, G., Stokes, E. J., Levine, D. M., & Moore, R. D. (1989). Characteristics, diagnosis, and treatment of alcoholism in elderly patients. *Journal of the American Geriatrics Society, 37,* 310–316.

Cyr, M. G., & Sherman, S. E. (1993). Screening, assessment, making the diagnosis. In J. Bigby (Ed.), *Substance abuse education in general internal medicine: A manual for faculty* (pp. 1–51). Washington, DC: Society for General Internal Medicine.

Department of Veterans Affairs. (1990). (*See* Stockford, Kelly, & Seitz, 1995.)

Douglass, R. (1980). Aged alcoholic widows in the nursing home. *Focus on Women, 1,* 258–265.

Dvoredsky, A. E., Suchinsky, R., & Speight, J. F. (1989). Chemical abuse among veterans. In A. J. Giannini & Andrew E. Slaby (Eds.), *Drugs of Abuse* (pp. 441–452). Oradell, NJ: Medical Economics Books.

Elon, R., & Pawlson, L. G. (1992). The impact of OBRA on medical practice within nursing facilities. *Journal of the American Geriatrics Society, 40,* 958–962.

Ferrell, B. A., Ferrell, B. R., & Osterweil, D. (1990). Pain in the nursing home. *Journal of the American Geriatrics Society, 38,* 409–414.

Fitzgerald, J. F., Moore, P. S., & Dittus, R. S. (1988). The care of elderly patients with hip fracture: Changes since implementation of the prospective payment system. *New England Journal of Medicine, 319,* 1392–1397.

Garrard, J., Dunham, T., Makris, L., Cooper, S., Heston, L. L., Ratner, E. R., Zelterman, D., & Kane, R. L. (1992). Longitudinal study of psychotropic drug use by elderly nursing home residents. *Journal of Gerontology, 47,* M183–188.

Garrard, J., Makris, L., Dunham, T., Heston, L. L., Cooper, S., Ratner, E. R., Zelterman, D., & Kane, R. L. (1991). Evaluation of neuroleptic drug use by nursing home elderly under proposed Medicare and Medicaid regulations. *JAMA, 265,* 463–467.

Gerety, M. B., Cornell, J. E., Plichta, D. T., & Eimer, M. (1993). Adverse events related to drugs and drug withdrawal in nursing home residents. *Journal of the American Geriatrics Society, 41,* 1326–1332.

Gilbert, A., Owen, N., Innes, J.M. & Sansom, L. (1993). Trial of an intervention to reduce chronic benzodiazepine use among residents of aged-care accomodation. *Australia and New Zealand Journal of Medicine, 23,* 343–347.

Gilleard, C. J., Smits, C., & Morgan, K. (1984). Changes in hypnotic usage in residential homes for the elderly: A longitudinal study. *Archives of Geronotology and Geriatrics, 3,* 223–228.

Graham, K. (1986). Identifying and measuring alcohol abuse among elderly: Serious problems with existing instrumentation. *Journal of Studies on Alcohol, 47,* 322–26.

Gurwitz, J., Noonan, J., & Soumerai, S. (1992). Reducing the use of H2-receptor antagonists in the long-term-care setting. *Journal of the American Geriatrics Society, 40,* 359–364.

Gurwitz, J. H., Soumerai, S. B., & Avorn, J. (1990). Improving medication prescribing and utilization in the nursing home. *Journal of the American Geriatrics Society, 38,* 542–552.

Hall, E. P. (1983). Substance abuse in the aging. In G. Bennett, C. Vouvrakis, & D. S. Woolf (Eds.), *Substance abuse: Pharmacologic, developmental and clinical perspectives* (pp. 192–206). New York: Wiley.

Harrington, C., Tompkins, C., Curtis, M., & Grant, L. (1992). Psychotropic drug use in long-term care facilities: A review of the literature. *Gerontologist, 6,* 822–833.

Health Care Financing Administration. (1989). Medicare and Medicaid: requirements for long term care facilities: Final rule with request for comments. *Federal Register, 54,* 5316–5336.

Heston, L. L., Garrard, J., Makris, L., Kane, R. L., Cooper, S., Dunham, T., & Zelterman, D. (1992). Inadequate treatment of depressed nursing home elderly. *Journal of the American Geriatrics Society, 40,* 1117–1122.

Hing, E. (1989a). Effects of the prospective payment system on nursing homes. *Vital and Health Statistics, 98,* 1–19.

Hing, E. (1989b). *Nursing home utilization by current residents: United States, 1985.* Hyattsville, MD: National Center for Health Statistics.

Horton, A., Jr., & Howe, N. (1982). Behavior therapy with an aged alcoholic: A case study. *International Journal of Behavioral Geriatrics, 1,* 17–18.

Hurt, R. D., Finlayson, R., Morse, R. M., & Davis, L. J. (1988). Alcoholism in elderly persons: Medical aspects and prognosis of 216 patients. *Mayo Clinic Proceedings, 63,* 753–760.

Institute of Medicine (1986). *Improving the quality of nursing home care.* Washington, DC: National Academy.

Institute of Medicine. (1986). *Improving the quality of nursing home care.* Washington, DC: National Academy.

James, D. S. (1985). Survey of hypnotic drug use in nursing homes. *Journal of the American Geriatrics Society, 33,* 436–439.

Janiri, L., DiGiovanni, A., Persico, A., Zeppetelli, E., Mannelli, P., Antico, L., & Tempesta, E. (1991). Benzodiazepine consumption and risk of dependence in institutionalized geriatric patients. *Minerva Psichiatrica, 32,* 151–63.

Joseph, C. L., Atkinson, R. M., Ganzini, L., & Edwards, A. (1992). Screening for alcohol problems in the nursing home [Abstract]. *Journal of the American Geriatrics Society, 40,* SA71.

Joseph, C. L., Barrington, R. N., Gardner, P., Atkinson, R. M., & Tolson, B. (1994, March). A peer volunteer program for extended-care clients with alcohol problems. Paper presented at the American Society on Aging Annual Meeting, San Francisco.

Joseph, C. L., Ganzini, L., & Atkinson, R. M. (1995). Screening for alcohol use disorders in the nursing home. *Journal of the American Geriatrics Society, 43,* 368–373.

Kane, R. A., & Kane, R. L. (1987). *Long-term care: Principles, programs and policies.* New York, NY: Springer Publishing.

Kastenbaum, R., & Slater, P. (1964). Effects of wine on the interpersonal behavior of geriatric patients: An exploratory study. In R. Kastenbaum (Ed.), *New thoughts on old age* (pp. 191–204). New York: Springer Publishing.

Kastenbaum, R. L., Sarley, V., & Stepto, R. C. (1968). The use of wine in hospitals and nursing homes. In S. Lucia (Ed.), *Wine and health* (pp. 25–32). Menlo Park, CA: Pacific Coast Publishers.

Keeler, E. B., Kane, R. L., & Solomon, D. H. (1981). Short- and long-term residents of nursing homes. *Medical Care, 19,* 363–369.

Keltner, N. L., & Folks, D. G. (1993). *Psychotropic drugs.* St. Louis: Mosby.

Kemper, P., & Murtaugh, C. (1991). Lifetime use of nursing home care. *New England Journal of Medicine, 324,* 595–600.

Kofoed, L. L., Tolson, R. L., Atkinson, R. M., Toth, R. L., & Turner, J. A. (1987). Treatment compliance of older alcoholics: An elder-specific approach is superior to "mainstreaming." *Journal of Studies on Alcohol, 48,* 47–51.

Koopmans, R.T., van Rossum, J.M., van den Hoogen, H.J., Hekster, Y.A., Willekens-Bogaers, M.A., & van Weel, C. (1993). Use of psychotropic drugs in a goup of nursing home patients with dementia: Many users, long-term use but low dosages. *Tijdschrift voor Gerontologie en Geriatrie, 24,* 214–219.

Koopmans, R.T., de Vaan, H.H., van den Hoogen, H.J., Gribnau, R.W., Hekster, Y.A., & van Wheel, C. (1993). Reduction of drug intake following admission to a psychgeriatric nursing home: discontinuation is possible. *Nederlands Tijdschrift voor Geneeskunde, 22,* 1049–1054.

Lakshmanan, M., Mion, L. C., & Frengley, J. D. (1986). Effective low dose tricyclic antidepressant treatment for depressed geriatric rehabilitation patients. *Journal of the American Geriatrics Society, 34,* 421–426.

Larson, E. B., Kukull, W. A., & Buchner, C. (1987). Adverse drug reactions associated with global cognitive impairment in elderly persons. *Annals of Internal Medicine, 107,* 169–73.

Linn, M. W., Linn, B. S., & Greenwald, S. R. (1972). The alcoholic patient in the nursing home. *Aging and Human Development, 3,* 273–277.

Liu, K., & Manton, K. G. (1984). The characteristics and utilization pattern of an admission cohort of nursing home patients. *Gerontologist, 24,* 70–76.

Mayfield, D., McLeod, G., & Hall, P. (1974). The CAGE questionnaire: Validation of a new alcoholism screening instrument. *American Journal of Psychiatry, 131,* 1121–1123.

McCusker, J., Cherubin, C. F., & Zimberg, S. (1971). Prevalence of alcoholism in a general municipal hospital population. *New York State Journal of Med, 71,* 751–754.

McGill, C. W., & Patterson, C. J. (1990). Former patients as peer counselors on locked psychiatric inpatient units. *Hospital and Community Psychiatry, 41,* 1017–1019.

Mehr, D. R., Fries, B. E., & Williams, B. C. (1993). How different are VA nursing home residents? *Journal of the American Geriatrics Society, 41,* 1095–1101.

Miller, N. S., Belkin, B. M., & Gold, M. S. (1991). Alcohol and drug dependence among the elderly: Epidemiology, diagnosis, and treatment. *Comprehensive Psychiatry, 32,* 153–165.

Miller, W. R. (1989). Increasing motivation for change. In R. K. Hester & W. R. Miller (Eds.), *Handbook of alcoholism treatment approaches: Effective alternatives* (pp. 67–80). New York: Pergamon.

Mishara, B. L., Kastenbaum, R., Baker, F., & Patterson, R. D. (1975). Alcohol effects in old age: An experimental investigation. *Social Science and Medicine, 9,* 535–547.

Moore, R. D., Bone, L. R., Geller, G., Mamon, J., Stokes, E. J., & Levine, D. (1989). Prevalence, detections, and treatment of alcoholism in hospitalized patients. *JAMA, 261,* 403–407.

Moos, R., Brennan, P. L., & Moos, B. S. (1991). Short-term processes of remission and nonremission among late-life problem drinkers. *Alcohol Clinical and Experimental Research, 15,* 948–955.

Office of Long-Term Care (1976). (*See* U.S. Department of Health, Education, and Welfare, 1976.)

Omnibus Budget Reconciliation Act. (1987). Public Law No. 100–203.

Ouslander, J. G. (1989). Medical care in the nursing home. *JAMA, 262,* 2582–2590.

Ouslander, J. G., Osterweil, D., & Morley, J. (1991). *Medical care in the nursing home.* New York: McGraw-Hill

Rango, N. (1982). Nursing-home care in the United States: Prevailing conditions and policy implications. *NEJM, 307,* 883–889.

Ray, W. A., Federspiel, C. F., & Schaffner, W. (1980). A study of antipsychotic drug use in nursing homes: Epidemiologic evidence suggesting misuse. *American Journal of Public Health, 70,* 485–91.

Ray, W. A., Griffin, M. R., Schaffner, W., Baugh, D. K., & Melton, L. J. (1987). Psychotropic drug use and the risk of hip fracture. *New England Journal of Medicine, 316,* 363–369.

Ray, W. A., Taylor, J. A., Meador, K. G., Lichtenstein, M. J., Griffin, M. R., Rought, R., Adams, M. L., & Blazer, D. G. (1993). Reducing antipsychotic drug use in nursing homes. *Archives of Internal Medicine, 153,* 713–721.

Rovner, B. W., Edelman, B. A., Cox, M. P., & Shmuely, Y. (1992). The impact of antipsychotic drug regulations on psychotropic prescribing practices in nursing homes. *American Journal of Psychiatry, 149,* 1390–1392.

Rubenstein, L. Z., Ouslander, J. G., & Wieland, D. (1988). Dynamics and clinical implications of the nursing home-hospital interface. *Clinics in Geriatric Medicine, 4,* 471–491.

Samet, J. M. (1992). The health benefits of smoking cessation. *Medical Clinics of North America, 76,* 399–414.

Schaschl, S., & Straw, D. (1989). Results of a model intervention program for physically impaired persons. *Alcohol Health and Research World, 13,* 150–153.

Schneider, E. L., & Guralnik, J. M. (1990). The aging of America: Impact on health care costs. *JAMA, 263,* 2335–2340.

Schuckit, M. A., & Miller, P. L. (1976). Alcoholism in elderly men: A survey of a general medical ward. *Annals of the NY Academy of Sciences, 273,* 558–571.

Schwartz, J. L. (1992). Methods of smoking cessation. *Medical Clinics of North America, 76,* 451–476.

Schweizer, E., Case, G., & Rickels, K. (1989). Benzodiazepine dependence and withdrawal in elderly patients. *American Journal of Psychiatry, 146,* 529–531.

Sherman, D., Avorn, J., & Campion, E. (1987). Cimetidine use in nursing homes: Prolonged therapy and excessive doses. *Journal of the American Geriatrics society, 35,* 1023–1027.

Shorr, R. I., Fought, R. L., & Ray, W. A. (1994). Changes in antipsychotic drug use in nursing homes during implementation of the OBRA-87 regulations. *JAMA, 271,* 358–362.

Simonson, W. (1991). *Consultant pharmacy practice.* Washington, DC: American Society of Consultant Pharmacists.

Solomon, K., Manepalli, J., Ireland, G. A., & Mahon, G. M. (1993). Alcoholism and prescription drug abuse in the elderly: St. Louis University Grand rounds. *Journal of the American Geriatrics Society, 41,* 57–69.

Sternberg, J., Spector, W. D., Drugovich, M. L., Fretwell, M. D., & Jackson, M. E. (1990). Use of psychoactive drugs in nursing homes: Prevalence and resident's characteristics. *Journal of Geriatric Drug Therapy, 4,* 47–60.

Stockford, D., Kelly, J., & Seitz, K. (1995). *Report on the 1990 and 1994 Surveys of VA nursing homes.* Washington, DC: Department of Veterans Affairs.

Svarstad, B. L., & Mount, J. K. (1991). Nursing home resources and tranquilizer use among the institutionalized elderly. *Journal of the American Geriatrics Society, 39,* 869–875.

Thompson, T. L. II, Moran, M. G., & Nies, A. S. (1983). Psychotropic drug use in the elderly. *New England Journal of Medicine, 308,* 134–138.

U.S. Department of Health, Education, and Welfare. (1976). *Physicians' drug prescribing patterns in skilled nursing facilities: Long-term care facility improvement campaign.* Public Health Service, Office of Long-Term Care, Monograph No. 2. Washington, DC: U.S. Government Printing Office.

U.S. Department of Health and Human Services (1989). Tobacco use by adults: United States, 1987. *Morbidity and Mortality Weekly Report, 38,* 685–687.

Walsh, D. C., Hingson, R. W., Merrigan, D. M., Levenson, S. M., Coffman, G. A., Heeren, T., & Cupples, L. A. (1992). The impact of a physician's warning on recovery after alcoholism treatment. *JAMA, 267,* 663–667.

Yip, B. Y., & Cumming, R. G. (1994). The association between medications and falls in Australian nursing-home residents. *Medical Journal of Australia, 160,* 14–18.

Glossary

Absorption—Intake of a drug or alcohol to the bloodstream; affected by the physicochemical properties of the drug, concentration and solubility of the drug, area and nature of absorbing surface, and blood circulation to the site of absorption (in the case of alcohol, usually the gastrointestinal tract).

Abstention—Using no alcohol.

Abstinence syndrome—Signs and symptoms experienced when a drug is withdrawn or the drug dose is lowered in an individual who is dependent on the drug.

ACTH (Adrenocorticotropic hormone)—A hormone secreted by the anterior pituitary gland, which stimulates the adrenal cortex to secrete corticosteroids.

Addict—Term of common usage, referring to an individual who exhibits compulsive behavior or loss of control or ability to inhibit or refrain from a particular substance or activity.

Affective disorder—Disorder of mood.

Age-specific treatment—Group treatment using age as a selection criterion to treat individuals of the same age group rather than in "mixed-age treatment." For example, problem drinkers age 55 or older may be placed in group treatment together, while those under age 55 would be excluded from their group.

Alcohol abuse—Maladaptive pattern of alcohol use manifested by recurrent and significant adverse consequences related to the repeated use of alcohol. There may be repeated failure to fulfill major role obligations, repeated use in situations in which it is physically hazardous, multiple legal problems, and recurrent social and interpersonal problems (DSM–IV)

Alcohol "abuse" subgroups—Three alcohol abuse subgroups are identified according to the age of onset: (a) *early-life* onset group comprises people who manifest their first alcohol problems at or before age 40; (b) *midlife* onset group ranges from 41 to 59 years; (c) *late-life* onset group exhibits signs of alcohol abuse at or after age 60 (Atkinson, Tolson, & Turner, 1990).

Alcohol dehydrogenase—Enzyme that performs the bulk of alcohol metabolism, predominantly in the liver, to a lesser degree in the stomach, and minimally in other tissues.

Alcohol dementia—Controversial disorder which entails global, persisting, and disabling cognitive impairment resulting from and temporally related to prolonged, heavy use of ethanol. Also referred to as *alcohol-induced persisting dementia* or *alcohol-related dementia.*

Alcohol dependence—Cluster of cognitive, behavioral, and psychological symptoms indicating that an individual continues to drink alcohol despite significant substance-related problems. There is a pattern of repeated self-administration that usually results in tolerance, withdrawal, and compulsive alcohol-using behavior. Often referred to loosely as alcoholism.

Alcohol-induced persisting amnestic disorder—Memory impairment, not exclusively occurring during the course of delirium or dementia, which is apparently due to the vitamin deficiency that is associated with prolonged, heavy ingestion of alcohol. Sometimes referred to as alcohol amnestic disorder, Korsakoff psychosis, *Korsakoff syndrome,* or *Korsakoff amnestic-confabulatroy state.*

Alcohol neurotoxicity—Controversial idea that chronic alcohol consumption can directly result in damage to cortical and subcortical brain regions distinct from pathology due to vitamin deficiency, liver disease, head trauma, and /or a variety of other causes of cognitive and neurological impairment which alcoholics are at risk. No underlying mechanism for this idea has been established, but it is supported by numerous imaging studies demonstrating ventricular enlargement and sulcal widening in alcoholics.

Alcohol withdrawal—Development of autonomic hyperactivity, increased tremor, insomnia, nausea or vomiting, transient visual, tactile, or auditory hallucinosis, illusions, agitation, anxiety, or seizures as a result of the cessation of or reduction in the prolonged, heavy use of alcohol. The period following alcohol withdrawal is not uncommonly associated with transient, often subtle cognitive deficits which stand in distinction to the persisting and disabling deficits of alcohol-induced dementia.

Alzheimer's disease—Degenerative brain disease characterized by specific pathologic findings, including neuritic plaques and neurofibrillary tangles.

Anomia—Difficulty with or inability to recall the names of persons or things. Also referred to as *dysnomia, nominal aphasia,* or *anomic aphasia.* This cognitive deficit is believed to be spared in alcohol-induced dementia.

Antecedents—Behaviors or events which precede a specified behavior. Behavioral and cognitive-behavioral treatments offer skills which teach the client to identify antecedents preceding drinking, to prevent a slip or a relapse.

Anticoagulant—Medication that decreases the tendency of blood to clot.

Antidepressant medication—Drugs used to treat depressive mood disorders, principally major depression.

Antigen—Substance, usually a protein, which when foreign to the bloodstream of an animal stimulates the formation of a specific antibody.

Antihypertensives—Medications that lower blood pressure.

Antipsychotic medication—Drugs used to treat serious mental illness or distress (also referred to as *neuroleptics* or *major tranquilizers*).

Anxiolytic medication—Drugs used in the management of anxiety disorders or for the short-term relief of the symptoms of anxiety.

Ataxia—Inability to coordinate the muscles in the execution of voluntary movement.

Aversion therapy—Use of classical conditioning principles to cause alcohol consumption to become aversive. An unpleasant state, produced by electric shock or injection of nausea-inducing drug, becomes associated with drinking during training sessions, making future alcohol consumption less likely.

Barbiturate—Salt or ester of barbituric acid, used as a sedative or hypnotic.

Behavior analysis—In both behavioral and cognitive-behavioral approaches, the use of direct observation or structured interview to identify the antecedents (prior events or behaviors) and consequences (reinforcers) of a high frequency problem behavior.

Behavior therapy—Treatment which focuses on overt, observable behaviors, and the use of principles of learning and reinforcement to modify those behaviors. Behavioral approaches attempt to identify antecedents to the behavior and consequences which reinforce it.

Benzodiazapine—Chemical compound commonly used to treat anxiety, to produce sedation, or as a muscle relaxant.

Biological markers—Three types of biological markers are used in alcohol research: (a) *trait markers* are designed to determine which individuals are at risk for alcohol dependence; (b) *state markers* reflect either chronic or acute consumption of alcohol; (c) *markers of organ damage* reflect the effect of alcohol consumption over time on specific organs such as the liver.

Biopsychosocial—Of or pertaining to the biological,psychological, and social factors that influence the development and course of an illness.

Bleeding time—Amount of time required for bleeding to stop spontaneously after intentional infliction of a standardized wound.

Brief interventions—Time-limited, directed prevention strategies that focus on reducing alcohol use in the nondependent drinker.

Cardiac arrhythmia—Variation from the normal rhythm of the heart beat.

Cardiovascular system—Heart and blood vessels.

Cerebral atrophy—Degeneration of cerebral neurons and loss of cerebral substance. Used sometimes to refer to sulcal widening and ventricular enlargement seen in imaging and post-mortem studies of chronic alcoholics.

Cerebrovascular system—The blood vessels of the brain.

Chemical restraints—Psychoactive drugs used to treat behavioral symptoms.

Clinical case model—As used in the text: treatment of the patient or client that is guided in an individualized manner by assessment, diagnosis, and problem-focused strategies.

Cognitive-behavioral therapy—Approaches used to teach individuals to observe and modify covert behaviors (i.e., those not observable to others, such as thoughts or feeling) as well as overt behaviors, using principles of learning and reinforcement.

Comorbidity—Refers to the presence of two or more illnesses, medical and psychiatric conditions, including alcohol and other drug use disorders, in the same person.

Confabulation—Bizarre and incorrect responses, and a readiness to give a fluent answer, with no regard whatever to facts, to any question put. Classically associated with alcohol-induced persisting amnestic disorder.

Confrontation—Method of interaction during treatment in which a therapist or peer-group members challenge statements, and label or confront individuals in treatment in an attempt to "break down" the client's use of defense mechanisms, and facilitate recognition of the problem.

Corticosteroid—Any of several hormones secreted by the adrenal cortex.

Cross-addiction—Phenomenon in which individuals who are dependent on one substance respond to another substance in a similarly addictive manner.

Cross-sectional study—Epidemiologic study for which all the data are collected at one time.

Delirium—Acute confusional state, characterized by sudden onset of mental status changes with disorganized thinking, fluctuating level of attention and often decreased consciousness, disorientation, hallucinations, and other changes.

Delusion—False belief that cannot be corrected by reason, argument or persuasion or even by evidence of the individual's own senses.

Dementia—Global decline in cognitive function of sufficient severity to interfere with usual functioning. Memory loss is always present; other features may include impairments in judgement, abstract thinking, language, recognition, and personality changes.

Dementia due to multiple etiologies—Dementia occurring with evidence from history, physical examination, or laboratory findings that the dementia has more than one etiology (e.g., head trauma plus chronic alcohol use, Alzheimer's dementia with subsequent development of vascular dementia). (DSM–IV)

Demographics—Characteristics of a particular population.

Detoxification—Clinical procedure by which a substance-dependent individual is withdrawn from a substance(s) in a manner that eliminates or minimizes psychological and physical distress.

Diagnostic and Statistical Manual of Mental Illness (3rd Ed. Revised, *DSM–III–R*; or 4th Ed., *DSM–IV*)—Manual of criteria for the diagnosis of mental illnesses, published by the American Psychiatric Association.

Diagnostic assessment—Making a diagnosis of alcohol abuse or dependence using complete diagnostic criteria, as opposed to screening, which makes a probability estimate that a given individual has a specific condition with incomplete diagnostic evidence.

Diagnostic criteria—Criteria used to ascertain alcohol abuse and dependence. In the United States, the accepted criteria appear in the *Diagnostic and Statistical Manual of Mental Disorders*. The World Health Organization's criteria appear in the International Classification of Diseases (ICD–10).

Diagnostic Interview Schedule—Research instrument that is considered the criterion standard measure to validate newly developed research instruments. The term "gold standard" is a misnomer when applied to alcohol abuse or dependence research.

Distribution—How a drug passes into various body compartments, e.g., body water or body fat; depends on its solubility, binding, and other properties.

Disulfiram—Antioxidant drug that inhibits several enzyme systems, including aldehyde dehydrogenase. When it is used concurrently with alcohol, high systemic levels of acetaldehyde cause headache, flushing, nausea, and dyspnea. In severe reactions, hypotension and ECG changes may occur.

Drink—Generally defined as an amount of an alcoholic beverage that contains approximately 12.5 grams of ethanol. This is approximately one 12 oz. bottle of "American beer," or a 3.5 oz. glass of 12% "table wine," or 1 oz. of 86-proof whisky.

Drug abuse—General term similar to the usage in the Diagnostic and *Statistical Manual of Mental Disorders–IV* in which drugs are specified, e.g., benzodiazepine abuse. It refers to inappropriate use of a substance leading to signifcant impairment or distress.

Drug addiction—Consistent physical or psychological craving for drugs.

Drug dependence—A general term similar to the usage in the *Diagnostic and Statistical Manual of Mental Disorders–IV* in which drugs are specified, e.g., benzodiazepine dependence. Some writers make a distinction between drug dependence and drug addiction, noting that an individual may have tolerance and dependence without addictive behaviors.

Drug tolerance—The need to provide more of a substance to obtain the desired effect.

DSM (Diagnostic and Statistical Manual of Mental Disorders): A manual, published by the American Psychiatric Association, that provides standardized criteria for the diagnosis of psychiatric conditions.

Dual diagnosis—Refers to a concomitant diagnosis of a psychiatric and a substance misuse disorder.

Dysphoria—Unpleasant mood characterized by an exaggerated feeling of depression and unrest.

Early onset—Age of onset topology in which problem drinking begins before midlife. The cutoff age is generally defined as before the age of about 40.

Elderly alcoholic—Term that is operationalized in various ways across research studies. The field of substance abuse research now uses terms from the field of social gerontology (e.g., "young-old," and "old-old," but use varying age breaks to signify these designators).

Environmental etiologic factors—Learned information from an individual's developmental surroundings that influences one's vulnerability to develop an illness.

Epidemiologic Catchment Area (ECA)—Key national survey, conducted in five sites in the United States, that assessed alcohol effects, consumption, related problems, and abuse or dependence; surveyed institutionalized and household population aged 18 years and older.

Epidemiology—Study of the relationship of various factors determining the frequency and distribution of diseases in a population.

Esophagitis—Inflammation of the esophagus.

Etiology—Factors associated with the development of an illness or type of illness.

Excretion—Elimination of a drug from the body, either unchanged or after metabolism. A function most often by the kidney.

Generalizability—Applicability of the findings from a research study to other settings.

Genetic etiologic factors—Inherited genes that influence one's vulnerability to develop an illness.

H2 blockers—Drug that inhibits the action of histamine at the histamine H2-receptors, which in turn inhibits the secretion of gastric acid.

Half-life—The time required by a living organism to eliminate half the quantity of the substance consumed or taken in.

Hallucination—Sense perception not founded on objective reality. In addition, these usually take the form of seeing or hearing people, animals or objects that are not really present.

Health Care Financing Administration (HCFA)—Agency of the United States government which provides oversight for the Medicare and

Medicaid programs and related federal medical care quality control
staff.

Heavy drinking—Variously defined and imprecise term used to describe the
amount of alcohol consumed by persons exhibiting alcohol-induced
mental disorders. Not useful unless a specific quantification is used to
describe amount of alcohol consumed per unit of time. Hemolytic syndrome—*Syndrome in which red blood cells are destroyed at a rate significantly greater than normal.*

Hemolytic sydrome—Syndrome in which red blood cells are destroyed at a
rate significantly greater than nornal.

Hepatic encephalopathy—Encephalopathy associated with cirrhosis of the
liver, attributed to the passage of nitrogenous substances from the portal to the systemic circulation. Also called portal-systemic
encephalopathy.

High-risk situations—According to the relapse prevention model of addictive
behaviors, these are situations which pose a threat to the person's sense
of control, and increase the risk of relapse.

Hustling—Robbery, theft, burglary and dealing drugs to obtain money for
drugs.

Iatrogenic—Caused by a physician's actions.

Incidence rate—Rate of newly occurring cases of a disease or condition in a
population over a defined period of time.

Intermediate care nursing facility—Nursing home providing care for residents who do not require the daily services of licensed professional
staff (as described under skilled nursing facility).

Korsakoff's syndrome—Organic mental syndrome resulting in chronic alcoholic dementia.

Late onset—Age of onset topology in which problem drinking begins in
midlife or beyond. The cutoff age is generally defined as after the age
of about 40.

Longitudinal studies—Studies which follow individual subjects over a period of time.

Macrocyte—Abnormally large red blood cell.

Malabsorption—Disorder of normal nutritive absorption, generally resulting
from abnormal functioning of the small intestine.

Mamillary bodies—Small round paired cell group that protrudes into the
interpeduncular fossa from the inferior aspect of the hypothalamus,

lesions of which are associated with alcohol-induced persisting amnestic disorder.

Marchiafava-Bignami disease—Uncommon degenerative disorder of the corpus callosum seen in alcoholics.

"Maturing out" hypothesis—Hypothesis that drug addicts mature out of their pattern of misuse.

Medicaid—Medical insurance provided by United States federal and State governments to low-income persons.

Medical morbidity and mortality—Disease and death rates associated with an illness or type of illness.

Medicare—Health care coverage for disabled persons and those *over 65, financed jointly by individual contributions and the United States government.*

Medicare Prospective Payment System (PPS)—System of hospital reimbursement enacted in the United States in 1983 to limit healthcare costs. The PPS system pays hospitals for care provided to Medicare beneficiaries based on the patient's diagnosis, rather than the cost of care.

Metabolism—Transformation of a drug into other, usually less active compounds, most often via enzymes in the liver.

Minimum data set—Uniform set of items and definitions mandated by OBRA (see below) for assessing all residents in nursing homes in the United States.

Misuse—Nonmedical term referring in this context to the use of a prescription drug by the patient or physician for the wrong purpose, in an inappropriate dose, or for an inappropriate time. It may also refer to coadministration with drugs with which it may interact unfavorably.

Mixed-age treatment—Treatment in which both older and younger problem drinkers participate in group treatment (as opposed to age-specific treatment).

Mucosa—Mucous membrane, lining various tubular structures inside the body, such as the mouth and intestines.

Myocardial cells—Heart muscle cells.

Myocardial infarction (heart attack)—Damage to the heart muscle due to insufficient blood supply

Neuroleptic medication—Drugs used to treat serious mental illness or distress (also referred to as *antipsychotics* or *major tranquilizers*).

Nonsteroidal antiinflammatory drugs (NSAIDs)—Drugs that control pain and inflammation. Often cause gastrointestinal side effects, including peptic ulcer disease.

Nursing home—Residential facility for persons who require nursing care and related medical or psychosocial services.

Omnibus Budget Reconciliation Act (OBRA)—United States federal government legislation containing provisions of the Nursing Home Reform Act and governing care provided in United States nursing homes.

Opiate—Derivative of opium.

Opioid—Synthetic drug with opiumlike properties.

Osteoporosis—Abnormal rarefaction of bone due to failure of osteoblasts to lay down bone matrix.

Pellagra—Syndrome of niacin deficiency characterized by gastrointestinal disturbance, erythema followed by desquamation, and dementia associated with poor diet or alcoholism.

Per capita consumption of alcohol —Amount of alcohol consumed per person in a designated population.

Peripheral neuropathy—Damage to multiple peripheral nerves characterized by absent or decreased reflexes, sensory loss and weakness. Also called polyneuropathy.

Pharmacodynamics—Action of drugs on body systems. Often dependent on age, sex, body weight, tolerance, and various physiologic variables.

Pharmacokinetics—Study of the absorption, metabolism, and action of drugs.

Physiologic—Of or pertaining to the biological functions of individuals.

Prescription drug Legally produced drug, obtained by the user either through illegal diversion or through a physician's prescription.

Prevalence—Number of existing cases of a disease or condition in a defined population over a given period of time.

Programmatic model—Understood in the context of this book as a treatment model for addictions in which all patients are exposed to the same strategies, for the same length of time.

Psychoactive medication—Any of a group of pharmacologic agents affecting mood, anxiety, behavior, or cognitive processes. Includes anxiolytics, antidepressants, neuroleptics, and sedative/hypnotics.

Psychodynamic approaches—Derived from classical psychoanalytic

(Freudian) theory, psychodynamic approaches have greater emphasis on ego functioning and personality disorders in the treatment of alcoholism.

Psychologic—Of or pertaining to the mental processes of individuals.

Psychopathologic—Mental and emotional disease states.

Remission—The marked decrease or abatement of symptoms of an illness.

Retrospective studies—Studies that look at data collected in the past (i.e. chart review studies).

Sample—A group of people selected for study to represent the population under study.

Screening—Activity that provides a probability estimate that a given person has a specific condition using incomplete diagnostic evidence. The goal of screening is to detect potential or developing alcohol problems. Compare the term with diagnostic assessment.

Secular trend Change in the environment or in societal attitudes that affect the phenomenon under investigation during the time period of a longitudinal study.

Sedative-hypnotic—Substance that induces a calm state or sleep.

Selection bias—Erroneous conclusions in a study that compares groups of subjects that results when the groups are systematically different in features other than those under study.

Self-management approaches—Procedures for teaching clients to monitor, modify, and reinforce their own behaviors. Several techniques are used, such as: self-monitoring (through logs and diaries), self-reinforcement, behavioral contracts with the therapist or family member, or tasks and assignments outside of the therapeutic environment.

Sensitivity—Term that refers to the accuracy of a test in identifying persons with a particular condition.

Skilled nursing facility—Nursing home providing skilled professional services to residents, i.e. daily observation and evaluation by a licensed professional nurse, daily physical, occupational, or speech therapy, or intensive medical therapy such as the intravenous administration of medications.

Sleep apnea—Period of cessation of spontaneous breathing activity during sleep.

Social support network—Those family members, friends, and acquaintances with whom a person interacts or relies on for assistance.

Social work-counseling approaches—Counseling techniques, often used by social workers and mental health counselors, which focus on family dynamics in helping a person with alcohol problems.

Specificity—Term that refers to a test's accuracy in identifying persons who do not have the problem.

Substance-use disorder—A *Diagnostic and Statistical Manual of Mental Disorder-IV* term encompassing substance abuse and substance dependence.

Thiamin—Vitamin B1, a heat labile vitamin, the deficiency of which results in beriberi. Thiamin deficiency is believed to play a role in the development of alcohol-induced persisting amnestic disorder.

Tolerance—Multifactorial phenomenon manifested by the use of increased amounts of alcohol to achieve intoxication or the desired effect; or by showing markedly diminished effect with continued use of the same amount of alcohol; or by demonstrating adequate functioning at doses or blood levels of alcohol that would produce significant impairment in a casual user.

Treatment outcome—Effect of a therapeutic intervention on variables that measure the severity of an illness.

True positives—Term that refers to the number of persons with the condition. Contrasted with the term *false positives* (persons falsely identified as having the condition).

Twelve Steps—Describes 12 "steps" or philosophies used by the self-help organization Alcoholics Anonymous. These include statements encouraging alcoholics to admit being powerless over drinking; seek a "higher power" to help overcome the problem; make amends to people harmed by their drinking; and help others to overcome their drinking problem.

Topology—Classification of an illness into different subtypes.

Vasodilators—Drugs that cause dilation of blood vessels.

Veterans Affairs—Department of the United States government operating a health care system of more than 170 hospitals and 120 nursing homes for persons who have served in the United States military.

Wernicke's encephalopathy—Reversible, thiamine-deficiency, alcohol-induced organic mental syndrome, causing dementia.

Index